BARRON'S

PRAXIS®

PPST/PLT

COMPUTERIZED PPST ELEMENTARY SCHOOL ASSESSMENTS
PARAPRO ASSESSMENT
PRAXIS II SUBJECT ASSESSMENTS OVERVIEW

5TH EDITION

Dr. Robert D. Postman
Professor
Mercy College
Westchester County, New York

BARRON'S

To my wife Liz,
who knows the way

And particularly to

my first grandchild, Quinn,
who calls me Pau Pau

Copyright © 2008 by Barron's Educational Series, Inc.

Previous editions Copyright © 2005, 2001, 1999, 1995 under the title *How to Prepare for PRAXIS/PPST/PLT* by Barron's Educational Series, Inc.

All inquiries should be addressed to:
Barron's Educational Series, Inc.
250 Wireless Boulevard
Hauppauge, New York 11788
www.barronseduc.com

ISBN-13 (book): 978-0-7641-3997-0
ISBN-10 (book): 0-7641-3997-5

ISBN-13 (book & CD-ROM Pkg): 978-0-7641-9487-0
ISBN-10 (book & CD-ROM Pkg): 0-7641-9487-9

Library of Congress Catalog Card No. 2008013367

Library of Congress Cataloging-in-Publication Data

Postman, Robert D.
    Praxis : PPST/PLT / Robert D. Postman.—5th ed.
        p. cm.
    Rev. ed. of: How to prepare for Praxis. 4th ed. c2005.
    Includes index.
    ISBN-13: 978-0-7641-3997-0
    ISBN-13: 978-0-7641-9487-0
    1. Teaching—United States—Examinations—Study guides. 2. PreProfessional Skills Tests—Study guides.
I. Postman, Robert D. How to prepare for Praxis. II. Title.
    LB1762.P67 2008
    370'.76—dc22

2008013367

PRINTED IN THE UNITED STATES OF AMERICA
9 8 7 6 5 4 3 2 1

Contents

10 Principles of Learning and Teaching Practice Test   329

PART V: ELEMENTARY EDUCATION INCLUDING FULL-LENGTH PRACTICE TESTS WITH EXPLAINED ANSWERS

11 Elementary Education: Curriculum, Instruction, and Assessment   370

12 Elementary Education: Content Area Exercises   419

13 Elementary Education: Content Knowledge   438

PART VI: PARAPRO ASSESSMENT OVERVIEW

14 ParaPro Assessment Overview   482

PART VII: OVERVIEW OF SELECTED SUBJECT ASSESSMENTS WITH SAMPLE QUESTIONS

15 Assessments in Biology and General Science, Early Childhood Education, English, French, and Fundamental Subjects: Content Knowledge   495

16 Assessments in Mathematics, Social Studies, Spanish, Special Education, and Education of Exceptional Students   542

Preface

This completely updated and expanded fifth edition shows you how to do your absolute best on the Praxis Teacher Certification examinations, and helps you get started in a teaching career. Hundreds of prospective teachers field-tested preliminary versions of this book, and dozens of experienced teachers and subject matter specialists reviewed the book to ensure that it provides you with the subject matter preparation and practice tests you need.

The practice tests in this book have the same question types and the same question-and-answer formats as the real tests. The practice tests also have the look and feel of the real thing—complete with uneven margins, open space, and the single and double columns found on the actual tests.

My wife Liz, a teacher, was a constant source of support and she made significant contributions to this book. I hope she accepts my regrets for the lost months and believes my promises that it won't happen again. My children Chad, Blaire, and Ryan have also been a source of support as I worked on this and other books over the years.

I can attest that Barron's is simply the best publisher of test preparation books. The editorial department spared no effort to ensure that this book will be most helpful to you, the test taker.

Anna E. Damaskos, my editor at Barron's, did another fine job with a mammoth and complex manuscript. Anna and I have worked on other books and, as usual, many of the special touches are due to her caring attention.

Special thanks to the undergraduate and graduate students and those changing careers who field-tested sections of this book, and to those at the Educational Testing Service and Metropolitan Museum of Art for their assistance. Special thanks also to Benjamin, Edith, and Pamela, who would have liked seeing their names in a book. I am also grateful to experts at state education departments for taking the time to talk with me about the teacher certification requirements in their states.

You are entering teaching during a time of tremendous opportunity and change, and I wish you well as you pursue a rewarding and fulfilling career. The next generation awaits. You will help them prepare for a vastly different, technological world.

Robert D. Postman

PRAXIS TEST DATES

Paper-based Praxis tests are offered on Saturdays in September, November, January, March, April, June, and July. However, Paper-based PPST tests are offered only in November, January, April, and July.

Computer-based PPST tests are offered virtually on demand at computer-based testing centers. Call 1-800-853-6773 to find the testing center nearest to you and to make an appointment.

For details and registration dates, check the ETS Praxis Bulletin, call ETS at 609-771-7395 or visit the Praxis Web site at *www.ets.org/praxis/*

PART I
TESTS AND STRATEGIES

Praxis Tests

CHAPTER 1

TEST INFO BOX

Most chapters begin with a Test Info Box. Read it for information about the Praxis tests.

The Educational Testing Service (ETS) offers the Praxis tests. Contact ETS for registration forms, admission tickets, testing accommodations, or test scores. You can register online.

Educational Testing Service
Praxis Series
Box 6501
Princeton, NJ 08541-6051
800-772-9476
TTY 609-771-7714
www.ets.org/praxis/
praxis@ets.org

PRAXIS TESTS REVIEWED IN THIS BOOK

PRAXIS I
  Preprofessional Skills Test (PPST)
  Computerized PPST
    Reading
    Writing
    Mathematics

PRAXIS II
  Principles of Learning and Teaching (PLT)
    Early Childhood Grades K–6, Grades 5–9, Grades 7–12
  Elementary Subject Assessments
    Curriculum, Instruction, and Assessment (0011*)
    Content Area Exercises (0012*)
    Content Knowledge (0014*)
    Curriculum, Instruction, and Assessment (K–5) (0016*)

PARAPRO ASSESSMENT

* Use these ETS test codes to help identify Elementary Subject Assessments.

Selected Subject Assessments (Overview)
  Biology, Science, Early Childhood, English, French, Fundamental Subjects: Content Knowledge, Mathematics, Social Studies, Spanish, Special Education

Passing Scores

Each state sets its own passing scores. See Chapter 17 for state certification testing requirements and an explanation of test scoring.

Read Me First!

This section explains the steps you should take in beginning your test preparation. Read it before going on.

WHAT'S GOING ON WITH PRAXIS?

Teacher certification examinations have been around for years. Until recently, most states relied on the National Teacher Examinations (NTE) developed by the Educational Testing Service (ETS), but the NTE is no longer given. Now, most states use the PPST, the PLT, and the Subject Assessments. There is an emphasis on Computer-based tests and more Computerized PPSTs are taken than any other Praxis test.

THE GOOD NEWS

The good news is that Praxis tests focus on a central core of information. In this book, we show you how to decide which tests to take and how to prepare successfully for each test. We show you how to review only the information you need.

At the end of the book we show you how to begin your career in teaching, how to write your perfect résumé, and how to look for your first job.

WHICH TESTS SHOULD I TAKE?

Check the tests you have to take in the following Review Checklist. It shows which part(s) of this book to use. Side tabs help you find the test review and the practice tests in this book. *Then read the rest of this chapter.*

REVIEW CHECKLIST AND TEST SECTION IDENTIFIER

Use this page to plan your study and to find the marked test preparation sections.

Praxis—The Inside Story

The official title is *The Praxis Series: Professional Assessment for Beginning Teachers.* The Praxis Series was developed by the Educational Testing Service (ETS), a giant educational testing organization that administers millions of tests yearly all over the world. The Praxis tests are described in the following sections.

PRAXIS I

PREPROFESSIONAL SKILLS TEST (PPST)

COMPUTERIZED PPST

The Computerized PPST and the Paper-based PPST each consists of three separate tests: (1) Reading, (2) Mathematics, and (3) Writing—multiple choice and essay.

The Computerized PPST and the Paper-based PPST are essentially the same test and have the same question types. However, the Computerized PPST can be taken almost on demand at test centers throughout the country, while the Paper-based PPST is given on scheduled test dates. ETS has even reduced the number of test dates on which the Paper-based PPST is given.

This has made the Computerized PPST the most popular choice among test takers. But there are still many people who take the paper-based test. One of the practice tests in this book will give you an idea of what the Computerized PPST is like, while the other practice test reflects the paper-based format. The computerized version of the PPST is found on page 182. The paper-based version of the PPST is found on page 224.

COMPUTERIZED PPST

You may take the Computerized PPST almost any day of the week and almost on demand at a center designed for computerized testing. You will sit in a cubicle in front of a computer screen, where your test session may be video recorded. Some scrap paper is available. You see the items one at a time, but can return to items later. A mouse is used to enter your answers directly on the test and you type your essay. A tutorial shows you how to use the computerized test, including the tool for marking items to return to. This extra practice may not be enough for every test taker to take the Computerized PPST. Your scores on the multiple-choice tests are available immediately, while the essay score is available about a month later.

PAPER-BASED PPST

The Paper-based PPST is taken on a scheduled test date. At press time the Paper-based PPST was given on just four of the seven Praxis paper-based test dates. For most people, it will be a very familiar test environment. You'll sit in a room, a gym, or an auditorium—usually at a college or a school—along with other people. That means there may be distractions. You'll be able to see the entire test and flip through the test pages. You will also be able to write on the test booklet and cross off answers you believe are incorrect. You will record your answers on a separate answer sheet, which increases the likelihood of making answer sheet marking errors. You won't know any of your scores for about a month.

SHOULD I TAKE THE COMPUTERIZED PPST OR THE PAPER-BASED PPST?

You will probably want to take the Computerized PPST, if for no reason other than the Computerized PPST is offered more frequently, and usually on shorter notice. You may even be able to get an appointment for the computerized test in a day. A primary reason for taking the Paper-based PPST is because there is not a Computerized PPST test center near you. There are about 300 centers for the computerized test, but there are many more sites for the paper-based test. Another main advantage of the computerized test is that you will not have to mark a separate answer sheet. Answer sheet marking errors are a main cause of problems on any paper-based test. It's a potential problem worth avoiding.

But there are other reasons for taking the Paper-based PPST. Some people have difficulty navigating the computerized test. If you are uncomfortable with computers, then paper may be the way to go. You may just like to work with a pencil and an eraser. It will usually be more familiar. You may enjoy the "social" atmosphere you'll find with a paper-based test. The cubicles for the computer-based test are not very friendly. And if you want to avoid any possibility that you will be video recorded, then paper is for you.

TEST SUMMARY

The table below summarizes the information about the Computerized PPST and the Paper-based PPST. Following that is a brief overview of the three individual tests.

Praxis I Summary		
Computerized PPST*		**PPST**
Reading	40 items—75 minutes	40 items—60 minutes
Mathematics	40 items—75 minutes	40 items—60 minutes
Writing Multiple choice	38 items—38 minutes	38 items—30 minutes
Essay	1 typed essay—30 minutes	1 handwritten essay—30 minutes

*Each Computerized PPST multiple-choice test includes six additional pretest items that are completed during the testing time.

READING

Each item has five answer choices. There are some long passages of about 200 words, some shorter passages of about 100 words, and some statements of a few sentences. According to ETS, test items are partitioned as follows: literal comprehension 55 percent, critical and inferential comprehension 45 percent.

WRITING

There are 38 scored multiple-choice items with five answer choices. According to ETS, multiple-choice items are partioned as follows: usage, 55 percent, and sentence correction, 45 percent. You are given a topic to write your essay. Each section contributes 50 percent to the final score.

MATHEMATICS

The mathematics test has 40 scored multiple-choice items. Each item has five answer choices. The test measures a wide range of mathematics topics primarily from the precollege curriculum. According to ETS, test items are partitioned as follows: number and operations 32 percent, algebra 20 percent, geometry and measurement 22 percent, data analysis and probability 26 percent.

PRAXIS II

PRINCIPLES OF LEARNING AND TEACHING (PLT)

The PLT consists of three separate tests, Elementary (K–6), Middle School (5–9), and Secondary (7–12). Each test has three scenarios that describe teaching situations. Each scenario is followed by seven multiple-choice and two short-answer (constructed-response) questions based on that scenario. In addition, there are 24 multiple-choice questions that are not based on any of the scenarios, making a total of 51 items. Test questions cover four broad areas: organizing content for student learning, creating an environment for student learning, teaching for student learning, and teacher professionalism.

Chapter 8 shows how to prepare for the PLT; Chapter 9 contains a practice PLT.

ELEMENTARY SUBJECT ASSESSMENTS

There are four elementary subject assessments. Each test is two hours long. Elementary Education: Curriculum, Instruction, and Assessment (0011) has 110 multiple-choice items about elementary school teaching. Elementary Education: Content Area Exercises (0012) has four constructed-response items about elementary school teaching.

Chapter 12 contains an overview and practice tests with explained answers.

Elementary Education: Content Knowledge has 120 multiple-choice items about content taught in the elementary school. Elementary Education: Curriculum, Instruction, and Assessment (K–5) (0011) has 120 multiple-choice items about elementary school teaching kindergarten through fifth grade.

Chapter 13 contains an overview and practice tests with explained answers.

OVERVIEW OF SELECTED SUBJECT ASSESSMENTS

Subject assessments are the revised form of the old specialty area tests. Subject assessments have been extensively revised and all are based on a job analysis. These tests feature a modularized format that usually includes modules for Content Knowledge, Content Essays, and Pedagogy (a combination of multiple choice and short answer).

Chapters 15 and 16 give an overview of selected tests with sample items.

ParaPro Assessment

The ParaPro Assessment is used by many states and school districts to meet paraprofessional requirements established by the No Child Left Behind Act. This test measures your knowledge in reading, mathematics, and writing and your ability to demonstrate teaching expertise in these areas. This book includes an overview for this test in Part VI beginning on page 486.

Taking the Praxis Tests

Register online at *www.ets.org* for all paper-based tests. For the Praxis I Computer-based PPST, register by calling 1-800-853-6773.

YOUR SCORES

Scores for paper-based tests are usually available one month after the test, scores for the multiple-choice items on the Computerized PPST are usually available immediately, while the essay score is available one month after the test.

The Praxis Bulletin lists a code for each organization that can receive scores. List the code for each certification agency or college you want to receive your scores. The scores are usually sent directly to the agencies from ETS.

You may want to wait until you know you have gotten a passing score before sending it in. That's not necessary. You will just slow the process and incur extra expense. Certification agencies do not use these scores for evaluative purposes. They just need to see a passing score, and ETS reports only your highest score.

You will receive your own report and you are entitled to have four score reports sent to the certification agency or colleges you choose. Any extra reports will be sent to you.

SPECIAL TEST ARRANGEMENTS

ETS offers special arrangements or considerations for the following categories. If you qualify for special test arrangements, take advantage of the opportunity. Go to *www.ets.org/disability* or call ETS for complete information.

Do You Have a Disability (a Learning Disability or a Physical, Visual, or Hearing Impairment)?

You may qualify for additional time to complete the test, for someone to read the test to you, or for other special circumstances to accommodate your disability. Written documentation is required. You must use the Certification of Disability form or write directly to ETS to receive these special considerations. Your letter should describe your disability and the special arrangements you desire. Also enclose a note from a school counselor or employer to verify that these arrangements have previously been made for you, or a note from a health professional documenting your disability. Contact ETS before you send in the form if you have any questions.

Is Your Primary Language Not English?

You may qualify for 50 percent additional testing time if your Primary Language is Not English (PLNE). Documentation is required. Contact ETS for more information.

Do You Celebrate Your Sabbath on Saturday? Do Your U.S. Military Duties Prevent You from Taking the Test on a Saturday?

You may qualify to take the test on the Monday following the Saturday administration. Complete the Praxis registration form indicating this special situation. If you are unable to take a test for religious reasons, include a note from the head of the religious group where you worship, on that group's letterhead, stating that your Sabbath is on Saturday. If you cannot take a test for military reasons, include a copy of your orders.

Do You Live More Than 100 Miles from a Test Site?

You may qualify for an alternative test site. Send in the registration form with a note explaining your circumstances. There is an additional fee for taking the test at an alternative test site. Contact ETS if you have any questions.

CHAPTER 2

Test-Preparation and Test-Taking Strategies

TEST INFO BOX

This chapter shows you how to set up a test preparation schedule and shows you some test-taking strategies that will help you improve your score. The important strategies are discussed below.

MULTIPLE CHOICE

Eliminate and then guess. There is no penalty for wrong answers. Never leave any answer blank.

Suppose a test has 40 items with four answer choices. If you eliminate two incorrect answer choices on all the items, guess every answer, and, on average, you would get 20 correct.

On paper-based tests, be sure to carefully mark your answer sheet. On the Computerized PPST, be sure to check that you have answered all the questions.

ESSAY

Write an outline first, then write the essay.

Topic Paragraph: Begin the written assignment with an introduction to orient the reader to the topic. The first paragraph should clearly state the main idea of your entire written assignment.

Topic Sentence: Begin each paragraph with a topic sentence that supports the main idea.

Details: Provide details, examples, and arguments to support the topic sentence.

Grammar, Punctuation, Spelling: Edit sentences to conform to standard usage.

Avoid Passive Construction: Write actively and avoid the passive voice.

Conclusion: End the written assignment with a paragraph that summarizes your main points.

PLT CONSTRUCTED RESPONSE

Use the PLT constructed-response strategies in Chapter 9. You have only about seven minutes to write each response. But still plan before you write.

Preparing for the Tests

By now, you know which tests you're going to take. You've sent in the registration form, and the test is probably six to eight weeks away. This section describes how to prepare for certification tests, and the next section describes test-taking strategies. Before we go on, let's think about what you are preparing for.

Wait! Why Test Me? I'm a Good Person!

Why indeed? Life would be so much easier without tests. If anyone tells you that they like to take tests, don't believe them. Nobody does. Tests are imperfect. Some people "pass" when they should have failed, while others "fail" when they should have passed. It may not be fair, but it is very real. So sit back and relax. You're just going to have to do it. And this book will show you how.

Who Makes Up These Tests and How Do They Get Written?

Consider the following scenario. It is late in the afternoon in Princeton, New Jersey. Around a table sit teachers, deans of education, parents, and representatives of state Education Departments. In front of each person is a preliminary list of skills and knowledge that teachers should possess. The list comes from comments by an even larger group of teachers and other educational professionals.

Those around the table are regular people just like the ones you might run into in a store or on the street. They all care about education. They also bring to the table their own strengths and weaknesses—their own perspectives and biases. What's that? An argument just broke out. People are choosing up sides and, depending on the outcome, one item on the list will stay or go.

This goes on for a few days until this group has drawn up a final list. Thousands of teachers and national teacher organizations receive the list. Each rates the importance of every item. The items rated important will be measured by the test.

The final list goes to professional test writers to prepare test items. These items are tried out, refined, and put through a review process. Eventually the test item bank is established, and a test is born. These test writers are not geniuses. They just know how to write questions. You might get a better score on this test than some of them would.

The test writers want to write a test that measures important concepts. They try not to ask dumb or obscure questions that have strange answers. For the most part, they are successful. You can count on the test questions to ask about things you should know.

You can also be sure that the test writers will ask questions that will make you think. Their questions will ask you to use what you know. They will not ask for rote responses.

Keep those people around the table and the test writers in mind as you use this book. You are preparing for their test. Soon, you will be like one of those people around the table. You may even contribute to a test like this one.

Proven Test-Preparation Strategies

Here are several strategies and steps to follow as you prepare for the test. These strategies take you right up to test day.

Get Yourself Ready for the Test

Most people feel at least a little bit uncomfortable about tests. You are probably one of them. No book is going to make you feel comfortable. But here are some suggestions.

Most people are less tense when they exercise. Set up a *reasonable* exercise program for yourself. The program should involve exercising in a way that is appropriate for you 30 to 45 minutes each day. This exercise may be just as important as other preparation.

Prepare with another person. You will feel less isolated if you have a friend or colleague to study with.

Accept these important truths. You are not going to get all the answers correct. You don't have to. You can take this test again if you have to. There is no penalty for taking the test again. This is not a do-or-die, life-or-death situation. You will survive.

Follow This Study Plan

Begin working four to ten weeks before the test. Use the longer time if you are very busy or you don't feel comfortable about the test.

Look in turn at each chapter you have to use. Review the description of each test you have to take. Then take each appropriate review quiz when one is available. Use the answer key to mark the review quiz. Each incorrect answer will point you to a specific portion of the review.

Use the subject matter review indicated by the review quiz. Don't spend your time reviewing things you already know.

Take the targeted test when one is available, after the review of each chapter is complete. It will let you know what further review may be necessary. Complete your review two weeks before the test. Then, complete the practice test. Have someone proctor the test. Take the test under exact test conditions. No television. No extra time. No breaks that are not normally included in the test. Nothing. We recommend that you take the practice test on the same day of the week and during the same time period that you will take the actual test.

Grade your own test or have someone do it for you. Either way, review each incorrect answer and read all the explanations. Every answer is explained in detail.

Two Weeks to Go

During this week look over those areas you got wrong on the practice test. Go over the answer explanations and go back to the review sections. Read the newspaper every day until the day before the test.

One Week to Go

The hard work is over. You're coasting in for a landing. You know the material on the test. You don't even have to get an A. You just have to pass.

Get up each day at the time you will have to get up the following Saturday. Sit down at the time the test will start and spend about one hour answering questions on targeted test or practice tests. It's okay that you have answered these questions before.

Four Days to Go

Make sure you:

- have your admission ticket.

- know where the test is given.

- know how you will get there.

Three Days to Go

- Write on 3×5 index cards any special terms or formulas you must remember for the test.

- Visit the test site or the test center, if you haven't done so already. You don't want any surprises this Saturday.

Two Days to Go

- Get some sharpened No. 2 pencils and a good big eraser and put them aside. If you're taking the paper-based test, you should also bring a watch.

One Day to Go

- Review your index cards one last time.

- Complete any forms you have to bring to the test.

- Prepare any snacks or food you want to bring with you.

- Talk to someone who makes you feel good or do something enjoyable and relaxing.

- Have a good night's sleep.

Test Day

- Most often you will be at the test site or center for at least four hours.

- Dress comfortably. There are no points for appearance.

- Don't stuff yourself. You want your blood racing through your brain, not your stomach.

- Get together things to bring to the test including: registration ticket, identification forms, pencils, eraser, and snacks.

- Take any extra clothing you need to be comfortable.

- Get to the test room or the test center, not the parking lot, about 10 to 15 minutes before the start time. Remember to leave time for parking and walking to the test site or test center.

- Hand in your forms. You're ready. This is the easy part.

- Follow the test-taking strategies in the next section.

Proven Test-Taking Strategies

Testing companies like to pretend that test-taking strategies don't help that much. They act like that because they want everyone to think that their tests only measure your knowledge of the subject. Of course, they are just pretending; test-taking strategies can make a big difference.

However, there is nothing better than being prepared for the subject matter on the test. These strategies will do you little good if you lack this fundamental knowledge. If you are prepared, then these strategies can make a difference. Use them. Other people will. Not using them may very well lower your score.

Be Comfortable

Get a good seat. Don't sit near anyone or anything that will distract you. Stay away from your friends. If you don't like where you are sitting, move or ask for another seat. You paid money for this test, and you have a right to favorable test conditions.

You Will Make Mistakes

You are going to make mistakes on this test. The people who wrote the test expect you to make them.

You Are Not Competing with Anyone

Don't worry about how anyone else is doing. Your score does not depend on theirs. When the score report comes out it doesn't say, "Nancy got a 661, but Blaire got a 670." You just want to get the score required for your certificate. If you can do better, that's great. Stay focused. Remember your goal.

MULTIPLE-CHOICE STRATEGIES

Some Questions Are Traps

Some questions include the words *not*, *least*, or *except*. You are being asked for the answer that doesn't fit with the rest. Be alert for these types of questions.

Save the Hard Questions for Last

You're not supposed to get all the questions correct, and some of them will be too difficult for you. Work through the questions and answer the easy ones. Pass the other ones by. Do these more difficult questions the second time through. If a question seems really hard, draw a circle around the question number in the test booklet. Save these questions until the very end.

They Show You the Answer

Every multiple-choice test shows you the correct answer for each question. The answer is staring right at you. You just have to figure out which one it is. There is a 20 or 25 percent chance you'll get it right by just closing your eyes and pointing.

Some Answers Are Traps

When someone writes a test question, they often include distracters. Distracters are traps—incorrect answers that look like correct answers. It might be an answer to an addition problem when you should be multiplying. It might be a correct answer to a different question. It might just be an answer that catches your eye. Watch out for this type of incorrect answer.

Eliminate the Incorrect Answers

If you can't figure out which answer is correct, then decide which answers can't be correct. Choose the answers you're sure are incorrect. Cross them off in the test booklet. Only one left? That's the correct answer.

Guess, Guess, Guess

If there are still two or more answers left, then guess. Guess the answer from those remaining. Never leave any item blank. There is no penalty for guessing.

PAPER-BASED TESTS

It's Not What You Know That Matters, It's Just Which Circle You Fill In

No one you know or care about will see your test. An impersonal machine scores all multiple-choice questions. The machine just senses whether the correct circle on the answer sheet is filled in. That is the way the test makers want it. If that's good enough for them, it should be good enough for you. Concentrate on filling in the correct circle.

You Can Be Right but Be Marked Wrong

If you get the right answer but fill in the wrong circle, the machine will mark it wrong. We told you that filling in the right circle was what mattered. We strongly recommend that you follow this strategy.

Write the letter for your answer big in the test booklet next to the number for the problem. If you change your mind about an answer, cross off the "old" letter and write the "new" one. At the end of each section, transfer all the answers together from the test booklet to the answer sheet.

Do Your Work in the Test Booklet

You can write anything you want in your test booklet. The test booklet is not used for scoring and no one will look at it. You can't bring scratch paper to the test so use your booklet instead. Some of the strategies we recommend involve writing in and marking up the booklet. These strategies work and we strongly recommend that you use them. Do your work for a question near that question in the test booklet. You can also do work on the cover or wherever else suits you. You may want to do calculations, underline important words, mark up a picture, or draw a diagram.

Watch That Answer Sheet

Remember that a machine does the marking. Fill in the correct answer circle completely. Don't put extra pencil marks on the answer section of the answer sheet. Stray marks could be mistaken for answers.

COMPUTERIZED PPST

Pay Attention During the Tutorial

The tutorial shows you how to use the computer, how to mark your answers, how to use a tool to mark items to return to, and how to use the review page to see the items to return to. Pay close attention. There is no way to get additional help once the test is underway.

You Don't Have to Answer Every Item When It First Appears

If you come across an item you're not ready to answer, mark it with the special marking tool you learned about during the tutorial. You can also mark an item you have not answered as a reminder to review the item later and/or perhaps change an answer.

All the items you mark are recorded on the review screen.

Use the Review Screen

Leave time at the end of the test to look at the review screen. The screen shows all the items you marked with the marking tool, as well as those items you revisited. Use the information on this screen to be sure you entered an answer for every item. There is no penalty for guessing.

It's Easy to Change Your Answer

You can change the answer to any multiple-choice item. Just click on the oval for another answer.

Use the Scrap Paper

The test center staff should provide you with scrap paper. Use the scrap paper to do calculations, draw diagrams, or to make any notes you need to arrive at the correct answer.

Take the Optional 15-Minute Break

You have the right to a 15-minute break between tests. Take it. You don't want to waste time during the next test to excuse yourself.

ESSAY STRATEGIES

The PPST Writing test has a 30-minute essay. The Elementary Education Content Area Exercises have constructed-response items. You have 30 minutes for each. The PLT has short constructed-response items, which are discussed on page 305.

Your Responses Are Graded Holistically

Holistic rating means the raters assign a score based on their informed sense about your writing. Raters read a lot of essays, and they do not do a detailed analysis.

ETS sends your essay to raters over the Internet. The raters score your essay online. These readers typically consist of teachers and college professors. At first, representatives of ETS show the readers the topics for the recent test and review the types of responses that should be rated 1–6. The rating guidelines are on page 62. The raters are trained to evaluate the responses according to the ETS guidelines.

Each written assignment is evaluated twice, without the second rater knowing the evaluation given by the first rater. If the two evaluations differ significantly, other raters review the assignment.

Raters have a tedious, tiring assignment, and they work quickly. Think about them as you write. Write a response that makes it easy for them to give you a high score.

Steps for Writing Passing Essays

Follow these steps to write a passing essay for the PPST essay and for each Elementary Subject Assessment constructed-response answer. You have 30 minutes for each essay.

1. **Understand the topic** (2 minutes).

   A topic is introduced and then described in more detail. Read the topic carefully to ensure that you understand it completely.

2. **Choose a thesis statement. Write it down** (2 minutes).

   Readers expect you to have one clear main point of view about the topic. Choose yours; make sure it addresses the entire topic, and stick to it.

3. **Write a brief outline** (6 minutes).

   Write a brief outline summarizing the following essay elements.

   - Thesis statement

   - Introduction

   - Topic sentence and details for each paragraph

   - Conclusion

   Use this time to plan your essay.

4. **Write the essay** (16 minutes).

   Essays rated in the upper third typically have three or four paragraphs totaling 150 to 250 words. Writing an essay this long does not guarantee a passing score, but most passing essays are about this long. Use this time to write well.

5. **Proofread and edit** (4 minutes).

   Leave four minutes to read your essay over and correct any errors in usage, spelling, or punctuation. The readers understand that your essay is a first draft and they expect to see corrections.

PART II

PPST SUBJECT MATTER PREPARATION

Writing

CHAPTER 3

USING THIS CHAPTER

This chapter prepares you to take the multiple-choice writing section and the essay section of the PPST. Use the Study Checklist below. You will need to find an English professor, teacher, or tutor to mark the essay portion of the review test. This person may also be able to help you prepare for the essay section of the test.

STUDY CHECKLIST

English Review

This review section targets the skills and concepts you need to know in order to pass the English parts of the PPST.

NOUNS AND VERBS

Every sentence has a subject and a predicate. Most sentences are statements. The sentence usually names something (subject). Then the sentence describes the subject or tells what that subject is doing (predicate). Sentences that ask questions also have a subject and a predicate. Here are some examples.

Subject	Predicate
The car	moved.
The tree	grew.
The street	was dark.
The forest	teemed with plants of every type and size.

Many subjects are nouns. Every predicate has a verb. A list of the nouns and verbs from the preceding sentences follows.

Noun	Verb
car	moved
tree	grew
street	was
forest, plants	teemed

NOUNS

Nouns name a person, place, thing, characteristic, or concept. Nouns give a name to everything that is, has been, or will be. Here are some simple examples.

Person (Idea)	Place	Thing	Characteristic	Concept
Abe Lincoln	Lincoln Memorial	beard	mystery	freedom
judge	courthouse	gavel	fairness	justice
professor	college	chalkboard	intelligence	number

Singular and Plural Nouns

Singular nouns refer to only one thing. Plural forms refer to more than one thing. Plurals are usually formed by adding an *s* or dropping a *y* and adding *ies*. Here are some examples.

Singular	Plural
college	colleges
professor	professors
Lincoln Memorial	Lincoln Memorials
mystery	mysteries

Possessive Nouns

Possessive nouns show that the noun possesses a thing or a characteristic. Make a singular noun possessive by adding *'s*. Here are some examples.

The *child's* sled was in the garage ready for use.
The *school's* mascot was loose again.
The rain interfered with *Jane's* vacation.
Ron's and *Doug's* fathers were born in the same year.
Ron and *Doug's* teacher kept them after school.

Make a singular noun ending in *s* possessive by adding *'s* unless the pronunciation is too difficult.

The teacher read *James's* paper several times.
The angler grabbed the *bass'* fin.

Make a plural noun possessive by adding an apostrophe (') only.

The *principals'* meeting was delayed.
The report indicated that *students'* scores had declined.

Practice

Write the plural of each singular noun.

1. sheaf
2. deer
3. fry
4. lunch
5. knee

6. lady
7. octopus
8. echo
9. foot
10. half

Answers on page 44

VERBS

Some verbs are action verbs. Other verbs are linking verbs that link the subject to words that describe it. Here are some examples.

Action Verbs	Linking Verbs
Blaire *runs* down the street.	Blaire *is* tired.
Blaire *told* her story.	The class *was* bored.
The crowd *roared*.	The players *were* inspired.
The old ship *rusted*.	It *had been* a proud ship.

Tense

A verb has three principal tenses: present tense, past tense, and future tense. The present tense shows that the action is happening now. The past tense shows that the action happened in the past. The future tense shows that something will happen. Here are some examples.

Present:	I *enjoy* my time off.
Past:	I *enjoyed* my time off.
Future:	I *will enjoy* my time off.
Present:	I *hate* working late.
Past:	I *hated* working late.
Future:	I *will hate* working late.

Regular and Irregular Verbs

Regular verbs follow the consistent pattern noted previously. However, a number of verbs are irregular. Irregular verbs have their own unique forms for each tense. A partial list of irregular verbs follows. The past participle is usually preceded by *had, has,* or *have.*

Some Irregular Verbs

Present Tense	Past Tense	Past Participle
am, is, are	was, were	been
begin	began	begun
break	broke	broken
bring	brought	brought
catch	caught	caught
choose	chose	chosen
come	came	come
do	did	done
eat	ate	eaten
give	gave	given
go	went	gone
grow	grew	grown
know	knew	known
lie	lay	lain
lay	laid	laid
raise	raised	raised
ride	rode	ridden
see	saw	seen
set	set	set
sit	sat	sat
speak	spoke	spoken
take	took	taken
tear	tore	torn
throw	threw	thrown
write	wrote	written

Tense Shift

Verbs in a sentence should reflect time sequence. If the actions represented by the verbs happened at the same time, the verbs should have the same tense.

Incorrect: Beth sits in the boat while she wore a life jacket.

Correct: Beth sits in the boat while she wears a life jacket.
[Both verbs are present tense.]

Correct:	Beth sat in the boat while she wore a life jacket.
	[Both verbs are past tense.]
Correct:	Beth wears the life jacket she wore last week.
	[The verbs show time order.]

Practice

Correct the tense errors. Some sentences may be correct.

1. Ryan driven to Florida.
2. Refereeing soccer games is not work.
3. Chad ride to the game with his team last week.
4. Why did Mary ran her errands now?
5. I have speak to my teacher about the grade.
6. Carl paddled across the river every Saturday.
7. Blaire thrown out the ball for the players to use.
8. Joann will lost her bag if she leaves it in the store.
9. Bob is standing on a stool next to the green table.
10. Liz begun to grasp the depth of her happiness.

Answers on page 45

Practice

Correct the tense shifts. Some sentences may be correct.

1. Lisa already went to the North Pole but she is not going there again.
2. Dennis will take his airline tickets with him because he is leaving for his flight.
3. The runner gasped as she crosses the finish line.
4. I like to hear music so I played the clarinet.
5. Chris wanted to be a producer so he puts in long hours every day.
6. Bertha sews five hours a day because she will need her dress by next month.
7. The car turns over and then bounced down the hill.
8. Lois handed over her money because she wants to buy the computer.
9. The captain wandered out on the deck as she calls to her friends on shore.
10. The sun sets in the west as the moon rose in the east.

Answers on page 45

PRONOUNS

Pronouns take the place of nouns or noun phrases and help avoid constant repetition of the noun or phrase. Here is an example.

Blaire is in law school. *She* studies in *her* room every day.
[The pronouns *she* and *her* refer to the noun *Blaire.*]

PRONOUN CASES

Pronouns take three case forms: subjective, objective, and possessive. The personal pronouns *I, he, she, it, we, they, you* refer to an individual or individuals. The relative pronoun *who* refers to these personal pronouns as well as to an individual or individuals. These pronouns change their case form depending on their use in the sentence.

Subjective Pronouns: *I, we, he, it, she, they, who, you*

Use the subjective form if the pronoun is, or refers to, the subject of a clause or sentence.

> *He* and *I* studied for the PPST.

> The proctors for the test were *she* and *I*.
> [*She* and *I* refer to the subject *proctors*.]

> She is the woman *who* answered every question correctly.

> I don't expect to do as well as *she*.
> [*She* is the subject for the understood verb *does*.]

Objective Pronouns: *me, us, him, it, her, them, whom, you*

Use the objective form if the pronoun is the object of a verb or preposition.

> Michelle helps both *him* and *me*.
> She wanted *them* to pass.
> I don't know *whom* she helped most.

Possessive Pronouns: *my, our, his, its, her, their, whose, your*

Use the objective form if the pronoun shows possession.

> I recommended they reduce the time they study with *their* friends.
> He was the person *whose* help they relied on.

CLEAR REFERENCE

The pronoun must clearly refer to a particular noun or noun phrase. Here are some examples.

Unclear

> Chris and Blaire took turns feeding *her* cat.
> [We can't tell which person *her* refers to.]

> Chris gave *it* to Blaire.
> [The pronoun *it* refers to a noun that is not stated.]

Clear

> Chris and Blaire took turns feeding Blaire's cat.
> [A pronoun doesn't work here.]

> Chris got the book and gave it to Blaire.
> [The pronoun works once the noun is stated.]

AGREEMENT

Each pronoun must agree in number (singular or plural) and gender (male or female) with the noun it refers to. Here are some examples.

Nonagreement in Number

> The children played all day, and *she* came in exhausted.
> [*Children* is plural, but *she* is singular.]

> The child picked up the hat and brought *them* into the house.
> [*Hat* is singular, but *them* is plural.]

Agreement

> The children played all day, and *they* came in exhausted.
> The child picked up the hat and brought *it* into the house.

Nonagreement in Gender

> The lioness picked up *his* cub.
> [*Lioness* is female, and *his* is male.]

> A child must bring in a doctor's note before *she* comes to school.
> [The child may be a male or female but *she* is female.]

Agreement

> The lioness picked up *her* cub.
> A child must bring in a doctor's note before *he or she* comes to school.

Practice

Correct the clear reference and case and number errors in these sentences. Some sentences may not have errors.

1. His was the best table tennis player.
2. Whom was the worst table tennis player?
3. Where are the table tennis balls?
4. Before the game everyone are going to choose teams.
5. The names of the winning team are sent to we.

6. Them are the best table tennis team.
7. Ron and Jeff wanted to use his skates.
8. Jeff went to get them.
9. The couch looked different, depending on how they were arranged.
10. Bob won most of his table tennis games.
11. The student waited for their school bus to come.
12. Either of the buses can arrive on time if they don't break down.
13. The book was most interesting near her beginning.
14. She read the book to find her most interesting parts.
15. I am the winner; victory is ours.
16. His friends got out of the car, and he went over to talk to them.
17. The rain clouds moved toward the pool, and the swimmers tried to wish it away.
18. Was Les disappointed that him team did not win?
19. Whom has more experience than Nicky does?
20. You play better after you have experience.

Answers on page 46

SUBJECT–VERB AGREEMENT

SINGULAR AND PLURAL

Singular nouns take singular verbs. Plural nouns take plural verbs. Singular verbs usually end in *s*, and plural verbs usually do not. Here are some examples.

Singular: My father wants me home early.
Plural: My parents want me home early.

Singular: Ryan runs a mile each day.
Plural: Ryan and Chad run a mile each day.

Singular: She tries her best to do a good job.
Plural: Liz and Ann try their best to do a good job.

CORRECTLY IDENTIFY SUBJECT AND VERB

The subject may not be in front of the verb. In fact, the subject may not be anywhere near the verb. Say the subject and the verb to yourself. If it makes sense, you probably have it right.

• Words may come between the subject and the verb.

Chad's final exam score, which he showed to his mother, improved his final grade.

The verb is *improved*. The word *mother* appears just before *improved*.

Is this the subject? Say it to yourself. [Mother improved the grade.]

That can't be right. *Score* must be the subject. Say it to yourself.
[Score improved the grade.]
That's right. *Score* is the subject, and *improved* is the verb.

The racer running with a sore arm finished first.

Say it to yourself. [Racer finished first.] *Racer* is the noun, and *finished* is the verb.

It wouldn't make any sense to say the arm finished first.

- The verb may come before the subject.

Over the river and through the woods romps the merry leprechaun.

Leprechaun is the subject, and *romps* is the verb. [Think: Leprechaun romps.]

Where are the car keys?

Keys is the subject, and *are* is the verb. [Think: The car keys are where?]

Examples of Subject–Verb Agreement

Words such as *each, neither, everyone, nobody, someone,* and *anyone* are singular pronouns. They always take a singular verb.

Everyone needs a good laugh now and then.
Nobody knows more about computers than Bob.

Words that refer to number such as *one-half, any, most,* and *some* can be singular or plural.

One-fifth of the students were absent. [*Students* is plural.]
One-fifth of the cake was eaten. [There is only one cake.]

Practice

Correct any subject-verb agreement errors. Some sentences may be correct.

1. The chess set are still on the shelf.
2. The shortest route to the college are shown in the catalog.
3. The golf pro drive a golf cart every day.
4. Derek and Ann walks every morning.
5. The tropical birds in the tree adds a festive air to the occasion.
6. No one, not even Rick or Ronnie, walk to school today.
7. Do you know who they is?
8. Ron prepare a paper for submission to the committee.
9. The 15 employees of the coffeehouse shows up each day at 6:00 A.M.
10. Each person who takes the 12 steps improve his or her view.

Answers on page 48

ADJECTIVES AND ADVERBS

ADJECTIVES

Adjectives modify nouns and pronouns. Adjectives add detail and clarify nouns and pronouns. Frequently, adjectives come immediately before the nouns or pronouns they are modifying. At other times, the nouns or pronouns come first and are connected directly to the adjectives by linking verbs. Here are some examples.

Direct	With a Linking Verb
That is a *large* dog.	That dog is *large*.
He's an *angry* man.	The man seems *angry*.

ADVERBS

Adverbs are often formed by adding *ly* to an adjective. However, many adverbs don't end in *ly* (e.g., *always*). Adverbs modify verbs, adjectives, and adverbs. Adverbs can also modify phrases, clauses, and sentences. Here are some examples.

Modify verb:	Ryan *quickly* sought a solution.
Modify adjective	That is an *exceedingly* large dog.
Modify adverb:	Lisa told her story *quite* truthfully.
Modify sentence:	*Unfortunately*, all good things must end.
Modify phrase:	The instructor arrived *just* in time to start the class.

Avoiding Adjective and Adverb Errors

• Don't use adjectives in place of adverbs.

Correct	Incorrect
Lynne read the book quickly.	Lynne read the book quick.
Stan finished his work easily.	Stan finished his work easy.

- Don't confuse the adjectives *good* and *bad* with the adverbs *well* and *badly*.

Correct	Incorrect
Adverbs	
She wanted to play the piano well.	She wanted to play the piano good.
Bob sang badly.	Bob sang bad.
Adjectives	
The food tastes good.	The food tastes well.
The food tastes bad.	The food tastes badly.

- Don't confuse the adjectives *real* and *sure* with the adverbs *really* and *surely*.

Correct	Incorrect
Chuck played really well.	Chuck played real well.
He was surely correct.	He was sure correct.

Comparison

Adjectives and adverbs can show comparisons. Avoid clumsy modifiers.

Correct	Incorrect
Jim is more clingy than Ray.	Jim is clingier than Ray.
Ray is much taller than Jim.	Ray is more taller than Jim.
Jim is more interesting than Ray	Jim is interesting than Ray.
Ray is happier than Jim.	Ray is more happy than Jim.

Word comparisons carefully to be sure that the comparison is clear.

Unclear:	Chad lives closer to Ryan than Blaire.
Clear:	Chad lives closer to Ryan than Blaire does.
Clear:	Chad lives closer to Ryan than he does to Blaire.
Unclear:	The bus engines are bigger than cars.
Clear:	The bus engines are bigger than cars' engines.

Practice

Correct the adjective and adverb errors. Some sentences may contain no errors.

1. The view of the Grand Canyon was real spectacular.
2. The trainer said the dog behaved very good today.
3. Unfortunate, the tickets for the concert were sold out.
4. Things went smooth.
5. The judge took extremely exception to the defendant's actions.
6. The accident was silly, particularly since driving more careful would have avoided the whole thing.
7. But the reviews said the performance was truly horrible.
8. The manager conveniently forgot that she promised the employee a raise.
9. The bonus was a welcome surprise; it was a real large check.
10. I didn't do good, but didn't do bad either.

Answers on page 49

Practice

Correct the comparison errors. Some sentences may be correct.

1. Leon was the happier chef in the restaurant.
2. But some of the people eating in the restaurant were happier than Leon.
3. The jet was the faster plane at the airport.
4. John was the fastest of the twins.
5. The taller of the apartment buildings is under repair.
6. The lightest of the two weights is missing.
7. Lonnie was among the most creative students in the school.
8. Ron is the least able of the two drivers.
9. His shoe size is the smallest in his class.
10. She was the more capable of the two referees.

Answers on page 49

MISPLACED AND DANGLING MODIFIERS

Modifiers may be words or groups of words. Modifiers change or qualify the meaning of another word or group of words. Modifiers belong near the words they modify.

Misplaced modifiers appear to modify words in a way that doesn't make sense.

The modifier in the following sentence is *in a large box*. It doesn't make sense for *in a large box* to modify *house*. Move the modifier near *pizza* where it belongs.

Misplaced: Les delivered pizza to the house in a large box.

Revised: Les delivered pizza in a large box to the house.

The modifier in the next sentence is *paid well. Paid well* can't modify *city*. Move it next to *the job* where it belongs.

Misplaced:	Gail wanted the job in the city that paid well.
Revised:	Gail wanted the well-paying job in the city.

Dangling modifiers modify words not present in the sentence. The modifier in the following sentence is *waiting for the concert to begin*.

This modifier describes the audience, but audience is not mentioned in the sentence. The modifier is left dangling with nothing to attach itself to.

Dangling:	Waiting for the concert to begin, the chanting started.
Revised:	Waiting for the concert to begin, the audience began chanting.
Revised:	The audience began chanting while waiting for the concert to begin.

The modifier in the next sentence is *after three weeks in the country*. The modifier describes the person, not the license. But the person is not mentioned in the sentence. The modifier is dangling.

Dangling:	After three weeks in the country, the license was revoked.
Revised:	After he was in the country for three weeks, his license was revoked.
Revised:	His license was revoked after he was in the country three weeks.

Practice

Correct the misplaced modifiers. Some sentences may be correct.

1. Les was reading his book through glasses with dirty lenses.
2. Jim left work early to go to the doctor on the train.
3. The first train car was crowded; which had to go to the next car.
4. Ron's car ran out of gas when on the way to the store.
5. Zena was jogging, when caused her to fall.
6. Derek wrapped the flowers and put them in the delivery van with colorful paper.
7. Which bus stops at the corner where the stop sign is?
8. Fran is going on the plane, which is just pulling up to the gate.
9. Lisa bought a shirt in the store, which was expensive.
10. The car turned around and the headlights shone quickly into the garage.

Answers on page 50

COMMA SPLICES AND RUN-ON SENTENCES

An *independent clause* is a clause that could be a sentence.

Independent clauses should be joined by a semicolon, or by a comma and a conjunction.

A *comma splice* consists of two independent clauses joined by just a comma.

A *run-on* sentence consists of two independent clauses incorrectly joined.

Correct: The whole family went on vacation; the parents took turns driving.
[Two independent clauses are joined by a semicolon.]

The whole family went on vacation, and the parents took turns driving.
[Two independent clauses are joined by a comma and a conjunction.]

Incorrect: The whole family went on vacation, the parents took turns driving.
[Comma splice. Two independent clauses are joined by just a comma.]

The whole family went on vacation the parents took turns driving.
[Run-on sentence. Two independent clauses are incorrectly joined.]

Practice

Correct the run-on sentences and comma splices. Some sentences may be correct.

1. It will be tomorrow before the sea is calm enough to go out.
2. It started to rain unexpectedly the boaters were soaked.
3. But right now my sneakers are soaking wet the towel is too wet to help me.
4. The Marine Police sounded the siren the boat stopped immediately.
5. I put the sneakers next to the fire to dry, although they started to steam after a while.
6. The Coast Guard monitors boats as they enter the river they use the data to monitor water pollution.
7. I like to use my compass when I go out on the boat.
8. When the boat breaks down, Liz calls Sea Tow.
9. The fire went out the sun came up.
10. Splashing through the waves, the water skier was covered with salt spray.

Answers on page 51

SENTENCE FRAGMENTS

English sentences require a subject and a predicate (see page 22). The predicate includes a verb. Fragments are parts of sentences written as though they were sentences. Fragments are writing mistakes that lack a subject, a predicate, or both subject and predicate. Here are some examples.

Since when.
To enjoy the summer months.
Because he isn't working hard.
If you can fix old cars.
What the principal wanted to hear.

Include a subject and/or a verb to rewrite a fragment as a sentence.

Fragment	Sentence
Should be coming up the driveway now.	The *car* should be coming up the driveway now.
Both the lawyer and her client.	Both the lawyer and her client *waited* in court.
Which is my favorite subject.	*I took math*, which is my favorite subject.
If you can play.	If you can play, *you'll improve with practice.*

Verbs such as *to be, to go, winning, starring,* etc., need a main verb.

Fragment	Sentence
The new rules to go into effect in April.	The new rules *will* go into effect in April.
The team winning every game.	The team *was* winning every game.

Often, a fragment is related to a complete sentence. Combine the two to make a single sentence.

Fragment: Reni loved vegetables. *Particularly corn, celery, lettuce, squash, and eggplant.*

Revised: Reni loved vegetables, particularly corn, celery, lettuce, squash, and eggplant.

Fragment: *To see people standing on Mars.* This could happen in this century.

Revised: To see people standing on Mars is one of the things that could happen in this century.

Sometimes short fragments can be used for emphasis. However, you should not use fragments in your essay. Here are some examples.

Stop! Don't take one more step toward that apple pie.

I need some time to myself. *That's why.*

Practice

Correct the sentence fragments. Some items may be correct.

1. A golf bag, golf clubs, and golf balls. That's what she needed to play.
2. As the rocket prepared for blast-off. Mary saw birds flying in the distance.
3. Jim is mowing the lawn. Then, the mower stopped.
4. The lawn looked lush and green. Like a golf course.
5. The polar bears swept across the ice. Like white ghosts in fur jackets.
6. Jim looked across at the igloo. Like an ice fort, it stood a lonely vigil.
7. Astronauts and their equipment went by. These were the people who would go into space.
8. This was what Joe had been waiting for. To graduate from college.
9. To be finished with this test. That's what I'm waiting for.
10. The test finished and done. The papers graded and good.

Answers on page 52

PARALLELISM

When two or more ideas are connected, use a parallel structure. Parallelism helps the reader follow the passage more clearly. Here are some examples.

Not Parallel: Toni stayed in shape by eating right and exercising daily.
Parallel: Toni stayed in shape by eating right and *by* exercising daily.

Not Parallel: Lisa is a student who works hard and has genuine insight.
Parallel: Lisa is a student who works hard and *who* has genuine insight.

Not Parallel: Art had a choice either to clean his room or take out the garbage.
Parallel: Art had a choice either to clean his room or *to* take out the garbage.

Not Parallel: Derek wanted a success rather than failing.
Parallel: Derek wanted a success rather than a failure.
Parallel: Derek wanted success rather than failure.

Practice

Correct any parallel form errors. Some sentences may not have errors.

1. I have to get to work, but first I have to find my way to breakfast.
2. The road was dry; the day was hot and sultry.
3. Jane likes to eat and go shopping when she is at the mall.
4. April chose to be a cameraperson rather than to be a technician who works the sound board.
5. Since I have not heard from you, I decided to write this letter.
6. Although she had driven the road before, Sally proceeded slowly, keeping her eye on the yellow line.
7. The tree withstood the hurricane, but the branches on the tree snapped off.
8. His work on the Board of Education revealed his dedication to the community.
9. Cars, taxis, and buses were my transportation to the airport.
10. The subject matter and the preparation for class created an excellent lesson.

Answers on page 53

DICTION

Diction is choosing and using appropriate words. Good diction conveys a thought clearly without unnecessary words. Good diction develops fully over a number of years; however, there are some rules and tips you can follow.

- Do not use slang, colloquialisms, or other nonstandard English. One person's slang is another person's confusion. Slang is often regional, and slang meanings change rapidly. We do not give examples of slang here for that very reason. Do not use slang words in your formal writing.

    Colloquialisms are words used frequently in spoken language. This informal use of terms such as *dog tired, kids,* and *hanging around* is not generally accepted in formal writing. Save these informal terms for daily speech and omit or remove them from your writing except as quotations.

    Omit any other nonstandard English. Always choose standard English terms that accurately reflect the thought to be conveyed.

- Avoid wordy, redundant, or pretentious writing. Good writing is clear and economical.

Wordy: I chose my career as a teacher because of its high ideals, the truly self-sacrificing idealism of a career in teaching, and for the purpose of receiving the myriad and cascading recognition that one can receive from the community as a whole and from its constituents.

Revised: I chose a career in teaching for its high ideals and for community recognition.

Given below is a partial list of wordy phrases and the replacement word.

Wordy Phrases and Replacements			
at the present time	now	because of the fact that	because
for the purpose of	for	in the final analysis	finally
in the event that	if	until such time as	until

HOMONYMS

Homonyms are words that sound alike but do not have the same meaning. These words can be confusing and you may use the incorrect spelling of a word. If words are homonyms, be sure you choose the correct spelling for the meaning you intend.

Homonyms	
accept (receive)	ascent (rise)
except (other than)	assent (agreement)
board (wood)	fair (average)
bored (uninterested)	fare (a charge)
led (guided)	lessen (make less)
lead (metal)	lesson (learning experience)
past (gone before)	peace (no war)
passed (moved by)	piece (portion)
rain (precipitation)	to (toward)
reign (rule)	too (also)
rein (animal strap)	two (a number)
their (possessive pronoun)	its (shows possession)
there (location)	it's (it is)
they're (they are)	

IDIOMS

Idioms are expressions with special meanings and often break the rules of grammar. Idioms are acceptable in formal writing, but they must be used carefully. Here are some examples.

Idioms	
in accordance with	inferior to
angry with	occupied by (someone)
differ from (someone)	occupied with (something)
differ about (an issue)	prior to
independent of	rewarded with (something)

Practice

Write the word or phrase that fits best in the blank.

1. Many _____ diseases, including pneumonia and swelling in cuts, are caused by bacteria.
   innocuous   unfortunate   infectious   ill-fated

2. Sigmund Freud's views of sexuality had become _____, and the country entered the sexual revolution.
   well known   all knowing   universal   inculcated

3. After crossing the land bridge near the Bering Strait, groups of Native Americans _____ spread throughout all of North, Central, and South America.
   inclusively   eventually   regardless   remotely

4. During the early 1500s Cortez and Pizarro opened up Central America to the Spanish who began _____ slaves from Africa.
   importing   exporting   imparting   immigrating

5. The Stamp Act requiring every legal paper to carry a tax stamp was vehemently _____ and eventually repealed by England.
   denied   deported   proclaimed   protested

Circle the underlined portion that is unnecessary in the passage.

6. No goal is more noble—no feat more revealing—than the strikingly brave exploration of space.
7. As many as a ton of bananas may have spoiled when the ship was stuck and delayed in the Panama Canal.

8. He <u>was concerned</u> about <u>crossing</u> the bridge, <u>but the officer</u> said that it was all right to cross <u>and he need not worry</u>.
9. A <u>professional</u> golfer told the <u>novice</u> beginning golfer that <u>professional instruction</u> or more practice <u>improves most golfers' scores</u>.
10. The soccer player's <u>slight</u> strain from the shot on goal <u>that won the game</u> led to a <u>pulled</u> muscle that <u>would</u> keep her from <u>playing</u> the next match.

Circle the word or words used incorrectly in the sentence.

11. He went to the bird's nest near the river, only too realize he missed its assent.
12. The rider pulled back on the horse's reign before the whether turned rainy.
13. The whether turned rainy as he led the hikers on there ascent.
14. The lessen was clear; it was fare, but not easy to accept.
15. They're board relatives were not fare too her father.

Correct the idiom errors. Some sentences may not have errors.

16. Her grades had everything to do of her efforts.
17. Joanie expected him to wait to the house until she arrived home.
18. She could spend months absorbed in her studies.
19. The two coaches differ significantly with each other's style.
20. That person is wearing the same coat from you.

Answers on page 53

PUNCTUATION

THE COMMA (,)

The comma may be the most used punctuation mark. This section details a few of these uses.

A clause is part of a sentence that could be a sentence itself. If a clause begins with a conjunction, use a comma before the conjunction.

Incorrect: I was satisfied with the food but John was grumbling.
Correct: I was satisfied with the food, but John was grumbling.

Incorrect: Larry was going fishing or he was going to paint his house.
Correct: Larry was going fishing, or he was going to paint his house.

A clause or a phrase often introduces a sentence. Introductory phrases or clauses should be set off by a comma. If the introductory element is very short, the comma is optional. Here are some examples.

However, there are other options you may want to consider.
When the deicer hit the plane's wing, the ice began to melt.
To get a driver's license, go to the motor vehicle bureau.
It doesn't matter what you want, you have to take what you get.

Parenthetical expressions interrupt the flow of a sentence. Set off the parenthetical expression with commas. Do not set off expressions that are essential to understanding the sentence. Here are some examples.

Tom, an old friend, showed up at my house the other day.

I was traveling on a train, in car 8200, on my way to Florida.

John and Ron, who are seniors, went on break to Florida.
[Use a comma. The phrase "who are seniors" is extra information.]

All the students who are seniors take an additional course.
[Don't use a comma. The phrase "who are seniors" is essential information.]

Commas are used to set off items in a list or series. Here are some examples.

Jed is interested in computers, surfing, and fishing.
[Notice the comma before the conjunction *and*.]

Mario drives a fast, red car.
[The sentence would make sense with *and* in place of the commas.]

Andy hoped for a bright, sunny, balmy day.
[The sentence would make sense with *and* in place of the commas.]

Lucy had a pale green dress.
[The sentence would not make sense with *and*. The word *pale* modifies *green*. Don't use a comma.]

Randy will go to the movies, pick up some groceries, and then go home.

Practice

Correct the comma errors. Some sentences may have no comma errors.

1. I had a slow day yesterday, but I worked hard in my junior year.
2. Passing calculus seems a difficult, but achievable, result.
3. After making the sandwich, I looked for some pickles, but the jar was empty.
4. Write an outline first and be sure to leave enough time to write the essay.
5. In the attic I found some old clothes, an old trunk, and a shoe.
6. Chad, Blaire, and Ryan have advanced degrees but they are still children at heart.
7. Using a computer the CBT tests reading, writing, and arithmetic.
8. Either walk the dog or wash the dishes.
9. Every pilot, who has flown over 20 missions, receives an award.
10. Each time I ate lunch at home, my mother made liverwurst sandwiches.

Answers on page 55

SEMICOLON AND COLON

The Semicolon (;)

Use the semicolon to connect main clauses not connected by a conjunction. Include a semicolon with very long clauses connected by a conjunction. Here are some examples.

The puck was dropped; the hockey game began.

The puck was dropped, and the hockey game began.

The general manager of the hockey team was not sure what should be done about the player who was injured during the game; but he did know that the player's contract stipulated that his pay would continue whether he was able to play or not.

The Colon (:)

Use the colon after a main clause to introduce a list. Here are some examples.

Liz kept these items in her car: spare tire, jack, flares, and a blanket.

Liz kept a spare tire, jack, flares, and a blanket in her car.

Practice

Correct any semicolon or colon errors. Some sentences may be correct.

1. Pack these other things for camp; a bathing suit, some socks and a shirt.
2. In your wallet put: your camp information card and your bus pass.
3. I have one thing left to do; say good-bye.
4. We went to the store; and the parking lot was filled with cars.
5. We fought our way through the crowds, the store was even more crowded than the parking lot.

Answers on page 56

PERIOD, QUESTION MARK, EXCLAMATION POINT

The Period (.)

Use a period to end every sentence, unless the sentence is a direct question, a strong command, or an interjection.

You will do well on the Praxis I test.

The Question Mark (?)

Use a question mark to end every sentence that is a direct question.

What is the passing score for the Praxis I test?

The Exclamation Point (!)

Use an exclamation point to end every sentence that is a strong command or interjection. Do not overuse exclamation points.

Interjection: Pass that test!
Command: Avalanche, head for cover!

Practice

Correct any punctuation errors.

1. I was so worn out after swimming!
2. Avalanche.
3. Who said that!
4. Warning. The danger signal blared in the background.
5. I can't believe this is the last day of camp?

Answers on page 56

Answers

Nouns, page 23

1. sheaves

2. deer

3. fries

4. lunches

5. knees

6. ladies

7. octopi

8. echoes

9. feet

10. halves

Verbs, page 26

has driven
drove
1. Ryan ~~driven~~ to Florida.

2. Refereeing soccer games is not work.
   [No tense errors.]

rode
3. Chad ~~ride~~ to the game with his team last week.
   [The words *last week* indicate that the verb must be past tense.]

run
4. Why did Mary ~~ran~~ her errands now?

spoken
5. I have ~~speak~~ to my teacher about the grade.

paddles
6. Carl ~~paddled~~ across the river every Saturday.
   [Use the present tense because it is a regular event.]

threw
had thrown
7. Blaire ~~thrown~~ out the ball for the players to use.

lose
8. Joann will ~~lost~~ her bag if she leaves it in the store.

9. Bob is standing on a stool next to the green table.
   [No tense errors.]

began
10. Liz ~~begun~~ to grasp the depth of her happiness.

Tense Shift, page 26

1. Lisa already went to the North Pole but she is not going there again.
   [No tense shift errors.]

took
2. Dennis ~~will take~~ his airline tickets with him because he is leaving for his flight.

3. The runner gasped as she crosses the finish line.

   The runner gasped as she crossed the finish line.
   The runner gasps as she crosses the finish line.

   play
4. I like to hear music so I ~~played~~ the clarinet.

   wants
5. Chris ~~wanted~~ to be a producer so he puts in long hours every day.

6. Bertha sews five hours a day because she will need her dress by next month. [No tense shift errors.]

7. The car turns over and then bounced down the hill.

   The car turned over and then bounced down the hill.
   The car turns over and then bounces down the hill.
   The car turned over and then bounced down the hill.

8. Lois handed over her money because she wants to buy the computer.

   Lois hands over her money because she wants to buy the computer.
   Lois handed over her money because she wanted to buy the computer.

9. The captain wandered out on the deck as she calls to her friends on shore.

   The captain wandered out on the deck as she called to her friends on shore.
   The captain wanders out on the deck as she calls to her friends on shore.

10. The sun sets in the west as the moon rose in the east.

    The sun set in the west as the moon rose in the east.
    The sun sets in the west as the moon rises in the east.

Pronouns, page 28

   He
1. ~~His~~ was the best table tennis player.

   Who
2. ~~Whom~~ was the worst table tennis player?

3. Where are the table tennis balls?
   [No errors.]

is
4. Before the game everyone ~~are~~ going to choose teams.

          us
5. The names of the winning team are sent to ~~we~~.

They
6. ~~Them~~ are the best table tennis team.

      Ron's
7. Ron and Jeff wanted to use ~~his~~ skates.
[Jeff's, or any other name, could be used in place of Ron's.]

      the skates
8. Jeff went to get ~~them~~.
[Other nouns that make sense in this context could be used in place of skates.]

      the pillows
9. The couch looked different, depending on how ~~they~~ were arranged.

10. Bob won most of his table tennis games.
[No errors.]

    her or his
11. The student waited for ~~their~~ school bus to come.

      it doesn't
12. Either of the buses can arrive on time if ~~they don't~~ break down.

      its
13. The book was most interesting near ~~her~~ beginning.

    the
14. She read the book to find ~~her~~ most interesting parts.

15. I am the winner; victory is ours.

    I am the winner; victory is mine.
    We are the winners; victory is ours.

16. His friends got out of the car, and he went over to talk to them.
[No errors.]

17. The rain clouds moved toward the pool and the swimmers tried to wish it away.

    The rain cloud moved toward the pool and the swimmers tried to wish it away.
    The rain clouds moved toward the pool and the swimmers tried to wish them away.

                    his
18. Was Les disappointed that ~~him~~ team did not win?

    Who
19. ~~Whom~~ has more experience than Nicky does?

20. You play better after you have experience.
    [No errors.]

Subject–Verb Agreement, page 30

          is
1. The chess set ~~are~~ still on the shelf.

                          is
2. The shortest route to the college ~~are~~ shown in the catalog.

              drives
3. The golf pro ~~drive~~ a golf cart every day.

                walk
4. Derek and Ann ~~walks~~ every morning.

                          add
5. The tropical birds in the tree ~~adds~~ a festive air to the occasion.

                        walks
6. No one, not even Rick or Ronnie, ~~walk~~ to school today.

                    are
7. Do you know who they ~~is~~?

        prepares
8. Ron ~~prepare~~ a paper for submission to the committee.

                        show
9. The 15 employees of the coffeehouse ~~shows~~ up each day at 6:00 a.m.

improves

10. Each person who takes the 12 steps ~~improve~~ his or her view.

Adjectives and Adverbs, page 33

really

1. The view of the Grand Canyon was ~~real~~ spectacular.

well

2. The trainer said the dog behaved very ~~good~~ today.

Unfortunately

3. ~~Unfortunate~~, the tickets for the concert were sold out.

smoothly

4. Things went ~~smooth~~.

extreme

5. The judge took ~~extremely~~ exception to the defendant's actions.

carefully

6. The accident was silly, particularly since driving more ~~careful~~ would have avoided the whole thing.

7. But the reviews said the performance was truly horrible.
[No adjective or adverb errors.]

8. The manager conveniently forgot that she promised the employee a raise.
[No adjective or adverb errors.]

really

9. The bonus was a welcome surprise; it was a ~~real~~ large check.

well   **badly**

10. I didn't do ~~good~~, but didn't do ~~bad~~ either.

Comparison, page 33

happiest

1. Leon was the ~~happieer~~ chef in the restaurant.

2. But some of the people eating in the restaurant were happier than Leon.
[No error.]

fastest

3. The jet was the ~~faster~~ plane at the airport.

faster
4. John was the ~~fastest~~ of the twins.

tallest
5. The ~~taller~~ of the apartment buildings is under repair.

lighter
6. The ~~lightest~~ of the two weights is missing.

7. Lonnie was among the most creative students in the school.
[No error.]

less
8. Ron is the ~~least~~ able of the two drivers.

9. His shoe size is the smallest in his class.
[No error.]

10. She was the more capable of the two referees.
[No error.]

Misplaced and Dangling Modifiers, page 34

1. Les was reading his book through glasses with dirty lenses.
[No modifier errors.]

2. Jim left work early to go to the doctor on the train.

Jim left work early to go on a train to the doctor.

3. The first train car was crowded; which had to go to the next car.

The first train car was crowded; someone (he) (she) had to go to the next car.

4. Ron's car ran out of gas when on the way to the store.

Ron's car ran out of gas when he was on the way to the store.
[Many other substitutions are possible for *he was.*]

5. Zena was jogging, when caused her to fall.

Zena was jogging, when a hole caused her to fall.
[Many other substitutions are possible for *a hole.*]

6. Derek wrapped the flowers and put them in the delivery van with colorful paper.

   Derek wrapped the flowers with colorful paper and put them in the delivery van.

7. Which bus stops at the corner where the stop sign is?
   [No modifier errors.]

8. Fran is going on the plane, which is just pulling up to the gate.
   [No modifier errors.]

9. Lisa bought a shirt in the store, which was expensive.

   Lisa bought an expensive shirt in the store.
   Lisa bought a shirt in an expensive store.
   Lisa bought an expensive shirt in an expensive store.

10. The car turned around and the headlights shone quickly into the garage.

    The car turned around quickly and the headlights shone into the garage.

Comma Splices and Run-On Sentences, page 35

There are three ways to remedy run-on sentence errors and comma splice errors. You can create two sentences, put a comma and a conjunction between the clauses, or put a semicolon between the two clauses. *Only one of these options is shown in the answers.*

1. It will be tomorrow before the sea is calm enough to go out.
   [No errors.]

2. It started to rain unexpectedly; the boaters were soaked.

3. But right now my sneakers are soaking wet; the towel is too wet to help me.

4. The Marine Police sounded the siren; the boat stopped immediately.

5. I put the sneakers next to the fire to dry, although they started to steam after a while.
   [No errors.]

6. The Coast Guard monitors boats as they enter the river; they use the data to monitor water pollution.

7. I like to use my compass when I go out on the boat.
   [No errors.]

8. When the boat breaks down, Liz calls Sea Tow.
   [No errors.]

9. The fire went out; the sun came up.

10. Splashing through the waves, the water skier was covered with salt spray.
    [No error.]

Sentence Fragments, page 37

1. A golf bag, golf clubs, and golf balls. That's what she needed to play.

   A golf bag, golf clubs, and golf balls were what she needed to play.

2. As the rocket prepared for blast-off. Mary saw birds flying in the distance.

   The rocket prepared for blast-off. Mary saw birds flying in the distance.
   As the rocket prepared for blast-off, Mary saw birds flying in the distance.

3. Jim is mowing the lawn. Then, the mower stopped.
   [No sentence fragment errors.]

4. The lawn looked lush and green. Like a golf course.

   The lawn looked lush and green, like a golf course.

5. The polar bears swept across the ice. Like white ghosts in fur jackets.

   The polar bears swept across the ice, like white ghosts in fur jackets.

6. Jim looked across at the igloo. Like an ice fort, it stood a lonely vigil.
   [No sentence fragment errors.]

7. Astronauts and their equipment went by. These were the people who would go into space.
   [No sentence fragment errors.]

8. This was what Joe had been waiting for. To graduate from college.

   This was what Joe had been waiting for, to graduate from college.

9. To be finished with this test. That's what I'm waiting for.

   To be finished with this test is what I'm waiting for.

10. The test finished and done. The papers graded and good.

    The tests were finished and done.
    The papers were graded and good.

Parallelism, page 38

1. I have to get to work, but first I have to ~~find my way~~ to breakfast.
   get

2. The road was dry; the day was hot and sultry.
   [No parallel form errors.]

3. Jane likes to eat and go shopping when she is at the mall.
   [No parallel form errors.]

4. April chose to be a cameraperson rather than to be a ~~technician who works the sound board~~.
   sound technician

5. Since I have not heard from you, I decided to write this letter.
   [No parallel form errors. The conjunction *since* shows subordination.]

6. Although she had driven the road before, Sally proceeded slowly, keeping her eye on the yellow line.
   [No parallel form errors. The conjunction *although* shows subordination.]

7. The tree withstood the hurricane, but ~~the branches on the tree~~ snapped off.
   tree branches

8. His work on the Board of Education revealed his dedication to the community.
   [No parallel form errors.]

9. Cars, taxis, and buses were my transportation to the airport.
   [No parallel form errors.]

10. The subject matter and the ~~preparation for class~~ created an excellent lesson.
    class preparation

Diction, page 40

1. Many <u>infectious</u> diseases, including pneumonia and swelling in cuts, are caused by bacteria.

   Infectious means a disease caused by bacteria. While the disease may be unfortunate, the context of the sentence calls for a word that means *caused by bacteria*.

2. Sigmund Freud's views of sexuality had become <u>well known</u>, and the country entered the sexual revolution.

   Well known means known by many people. *Universal* means known everywhere, which does not fit the context of this sentence.

3. After crossing the land bridge near the Bering Strait, groups of Native Americans <u>eventually</u> spread throughout all of North, Central, and South America.

   Eventually means over a period of time. The other words do not make sense in this context.

4. During the early 1500s Cortez and Pizarro opened up Central America to the Spanish who began <u>importing</u> slaves from Africa.

   Importing means to bring in. Exporting means to send out, which does not fit the context of the sentence.

5. The Stamp Act requiring every legal paper to carry a tax stamp was vehemently <u>protested</u> and eventually repealed by England.

   The act could only be *protested* in this context. It was not *denied*, and it does not make sense to say it was *vehemently* denied.

The circled phrases make the sentence too wordy.

6. <u>No</u> goal <u>is more noble</u>—<u>no feat more reveal-ing</u>—than the (strikingly) brave <u>exploration of space</u>.

7. <u>As many</u> as a <u>ton of</u> bananas <u>may have</u> spoiled when <u>the ship</u> was stuck (and delayed) in the Panama Canal.

8. He <u>was concerned</u> about <u>crossing</u> the bridge, <u>but the officer</u> said that it was all right to cross (and he need not worry).

9. A <u>professional</u> golfer told the (novice) beginning golfer that <u>professional instruction</u> or more practice <u>improves most golfers' scores</u>.

10. The soccer player's <u>slight</u> strain from the shot on goal <u>that won the game</u> led to a <u>pulled</u> muscle that <u>would</u> keep her from <u>playing</u> the next match.

The circled words are homonym errors.

11. He went to the bird's nest near the river, only (too) realize he missed its (assent).

12. The rider pulled back on the horse's (reign) before the (whether) turned rainy.

13. The (whether) turned rainy as he led the hikers on there ascent.

14. The (lessen) was clear; it was (fare), but not easy to accept.

15. (They're) (board) relatives were not (fare), (too) her father.

Refer to page 40 for a list of idioms.

with

16. Her grades had everything to do ~~of~~ her efforts.

at

17. Joanie expected him to wait ~~to~~ the house until she arrived home.

18. She could spend months absorbed in her studies.
[No idiom error.]

from

19. The two coaches differ significantly ~~with~~ each other's style.

as

20. That person is wearing the same coat ~~from~~ you.

Commas, page 41

1. I had a slow day yesterday, but I worked hard in my junior year.
[No comma errors.]

2. Passing calculus seems a difficult, but achievable, result.
[No comma errors.]

3. After making the sandwich, I looked for some pickles, but the jar was empty.
[No comma errors.]

4. Write an outline first, and be sure to leave enough time to write the essay.
[Add a comma before the conjunction to separate the two clauses.]

5. In the attic I found some old clothes, an old trunk, and a shoe.
[No comma errors.]

6. Chad, Blaire, and Ryan have advanced degrees, but they are still children at heart.
[Add a comma to separate the clauses.]

7. Using a computer, the CBT tests reading, writing, and arithmetic.
[Add a comma to set off the introductory phrase.]

8. Either walk the dog or wash the dishes.
   [No comma errors.]

9. Every pilot who has flown over 20 missions receives an award.
   [Remove the commas.]

10. Each time I ate lunch at home my mother made liverwurst sandwiches.
    [Remove the comma.]

Semicolons and Colons, page 43

1. Pack these other things for camp: a bathing suit, some socks, and a shirt.
   [Replace the semicolon with a colon.]

2. In your wallet put your camp information card and your bus pass.
   [Remove the colon.]

3. I have one thing left to do: say good-bye.
   [Replace the semicolon with a colon.]

4. We went to the store, and the parking lot was filled with cars.
   [Replace the semicolon with a comma.]

5. We fought our way through the crowds; the store was even more crowded than the parking lot.
   [Replace the comma with a semicolon.]

Period, Question Mark, and Exclamation Point, page 44

1. I was so worn out after swimming.
   [Change the exclamation point to a period.]

2. Avalanche!
   [Change the period to an exclamation point.]

3. Who said that?
   [Change the exclamation point to a question mark.]

4. Warning! The danger signal blared in the background.
   [Change the period to an exclamation point.]

5. I can't believe this is the last day of camp.
   [Change the question mark to a period.]

Strategies for Taking the Multiple-Choice Writing Test

This section shows you how to pass the multiple-choice writing portion of the PPST writing test.

TYPES OF QUESTIONS

The multiple-choice writing test is very similar to the old Test of Standard Written English (TSWE). You may have taken the TSWE along with the old Scholastic Aptitude Test. Educational Testing Service did away with the TSWE in 1994, but they kept this test.

This test gives you a chance to show what you know about grammar, sentence structure, and word usage. You should be familiar with the topics in the English Review section.

The following topics may be particularly important:

- subject-verb and noun-pronoun agreement

- correct verb tense

- the best word or phrase for a sentence

- parallel verb forms and parallel sentence structure

- sentence fragments and wordy sentences

- distinguishing clear and exact sentences from awkward or ambiguous ones

You may be able to get the correct answer from your sense or feel about the sentence. If you are someone who has an intuitive grasp of English usage, you should rely on your intuition as you complete this section of the tests.

There are two types of questions on the PPST. These examples are from the Review Questions that follow.

Usage

You are shown a sentence with four parts underlined and lettered (A), (B), (C), and (D). There is a fifth choice: (E) No error. You choose the letter of the flawed part, or (E) if there is no error. You do not have to explain what the error is or what makes the other parts correct. No sentence contains more than one error. You just have to recognize the error or realize that there is no error.

EXAMPLE: Every week, Doug took a child from the class on a visit to the
              (A)   (B)   (C)
          art room until he got tired. No error.
                       (D)   (E)

Sentence Correction

You are shown a sentence with one part underlined. Choice (A) repeats the underlined selection exactly. Choices (B) through (E) give suggested changes for the underlined part. You choose the letter of the best choice that does not change the meaning of the original sentence. If the original is best, choose (A). Otherwise, select one of the suggested changes.

> **EXAMPLE:** Many times a shopper will prefer value <u>to price</u>.
> (A) to price
> (B) instead of price
> (C) rather than price
> (D) more than price
> (E) than price

STRATEGIES FOR PASSING THE MULTIPLE-CHOICE TEST

Read Carefully

It is often the small details that count on this test. Read each passage carefully. Read the whole sentence, not just the underlined sections. Remember that an underlined section by itself can look fine but be incorrect in the whole sentence or passage. Read each sentence a few times until you get a sense for its rhythm and flow.

This Is a Test of Written English

Evaluate each sentence as written English. Do not apply the more informal rules of spoken English.

Don't Focus on Punctuation

Use the English rules discussed in the English Review section. However, don't be overly concerned about punctuation. Punctuation rules are seldom tested.

Eliminate and Guess

Eliminate the answers you know are incorrect. If you can't pick out the correct answer, guess from among the remaining choices.

Practice

Usage

Choose the letter that indicates an error, or choose (E) for no error.

1. <u>Every week</u>, Doug took <u>a child from</u> the class on <u>a visit to the</u> art room
   (A)   (B)   (C)

   <u>until he</u> got tired. <u>No error</u>.
   (D)   (E)

2. Doug <u>walks</u> two miles <u>every day</u> and he rubbed off <u>the dirt</u> on <u>his shoes</u> as
   (A)   (B)   (C)   (D)

   he went. <u>No error</u>.
           (E)

3. Jim and Tom, <u>the salesmen</u>, <u>was doing</u> a good job <u>directing</u> the <u>under twelve</u>
              (A)   (B)   (C)   (D)

   soccer league. <u>No error</u>.
              (E)

4. The <u>students</u> were <u>greatly</u> <u>effected</u> by the retirement of a <u>very popular</u>
        (A)   (B)   (C)   (D)

   teacher. <u>No error</u>.
         (E)

5. The Rathburn is a <u>high rated</u> and <u>singularly successful</u> <u>Italian restaurant</u> near
               (A)   (B)   (C)

   <u>the beach</u> in Avalon. <u>No error</u>.
   (D)   (E)

Sentence Correction

Choose the letter of the best choice for the underlined section, without changing the meaning of the sentence. If the original is best, choose (A). Otherwise, select one of the suggested changes.

6. Many times a shopper will prefer value <u>to price</u>.

   (A) to price
   (B) instead of price
   (C) rather than price
   (D) more than price
   (E) than price

7. The tug boat strained against the ship, revved up its engines <u>and was able to maneuver the ship into the middle of the channel</u>.

   (A) and was able to maneuver the ship into the middle of the channel.
   (B) and moves the ship into the middle of the channel.
   (C) moving the ship into the middle of the channel.
   (D) and moved the ship into the middle of the channel.
   (E) with the ship moved into the middle of the channel.

8. After it had snowed steadily for days, the snow plows and snow blowers <u>most important priorities</u>.

   (A) most important priorities.
   (B) were ready for action.
   (C) concentrated on the most important priorities.
   (D) most significant priorities.
   (E) most frequent difficulties.

9. The zoo opened for <u>the day, the children ran</u> to the exhibits.

   (A) the day, the children ran
   (B) the day. the children ran
   (C) the day; the children ran
   (D) the day: the children ran
   (E) the day the children ran

Answer Explanations

Usage

1. **(D)** Pronoun error—it is not clear which noun the pronoun *he* refers to.

2. **(A)** Verb tense error—the verb *walks* should be *walked* to agree with the verb *rubbed*.

3. **(B)** Number error—the subject, *Jim and Tom*, is plural. The verb *was* should be the plural verb *were*.

4. **(C)** Diction error—the word *effected* should be replaced by the word *affected*.

5. **(A)** Adjective-adverb error—the adjective *high* should be changed to the adverb *highly*.

Sentence Correction

6. **(A)** No error—Always choose (A) if there is no error.

7. **(D)** Parallelism error—Choice (D) maintains the parallel development of the sentence.

8. **(C)** Sentence fragment error—The original choice is a sentence fragment. There is no verb for the subject *snow plows and snow blowers*. Choice (B) is grammatically correct but changes the meaning of the sentence.

9. **(C)** Run-on sentence error—Use a semicolon to separate two independent clauses.

Strategies for Taking the Essay Writing Test

FORM OF THE TEST

You will have 30 minutes to write an essay. Your essay is graded holistically by two raters using the six-point scale described on the next page. Holistic grading means that the raters use their informed sense about your writing and not a detailed analysis.

STRATEGIES FOR PASSING THE ESSAY TEST

Read the Topic

Take a few minutes to read and understand the topic. Part of your rating will depend on how well you address the topic.

Make Notes and Sketch a Brief Outline

The page listing the topic has room for an outline. Think for a few minutes and take up to five more minutes to write a brief outline showing how you will structure each of the three or four paragraphs in the essay.

Use the time writing the outline to plan your essay. Use the time working on the essay to write well.

Follow These Rules as You Write

You should have a little more than 15 minutes to write your essay. Plan to write three or four paragraphs. Essays scored 6 are usually longer than those scored 5 or less. Your essay should be a maximum of 350 words.

This does not mean that longer is necessarily better. It does mean that you will need at least four well-written paragraphs to receive a 6 and three or four well-written paragraphs to receive a 5.

Compose and write the topic sentence for your first paragraph. Write two more sentences that develop the topic sentence. These sentences may contain examples, illustrations, and other supporting facts or arguments. You can close your paragraph with a summary sentence.

If you follow this plan for the remaining paragraphs, you should be able to get a 4 or higher.

Use the rules of grammar as you write. Punctuate as carefully as you can but do not spend an inordinate amount of time on punctuation. Raters will often ignore minor grammatical or spelling errors if the essay is well developed.

Refer to your outline as you write.

PART II—ESSAY

Evaluation Guidelines

Find an English professor or a high school English teacher and ask that person to correct your essay and to rate it rigorously 6 through 1 using these criteria.

A rating of 6 or 5 indicates that your writing is acceptable. A rating of 4 or 3 shows you need to work on the errors identified by the raters. A rating of 2 or 1 indicates that you will benefit from English tutoring or additional English coursework.

RATING SCALE

6 This essay is extremely well written. It is the equivalent of an A in-class assignment. The essay addresses the question and provides clear supporting arguments, illustrations, or examples. The paragraphs and sentences are well organized and show a variety of language and syntax. The essay may contain some minor errors.

5 This essay is well written. It is the equivalent of a B+ in-class assignment. The essay addresses the question and provides some supporting arguments, illustrations, or examples. The paragraphs and sentences are fairly well organized and show a variety of language and syntax. The essay may contain some minor mechanical or linguistic errors.

4 This essay is fairly well written. It is the equivalent of a B in-class assignment. The essay adequately addresses the question and provides some supporting arguments, illustrations, or examples for some points. The paragraphs and sentences are acceptably organized and show a variety of language and syntax. The essay may contain mechanical or linguistic errors but is free from an identifiable pattern of errors.

3 This essay may demonstrate some writing ability, but it contains obvious errors. It is the equivalent of a C or C+ in-class assignment. The essay may not clearly address the question and may not give supporting arguments or details. The essay may show problems in diction including inappropriate word choice. The paragraphs and sentences may not be acceptably developed. There will be an identifiable pattern or grouping of errors.

2 This essay shows only the most limited writing ability. It is the equivalent of a D in-class assignment. It contains serious errors and flaws. This essay may not address the question, be poorly organized, or provide no supporting arguments or detail. It usually shows serious errors in diction, usage, and mechanics.

1 This essay does not demonstrate minimal writing ability. It is equivalent of an F in-class assignment. This essay may contain serious and continuing errors, or it may not be coherent.

Targeted Writing Test

This targeted test is designed to help you practice the strategies presented in this chapter. For that reason, questions may have a different emphasis than the actual test, and the actual test will certainly be more complete.

Mark your choice, then check your answers.

Use the strategies on page 57.

PART A

Choose the letter that indicates an error, or choose (E) for no error.

1. <u>Kitty and Harry's</u> <u>anniversary will fall on</u> <u>Father's Day</u> <u>this year</u>. <u>No error.</u>
   (A)   (B)   (C)   (D)   (E)

2. <u>The trees leaves</u> <u>provide</u> a fall festival called <u>"Fall Foliage"</u>
   (A)   (B)   (C)

   <u>in most New England states</u>. <u>No error.</u>
          (D)   (E)

3. <u>Most colleges</u> <u>require</u> <u>a specific number</u> <u>of academic credits for admission.</u>
   (A)   (B)   (C)   (D)

   <u>No error.</u>
   (E)

4. <u>My brother Robert</u> <u>loves to read novels</u> <u>but would enjoy</u>
        (A)   (B)   (C)

   <u>good mystery's more</u>. <u>No error</u>.
        (D)   (E)

5. <u>Louise had lay</u> <u>her mitt on</u> <u>the bench</u> <u>when she got a glass of water</u>.
      (A)   (B)   (C)   (D)

   <u>No error</u>.
    (E)

6. <u>It seems to me</u> that <u>I had spoke</u> to my landlord <u>about the crack</u> in the ceiling
      (A)   (B)   (C)

   <u>about two months ago</u>. <u>No error</u>.
       (D)   (E)

7. <u>The committee</u> <u>on fund-raising</u> <u>gathers in the hall</u>, <u>but Joe went to the</u>
      (A)   (B)   (C)   (D)

   room. <u>No error</u>.
       (E)

8. The <u>administrator</u> <u>wanted</u> <u>all lesson plan books</u> <u>handed in by Friday</u>.
         (A)   (B)   (C)   (D)

   <u>No error</u>.
    (E)

9. <u>Behind the tree</u>, she was <u>reading a book</u>, <u>eating a banana</u>, <u>and she waited</u> for
      (A)   (B)   (C)   (D)

   the sunset. <u>No error</u>.
        (E)

10. <u>Is</u> <u>Washington, D. C.</u> <u>closer</u> to Arlington Cemetery <u>than Charleston</u>?
  (A)   (B)   (C)   (D)

   <u>No error</u>.
    (E)

11. The <u>student</u> <u>would not do nothing</u> <u>to redeem</u> himself
          (A)   (B)   (C)

    <u>in the eyes of the principal</u>. <u>No error.</u>
              (D)   (E)

12. <u>Good teachers</u> <u>are distinguished</u> by their <u>enthusiasm</u> and <u>organization.</u>
         (A)   (B)   (C)   (D)

    <u>No error.</u>
      (E)

13. <u>The principle</u> <u>of the middle</u> school <u>wanted</u> to reorganize <u>the lunch schedule</u>.
         (A)   (B)   (C)   (D)

    <u>No error.</u>
      (E)

14. <u>Grandmother's</u> shopping list <u>consisted of</u> mustard, green beans, <u>buttermilk,</u>
         (A)   (B)   (C)

    and <u>included some eggs.</u> <u>No error.</u>
          (D)   (E)

15. Unless <u>you arm yourself</u> with <u>insect repellent,</u> you <u>will get</u> <u>a bite.</u>
            (A)   (B)   (C) (D)

    <u>No error.</u>
      (E)

16. Graduation <u>exercises</u> will be held on __ Friday __ June 19th, at <u>7:00</u> P.M.
             (A)   (B) (C)   (D)

    <u>No error.</u>
      (E)

17. <u>With a quick</u> <u>glance</u> <u>the noisy room</u> <u>was silenced.</u> <u>No error.</u>
        (A)   (B)   (C)   (D)   (E)

18. <u>Without even trying,</u> <u>the sprinter</u> <u>passed the world record</u> <u>by five tenths</u> of a
         (A)   (B)   (C)   (D)

    second. <u>No error.</u>
          (E)

19. Prior to the passage of PL 94-142, special education students

       (A)   (B)   (C)

    were not unrepresented legally. No error.

             (D)   (E)

20. Combine the sugar, waters, cornstarch, and eggs. No error.

      (A)   (B)   (C)   (D)   (E)

PART B

Choose the letter of the best choice for the underlined section, without changing the meaning of the sentence. If the original is best, choose (A). Otherwise, select one of the suggested changes.

21. Postman's talents were missed not any more as a student but also in his extracurricular activities on campus.

    (A) not any more
    (B) not
    (C) not only
    (D) never any
    (E) any

22. Piled on the table, the students started sorting through their projects.

    (A) Piled on the table, the students started sorting through their projects.
    (B) The students started sorting through their projects, which were piled on the table.
    (C) Piled on the table, the students sorted through their projects.
    (D) The students sorted through their projects as they piled on the table.
    (E) Students started sorting through the table piled with projects.

23. All the soccer players, who are injured, must not play the game.

    (A) ,who are injured,
    (B) ,who are injured
    (C) who are injured,
    (D) who are injured
    (E) (who are injured)

24. The plumber kept these tools in his truck; plunger, snake, washers and faucets.

    (A) truck; plunger, snake, washers and faucets
    (B) truck (plunger, snake, washers and faucets)
    (C) truck: plunger; snake; washers and faucets
    (D) truck; plunger, snake, washers, and faucets
    (E) truck: plunger, snake, washers, and faucets.

25. The two <u>attorneys meet</u> and agreed on an out-of-court settlement.

   (A) attorneys meet
   (B) attorney's meet
   (C) attorney's met
   (D) attorneys met
   (E) attorney meets

PART C

Use the lined pages to write a brief essay based on this topic.

Elementary school teachers provide a model of appropriate and inappropriate classroom practices that their students can in turn learn from when they become teachers.

Describe the extent to which you agree or disagree with this statement. Support your response with specific details, examples, and experiences.

_____

_____

_____

_____

_____

_____

_____

_____

_____

_____

_____

_____

_____

_____

_____

_____

_____

_____

_____

_____

_____

_____

_____

_____

_____

_____

_____

_____

_____

_____

_____

_____

TARGETED TEST
EXPLAINED ANSWERS

Part A

1. **(E)** The underlined sections are all correct.

2. **(A)** Replace the word *trees* with the possessive *tree's*.

3. **(E)** The underlined sections are all correct.

4. **(D)** Replace the word *mystery's* with the plural *mysteries*.

5. **(A)** Replace the words *had lay* with *laid* to show the past tense.

6. **(B)** Replace the words *had spoke* with *spoke* or *had spoken* to show the past tense.

7. **(C)** Replace *gathers* with *gathered* to show past tense and agree with the singular *committee*.

8. **(E)** The underlined sections are all correct.

9. **(D)** Replace the phrase with *and waiting* to maintain the parallel form.

10. **(D)** Replace the phrase with *than to Charleston* to maintain the parallel form.

11. **(B)** Replace the phrase with *would do nothing* and similar phrases to eliminate the double negative.

12. **(E)** The underlined sections are all correct.

13. **(A)** Replace the word *principle* with the correct spelling *principal*.

14. **(D)** Replace the phrase with *eggs* to maintain the parallel form.

15. **(D)** Replace the phrase with *bitten* to show the future tense.

16. **(C)** Replace the blank space with a comma.

17. **(E)** The underlined sections are all correct.

18. **(D)** Replace *five tenths* with the hyphenated *five-tenths*.

19. (**D**) Replace *unrepresented* with *represented* to eliminate the double negative.

20. (**C**) Replace the word *waters* with the singular *water*.

Part B

21. (**C**) The conjunction pair *not only . . . but also* is the correct coordination for this sentence.

22. (**B**) This wording conveys the meaning of students sorting through projects, which are piled on the table.

23. (**D**) The phrase *who are injured* is essential to the sentence, and it is not set off by commas.

24. (**E**) This choice shows the correct combination of punctuation, a colon and three commas.

25. (**D**) This choice shows the correct combination of a plural noun and a past tense verb.

Part C

Show your essay to an English teacher or an English professor for evaluation. Use the rating scale shown on page 62, and the following sample essays.

SAMPLE ESSAY I

The essay below would likely receive a total score of 5 or 6 out of 6. This well-written essay is long enough to earn a rating in the upper third. The essay is very well developed, and it directly addresses each point in the essay prompt. The essay provides excellent supporting details, including extra details about the essay writer and the teacher discussed in the essay. The heading helps the reader understand the essay topic and prepares the reader for the essay to follow.

Miss Stendel — The Teacher I Want to be Like

I agree completely that elementary school teachers can shape what their students will be like as teachers. Miss Dorothea T. Stendel is the teacher I want to be like. She was my fifth grade teacher in Emerson School. She liked to visit Native American reservations. She used to spend a lot of time in the western states.

The main appropriate technique she used was to be very nice to me. She seemed to understand boys, which many teachers do not. I worked hard because she was nice to me and I would try to use that same approach in my classroom. This may not be a scientific approach but it certainly was a very appropriate approach for me.

The approach motivated me. I guess you would call it intrinsic motivation. I did not want to work hard for grades. I was interested. I wanted to work hard just for the work itself.

Miss Stendel used an approach that I thought was not appropriate. She had piles of mathematics worksheets all around the windowsill. You had to work your way around the windowsill to do the math program. When you reached the last window, you were done.

The approach was inappropriate because it did not it did not show real world applications of mathematics and did not show how mathematical ideas were connected. The sheets were boring and you really got nothing out of them. There were just a lot of exercises and skill problems on the sheets. You could do the entire windowsill and not learn anything.

In my classroom, I would try to make sure students mastered mathematics concepts and be sure to show how to transfer the learning to real world situations. I would emphasize the meaning of mathematics and show students how mathematics ideas were connected.

I do not know where Miss Stendel is today, but I would like to thank her for helping me so much. It seems motivating someone to learn is more important than teaching them mathematics. The more I think about it, the more I realize how much she understood and how strategic she was. I want to be like that.

SAMPLE ESSAY II

This essay would likely receive a total score of 2 or 3 out of 6. This essay is not long enough to earn a rating in the upper third. The essay is not just fairly well developed, and it contains some obvious errors in grammar and usage. The essay never directly addresses the main point of the essay prompt. The essay provides very few supporting details. The absence of a heading makes it more difficult for the reader to understand the essay topic.

Miss Willis was my second grade teacher, who I respected very much.

I remember her most of all of my teachers. Good teachers are very important if we expect to have good students.

Miss Willis would have come to school every day with a very sunny attitude even when there was some other problem at home or in school. She never got mad at us or yeled at us when we did stuff that was not good.

That was the style which Miss Willis had that I would use if I was a teacher. She never made me feel bad and she was always trying to be helpful and nice. I would try my very best to be as nice as she was and to follow her examples to. If I could be as good a teacher as she was when I was a teacher my supervisor would have to say that she thought I was doing all the things that she had done to make her a good teacher.

SO, Miss Willis is the most favorite teacher I can remember.

CHAPTER 4

Mathematics

USING THIS CHAPTER

This chapter prepares you to take the mathematics part of the PPST. Use this study checklist to mark your review topics.

STUDY CHECKLIST

Mathematics Review

This review section targets the skills and concepts you need to know to pass the Mathematics part of the PPST.

UNDERSTANDING AND ORDERING WHOLE NUMBERS

Whole numbers are the numbers you use to tell how many. They include 0, 1, 2, 3, 4, 5, 6, . . . The dots tell us that these numbers keep going on forever. There are an infinite number of whole numbers, which means you will never reach the last one.

Cardinal numbers such as 1, 9, and 18 tell how many. There are 9 players on the field in a baseball game. Ordinal numbers such as 1st, 2nd, 9th, and 18th tell about order. For example, Lynne batted 1st this inning.

You can visualize whole numbers evenly spaced on a number line.

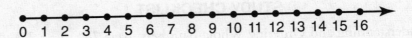

You can use the number line to compare numbers. Numbers get smaller as we go to the left and larger as we go to the right. We use the terms *equal to* (=), *less than* (<), *greater than* (>), and *between* to compare numbers.

12 equals 10 + 2	2 is less than 5	9 is greater than 4	6 is between 5 and 7
12 = 10 + 2	2 < 5	9 > 4	5 < 6 < 7

PLACE VALUE

We use ten digits, 0–9, to write out numerals. We also use a place value system of numeration. The value of a digit depends on the place it occupies. Look at the following place value chart.

millions	hundred thousands	ten thousands	thousands	hundreds	tens	ones
3	5	7	9	4	1	0

The value of the 9 is 9,000. The 9 is in the thousands place. The value of the 5 is 500,000. The 5 is in the hundred thousands place. Read the number three million, five hundred seventy-nine thousand, four hundred ten.

Some whole numbers are very large. The distance from Earth to the planet Pluto is about six trillion (6,000,000,000,000) yards. The distance from Earth to the nearest star is about 40 quadrillion (40,000,000,000,000,000) yards.

Completed Examples

A. What is the value of 8 in the numeral 47,829?

The value of the 8 is 800; this is because the 8 is in the hundreds place.

B. Use >, <, or = to compare 2 and 7.

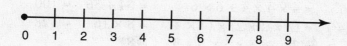

Use the number line to see that 2 < 7 (2 is less than 7).

Practice

Fill in the space with =, <, or > to make each statement true.

1. 2 _____ 3
2. 4 _____ 1
3. 8 _____ 9
4. 1 _____ 1
5. 7 _____ 6
6. Write a numeral in which the value of 7 is seven, the value of 9 is nine thousand, the value of 3 is thirty, and the 0 is in the hundreds place.
7. Write a numeral in which the value of 5 is fifty, the value of 2 is two thousand, the value of 1 is one, and the value of 8 is eight hundred.
8. What place values in the numeral 65,747 contain the same digit?
9. Write the whole numbers between 0 and 15.
10. How many whole numbers are there between 0 and 50?

Answers on page 129

POSITIVE EXPONENTS

You can show repeated multiplication as an exponent. The exponent shows how many times the factor appears.

$$\text{Base} \rightarrow 3^5 = 3 \times 3 \times 3 \times 3 \times 3 = 243$$
[Exponent]
[Factors]

RULES FOR EXPONENTS

$$a^0 = 1 \qquad a^1 = a$$

Use these rules to multiply and divide exponents with the *same base*.

$$7^8 \times 7^5 = 7^{13} \qquad a^n \times a^m = a^{m+n} \qquad 7^8 \div 7^5 = 7^3 \qquad a^n \div a^m = a^{n-m}$$

Keep the base.   Keep the base.
Add the exponents.   Subtract the exponents.

Completed Examples

A. $4^3 + 6^2$ $= 4 \times 4 \times 4 + 6 \times 6$ $= 64 + 36$ $= 100$
B. $(2^3)(4^2)$ $= (2 \times 2 \times 2) \times (4 \times 4)$ $= 8 \times 16$ $= 128$
C. $(3^2)^2$ $= 3^4 = 3 \times 3 \times 3 \times 3$ $= 81$
D. $(10 - 9)^2 = 1^2$ $= 1$

Practice

1. $5^2 + 6^3 =$
2. $(3^2)^2 =$
3. $(8 - 6)^3 =$
4. $(5^2)(6^2) =$
5. $3^3 + 2^3 =$
6. $10^2 - 7^2 =$
7. $(4^3)^2 =$
8. $(2^1)^5 =$
9. $6^2 + 2^3 =$
10. $(25 - 15)^3 =$
11. $(4^2)^2 =$
12. $(2^3)(3^2) =$

Answers on page 129

ORDER OF OPERATIONS

Use this phrase to remember the order in which we do operations:

Please Excuse My Dear Aunt Sally

(1) **P**arentheses
(2) **E**xponents
(3) **M**ultiplication or **D**ivision
(4) **A**ddition or **S**ubtraction

For example,

$$4 + 3 \times 7^2 \quad = 4 + 3 \times 49 \quad = 4 + 147 \quad = 151$$
$$(4 + 3) \times 7^2 = 7 \times 7^2 \quad\quad = 7 \times 49 \quad = 343$$
$$(6 - 10 \div 5) + 6 \times 3 = (6 - 2) + 6 \times 3 = 4 + 6 \times 3 = 4 + 18 = 22$$

Completed Example

$$7 + 3 \times 6 + 4^2 - (8 + 4) \quad = 7 + 3 \times 6 + 4^2 - \underline{12} \quad =$$
$$7 + 3 \times 6 + \underline{16} - 12 \quad\quad = 7 + \underline{18} + 16 - 12 \quad\quad = 29$$

Practice

Find the answer.

1. $4 \times 5 + 4 \div 2 =$
2. $(5 + 7 - 9) \times 8^2 + 2 =$
3. $((7 + 4) - (1 + 4)) \times 6 =$
4. $6^2 + 3(9 - 5 + 7)^2 =$
5. $(12 + 5) \times 3 - 6^2 =$
6. $8 \times 5 + 4 - 8 \div 2 =$
7. $100 - 30 \times 5 + 7 =$
8. $((5 + 2)^2 + 16) \times 8 =$

Answers on page 130

UNDERSTANDING AND ORDERING DECIMALS

Decimals are used to represent numbers between 0 and 1. Decimals can also be shown on a number line.

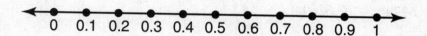

We also use ten digits, 0–9, and a place value system of numeration to write decimals. The value of a digit depends on the place it occupies. Look at the following place value chart.

ones	tenths	hundredths	thousandths	ten thousandths	hundred thousandths	millionths	ten millionths	hundred millionths	billionths
0 .	3	6	8	7					

The value of 3 is three tenths. The 3 is in the tenths place. The value of 8 is eight thousandths. The 8 is in the thousandths place.

COMPARING WHOLE NUMBERS AND DECIMALS

To compare two numbers, compare the value of the digits in each place.

Compare	9,879 and 16,459	23,801 and 23,798	58.1289 and 58.132
	9,879	23,**8**01	58.1289
	16,459	23,798	58.1**3**2
	9,879 < 16,459	23,801 > 23,798	58.1289 < 58.132
	Less than	Greater than	Less than

Completed Examples

A. What is the value of the digit 2 in the decimal 35.6829?

The 2 is in the thousandths place. 2 × 0.001 = 0.002.
The value of the 2 is 0.002 or 2 thousandths.

B. Use <, >, or = to compare 1,248.9234 and 1,248.9229

1,248.9234 and 1,248.9229 The digits in the numerals are the same
until you reach the thousandths place where 3 > 2. Since 3 > 2, then
1,248.9234 > 1,248.9229.

Practice

Use <, >, or = to compare.

1. 0.02 _____ 0.003
2. 4.6 _____ 1.98
3. 0.0008 _____ 0.00009
4. 1.0 _____ 1
5. 7.6274 _____ 7.6269

Write the answer.

6. Write a numeral in which the value of 5 is five tenths, the value of 2 is two, the value of 6 is six thousandths, and the value of 8 is eight hundredths.

_____

7. Write a numeral in which the value of 4 is in the ten thousandths place, the value of 3 is three hundred, the 7 is in the hundredths place, the 1 is in the tens place, the 9 is in the ten thousands place, and the rest of the digits are zeros.

_____

8. In the numeral 6.238935, which place values contain the same digit?

_____

9. Using only the tenths place, write all the decimals from 0 to 1.

_____

10. If you used only the tenths and hundredths places, how many decimals are between 0 and 1?

_____

Answers on page 130

ADD, SUBTRACT, MULTIPLY, AND DIVIDE DECIMALS

Estimate first. Then add, subtract, multiply, or divide.

ADD AND SUBTRACT DECIMALS

Line up the decimal points.

Add: 14.9 + 3.108 + 0.16

```
  14.9
  3.108
+ 0.16
 18.168
```

Subtract: 14.234 − 7.14

```
 14.234
− 7.14
  7.094
```

MULTIPLY DECIMALS

Multiply decimals as you would whole numbers. Count the total number of decimal places in the factors. Put that many decimal places in the product. You may have to write leading zeros.

Multiply: 17.4 × 1.3

```
   17.4
 × 1.3
   522
  174
  22.62
```

Multiply: 0.016 × 1.7

```
   0.016
 × 1.7
   112
  16
  .0272
```

DIVIDE DECIMALS

Move the decimal point to make the divisor a whole number. Move the decimal point in the dividend the same number of places. Then divide.

0.16)1.328   016.)132.8

```
        8.3
  16)132.8
     128
      48
      48
       0
```

Practice

1.
```
  12.79
   8.1
+  5.2
```

2.
```
  40.267
  23.2
+  9.15
```

3.
```
  940.17
  36.15
+ 12.07
```

4.
```
  5290.3
  167.8
+  15.09
```

5.
```
   37.9
−  29.7
```

6.
```
  136.804
−  65.7944
```

7.
```
  513.72
−  59.75
```

8.
```
  2451.06
−  683.19
```

9.	0.249	10.	46.7	11.	56.2	12.	93.57
	× 2.5		× 3.5		× 65.49		× 40.2

13. $10.08 \div 2.1 =$ **14.** $16.32 \div 1.7 =$ **15.** $248.64 \div 7.4 =$ **16.** $653.276 \div 5.2 =$

Answers on page 131

UNDERSTANDING AND ORDERING FRACTIONS

A fraction names a part of a whole or of a group. A fraction has two parts, a numerator and a denominator. The denominator tells how many parts in all. The numerator tells how many parts you identified.

$$\frac{3}{4} \quad \begin{array}{l}\text{Numerator}\\\text{Denominator}\end{array}$$

MIXED NUMBERS AND IMPROPER FRACTIONS

Change an improper fraction to a mixed number:

Change a mixed number to an improper fraction:

Multiply denominator and whole number. Then add the numerator.

$$\frac{(3 \times 5) + 2}{5} = \frac{15 + 2}{5} = \frac{17}{5}$$

EQUIVALENT FRACTIONS

Two fractions that stand for the same number are called equivalent fractions. Multiply or divide the numerator and denominator by the same number to find an equivalent fraction.

$$\frac{2 \times 3}{5 \times 3} = \frac{6}{15} \qquad \frac{6 \div 3}{9 \div 3} = \frac{2}{3} \qquad \frac{6 \times 4}{8 \times 4} = \frac{24}{32} \qquad \frac{8 \div 2}{10 \div 2} = \frac{4}{5}$$

$\dfrac{1}{2}$ is equivalent to $\dfrac{2}{4}$ $\dfrac{2}{3}$ is less than $\dfrac{3}{4}$

$$\dfrac{1}{2} = \dfrac{2}{4} \qquad\qquad \dfrac{2}{3} < \dfrac{3}{4}$$

$\dfrac{5}{8}$ is greater than $\dfrac{1}{2}$ $\dfrac{1}{3}$ is between $\dfrac{1}{4}$ and $\dfrac{3}{8}$

$$\dfrac{5}{8} > \dfrac{1}{2} \qquad\qquad \dfrac{1}{4} < \dfrac{1}{3} < \dfrac{3}{8}$$

COMPARE TWO FRACTIONS

Use this method to compare two fractions. For example, compare $\dfrac{13}{18}$ and $\dfrac{5}{7}$. First, write the two fractions and cross multiply as shown. The larger cross product appears next to the larger fraction. If cross products are equal, then the fractions are equivalent.

$$91 = \qquad\qquad = 90$$

$$\dfrac{13}{18} \times \dfrac{5}{7}$$

$$91 > 90 \text{ so } \dfrac{13}{18} > \dfrac{5}{7}$$

Completed Examples

A. Compare $\dfrac{5}{7}$ and $\dfrac{18}{19}$,

Use cross multiplication.

$\dfrac{5}{7} \times \dfrac{18}{19}$, $5 \times 19 = 95$ and $7 \times 18 = 126$, therefore $\dfrac{5}{7} < \dfrac{18}{19}$.

B. Write $\dfrac{27}{7}$ as a mixed number.

$$\begin{array}{r} 3\,\text{R}6 \\ 7\overline{)27} \\ \underline{21} \\ 6 \end{array}$$

$$\dfrac{27}{7} = 3\dfrac{6}{7}$$

C. Write $6\frac{5}{8}$ as a fraction.

$6 \times 8 = 48$. Multiply the denominator and the whole number.
$48 + 5 = 53$. Add the numerator to the product.

$$6\frac{5}{8} = \frac{53}{8}$$

Practice

Write the improper fraction as a mixed number.

1. $\frac{5}{3}$ 2. $\frac{15}{7}$ 3. $\frac{24}{9}$

Write the mixed number as an improper fraction.

4. $8\frac{1}{5}$ 5. $6\frac{7}{8}$ 6. $9\frac{5}{7}$

Use >, <, = to compare the fractions.

7. $\frac{3}{7}, \frac{4}{9}$ 8. $\frac{5}{6}, \frac{25}{30}$ 8. $\frac{4}{5}, \frac{7}{8}$

Answers on page 131

MULTIPLY, DIVIDE, ADD, AND SUBTRACT FRACTIONS AND MIXED NUMBERS

MULTIPLY FRACTIONS AND MIXED NUMBERS

To write any mixed number as an improper fraction, multiply the numerator and the denominator. Write the product in simplest form. For example, multiply $\frac{3}{4}$ and $\frac{1}{6}$.

$$\frac{3}{4} \times \frac{1}{6} = \frac{3}{24} = \frac{1}{8}$$

Now, multiply $3\frac{1}{3}$ by $3\frac{3}{5}$.

$$3\frac{1}{3} \times 3\frac{3}{5} = \frac{10}{3} \times \frac{3}{5} = \frac{30}{15} = 2$$

DIVIDE FRACTIONS AND MIXED NUMBERS

To divide $1\frac{4}{5}$ by $\frac{3}{8}$:

$$1\frac{4}{5} \div \frac{3}{8} = \frac{9}{5} \div \frac{3}{8} = \qquad \frac{9}{5} \times \frac{8}{3} = \frac{72}{15} = \qquad 4\frac{12}{15} = \qquad 4\frac{4}{5}$$

Write mixed numbers as improper fractions.　　Invert the divisor and multiply.　　Write the product.　　Write the quotient in simplest form.

ADD FRACTIONS AND MIXED NUMBERS

To add, write fractions with common denominators. Then write in simplest form.

Add: $\frac{3}{8} + \frac{1}{4}$　　　　Add: $\frac{7}{8} + \frac{5}{12}$　　　　Add: $2\frac{1}{3} + \frac{5}{7}$

$$\begin{aligned} \frac{3}{8} &= \frac{3}{8} \\ +\frac{1}{4} &= \frac{2}{8} \\ \hline &\ \ \frac{5}{8} \end{aligned}$$

$$\begin{aligned} \frac{7}{8} &= \frac{21}{24} \\ +\frac{5}{12} &= \frac{10}{24} \\ \hline \frac{31}{24} &= 1\frac{7}{24} \end{aligned}$$

$$\begin{aligned} 2\frac{1}{3} &= 2\frac{7}{21} \\ +\frac{5}{7} &= \frac{15}{21} \\ \hline 2\frac{22}{21} &= 3\frac{1}{21} \end{aligned}$$

SUBTRACT FRACTIONS AND MIXED NUMBERS

Write fractions with common denominators. Subtract and then write in simplest form.

Subtract: $\frac{5}{6} - \frac{1}{3}$　　Subtract: $\frac{3}{8} - \frac{1}{5}$　　Subtract: $3\frac{1}{6} - 1\frac{1}{3}$

$$\begin{aligned} \frac{5}{6} &= \frac{5}{6} \\ \frac{1}{3} &= \frac{2}{6} \\ \hline \frac{3}{6} &= \frac{1}{2} \end{aligned}$$

$$\begin{aligned} \frac{3}{8} &= \frac{15}{40} \\ \frac{1}{5} &= \frac{8}{40} \\ \hline &\ \ \frac{7}{40} \end{aligned}$$

$$\begin{aligned} 3\frac{1}{6} &= 3\frac{1}{6} = 2\frac{7}{6} \\ 1\frac{1}{3} &= 1\frac{2}{6} = 1\frac{2}{6} \\ \hline &\qquad\qquad 1\frac{5}{6} \end{aligned}$$

Practice

1. $\dfrac{1}{3} \times \dfrac{5}{9} =$ 2. $\dfrac{2}{3} \times \dfrac{1}{4} =$ 3. $3\dfrac{3}{8} \times 4\dfrac{1}{8} =$ 4. $3\dfrac{1}{5} \times 2\dfrac{4}{7} =$

5. $\dfrac{3}{4} \div \dfrac{7}{8} =$ 6. $\dfrac{2}{5} \div \dfrac{7}{9} =$ 7. $9\dfrac{5}{7} \div 4\dfrac{1}{3} =$ 8. $8\dfrac{4}{5} \div 7\dfrac{3}{5} =$

9. $\dfrac{5}{9} + \dfrac{2}{3} =$ 10. $\dfrac{7}{10} + \dfrac{2}{4} =$ 11. $1\dfrac{6}{7} + 2\dfrac{3}{14} =$ 12. $5\dfrac{2}{3} + 6\dfrac{5}{6} =$

13. $\dfrac{2}{7} - \dfrac{5}{21} =$ 14. $\dfrac{2}{5} - \dfrac{3}{8} =$ 15. $3\dfrac{4}{5} - 3\dfrac{2}{15} =$ 16. $8\dfrac{1}{7} - 4\dfrac{2}{9} =$

Answers on page 132

NUMBER THEORY

Number theory explores the natural numbers [1, 2, 3, 4, . . .]. We'll review just a few important number theory concepts.

FACTORS

The factors of a number evenly divide the number with no remainder. For example, 2 is a factor of 6, but 2 is not a factor of 5.

The number 1 is a factor of every number. Each number is a factor of itself.

1 The only factor is 1	6 1, 2, 3, 6
2 Factors 1, 2	7 1, 7
3 1, 3	8 1, 2, 4, 8
4 1, 2, 4	9 1, 3, 9
5 1, 5	10 1, 2, 5, 10

PRIME NUMBERS AND COMPOSITE NUMBERS

A prime number has exactly two factors, itself and 1.

2 is prime. The only factors are 1 and 2.   5 is prime. Factors: 1, 5
3 is prime. Factors: 1, 3   7 is prime. Factors: 1, 7

A composite number has more than two factors.

4 is composite. The factors are 1, 2, 4.   9 is composite. Factors: 1, 3, 9
6 is composite. Factors: 1, 2, 3, 6   10 is composite. Factors: 1, 2, 5, 10

The number 1 has only one factor, itself. The number 1 is neither prime nor composite.

LEAST COMMON MULTIPLE (LCM), GREATEST COMMON FACTOR (GCF)

Multiples. The multiples of a number are all the numbers you get when you count by that number. Here are some examples.

Multiples of 1: 1, 2, 3, 4, 5, . . .

Multiples of 2: 2, 4, 6, 8, 10, . . .

Multiples of 3: 3, 6, 9, 12, 15, . . .

Multiples of 4: 4, 8, 12, 16, 20, . . .

Least common multiple is the smallest multiple shared by two numbers.

The least common multiple of 6 and 8 is 24.

List the multiples of 6 and 8. Notice that 24 is the smallest multiple common to both numbers.

Multiples of 6: 6, 12, 18, **24**, 30, 36

Multiples of 8: 8, 16, **24**, 32, 40

Greatest common factor is the largest factor shared by two numbers.

The greatest common factor of 28 and 36 is 4.

List the factors of 28 and 36.

Factors of 28: 1, 2, **4**, 7, 28

Factors of 36: 1, 2, 3, **4**, 6, 9, 12, 18, 36

Completed Examples

A. Find the factors of 24.

The factors are 1, 2, 3, 4, 6, 8, 12, and 24.
These are the only numbers that divide 24 with no remainder.

B. Find the GCF of 14 and 22.

Write out the factors of each number.
14: 1, 2, 7, 14
22: 1, 2, 11, 22

The greatest common factor is 2.

C. Find the LCM of 6 and 9.

List some of the multiples of each number.
6: 6, 12, 18, 24, . . .
9: 9, 18, 27, . . .

The least common multiple is 18.

Practice

Write the factors of each number.

1. 13   **2.** 26   **3.** 40   **4.** 23

Find the LCM of the two numbers.

5. 6 and 8   **6.** 5 and 12   **7.** 7 and 35   **8.** 4 and 14

Find the GCF of the two numbers.

9. 24 and 30   **10.** 15 and 40   **11.** 32 and 64   **12.** 56 and 84

Answers on page 133

RATIO AND PROPORTION

RATIO

A ratio is a way of comparing two numbers with division. It conveys the same meaning as a fraction. There are three ways to write a ratio.

Using words 3 to 4   As a fraction $\frac{3}{4}$ Using a colon 3:4

PROPORTION

A proportion shows two ratios that have the same value; that is, the fractions representing the ratios are equivalent. Use cross multiplication. If the cross products are equal, then the two ratios form a proportion.

$\frac{3}{8}$ and $\frac{27}{72}$ form a proportion. The cross products are equal. ($3 \times 72 = 8 \times 27$)

$\frac{3}{8}$ and $\frac{24}{56}$ do not form a proportion. The cross products are not equal.

Writing a Proportion: You may be able to write a proportion to solve a problem. For example, the mason mixes cement and sand using a ratio of 2:5. Twelve bags of cement will be used. How much sand is needed? To solve, use the numerator to stand for cement. The denominator will stand for sand.

$$\frac{2}{5} = \frac{12}{S}$$
$$2 \times S = 5 \times 12$$
$$2S = 60$$
$$S = 30$$

Cross multiply to solve.

Thirty bags of sand are needed.

Completed Example

The problem compares loaves of whole wheat bread with loaves of rye bread. Let the numerators stand for loaves of whole wheat bread. The denominators stand for loaves of rye bread.

Ratio of whole wheat to rye. $\dfrac{3}{7}$ Ratio of whole wheat to rye for 51 loaves of whole wheat. $\dfrac{51}{R}$

Write a proportion. $\dfrac{3}{7} = \dfrac{51}{R}$

Solution: $3R = 357$ $R = 119$

There are 119 loaves of bread.

Practice

1. A salesperson sells 7 vacuum cleaners for every 140 potential buyers. If there are 280 potential buyers, how many vacuums are sold?
2. There is one teacher for every 8 preschool students. How many teachers are needed if there are 32 preschool students?
3. There are 3 rest stops for every 20 miles of highway. How many rest stops would there be on 140 miles of highway?
4. Does $\dfrac{7}{9}$ and $\dfrac{28}{36}$ form a proportion? Explain.

Answers on page 134

PERCENT

Percent comes from *per centum*, which means per hundred. Whenever you see a number followed by a percent sign it means that number out of 100.

DECIMALS AND PERCENTS

To write a decimal as a percent, move the decimal point two places to the right and write the percent sign.

$0.34 = 34\%$ $0.297 = 29.7\%$ $0.6 = 60\%$ $0.001 = 0.1\%$

To write a percent as a decimal, move the decimal point two places to the left and delete the percent sign.

$51\% = 0.51$ $34.18\% = 0.3418$ $0.9\% = 0.009$

FRACTIONS AND PERCENTS

Writing Fractions as Percents

- Divide the numerator by the denominator. Write the answer as a percent.

Write $\frac{3}{5}$ as a percent   Write $\frac{5}{8}$ as a percent.

$$5\overline{)3.0}^{\,0.6} \qquad 0.6 = 60\% \qquad\qquad 8\overline{)5.00}^{\,0.625} \qquad 0.625 = 62.5\%$$

- Write an equivalent fraction with 100 in the denominator. Write the numerator followed by a percent sign.

Write $\frac{13}{25}$ as a percent.

$$\frac{13}{25} = \frac{52}{100} = 52\%$$

- Use these equivalencies.

$$\frac{1}{4} = 25\% \qquad\qquad \frac{1}{2} = 50\% \qquad\qquad \frac{3}{4} = 75\% \qquad\qquad \frac{4}{4} = 100\%$$

$$\frac{1}{5} = 20\% \qquad\qquad \frac{2}{5} = 40\% \qquad\qquad \frac{3}{5} = 60\% \qquad\qquad \frac{4}{5} = 80\%$$

$$\frac{1}{6} = 16\frac{2}{3}\% \qquad \frac{1}{3} = 33\frac{1}{3}\% \qquad \frac{2}{3} = 66\frac{2}{3}\% \qquad \frac{5}{6} = 83\frac{1}{3}\%$$

$$\frac{1}{8} = 12\frac{1}{2}\% \qquad \frac{3}{8} = 37\frac{1}{2}\% \qquad \frac{5}{8} = 62\frac{1}{2}\% \qquad \frac{7}{8} = 87\frac{1}{2}\%$$

Writing Percents as Fractions

Write a fraction with 100 in the denominator and the percent in the numerator. Simplify.

$$18\% = \frac{18}{100} = \frac{9}{50} \qquad\qquad 7.5\% = \frac{7.5}{100} = \frac{75}{1000} = \frac{3}{40}$$

Completed Examples

A. Write 0.567 as a percent.

Move the decimal two places to the right and write a percent sign; therefore, 0.567 = 56.7%.

B. Write $\frac{1}{4}$ as a percent.

Write $\frac{1}{4}$ as a decimal (1 ÷ 4) = 0.25

Write 0.25 as a decimal 0.25 = 25%

C. Write 26% as a fraction.

Place the percent number in the numerator and 100 in the denominator.

$26\% = \frac{26}{100} = \frac{13}{50}$.

Simplify: $\frac{26}{100} = \frac{13}{50}$.

Practice

Write the decimal as a percent.

1. 0.359   **2.** 0.78   **3.** 0.215   **4.** 0.041

Write the fraction as a percent.

5. $\frac{1}{9}$ **6.** $\frac{5}{8}$ **7.** $\frac{3}{10}$ **8.** $\frac{4}{9}$

Write the percents as fractions in simplest form.

9. 58%   **10.** 79%   **11.** 85.2%   **12.** 97.4%

Answers on page 134

THREE TYPES OF PERCENT PROBLEMS

FINDING A PERCENT OF A NUMBER

To find a percent of a number, write a number sentence with a decimal for the percent and solve.

Find 40% of 90.
0.4 × 90 = 36

It may be easier to write a fraction for the percent. Use the fraction equivalencies.

$$\text{Find } 62\frac{1}{2}\% \text{ of } 64.$$

$$\frac{5}{8} \times 64 = 5 \times 8 = 40$$

FINDING WHAT PERCENT ONE NUMBER IS OF ANOTHER

To find what percent one number is of another, write a number sentence and solve to find the percent.

What percent of 5 is 3?

$$n \times 5 = 3$$

$$n = \frac{3}{5} = 0.6 = 60\%$$

FINDING A NUMBER WHEN A PERCENT OF IT IS KNOWN

To find a number when a percent of it is known, write a number sentence with a decimal or a fraction for the percent and solve to find the number.

5% of what number is 2?

$$0.05 \times n = 2$$
$$n = 2 \div 0.05$$
$$n = 40$$

Completed Examples

A. What percent of 70 is 28?

$$\square \times 70 = 28$$

$$\square = \frac{28}{70} = \frac{4}{10}$$

$$\square = 40\%$$

B. 30% of 60 is what number?

$$30\% \times 60 = \square$$
$$0.3 \times 60 = \square$$
$$\square = 18$$

C. 40% of what number is 16?

$$0.40 \times \square = 16$$

$$\square = \frac{16}{0.4}$$

$$\square = 40$$

Practice

1. 120 is what percent of 240?
2. 15% of 70 is what number?
3. 60% of 300 is what number?
4. What percent of 60 is 42?
5. What percent of 25 is 2.5?
6. 40% of what number is 22?
7. 70% of what number is 85?
8. 25% of 38 is what number?
9. 35% of what number is 24?
10. 24 is what percent of 80?

Answers on page 135

PERCENT OF INCREASE AND DECREASE

PERCENT OF INCREASE

A price increases from $50 to $65. What is the percent of increase?

Subtract to find the amount of increase.

$$\$65 - \$50 = \$15$$
$15 is the amount of increase

Write a fraction. The amount of increase is the numerator. The original amount is the denominator.

$$\frac{\$15}{\$50} \quad \frac{\text{Amount of increase}}{\text{Original amount}}$$

Write the fraction as a percent.
The percent of increase is 30%.

$$\begin{array}{r} 0.3 \\ 50\overline{)15.00} \end{array} \qquad 0.3 = 30\%$$

PERCENT OF DECREASE

A price decreases from $35 to $28. What is the percent of decrease?

Subtract to find the amount of decrease. $35 − $28 = $7
                                                        $7 is the amount of decrease

Write a fraction. The amount of decrease $7   Amount of decrease
is the numerator. The original amount is   ————   —————————————
the denominator. $35   Original amount

Write the fraction as a percent. $\frac{7}{35} = \frac{1}{5} = 20\%$
The percent of decrease is 20%.

Completed Examples

A. The price increased from $30 to $36. What is the percent increase?

   $36 − $30 = $6

   $\frac{6}{30} = \frac{1}{5} = 20\%$

B. An $80 item goes on sale for 25% off. What is the sale price?

   $80 × 25% = $80 × 0.25 = $20
   $80 − $20 = $60. $60 is the sale price.

Practice

1. The price increased from $25 to $35. What is the percent of increase?
2. A sale marks down a $100 item 25%. What is the sale price?
3. The price decreases from $80 by 15%. What is the new price?
4. The price increased from $120 to $150. What is the percent of increase?
5. A sale marks down a $75 item 10%. What is the sale price?
6. The price decreases from $18 to $6. What is the percent of decrease?
7. A sale marks down a $225 item to $180. What is the percent of decrease?
8. A sale price of $150 was 25% off the original price. What was the original price?

Answers on page 136

PROBABILITY

The probability of an occurrence is the likelihood that it will happen. Most often, we write probability as a fraction.

Flip a fair coin and the probability that it will come up heads is $\frac{1}{2}$. The same is true for tails. Write the probability this way.

$$P(H) = \frac{1}{2} \qquad P(T) = \frac{1}{2}$$

H T

If something will never occur the probability is 0. If something will always occur, the probability is 1. Therefore, if you flip a fair coin,

$$P(7) = 0 \qquad P(H \text{ or } T) = 1$$

Write the letters A, B, C, D, and E on pieces of paper. Pick them randomly without looking. The probability of picking any letter is $\frac{1}{5}$.

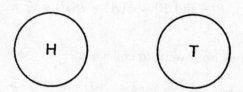

$$P(\text{vowel}) = \frac{2}{5} \qquad P(\text{consonant}) = \frac{3}{5}$$

RULES FOR COMPUTING PROBABILITY

$$P(A \text{ or } B) = P(A) + P(B) = \frac{1}{5} + \frac{1}{5} = \frac{2}{5}$$

when A and B have no common elements

$$P(A \text{ and } B) = P(A) \times P(B) = \frac{1}{5} \times \frac{1}{5} = \frac{1}{25}$$

$$P(\text{not } C) = 1 - P(C) = 1 - \frac{1}{5} = \frac{4}{5}$$

Completed Example

In one high school, 40% of the students go on to college. Two graduates of the high school are chosen at random. What is the probability that they both went to college?

Write the probabilities you know. $P(\text{college}) = \dfrac{40}{100} = \dfrac{2}{5}$

Solve the problem. $P(A \text{ and } B)$ probability the two students went to college.

$$P(A \text{ and } B) = P(A) \times P(B) = \frac{2}{5} \times \frac{2}{5} = \frac{4}{25}$$

The probability that they both went to college is $\dfrac{4}{25}$.

Practice

1. There are 3 black, 2 white, 2 gray, and 3 blue socks in a drawer. What is the probability of drawing a sock that is not black?
2. Six goldfish are in a tank; 4 are female and 2 are male. What is the probability of scooping out a male?
3. A standard deck of 52 playing cards is spread facedown on a table. What is the probability of choosing a card that is a king or a queen?
4. Six names are written on pieces of paper. The names are Aaron, Ben, Carl, Edith, Elizabeth, and Phyllis. One name is picked and replaced. Then another name is picked. What is the probability that the names were Carl and Phyllis?
5. A fair die having six sides is rolled. What is the probability that the side facing up is a prime number?
6. A fair coin is tossed in the air 5 times. What is the probability of getting five tails?

Answers on page 137

STATISTICS

Descriptive statistics are used to explain or describe a set of numbers. Most often we use the mean, median, or mode to describe these numbers.

MEAN (AVERAGE)

The mean is a position midway between two extremes. To find the mean:

1. Add the items or scores.
2. Divide by the number of items.

For example, find the mean of 23, 17, 42, 51, 37.

$$23 + 17 + 42 + 51 + 37 = 170 \quad 170 \div 5 = 34$$

The mean or average is 34.

MEDIAN

The median is the middle number. To find the median:

1. Arrange the numbers from least to greatest.
2. If there are an odd number of scores, then find the middle score.
3. If there is an even number of scores, average the two middle scores.

For example, find the median of these numbers.

$$6, 9, 11, 17, 21, 33, 45, 71$$

There are an even number of scores.

$$17 + 21 = 38 \quad 38 \div 2 = 19$$

The median is 19.

Don't forget to arrange the scores in order before finding the middle score!

MODE

The mode is the number that occurs most often. For example, find the mode of these numbers.

$$6, 3, 7, 6, 9, 3, 6, 1, 2, 6, 7, 3$$

The number 6 occurs most often, so 6 is the mode.

Not all sets of numbers have a mode. Some sets of numbers may have more than one mode.

Completed Example

What is the mean, median, and mode of 7, 13, 18, 4, 14, 22?

Mean   Add the scores and divide by the number of scores.
$7 + 13 + 18 + 4 + 14 + 22 = 78 \div 6 = 13$ The mean is 13.

Median Arrange the scores in order. Find the middle score.
$4, 7, 13, 14, 18, 22 \quad 13 + 14 = 27 \div 2 = 13.5$ The median is 13.5.

Mode   Find the score that occurs most often.
Each score occurs only once.   There is no mode.

Practice

1. A group of fourth graders received the following scores on a science test.

80, 87, 94, 100, 75, 80, 98, 85, 80, 95, 92

Which score represents the mode?

2. What is the mean of the following set of data?

   44, 13, 84, 42, 12, 18

3. What is the median of the following set of data?

   8, 9, 10, 10, 8, 10, 7, 6, 9

4. What measure of central tendency does the number 16 represent in the following data?

   14, 15, 17, 16, 19, 20, 16, 14, 16

5. What is the mean of the following set of scores?

   100, 98, 95, 70, 85, 90, 94, 78, 80, 100

6. What is the mode of the following data?

   25, 30, 25, 15, 40, 45, 30, 20, 30

Answers on page 137

PERMUTATIONS, COMBINATIONS, AND THE FUNDAMENTAL COUNTING PRINCIPLE

PERMUTATIONS

A permutation is the way a set of things can be arranged in order. There are 6 permutations of the letters A, B, and C.

    ABC   **ACB**   **BAC**   **BCA**   **CAB**   **CBA**

Permutation Formula

The formula for the number of permutations of *n* things is **n! (n factorial)**.

$$6! = 6 \times 5 \times 4 \times 3 \times 2 \times 1 \qquad 4! = 4 \times 3 \times 2 \times 1 \qquad 2! = 2 \times 1$$

There are 120 permutations of 5 things.

$$n! = 5! = 5 \times 4 \times 3 \times 2 \times 1 = 120$$

COMBINATIONS

A combination is the number of ways of choosing a given number of elements from a set. The order of the elements does not matter. There are 3 ways of choosing 2 letters from the letters A, B, and C.

AB AC BC

FUNDAMENTAL COUNTING PRINCIPLE

The fundamental counting principle is used to find the total number of possibilities. Multiply the number of possibilities from each category.

Completed Example

An ice cream stand has a sundae with choices of 28 flavors of ice cream, 8 types of syrups, and 5 types of toppings. How many different sundae combinations are available?

28	×	8	×	5	=	1,120
flavors		syrups		toppings		sundaes

There are 1,120 possible sundaes.

Practice

1. There are 2 chairs left in the auditorium, but 4 people are without seats. In how many ways could 2 people be chosen to sit in the chairs?
2. The books *Little Women, Crime and Punishment, Trinity, The Great Santini, Pygmalion, The Scarlet Letter,* and *War and Peace* are on a shelf. In how many different ways can they be arranged?
3. A license plate consists of 2 letters and 2 digits. How many different license plates can be formed?
4. There are four students on line for the bus, but there is only room for three students on this bus. How many different ways can 3 of the 4 students get on the bus?

Answers on page 138

INTEGERS

The number line can also show negative numbers. There is a negative whole number for every positive whole number. Zero is neither positive nor negative. The negative whole numbers, the positive whole numbers, and zero, together, are called integers.

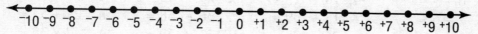

ADD AND SUBTRACT INTEGERS

Add

When the signs are the same, keep the sign and add.

$$\begin{array}{r} {}^+7 \\ + \ {}^+8 \\ \hline {}^+15 \end{array} \qquad \begin{array}{r} {}^-3 \\ + \ {}^-11 \\ \hline {}^-14 \end{array}$$

When the signs are different, disregard the signs, subtract the numbers, and keep the sign of the larger number.

$$\begin{array}{r} {}^+28 \\ + \ {}^-49 \\ \hline {}^-21 \end{array} \qquad \begin{array}{r} {}^-86 \\ + \ {}^+135 \\ \hline {}^+49 \end{array}$$

Subtract

Change the sign of the number being subtracted. Then add using the preceding rules.

$$
\begin{array}{cccc}
^{+}13 & ^{-}43 & ^{+}29 & ^{-}92 \\
- \ ^{-}18 & - \ ^{-}17 & - \ ^{-}49 & - \ ^{+}135 \\
\hline
\Downarrow & \Downarrow & \Downarrow & \Downarrow \\
^{+}13 & ^{-}43 & ^{+}29 & ^{-}92 \\
+ \ ^{+}18 & + \ ^{+}17 & + \ ^{+}49 & + \ ^{-}135 \\
\hline
31 & ^{-}26 & ^{+}78 & ^{-}227
\end{array}
$$

MULTIPLY AND DIVIDE INTEGERS

Multiply

Multiply as you would whole numbers. The product is *positive* if there are an even number of negative factors. The product is *negative* if there are an odd number of negative factors.

$$^{-}2 \times {}^{+}14 \times {}^{-}6 \times {}^{+}3 = {}^{+}144 \qquad {}^{-}2 \times {}^{-}4 \times {}^{+}6 \times {}^{-}3 = {}^{-}144$$

Divide

Forget the signs and divide. The quotient is *positive* if both integers have the same sign. The quotient is *negative* if the integers have different signs.

$$^{+}24 \div {}^{+}4 = {}^{+}6 \qquad {}^{-}24 \div {}^{-}4 = {}^{+}6 \qquad {}^{+}24 \div {}^{-}4 = {}^{-}6 \qquad {}^{-}24 \div {}^{+}4 = {}^{-}6$$

Practice

1. $6 + 9 =$ 2. $18 + {}^{-}17 =$ 3. $^{-}24 + {}^{-}45 =$ 4. $^{-}38 + 29 =$
5. $7 - 6 =$ 6. $15 - {}^{-}39 =$ 7. $^{-}36 - {}^{-}58 =$ 8. $^{-}27 - 53 =$
9. $9 \times 11 =$ 10. $26 \times {}^{-}25 =$ 11. $^{-}31 \times {}^{-}59 =$ 12. $^{-}42 \times 35 =$
13. $120 \div 8 =$ 14. $68 \div {}^{-}4 =$ 15. $^{-}352 \div {}^{-}8 =$ 16. $^{-}66 \div 3 =$

Answers on page 138

SCIENTIFIC NOTATION

Scientific notation uses powers of 10. The power shows how many zeros to use.

$$10^0 = 1 \quad 10^1 = 10 \quad 10^2 = 100 \quad 10^3 = 1{,}000 \quad 10^4 = 10{,}000 \quad 10^5 = 100{,}000$$
$$10^{-1} = 0.1 \quad 10^{-2} = 0.01 \quad 10^{-3} = 0.001 \quad 10^{-4} = 0.0001 \quad 10^{-5} = 0.00001$$

Write whole numbers and decimals in scientific notation. Use a decimal with one numeral to the left of the decimal point.

2,345 = 2.345×10^3 The decimal point moved three places to the left. Use 10^3.

176.8 = 1.768×10^2 The decimal point moved two places to the left. Use 10^2.

0.0034 = 3.4×10^{-3} The decimal point moved three places to the right. Use 10^{-3}.

2.0735 = 2.0735×10^0 The decimal is in the correct form. Use 10^0 to stand for 1.

Completed Examples

A. Write 7,952 in scientific notation.
Move the decimal point three places to the left and write
$7,952 = 7.952 \times 10^3$.

B. Write 0.03254 in scientific notation.
Move the decimal point two places to the right and write 3.254×10^{-2}.

Practice

Rewrite using scientific notation.

1. 0.0564
2. 0.00897
3. 0.06501
4. 0.000354
5. 545
6. 7,790
7. 289,705
8. 1,801,319

Answers on page 139

EQUATIONS

The whole idea of solving equations is to isolate the variable on one side of the equal sign. The value of the variable is what's on the other side of the equal sign. Substitute your answer in the original equation to check your solution.

SOLVING EQUATIONS BY ADDING OR SUBTRACTING

Solve: $y + 19 = 23$
Subtract 19 $y + 19 - 19 = 23 - 19$
$y = 4$

Check: Does $4 + 19 = 23$? Yes. It checks.

Solve: $x - 23 = 51$
Add 23 $x - 23 + 23 = 51 + 23$
$x = 74$

Check: Does $74 - 23 = 51$? Yes. It checks.

SOLVING EQUATIONS BY MULTIPLYING OR DIVIDING

Solve: $\dfrac{z}{7} = 6$

Multiply by 7 $\quad\quad \dfrac{z}{7} \times 7 = 6 \times 7$

$z = 42$

Check: Does $\dfrac{42}{7} = 6$? Yes. It checks.

Solve: $\quad\quad\quad 21 = -3x$

Divide by -3 $\quad\quad \dfrac{21}{-3} = \dfrac{-3x}{-3}$

$-7 = x$

Check: Does $21 = (-3)\,(-7)$?
Yes. It checks.

SOLVING TWO-STEP EQUATIONS

Add or subtract before you multiply or divide.

Solve: $\quad\quad\quad 3x - 6 = 24$

$3x - 6 + 6 = 24 + 6$

$3x = 30$

Divide by 3 $\quad\quad \dfrac{3x}{3} = \dfrac{30}{3}$

$x = 10$

Check: Does $3 \times \mathbf{10} - 6 = 24$? Yes. It checks.

Solve: $\quad\quad\quad \dfrac{y}{7} + 4 = 32$

Subtract 4 $\quad\quad \dfrac{y}{7} + 4 - 4 = 32 - 4$

$\dfrac{y}{7} = 28$

Multiply by 7 $\quad\quad \dfrac{y}{7} \times 7 = (28)(7)$

$y = 196$

Check: Does $\dfrac{196}{7} + 4 = 32$? Yes. It checks.

Check: Does $28 + 4 = 32$? Yes. It checks.

Practice

Solve.

1. $w - 3 = 5$ 2. $x + 9 = 24$ 3. $y - 10 = 60$ 4. $z + 50 = 46$

5. $3w = 12$ 6. $\dfrac{x}{18} = 7$ 7. $^{-}9y = 45$ 8. $\dfrac{z}{6} = {}^{-}11$

9. $5w + 6 = 41$ 10. $^{-}3 - 2x = 23$ 11. $\dfrac{x}{19} + 11 = 35$ 12. $26z - 13 = 65$

Answers on page 139

GEOMETRY

We can think of geometry in two or three dimensions. A two-dimensional model is this page. A three-dimensional model is the room you'll take the test in.

Definition	Model	Symbol
Point—a location	· A	A
Plane—a flat surface that extends infinitely in all directions		plane ABC
Space—occupies three dimensions and extends infinitely in all directions		space xyz
Line—a set of points in a straight path that extends infinitely in two directions		$\overleftrightarrow{AB}$
Line segment—part of a line with two endpoints		$\overline{AB}$
Ray—part of a line with one endpoint		$\overrightarrow{AB}$
Parallel lines—lines that stay the same distance apart and never touch		
Perpendicular lines—lines that meet at right angles		

Definition	**Model**	**Symbol**

Angle—two rays with a common endpoint, which is called the vertex.

∠*ABC*

Acute angle—angle that measures between 0° and 90°

Right angle—angle that measures 90°

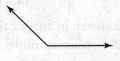

Obtuse angle—angle that measures between 90° and 180°

Complementary angles—angles that have a total measure of 90°

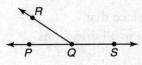

Supplementary angles—angles that have a total measure of 180°

Polygon—a closed figure made up of line segments; if all sides are the same length, the figure is a regular polygon

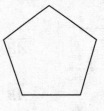

Pentagon
(Five Sides)

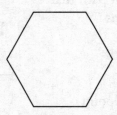

Hexagon
(Six Sides)

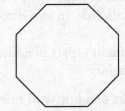

Octagon
(Eight Sides)

Triangle—polygon with three sides and three angles; the sum of the angles is always 180°

Equilateral triangle—all the sides are the same length; all the angles are the same size, 60°

Definition	**Model**	**Symbol**

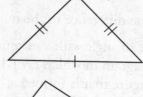

Isosceles triangle—two sides the
same length; two angles the same size

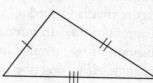

Scalene triangle—all sides different
lengths; all angles different sizes

Quadrilateral—polygon with four sides

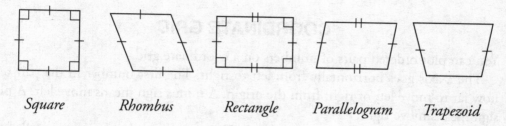

Square   Rhombus   Rectangle   Parallelogram   Trapezoid

Completed Example

Which types of quadrilaterals can be constructed using four congruent line segments
AB, *BC*, *CD*, and *DA*?

You can create a square and a rhombus.

Practice

Be certain to use proper markings to indicate congruent segments and congruent
angles.

1. What is the name of a quadrilateral that has exactly one pair of parallel sides?
2. Use the figure below. The m∠1 = 45°. What is m∠2?

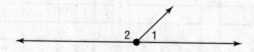

3. In the triangle below, *AB* = *AC* and m∠*BAC* = 80°.

   What are the measures of ∠*ABC* and ∠*ACB*?

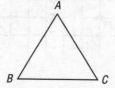

4. Draw a diagram of an equilateral triangle.
5. Which has more sides, an octagon or a hexagon?

   What is the difference in the number of sides for these figures?

6. What type of angle with a measure less than 180° is neither obtuse nor acute?
7. Draw a diagram in which ray (*AB*) intersects ray (*AC*) at point *A*, and name the new figure that is formed.
8. Draw a diagram of line *AB* intersecting line segment *CD* at point *E*.
9. Draw a diagram of two parallel lines perpendicular to a third line.
10. Given a triangle *ABC*, describe the relationship among the measures of the three angles.

Answers on page 140

COORDINATE GRID

You can plot ordered pairs of numbers on a coordinate grid.

The *x*-axis goes horizontally from left to right. The first number in the pair tells how far to move left or right from the origin. A minus sign means move left. A plus sign means move right.

The *y*-axis goes vertically up and down. The second number in the pair tells how far to move up or down from the origin. A minus sign means move down. A plus sign means move up.

Pairs of numbers show the *x*-coordinate first and the *y*-coordinate second (*x, y*). The origin is point (0, 0) where the *x*-axis and the *y*-axis meet.

Plot these pairs of numbers on the grid.

A (3, ⁻7) B (⁺5, ⁺3) C (⁻6, ⁺2) D (⁻3, ⁻6)

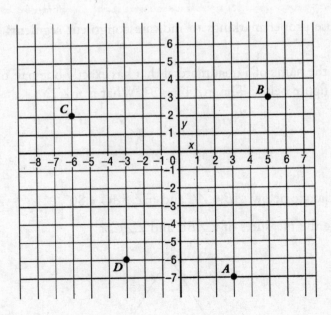

Practice

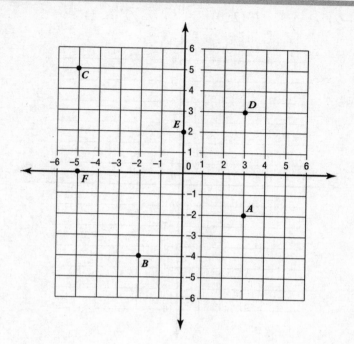

1. Write the coordinates of the points on the grid.

   A _____ B _____ C _____ D _____ E _____ F _____

2. Plot these points on the grid below.

   G (3, –1)   H (2, –3)   I (5, 6)   J (–4, 0)
   K (–5,–2)   L (–1, 6)   M (0, 3)   N (–5, 2)

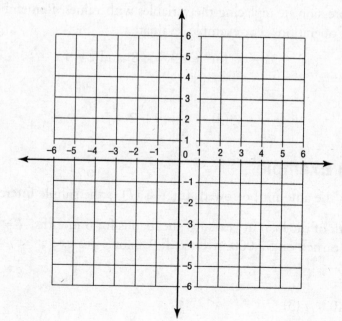

3. Plot these points on the grid below and connect them in the order shown.

Z (–5, 5)	Y (–2, 0)	X (2, –6)	W (3, 5)
V (–6, –2)	U (2, 0)	T (6, 1)	S (–5, 5)

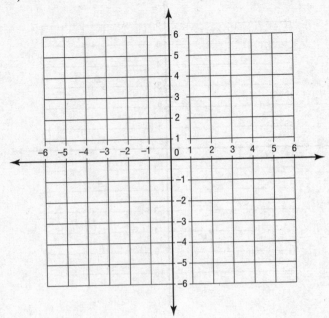

Answers on page 141

FORMULAS

EVALUATING AN EXPRESSION OR FORMULA

Evaluate an expression by replacing the variables with values. Remember to use the correct order of operations. For example, evaluate

$$3x - \frac{y}{z} \text{ for } x = 3, y = 8, \text{ and } z = 4$$

$$3(3) - \frac{8}{4} = 9 - 2 = 7$$

Completed Example

Principle (*P*) is the amount borrowed. Interest (*I*) is the simple interest rate. Time (*T*) is the length of the loan in **years**. (If the loan is for 6 months, $T = \frac{1}{2}$.) Find the simple interest earned on $2,000 invested at 9% for 3 years.

$I = PRT$

$I = (2,000) (0.09) (3)$

$I = 180 \times 3 \ I = 540$

The investment earns $540 in interest.

DISTANCE AND AREA

Perimeter   The distance around a figure. The perimeter of a circle is called the circumference.

Area   The amount of space occupied by a two-dimensional figure.

FORMULAS FOR PERIMETER AND AREA

Figure	Formula	Description
Triangle	Area = $\dfrac{1}{2} bh$ Perimeter = $s_1 + s_2 + s_3$	
Square	Area = s^2 Perimeter = $4s$	
Rectangle	Area = lw Perimeter = $2l + 2w$	
Parallelogram	Area = bh Perimeter = $2b + 2s$	
Trapezoid	Area = $\dfrac{1}{2} h (b_1 + b_2)$ Perimeter = $b_1 + b_2 + s_1 + s_2$	
Circle	Area = πr^2 Circumference = $2\pi r$ or = πd	

Pythagorean Theorem

The Pythagorean theorem for right triangles states that the sum of the square of the legs equals the square of the hypotenuse.

$$a^2 + b^2 = c^2$$

Completed Examples—Distance and Area

Let's solve the distance and area problems.

A. How many meters is it around a regular hexagon with a side of 87 centimeters? A hexagon has 6 sides. It's a regular hexagon, so all the sides are the same length. 6 × 87 = 522. The perimeter is 522 centimeters, which equals 5.22 meters.

B. What is the area of this figure?

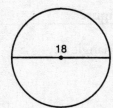

The formula for the area of a circle is πr^2.
The diameter is 18, so the radius is 9. Use 3.14 for π.
A = 3.14 × (9)² = 3.14 × 81 = 254.34 or about 254.

VOLUME

Volume—The amount of space occupied by a three-dimensional figure.

Formulas for Volume

Figure	Formula	Description
Cube	Volume = s^3	
Rectangular Prism	Volume = lwh	
Sphere	Volume = $\dfrac{4}{3}\pi r^3$	
Cone	Volume = $\dfrac{1}{3}\pi r^2 h$	
Cylinder	Volume = $\pi r^2 h$ Surface Area = $2\pi r(h+r)$	

Completed Example—Volume

A circular cone has a radius of 8 cm and a height of 10 cm. What is the volume?

Formula for the volume of a cone = $\frac{1}{3} \pi r^2 h$.

$$V = \left(\frac{1}{3}\right)(3.14)(8^2)(10) = \left(\frac{1}{3}\right)(3.14)(64)(10) = \left(\frac{1}{3}\right)(3.14)(640) = 669.87$$

The volume of the cone is 669.87 cubic centimeters or about 670 cubic centimeters.

Practice

1. A circle has a radius of 9 meters. What is the area?
2. The faces of a pyramid are equilateral triangles. What is the surface area of the pyramid if the sides of the triangles equal 3 inches and the height is 2.6 inches?
3. A regular hexagon has one side 5 feet long. What is the distance around its edge?
4. What is the surface area of the side of a cylinder (not top and bottom) with a height of 10 cm and a diameter of 2.5 cm?
5. A rectangle has a width x and a length $(x + 5)$. If the perimeter is 90 feet, what is the length?
6. The perimeter of one face of a cube is 20 cm. What is the surface area?
7. What is the length of the third side in the right triangle below?

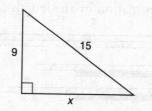

8. What is the area of a trapezoid whose height is 5 inches, the length of one base is 5 inches, and the length of the other base is 8 inches?
9. What is the volume of a sphere that has a diameter of length 20 cm?
10. What is the volume of a cube having a side length of 15 inches.

Answers on page 142

GRAPHS

You will encounter four main types of graphs on the test.

THE PICTOGRAPH

The pictograph uses symbols to stand for numbers. In the following graph, each picture represents 1,000 phones.

Number of Phones in Five Towns

Find the number of phones in Emerson.

Count the number of phones on the pictograph for Emerson. There are $7\frac{1}{2}$. That means there are $7.5 \times 1,000 = 7,500$ phones in Emerson.

THE BAR GRAPH

The bar graph represents information by the length of a bar.

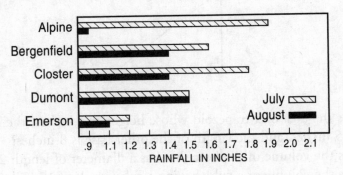

Rainfall in July and August for Five Towns

Find the August rainfall for Emerson and the July rainfall for Closter.

Follow the bar across and then read down to find that 1.1 inches of rain fell in Emerson during August.

Read down from the striped bar for Closter to find that 1.8 inches of rain fell in Closter during July.

THE LINE GRAPH

The line graph plots information against two axes.

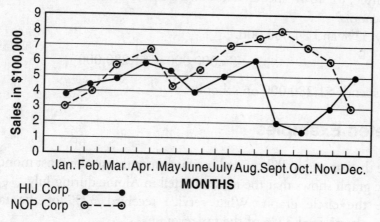

HIJ Corp
NOP Corp

Sales for Two Companies During the Year

Find the June sales for HIJ Corp.

Read up from June and across from Sales to find that the HIJ Corp. had $400,000 in sales during June.

THE CIRCLE GRAPH

The circle represents an entire amount. Each wedge-shaped piece of the graph represents some percent of that whole.

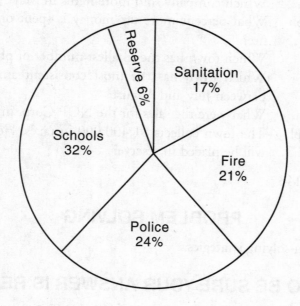

Percent of Tax Money Spent for Town Services

Multiply the percent and the entire budget amount to find the amount spent in a budget area.

For example, the town spends $4,000,000 on services. How much does the town spend on schools?

Multiply 32% and $4,000,000.

$$0.32 \times \$4,000,000 = \$1,280,000$$

The town spends $1,280,000 on schools.

Completed Examples

A. Use the bar graph. Where and in which month was the most monthly rainfall? The graph shows that the most rain fell in Alpine during July.

B. Use the circle graph. What service received 32% of the tax revenue? Schools received 32% of the tax revenue.

Practice

Use the graphs shown earlier in this section to answer these practice items.

1. Pictograph — How many more phones are there in Bergenfield than in Closter?

2. Bar Graph — Which town has the greatest rainfall difference between July and August?

3. Line Graph — Which company sold more items in May?

4. Circle Graph — What percent more tax money is spent on police than on fire?

5. Pictograph — Which town has the smallest number of phones?

6. Bar Graph — Which town has the most consistent amount of rainfall between July and August?

7. Line Graph — What were the sales for the NOP Corp. in September?

8. Circle Graph — The town collects $1,400,000 in taxes. How much money will be placed in reserve?

Answers on page 143

PROBLEM SOLVING

Use these problem-solving strategies.

ESTIMATE TO BE SURE YOUR ANSWER IS REASONABLE

You can use estimation and common sense to be sure that the answer is reasonable. You may make a multiplication error or misalign decimal points. You may be so engrossed in a problem that you miss the big picture because of the details. These difficulties can be headed off by making sure your answer is reasonable.

A few examples follow.

A question involves dividing or multiplying. Multiply: 28 × 72.

Estimate first: 30 × 70 = 2,100. Your answer should be close to 2,100. If not, then your answer is not reasonable. A mistake was probably made in multiplication.

A question involves subtracting or adding. Add: 12.9 + 0.63 + 10.29 + 4.3.

Estimate first: 13 + 1 + 10 + 4 = 28. Your answer should be close to 28. If not, then your answer is not reasonable. The decimal points may not have been aligned.

A question asks you to compare fractions to $\frac{11}{10}$.

Think: $\frac{11}{10}$ is more than 1. Any number 1 or less will be less than $\frac{11}{10}$. Any number $\frac{1}{8}$ or larger will be more than $\frac{11}{10}$. You have to look closely only at numbers between 1 and $1\frac{1}{8}$.

A question asks you to multiply two fractions or decimals.

The fractions or decimals are less than 1. The product of two fractions or decimals less than one is less than either of the two fractions or decimals. If not, you know that your answer is not reasonable.

Stand back for a second after you answer each question and ask, "Is this reasonable? Is this at least approximately correct? Does this make sense?"

Check answers to computation, particularly division and subtraction. When you have completed a division or subtraction example, do a quick, approximate check. Your check should confirm your answer. If not, your answer is probably not reasonable.

WORDS TO SYMBOLS PROBLEMS

Before you solve a problem, you may have to decide which operation to use. You can use key words to help you decide which operation to use.

Key Words

Addition	sum, and, more, increased by
Subtraction	less, difference, decreased by
Multiplication	of, product, times
Division	per, quotient, shared, ratio
Equals	is, equals

You can't just use these key words without thinking. You must be sure that the operation makes sense when it replaces the key word. For example,

19 and 23 is 42	16 is 4 more than 12	30% of 19 is 57?
$19 + 23 = 42$	$16 = 4 + 12$	$0.3 \times 19 = 57$

three more than y	$y + 3$	The product of 3 and y	$3y$
y increased by 3	$y + 3$	3 times y	$3y$
y more than 3	$3 + y$	3% of y	$0.03y$
3 less than y	$y - 3$	3 divided by y	$\dfrac{3}{y}$
y decreased by 3	$y - 3$	y divided by 3	$\dfrac{y}{3}$
3 decreased y	$3 - y$	ratio of 3 to y	$\dfrac{3}{y}$
The opposite of y	$-y$	The reciprocal of y	$\dfrac{1}{y}$

Completed Examples

A. 18 divided by what number is 3?

$18 \div y = 3$ $18 = 3y$ $y = 6$

B. 25 less 6 is what number?

$25 - 6 = y$ $y = 19$

C. A student correctly answered 80% of 120 mathematics problems. How many mathematics problems did he answer correctly?

$0.8 \times 120 = y$ $y = 96$

The student correctly answered 96 problems.

D. The product of a number and its opposite is −25. What is the number?

$(y) \times (-y) = 25$ $y = 5$

The number is 5.

Practice

Solve the problem.

1. What number decreased by 9 is 25?
2. What is 60% of 90?
3. Bob lives $\frac{2}{3}$ mile from Gina and $\frac{1}{2}$ mile from Sam. Bob's walk to the school is three times the sum of these distances. How far is Bob's walk to school?
4. The ratio of two gears is 20 to y. If the ratio equals 2.5, what is the value of y?
5. The sum of 5 and the reciprocal of another number is $5\frac{1}{8}$. What is the other number?
6. Car A travels at a constant speed of 60 mph for 2.5 hours. Car B travels at a constant speed of 70 mph for 2 hours. What is the total distance traveled by both cars?

Answers on page 143

FINDING AND INTERPRETING PATTERNS

Sequences

Arithmetic Sequence

A sequence of numbers formed by adding the same nonzero number.

3, 11, 19, 27, 35, 42, 50	Add 8 to get each successive term
52, 48, 44, 40, 36, 32	Add (−4) to get each successive term

Geometric Sequence

A sequence of numbers formed by multiplying the same nonzero number.

3, 15, 75, 375	Multiply by 5 to get each successive term.
160, 40, 10, $2\frac{1}{2}$	Multiply by $\frac{1}{4}$ to get each successive term.

Harmonic Sequence

A sequence of fractions with a numerator of 1 in which the denominators form an arithmetic sequence.

$$\frac{1}{2} \quad \frac{1}{9} \quad \frac{1}{16} \quad \frac{1}{23} \quad \frac{1}{30}$$

Each numerator is 1. The denominators form an arithmetic sequence.

Relationships

Linear Relationships

Linear relationships are pairs of numbers formed by adding or multiplying the same number to the first term in a pair. Here are some examples.

(3, 12), (5, 14), (11, 20), (15, 24)   Add 9 to the first term to get the second.

(1, 6), (2, 12), (3, 18), (4, 24), (5, 30)   Multiply the first term by 6 to get the second.

(96, 12), (72, 9), (56, 7), (24, 3), (16, 2)   Multiply the first term by $\frac{1}{8}$ to get the second.

Completed Examples

A. What term is missing in this number pattern?

2   5   10   17   ____

   +3   +5   +7   +9

26 is the missing term.

B. These points are all on the same line.

Find the missing term.

(–7, –15) $\left(\frac{2}{3}, \frac{1}{3}\right)$ (2, 3) (4, 7) (8, ____)

Multiply the first term by 2 and subtract 1.

The missing term is (8, 15).

Practice

Find the missing term in each pattern below.

1. 4, 2, 0, –2, –4, ____ –8, –10
2. 4, 6.5, 9, 11.5, ____
3. 120, 60, 30, 15, ____
4. 1, 2, 6, 24, 120, ____
5. 5, 9, 13, 17, ____

The points in each sequence below are on the same line. Find the missing term.

6. (4, 12), (2, 10), (10, 18), (18, 26), (22, ____)
7. (100, 11), (70, 8), (90, 10), (40, 5), (30, ____)
8. (3, 9), (7, 49), (2, 4), (100, 10,000), (5, ____)

9. A meteorologist placed remote thermometers at sea level and up the side of the mountain at 1,000, 2,000, 5,000, and 6,000 feet. Readings were taken simultaneously and entered in the following table. What temperatures would you predict for the missing readings?

Temperature

0	1,000	2,000	3,000	4,000	5,000	6,000	7,000	8,000	9,000	10,000
52°	49°	46°			37°	34°				

10. Consider another example. A space capsule is moving in a straight line and is being tracked on a grid. The first four positions on the grid are recorded in the following table. Where will the capsule be on the grid when the x position is 13?

x-value	1	2	3	4
y-value	1	4	7	10

Answers on page 144

FREQUENCY TABLE PROBLEMS

Percent

Percent tables show the percent or proportion of a particular score or characteristic. We can see from Table 1 that 13% of the students got a score from 90 through 100.

Completed Example

Table 1	
Scores	**Percent of Students**
0–59	2
60–69	8
70–79	39
80–89	38
90–100	13

Which score interval contains the mode?

The largest percentage is 39% for 70–79. The interval 70–79 contains the mode.

Which score interval contains the median?

The cumulative percentage of 0–79 is 49%.

The median is in the interval in which the cumulative percentage of 50% occurs. The score interval 80–89 contains the median.

What percent of the students scored above 79?

Add the percentiles of the intervals above 79.   38 + 13 = 51

51% of the students scored above 79.

Percentile Rank

The percentile rank shows the percent of scores below a given value. We can see from Table 2 that 68% of the scores fell below 60.

Completed Example

Table 2	
Standardized Score	Percentile Rank
80	99
70	93
60	68
50	39
40	22
30	13
20	2

What percent of the scores are below 50?

The percentile rank next to 50 is 39. That means 39% of the scores are below 50.

What percent of the scores are between 30 and 70?

Subtract the percentile rank for 30 from the percentile rank for 70. 93% – 13% = 80%. 80% of the scores are between 30 and 70.

What percent of the scores are at or above 60?

Subtract the percentile rank for 60 from 100%. 100% – 68% = 32%. 32% of the scores are at or above 60.

Practice

Use Table 1 and Table 2 on pages 117 and 118.

Table 1

1. What percent of the scores are below 70?
2. In which score interval is the median?
3. What percent of the scores are from 80 to 100?

Table 2

4. The lowest passing score is 50. What percent of the scores are passing?
5. What percent of the scores are from 20 to 50?

Answers on page 145

GEOMETRIC FIGURE PROBLEMS

Follow these steps to solve this type of problem.

1. Identify the figure or figures involved.
2. Use the formulas for these figures.
3. Use the results of the formulas to solve the problem.

Completed Example

A circular pool with a radius of 10 feet is inscribed inside a square wall. What is the area of the region outside the pool but inside the fence?

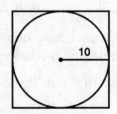

1. There is a square with $s = 20$ and a circle with $r = 10$. The side of the square is twice the radius of the circle.

2. Find the areas.
   Square: $(A = s^2)$ (20) × (20) = 400
   Circle: $(A = \pi r^2)$ 3.14 × 10^2 = 3.14 × 100 = 314

3. Subtract to find the area inside the square but outside the circle.
   400 − 314 = 86

Practice

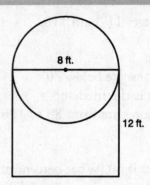

1. The dimensions of part of a basketball court are shown in the diagram above. One pint of paint covers 35 square feet. How much paint would it take to paint the inside region of this part of the court?

2. A roofer uses one bushel of shingles to cover 1,200 square feet. How many bushels of shingles are needed to cover these three rectangular roofs?

   Roof 1: 115 ft by 65 ft
   Roof 2: 112 ft by 65 ft
   Roof 3: 72 ft by 52 ft

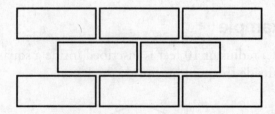

3. The bricks in the wall pictured here measure 2 inches by 4 inches by 8 inches. What is the volume of the bricks in this section of the wall?

4. A circular cone has a radius of 4 cm. If the volume is 134 cm³, what is the height?

5. The official basketball has a radius of 6.5 inches. What is the volume?

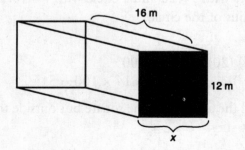

6. The rectangular solid shown here has a volume of 1,920 m³. What is the area of the shaded side?

Answers on page 145

INTERPRETING REMAINDER PROBLEMS

When you divide to solve a problem there may be both a quotient and a remainder. You may need to (1) use only the quotient, (2) round the quotient to the next greater whole number, or (3) use only the remainder.

Completed Example

Stereo speakers are packed four to a box. There are 315 stereo speakers to be packed.

Questions:

1. How many boxes can be filled?
2. How many boxes would be needed to hold all the stereo speakers?
3. How many stereo speakers will be in the box that is not completely full? Divide 315 by 4.

$$
\begin{array}{r}
78 \text{ R}3 \\
4{\overline{)315}} \\
28 \\
\hline
35 \\
32 \\
\hline
3
\end{array}
$$

Answers:

1. Use only the quotient—78 of the boxes can be filled.
2. Round the quotient to the next higher number. It would take 79 boxes to hold all the stereo speakers.
3. Use only the remainder. Three stereo speakers would be in the partially filled box.

Practice

At the quarry, workers are putting 830 pounds of sand into bags that hold 25 pounds.

1. How much sand is left over after the bags are filled?
2. How many bags are needed to hold all the sand?
3. How many bags can be filled with sand?

Answers on page 146

Strategies for Taking the Mathematics Test

The mathematics tested is the kind you probably had in high school and in college. It is the kind of mathematics you will use as you teach and go about your everyday life. Computational ability, alone, is expected but is held to a minimum. Remember to use the general test strategies discussed in the Introduction.

Work from the Answers

If you don't know how to solve a formula or relation, try out each answer choice until you get the correct answer. Look at this example.

What percent times $\frac{1}{4}$ is $\frac{1}{5}$?

(A) 25%
(B) 40%
(C) 80%
(D) 120%
(E) None of the above

Just take each answer in turn and try it out.

$$0.25 \times \frac{1}{4} = \frac{1}{4} \times \frac{1}{4} = \frac{1}{16} \qquad \text{That's not it.}$$

$$0.40 \times \frac{1}{4} = \frac{4}{10} \times \frac{1}{4} = \frac{4}{40} = \frac{1}{10} \qquad \text{That's not it either.}$$

$$0.8 \times \frac{1}{4} = \frac{4}{5} \times \frac{1}{4} = \frac{4}{20} = \frac{1}{5}$$

You know that 0.8 is the correct answer, and so choice (C) is correct.

Try Out Numbers

Look at the preceding question.

Work with fractions at first. Ask: What number times $\dfrac{1}{4}$ equals $\dfrac{1}{5}$?

Through trial and error you find out that $\dfrac{4}{5} \times \dfrac{1}{4} = \dfrac{1}{5}$.

The answer in fractions is $\dfrac{4}{5}$.

$$\dfrac{4}{5} = 0.8 = 80\%$$

The correct choice is (C).

In this example, we found the answer without ever solving an equation. We just tried out numbers until we found the one that works.

Eliminate and Guess

Use this approach when all else has failed. Begin by eliminating the answers you know are wrong. Sometimes you know with certainty that an answer is incorrect. Other times, an answer looks so unreasonable that you can be fairly sure that it is not correct.

Once you have eliminated incorrect answers, a few will probably be left. Just guess among these choices. There is no method that will increase your chances of guessing correctly.

PAPER-BASED TESTS

WRITE IN THE TEST BOOKLET

It is particularly important to write in the test booklet while taking the mathematics portion of the test. Use these hints for writing in the test booklet.

Do Your Calculations in the Test Booklet

Do all your calculations in the PPST test booklet to the right of the question. This makes it easy to refer to the calculations as you choose the correct answer.

This example should make you feel comfortable about writing in the test booklet.

What number times 0.00708 is equal to 70.8?

(A) 100,000 ×   ~~0.00708~~ ~~700.8~~
(B) 10,000 ×   ~~0.00708~~ = 70.8
(C) 1,000
(D) 0.01
(E) 0.0001

The correct answer is (B) 10,000.

Draw Diagrams and Figures in the Test Booklet or on Scrap Paper

When you come across a geometry problem or related problem, draw a diagram in the PPST test booklet to help.

All sides of a rectangle are shrunk in half. What happens to the area?

(A) Divided by two
(B) Divided by four
(C) Multiplied by two
(D) Multiplied by six
(E) Does not change

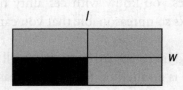

Answer (B), divided by 4, is the correct answer. The original area is evenly divided into four parts.

Targeted Mathematics Test

This targeted test is designed to help you practice the problem-solving and test-taking strategies presented in this chapter. For that reason, questions may have a different emphasis than the actual test, and the actual test will certainly be more complete.

Mark your choice, then check your answers on page 147.

Use the strategies on pages 122–124.

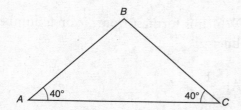

1. What is the measure of angle *B*?

   (A) 10
   (B) 40
   (C) 80
   (D) 100
   (E) 180

2. After a discount of 25%, the savings on a pair of roller blades was $12.00. What was the sale price?

   (A) $48.00
   (B) $36.00
   (C) $24.00
   (D) $25.00
   (E) $60.00

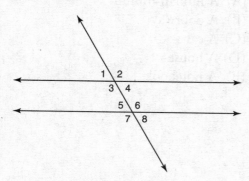

3. Which two angles are supplementary?

   (A) 6 and 7
   (B) 1 and 4
   (C) 3 and 6
   (D) 2 and 4
   (E) 4 and 8

4. Chad rolls a fair die. The sides of the die are numbered from 1 to 6. Ten times in a row he rolls a 5. What is the probability that he will roll a 5 on his next roll?

   (A) $\dfrac{1}{5}$

   (B) $\dfrac{1}{6}$

   (C) $\dfrac{1}{50}$

   (D) $\dfrac{1}{11}$

   (E) $\dfrac{1}{10}$

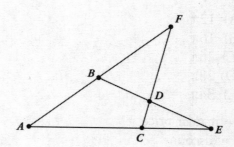

5. Which of the following set of points do not form an angle in the diagram?

   (A) *ABF*
   (B) *ABE*
   (C) *AFC*
   (D) *ABC*
   (E) *CDE*

6. An apple costs (*C*). You have (*D*) dollars. What equation would represent the amount of apples you could buy for the money you have?

(A) *C/D*
(B) *CD*
(C) *C* + *D*
(D) *D/C*
(E) *C* + 2*D*

7. If a worker gets $144.00 for 18 hours' work, how much would that worker get for 32 hours' work?

(A) $200.00
(B) $288.00
(C) $400.00
(D) $432.00
(E) $256.00

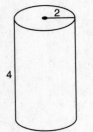 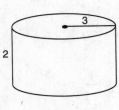

$V = \pi r^2 h$

8. What is the combined volume of these two cylinders?

(A) 12π
(B) 16π
(C) 26π
(D) 28π
(E) 34π

9. *r* = regular price
d = discount
s = sale price

What equation would represent the calculations for finding the discount?

(A) $d = r - s$
(B) $d = s - r$
(C) $d = sr$
(D) $d = s + r$
(E) $d = \frac{1}{2}r$

10. A printing company makes pamphlets that cost $.75 per copy plus $5.00 as a setter's fee. If $80 were spent printing a pamphlet, how many pamphlets were ordered?

(A) 50
(B) 75
(C) 100
(D) 150
(E) 225

11. Which is furthest from $\frac{1}{2}$ on a number line?

(A) $\frac{1}{12}$

(B) $\frac{7}{8}$

(C) $\frac{3}{4}$

(D) $\frac{2}{3}$

(E) $\frac{5}{6}$

12. Which of the following could be about 25 centimeters long?

(A) A human thumb
(B) A doorway
(C) A car
(D) A house
(E) A notebook

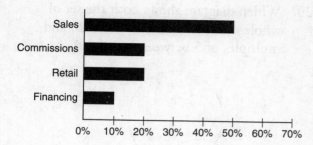

13. The sales department staff draws its salary from four areas of the company's income. Using the above graph, determine what percentage is drawn from the retail fund.

    (A) 10%
    (B) 20%
    (C) 25%
    (D) 30%
    (E) 15%

14. What percentage of 250 is 25?

    (A) 5%
    (B) 10%
    (C) 20%
    (D) 25%
    (E) 50%

15. For a fund raiser the Science and Technology Club is selling raffles at the cost of six raffles for $5.00. It cost the club $250.00 for the prizes and tickets that will be given away. How many raffles will the club have to sell in order to make $1,000.00?

    (A) 300
    (B) 600
    (C) 750
    (D) 1,200
    (E) 1,500

16. $5.3 \times 10^4 =$

    (A) 0.0053
    (B) 0.00053
    (C) 5,300
    (D) 53,000
    (E) 530,000

17. Which of the following represents supplementary angles?

    (A)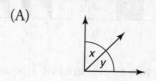

    (B)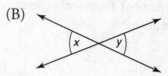

    (C)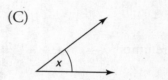

    (D)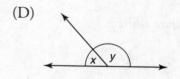

    (E)

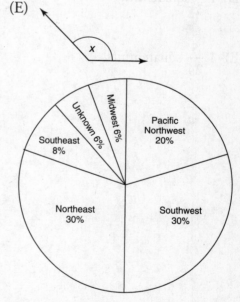

18. The above graph shows the percentage of students who attend college by the location of their home towns. How many more college students come from the Northeast than come from the Midwest?

    (A) Twice as many
    (B) Three times as many
    (C) Half as many
    (D) Five times as many
    (E) Ten times as many

19. Each rectangle has a total area of 1 square unit. What number represents the area of the shaded regions?

    (A) $\dfrac{5}{6}$ square units

    (B) $\dfrac{7}{8}$ square units

    (C) $1\dfrac{3}{4}$ square units

    (D) $1\dfrac{1}{3}$ square units

    (E) $1\dfrac{5}{24}$ square units

20. Which diagram shows both the set of whole numbers between 1 and 20 and multiples of 5 between 1 and 20?

    (A)

    (B)

    (C)

    (D)

    (E)

Answers
Mathematics Practice

Understanding and Ordering Whole Numbers, page 75

1. $2 < 3$

2. $4 > 1$

3. $8 < 9$

4. $1 = 1$

5. $7 > 6$

6. 9,037

7. 2,851

8. The hundreds place and the ones place each contain a 7.

9. 1, 2, 3, 4, 5, 6, 7, 8, 9, 10, 11, 12, 13, 14

    The problem asks for the numbers between 0 and 15, so 0 and 15 are not included.

10. There are 49. (1, 2, 3, . . . , 47, 48, 49)

Positive Exponents, page 76

1. 241

2. 81

3. 8

4. 900

5. 35

6. 51

7. $4^6 = 4,096$

8. $2^5 = 32$

9. 44

10. 1,000

11. $4^4 = 256$

12. 72

Order of Operations, page 77

1. $4 \times 5 + 4 \div 2 = 20 + 2 = 22$

2. $(5 + 7 - 9) \times 8^2 + 2 = 3 \times 8^2 + 2 = 194$

3. $((7 + 4)-(1 + 4)) \times 6 = (11- 5) \times 6 = 36$

4. $6^2 + 3(9 - 5 + 7)^2 = 36 + 3 \times 11^2 = 399$

5. $51 - 36 = 15$

6. $40 + 4 - 4 = 40$

7. $^-50 + 7 = ^-43$

8. $(49 + 16) \times 8 = 520$

Understanding and Ordering Decimals, page 78

1. $0.02 > 0.003$

2. $4.6 > 1.98$

3. $0.0008 > 0.00009$

4. $1.0 = 1$

5. $7.6274 > 7.6269$

6. 2.586

7. 90,310.0704

8. The hundredths place and the hundred thousandths place each contain a 3.

9. 0, 0.1, 0.2, 0.3, 0.4, 0.5, 0.6, 0.7, 0.8, 0.9, 1.0

10. There are 99—0.01, 0.02, 0.03, . . . , 0.50, 0.51, 0.52, . . . , 0.97, 0.98, 0.99

Add, Subtract, Multiply, and Divide Decimals, page 80

1. 26.09
2. 72.617
3. 988.39
4. 5,473.19
5. 8.2
6. 71.0096
7. 453.97
8. 1,767.87
9. .6225
10. 163.45
11. 3,680.538
12. 3,761.514
13. 4.8
14. 9.6
15. 33.6
16. 125.63

Understanding and Ordering Fractions, page 82

1. $1\frac{2}{3}$

2. $2\frac{1}{7}$

3. $2\frac{2}{3}$

4. $\frac{41}{5}$

5. $\dfrac{55}{8}$

6. $\dfrac{68}{7}$

7. $\dfrac{3}{7} < \dfrac{4}{9}$

8. $\dfrac{5}{6} = \dfrac{25}{30}$

9. $\dfrac{4}{5} < \dfrac{7}{8}$

Multiply, Divide, Add, and Subtract Fractions and Mixed Numbers, page 84

1. $\dfrac{5}{27}$

2. $\dfrac{1}{6}$

3. $13\dfrac{59}{64}$

4. $8\dfrac{8}{35}$

5. $\dfrac{6}{7}$

6. $\dfrac{18}{35}$

7. $2\dfrac{22}{91}$

8. $\dfrac{7}{19}$

9. $1\frac{2}{9}$

10. $1\frac{1}{5}$

11. $4\frac{1}{14}$

12. $12\frac{1}{2}$

13. $\frac{1}{21}$

14. $\frac{1}{40}$

15. $\frac{2}{3}$

16. $3\frac{58}{63}$

Number Theory, page 86

1. 13: 1 and 13

2. 26: 1, 2, 13, and 26

3. 40: 1, 2, 4, 5, 8, 10, 20, 40

4. 23: 1 and 23

5. 24

6. 60

7. 35

8. 28

9. 6

10. 5

11. 32

12. 28

Ratio and Proportion, page 87

1. 14 vacuum cleaners for 280 houses

2. 4 teachers for 32 children

3. 21 rest stops for 140 miles

4. Yes. $\dfrac{7}{9} = \dfrac{28}{36}$ because $7 \times 36 = 252 = 9 \times 28$

Percent, page 89

1. 35.9%

2. 78%

3. 21.5%

4. 4.1%

5. $11\dfrac{1}{9}\%$

6. 62.5%

7. 30%

8. $44\dfrac{4}{9}\%$

9. $\dfrac{29}{50}$

10. $\dfrac{79}{100}$

11. $\dfrac{213}{250}$

12. $\dfrac{487}{500}$

Three Types of Percent Problems, page 91

1. $\square \times 240 = 120$

    $\square = \dfrac{120}{240}$

    $\square = .5 = 50\%$

2. $.15 \times 70 = \square$

    $.15 \times 70 = 10.5$

    $\square = 10.5$

3. $.6 \times 300 = \square$

    $.6 \times 300 = 180$

    $\square = 180$

4. $\square \times 60 = 42$

    $\square = \dfrac{42}{60}$

    $\square = 70\%$

5. $\square \% \times 25 = 2.5$

    $\square \% = \dfrac{2.5}{25}$

    $\square = 10\%$

6. $40\% \times \square = 22$

    $\square = \dfrac{22}{.4}$

    $\square = 55$

7. $.7 \times \square = 85$

    $\square = \dfrac{85}{.7}$

    $\square = 121\dfrac{3}{7}$

8. $25\% \times 38 = \square$

    $.25 \times 38 = 9.5$

    $\square = 9.5$

9. $.35 \times \square = 24$

$$\square = \frac{24}{.35}$$

$$\square = 68\frac{4}{7}$$

10. $24 = \square \times 80$

$$\frac{24}{80} = \square$$

$$\square = 30\%$$

Percent of Increase and Decrease, page 92

1. Amount of increase $35 - 25 = \$10$

$$\frac{10}{25} = 0.4 = 40\%$$

Percent of increase = 40%

2. Discount: $\$100 \times .25 = \$25$
$\$100 - \$25 = \$75$
Sale price = $75

3. Discount $\$80 \times 15\% = \$12$
$\$80 - \$12 = \$68$
New price = $68

4. Amount of increase $\$150 - \$120 = \$30$

$$\frac{30}{120} = \frac{1}{4} = 25\%$$

Percent of increase = 25%

5. Discount $\$75 \times 10\% = \$7.50$
$\$75 - \$7.50 = \$67.50$
Sale price = $67.50

6. Amount of decrease $\$18 - \$6 = \$12$

$$\frac{12}{18} = \frac{2}{3} = 66\frac{2}{3}\%$$

Percent of decrease = $66\frac{2}{3}\%$

7. Amount of decrease $225 − $180 = $45

$$\frac{45}{225} = 0.2 = 20\%$$

Percent of decrease = 20%

8. Discount $150 = x − 0.25x
$150 = 0.75x
x = $200
Original price: $200

Probability, page 94

1. There are 10 socks in the drawer. 7 of the 10 are not black.

$$P \text{ (not black)} = \frac{7}{10}$$

2. There are 6 goldfish; 2 of the 6 are male

$$P \text{ (male)} = \frac{2}{6} = \frac{1}{3}$$

3. There are 52 cards in a deck. There are 4 kings and 4 queens.
P (king or queen) = P (king) + P (queen) =

$$\frac{4}{52} + \frac{4}{52} = \frac{8}{52} = \frac{2}{13}$$

4. There are 6 different names.
P (Carl and Phyllis) =
P (Carl) × P (Phyllis) =

$$\frac{1}{6} \times \frac{1}{6} = \frac{1}{36}$$

5. $\dfrac{1}{2}$

6. This is an "and" problem. Multiply the probability.

$$\left(\frac{1}{2}\right)\left(\frac{1}{2}\right)\left(\frac{1}{2}\right)\left(\frac{1}{2}\right)\left(\frac{1}{2}\right) = \frac{1}{32}$$

Statistics, page 96

1. mode 80

2. mean (average) 35.5

3. median 9 (Remember to arrange the numbers in order.)

4. 16 is the median, the mode, and very close to the mean.

5. mean 89

6. mode 30

Permutations, Combinations, and the Fundamental Counting Principle, page 97

1. There are 6 combinations of 2 people to sit in the chairs.

2. There are 5,040 possible arrangements of the 7 books on the shelf.

3. 67,600 (26 × 26 × 10 × 10)

4. The positions on the bus are not specified. Order does not matter. This is a combination problem.

   Four students A B C D

   ABC   ABD   ACD   BCD

   There are four ways for three of four students to board the bus.

Integers, page 98

1. 15

2. 1

3. −69

4. −9

5. 1

6. 54

7. 22

8. −80

9. 99

10. −650

11. 1,829

12. −1,470

13. 15

14. −17

15. 44

16. −22

Scientific Notation, page 99

1. $0.0564 = 5.64 \times 10^{-2}$

2. $0.00897 = 8.97 \times 10^{-3}$

3. $0.06501 = 6.501 \times 10^{-2}$

4. $0.000354 = 3.54 \times 10^{-4}$

5. $545 = 5.45 \times 10^{2}$

6. $7,790 = 7.79 \times 10^{3}$

7. $289,705 = 2.89705 \times 10^{5}$

8. $1,801,319 = 1.801319 \times 10^{6}$

Equations, page 101

1. $w = 8$

2. $x = 15$

3. $y = 70$

4. $z = -4$

5. $w = 4$

6. $x = 126$

7. $y = -5$

8. $z = -66$

9. $w = 7$

10. $x = -13$

11. $y = 456$

12. $z = 3$

Geometry, page 103

1. trapezoid

2. $m\angle 2 = 135°$

3. $m\angle ABC = 50° = m\angle ACB$

4.

5. An octagon (8 sides) has two more sides than a hexagon (6 sides).

6. A right angle, which has a measure of 90°.

7. (Picture may vary)

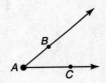

The new figure is $\angle BAC$.

8. (Picture may vary)

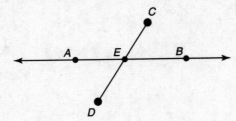

9. (Picture may vary)

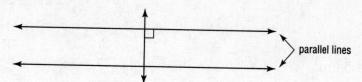

parallel lines

10. The sum of the measures is 180° (m∠A + m∠B + m∠C = 180°).

Coordinate Grid, page 105

1. A(3, −2)
   B(−2, −4)
   C(−5, 5)
   D(3, 3)
   E(0, 2)
   F(−5, 0)

2.

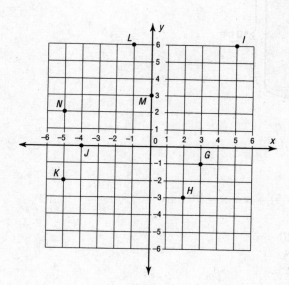

3.

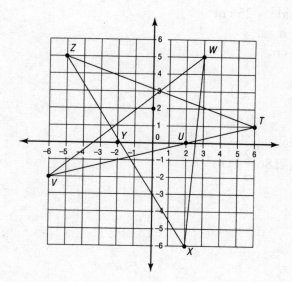

Formulas, page 109

1. πr^2
    $3.14 \times (9)^2 =$
    $3.14 \times 81 = 254.34$ m^2

2. $b = 3$, $h = 2.6$
    $(\frac{1}{2})(3)(2.6) = 3.9$
    $4 \times 3.9 = 15.6$ in^2

3. Hexagon is 6-sided.
    6×5 ft $= 30$ ft perimeter

4.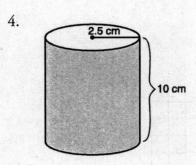

    $\quad 2 \quad \pi \quad r \quad h$
    $2 \, (3.14)(1.25)(10)$
    $= 78.5$ cm^2

5. $(x + 5) + (x + 5) + x + x = 90$
    $4x + 10 = 90$
    $4x = 80 \quad x = 20$
    length $= x + 5$
    length $= 25$ ft

6. Area of each side $= 25$ cm^2
    Cube is 6-sided.
    $6 \times 25 = 150$ cm^2

7. $x = 12$

8. $A = 32.5$ in.^{2}

9. $V = 4186.\overline{6}$ $(4186\frac{2}{3})$ cm^3

10. $V = 3375$ in^3

Graphs, page 112

1. 1,000 phones

2. Alpine

3. HIJ Corp.

4. 3%

5. Alpine

6. Dumont

7. $800,000

8. $84,000

Words to Symbols Problems, page 115

1. $34; 34 - 9 = 25$

2. $0.6 \times 90 = 54$

3. Add: $\dfrac{2}{3} + \dfrac{1}{2} = \dfrac{7}{6}$

   Multiply: $\dfrac{7}{6} \times 3 = \dfrac{21}{6}$

   Divide: $\dfrac{21}{6} \div 3\dfrac{3}{6} = 3\dfrac{1}{2}$.

   Bob's walk to school is $3\dfrac{1}{2}$ miles.

4. $\dfrac{20}{y} = 2.5 \quad 20 = 2.5y \quad y = 8$

5. $5\dfrac{1}{x} = 5\dfrac{1}{8} \quad x = 8$

   The number is 8.

6. Multiply: $60 \times 2.5 = 150$

   $70 \times 2 = 140$

   Add: $150 + 140 = 290$

   The cars traveled a total distance of 290 miles.

Finding and Interpreting Patterns, page 117

1. **−6** is the missing term. Subtract 2 from each term.

2. **14** is the missing term. Add 2.5 to each term.

3. **7.5** is the missing term. Divide each term by 2 to get the next term.

4. **720** is the missing term. The sequence follows the pattern $(1 \times 1)(1 \times 2)$ $(1 \times 2 \times 3)(1 \times 2 \times 3 \times 4)\ldots$

5. **21** is the missing term. Add 4 to find the next term.

6. (22, **30**) is the missing term. Add 8 to the first term to find the second term.

7. (30, **4**) is the missing term. Divide the first term by 10 and add 1 to find the second term.

8. (5, **25**) is the missing term. Square the first term to get the second term.

9. The temperatures drops 3° from 52° to 49° and from 49° to 46°. If it drops at the same rate, the temperature drop at 3,000 feet would be 43° and 4,000 feet would be 40° (followed by 37° and 34°). Continue to fill in the table accordingly, as follows.

Temperature

0	1,000	2,000	3,000	4,000	5,000
52°	49°	46°	43°	40°	37°
6,000	7,000	8,000	9,000	10,000	
34°	31°	28°	25°	22°	

10. Multiply three times the *x* value, subtract 2, and that gives the *y* value. The rule is *y* equals three times *x* − 2 so that the equation is $y = 3x - 2$. Substitute 13 for *x*:

    $$y = 3(13) - 2 = 39 - 2 = 37$$

    The capsule will be at position (13, 37).

Frequency Table Problems, page 119

1. Add the percentiles of the intervals below 70.

   $2 + 8 = 10$ 10% of the students scored below 70.

2. The median score is in the interval 80–89.

3. The percent of scores from 80 to 100 is $38 + 13 = 51$

   51% of the students scored from 80 to 100.

4. The question is asking for the number of scores that are above 50. The percentile rank next to 50 is 39. So 39% of the scores are below 50, 39% failed. $100 - 39 = 61$. 61% passed.

5. The percent of the scores from 20 to 50 is the percentile rank for 50, less the percentile rank for 20.

   $39 - 2 = 37$

   37% of the scores are from 20 to 50.

Geometric Figure Problems, page 120

1. Area of half the circle ($r = 4$)

   $\frac{1}{2} (3.14)(16) = (3.14)(8)$ is

   approximately 25.12 sq ft

   Area of the rectangle
   $12 \times 8 = 96$ sq ft

   Area of the entire figure
   $25.12 + 96 = 121.12$ sq ft

   $121.12 \div 35$ is approximately 3.5 pints
   Round up. You need 4 pints of paint.

2. Find the area of the roofs.
   Roof 1: $115 \times 65 = $ 7,475 sq ft
   Roof 2: $112 \times 65 = $ 7,280 sq ft
   Roof 3: $72 \times 52 \ \ = $ <u>2,744 sq ft</u>
   TOTAL   18,499 sq ft
   $18,499 \div 1,200 = 15.4$
   Round up. You need 16 bushels.

3. Volume of a brick = *lwh*

$V = 2 \times 4 \times 8 = 64 \text{ in}^3$

$8 \times 64 \text{ in}^3 = 512 \text{ in}^3$

4. Volume of a cone = $\frac{1}{3} \pi r^2 h$

$134 = \frac{1}{3} (3.14)(4)^2 h$

$134 = 16.7 h$
$h = 8 \text{ cm}$

5. Volume of a sphere = $\frac{4}{3} \pi r^3$

$V = \frac{4}{3}(3.14)(274.6)$

$V = 1{,}149.76 \text{ in}^3$

6. Volume of a rectangular solid = *lwh*
$1{,}920 = (16)(12) \ w$
$1{,}920 = 192 \ w \quad w = 10$

Shaded area = $12 \times 10 = 120 \ m^2$

Interpreting Remainder Problems, page 121

1. 5 pounds

2. 34 bags

3. 33 bags

TARGETED TEST
EXPLAINED ANSWERS

1. **(D)** $40° + 40° + 100° = 180°$. There is a total of 180° in a triangle.

2. **(B)** 25% of $48 = $12. $48 – $12 = $36.

3. **(D)** Supplementary angles total 180°, which is the number of degrees on this line.

4. **(B)** The probability of rolling a 5 is 1/6, regardless of what happened on previous rolls.

5. **(D)** An angle is not formed because point *B* and point *C* are not connected in this diagram.

6. **(D)** Divide the money by the cost of an item to find the number of items you can afford.

7. **(E)** Estimate. 32 hours is not twice 18 hours, so eliminate choices (B), (C), and (D). 32 hours is about 75% more than 18 hours. 75% more than $144 is about $250. Choice E must be correct.

8. **(E)** $\pi(2^2 \times 4) + \pi(3^2 \times 2) = (4 \times 4 + 9 \times 2)\pi = 34\pi$

9. **(A)** The discount is the regular price less the sale price.

10. **(C)** $80 – $5 = $75. $75 ÷ $0.75 = 100.

11. **(A)** The fraction farthest from $\frac{1}{2}$ is closest to 0 or closest to 1. The answer is $\frac{1}{12}$ from 0. The other answers are greater than $\frac{1}{2}$ but farther than $\frac{1}{12}$ from 1.

12. **(E)** 25 centimeters is about 10 inches, a reasonable length for a notebook.

13. **(B)** The end of the retail bar matches 20% on the scale.

14. **(B)** $25 ÷ 250 = 0.1.   0.1 = 10%.$

15. **(E)** $1,000 + $250 = $1,250, needed to make $1,000. $1,250 ÷ $5 = 250. $250 \times 6 = 1,500$ tickets.

16. **(D)** $5.3 \times 10^4 = 5.3000 = 53,000$

17. **(D)** Supplementary angles total 180°, the number of degrees in a straight line.

18. **(D)** Northeast, 30%; Midwest, 6%. 30% ÷ 6% = 5, or five times as many students from the Northeast.

19. **(E)** $\frac{1}{2} + \frac{1}{3} + \frac{3}{8} = \frac{12}{24} + \frac{8}{24} + \frac{3}{8} = \frac{27}{24} = 1\frac{5}{24}$.

20. **(B)** The outer circle and the inner circle show the whole numbers from 1 to 20. The inner circle shows the multiples of 5 from 1 to 20.

Reading

CHAPTER 5

USING THIS CHAPTER

This chapter prepares you to take the PPST reading comprehension tests. Choose one of these approaches.

- **I want vocabulary and reading help**. Review the entire chapter and take the targeted test at the end.

- **I just want reading help.** Read Strategies for Taking the Reading Test beginning on page 161. Take the targeted test at the end of the chapter.

- **I want to practice reading items.** Take the targeted test at the end of the chapter.

Vocabulary Review

You can't read if you don't know the vocabulary. But you don't have to know every word in the dictionary. Follow this reasonable approach to developing a good vocabulary for these tests.

CONTEXT CLUES

Many times you can figure out a word from its context. Look at these examples. Synonyms, antonyms, examples, or descriptions may help you figure out the word.

1. The woman's mind wandered as her two friends **prated** on. It really did not bother her though. In all the years she had known them, they had always <u>babbled</u> about their lives. It was almost comforting.
2. The wind **abated** in the late afternoon. Things were different yesterday when the wind had <u>picked up</u> toward the end of the day.
3. The argument with her boss had been her **Waterloo**. She wondered if the <u>defeat</u> suffered by Napoleon <u>at this famous place</u> had felt the same.
4. The events swept the politician into a **vortex** of controversy. The politician knew what it meant to be spun around like a toy boat in the <u>swirl of water</u> that swept down the bathtub drain.

Passage 1 gives a synonym for the unknown word. We can tell that *prated* means babbled. *Babbled* is used as a synonym of *prated* in the passage.

Passage 2 gives an antonym for the unknown word. We can tell that *abated* means slowed down or diminished because *picked up* is used as an antonym of *abated*.

Passage 3 gives a description of the unknown word. The description of *Waterloo* tells us that the word means *defeat*.

Passage 4 gives an example of the unknown word. The example of a *swirl of water* going down the bathtub drain gives us a good idea of what a *vortex* is.

ROOTS

A root is the basic element of a word. The root is usually related to the word's origin. Roots can often help you figure out the word's meaning. Here are some roots that may help you.

Root	Meaning	Examples
bio	life	biography, biology
circu	around	circumference, circulate
frac	break	fraction, refract
geo	earth	geology, geography
mal	bad	malicious, malcontent
matr, mater	mother	maternal, matron
neo	new	neonate, neoclassic
patr, pater	father	paternal, patron
spec	look	spectacles, specimen
tele	distant	telephone, television

PREFIXES

Prefixes are syllables that come at the beginning of a word. Prefixes usually have a standard meaning. They can often help you figure out the word's meaning. Here is a list of prefixes that may help you figure out a word.

Prefix	Meaning	Examples
a-	not	amoral, apolitical
il-, im-, ir-	not	illegitimate, immoral, incorrect
un-	not	unbearable, unknown
non-	not	nonbeliever, nonsense
ant-, anti-	against	antiwar, antidote
de-	opposite	defoliate, declaw
mis-	wrong	misstep, misdeed
ante-	before	antedate, antecedent
fore-	before	foretell, forecast
post-	after	postfight, postoperative
re-	again	refurbish, redo
super-	above	superior, superstar
sub-	below	subsonic, subpar

THE VOCABULARY LIST

Here is a list of a few hundred vocabulary words. The list includes everyday words and a few specialized education terms. Read through the list and visualize the words and their definitions. After a while you will become very familiar with them.

Of course, this is not anywhere near all the words you need to know for the exams. But they will give you a start. These words also will give you some idea of the kinds of words you may encounter on the examinations.

Another great way to develop a vocabulary is to read a paper every day and a news magazine every week, in addition to the other reading you are doing. There are also several inexpensive books, including *1100 Words You Need to Know* and *Pocket Guide to Vocabulary* from Barron's, which may help you develop your vocabulary further.

abhor To regard with horror
I abhor violence.

abstain To refrain by choice
Ray decided to abstain from fattening foods.

abstract Not related to any object, theoretical
Mathematics can be very abstract.

acquisition An addition to an established group or collection
The museum's most recent acquisition was an early Roman vase.

admonish To correct firmly but kindly
The teacher admonished the student not to chew gum in class.

adroit Skillful or nimble in difficult circumstances
The nine year old was already an adroit gymnast.

adversary A foe or enemy
The wildebeest was ever-alert for its ancient adversary, the lion.

advocate To speak for an idea; a person who speaks for an idea
Lou was an advocate of gun control.

aesthetic Pertaining to beauty
Ron found the painting a moving aesthetic experience.

affective To do with the emotional or feeling aspect of learning
Len read the Taxonomy of Educational Objectives: Affective Domain.

alias An assumed name
The check forger had used an alias.

alleviate To reduce or make more bearable
The hot shower helped alleviate the pain in her back.

allude To make an indirect reference to, hint at
Elaine only alluded to her previous trips through the state.

ambiguous Open to many interpretations
That is an ambiguous statement.

apathy Absence of passion or emotion
The teacher tried to overcome their apathy toward the subject.

apprehensive Fear or unease about possible outcomes
Bob was apprehensive about visiting the dentist.

aptitude The ability to gain from a particular type of instruction
The professor pointed out that aptitude, alone, was not enough for success in school.

articulate To speak clearly and distinctly, present a point of view
Chris was chosen to articulate the group's point of view.

assess To measure or determine an outcome or value
There are many informal ways to assess learning.

attest To affirm or certify
I can attest to Cathy's ability as a softball pitcher.

augment To increase or add to
The new coins augmented the already large collection.

belated Past time or tardy
George sent a belated birthday card.

benevolent Expresses goodwill or kindly feelings
The club was devoted to performing benevolent acts.

biased A prejudiced view or action
The judge ruled that the decision was biased.

bolster To shore up, support
The explorer sang to bolster her courage.

candid Direct and outspoken
Lee was well known for her candid comments.

caricature Exaggerated, ludicrous picture, in words or a cartoon
The satirist presented world leaders as caricatures.

carnivorous Flesh eating or predatory
The lion is a carnivorous animal.

censor A person who judges the morality of others; act on that judgment
Please don't censor my views!

censure Expression of disapproval, reprimand
The senate acted to censure the congressman.

cessation The act of ceasing or halting
The eleventh hour marked the cessation of hostilities.

chronic Continuing and constant
Asthma can be a chronic condition.

clandestine Concealed or secret
The spy engaged in clandestine activities.

cogent Intellectually convincing
He presented a cogent argument.

cognitive Relates to the intellectual area of learning
Lou read the Taxonomy of Educational Objectives: Cognitive Domain.

competency Demonstrated ability
Bert demonstrated the specified mathematics competency.

complacent Unaware self-satisfaction
The tennis player realized she had become complacent.

concept A generalization
The professor lectured on concept development.

congenital Existing at birth but nonhereditary
The baby had a small congenital defect.

contemporaries Belonging in the same time period, about the same age
Piaget and Bruner were contemporaries.

contempt Feeling or showing disdain or scorn
She felt nothing but contempt for their actions.

contentious Argumentative
Tim was in a contentious mood.

corroborate To make certain with other information, to confirm
The reporter would always corroborate a story before publication.

credence Claim to acceptance or trustworthiness
They did not want to lend credence to his views.

cursory Surface, not in depth
Ron gave his car a cursory inspection.

daunt To intimidate with fear
Harry did not let the difficulty of the task daunt him.

debacle Disastrous collapse or rout
The whole trip had been a debacle.

debilitate To make feeble
He was concerned that the flu would debilitate him.

decadent Condition of decline/decay
Joan said in frustration, "We live in a decadent society."

deductive Learning that proceeds from general to specific
He proved his premise using deductive logic.

demographic Population data
The census gathers demographic information.

denounce To condemn a person or idea
The diplomat rose in the United Nations to denounce the plan.

deter To prevent or stop an action, usually by some threat
The president felt that the peace conference would help deter aggression.

diligent A persistent effort; a person who makes such an effort
The investigator was diligent in her pursuit of the truth.

discern To perceive or recognize, often by insight
The principal attempted to discern which student was telling the truth.

discord Disagreement or disharmony
Gail's early promotion led to discord in the office.

discriminate To distinguish among people or groups based on their characteristics
It is not appropriate to discriminate based on race or ethnicity.

disdain To show or act with contempt
The professional showed disdain for her amateurish efforts.

disseminate To send around, scatter
The health organization will disseminate any new information on the flu.

divergent Thinking that extends in many directions, is not focused
Les was an intelligent but divergent thinker.

diverse Not uniform, varied
Alan came from a diverse neighborhood.

duress Coercion
He claimed that he confessed under duress.

eccentric Behaves unusually, different from the norm
His long hair and midnight walks made Albert appear eccentric.

eclectic Drawing from several ideas or practices
Joe preferred an eclectic approach to the practice of psychology.

eloquent Vivid, articulate expression
The congregation was held spellbound by the eloquent sermon.

emanate To flow out, come forth
How could such wisdom emanate from one so young?

embellish To make things seem more than they are
Art loved to embellish the facts.

empirical From observation or experiment
The scientist's conclusions were based on empirical evidence.

employment A job or professional position (paid)
You seek employment so you can make the big bucks.

enduring Lasting over the long term
Their friendship grew into an enduring relationship.

enhance To improve or build up
The mechanic used a fuel additive to enhance the car's performance.

enigma A mystery or puzzle
The communist bloc was an "enigma wrapped inside a mystery." (Churchill)

equity Equal attention or treatment
The workers were seeking pay equity with others in their industry.

equivocal Uncertain, capable of multiple interpretations
In an attempt to avoid conflict the negotiator took an equivocal stand.

expedite To speed up, facilitate
Hal's job at the shipping company was to expedite deliveries.

exploit Take maximum advantage of, perhaps unethically
Her adversary tried to exploit her grief to gain an advantage.

extrinsic Coming from outside
The teacher turned to extrinsic motivation.

farce A mockery
The attorney objected, saying that the testimony made the trial a farce.

feign To pretend, make a false appearance of
Some people feign illness to get out of work.

fervent Marked by intense feeling
The spokesman presented a fervent defense of the company's actions.

fiasco Total failure
They had not prepared for the presentation, and it turned into a fiasco.

formidable Difficult to surmount
State certification requirements can present a formidable obstacle.

fracas A noisy quarrel or a scrap
The debate turned into a full-fledged fracas.

gamut Complete range or extent
Waiting to take the test, her mind ran the gamut of emotions.

glib Quickness suggesting insincerity
The glib response made Rita wonder about the speaker's sincerity.

grave Very serious or weighty
The supervisor had grave concerns about the worker's ability.

guile Cunning, craftiness, duplicity
When the truth failed, he tried to win his point with guile.

handicapped Having one or more disabilities
The child study team classified Loren as handicapped.

harass Bother persistently
Some fans came to harass the players on the opposing team.

heterogeneous A group with normal variation in ability or performance
Students from many backgrounds formed a heterogeneous population.

homogeneous A group with little variation in ability or performance
The school used test scores to place students in homogeneous groups.

hypocrite One who feigns a virtuous character or belief
Speaking against drinking and then driving drunk made him a hypocrite!

immune Protected or exempt from disease or harm
The vaccination made Ray immune to measles.

impartial Fair and objective
The contestants agreed on an objective, impartial referee.

impasse Situation with no workable solution
The talks had not stopped, but they had reached an impasse.

impede To retard or obstruct
Mason did not let adversity impede his progress.

implicit Understood but not directly stated
They never spoke about the matter, but they had an implicit understanding.

indifferent Uncaring or apathetic
The teacher was indifferent to the student's pleas for an extension.

indigenous Native to an area
The botanist recognized it as an indigenous plant.

inductive Learning that proceeds from specific to general
Science uses an inductive process, from examples to a generalization.

inevitable Certain and unavoidable
After the rains, the collapse of the dam was inevitable.

infer To reach a conclusion not explicitly stated
The viewer could infer that this product is superior to all others.

inhibit To hold back or restrain
The hormone was used to inhibit growth.

innovate To introduce something new or change established procedure
Mere change was not enough, they had to innovate the procedure.

inquiry Question-based Socratic learning
Much of science teaching uses inquiry-based learning.

intrinsic Inherent, the essential nature
The teacher drew on the meaning of the topic for an intrinsic motivation.

inundate To overwhelm, flood
It was December, and mail began to inundate the Post Office.

jocular Characterized by joking or good nature
The smiling man seemed to be a jocular fellow.

judicial Relating to the administration of justice
His goal was to have no dealings with the judicial system.

knack A talent for doing something
Ron had a real knack for mechanical work.

languid   Weak, lacking energy
The sunbather enjoyed a languid afternoon at the shore.

liaison   An illicit relationship or a means of communication
The governor appointed his chief aid liaison to the senate.

lucid   Clear and easily understood
The teacher answered the question in a direct and lucid way.

magnanimous   Generous in forgiving
Loretta is magnanimous to a fault.

malignant   Very injurious, evil
Crime is a malignant sore on our society.

malleable   Open to being shaped or influenced
He had a malleable position on gun control.

meticulous   Very careful and precise
Gina took meticulous care of the fine china.

miser   A money hoarder
The old miser had more money than he could ever use.

monotonous   Repetitive and boring
Circling the airport, waiting to land, became dull and monotonous.

mores   Understood rules of society
Linda made following social mores her goal in life.

motivation   Something that creates interest or action
Most good lessons begin with a good motivation.

myriad   Large indefinite number
Look skyward and be amazed by the myriad of stars.

naive   Lacking sophistication
Laura is unaware, and a little naive, about the impact she has on others.

nemesis   A formidable rival
Lex Luthor is Superman's nemesis.

novice   A beginner
Her unsteady legs revealed that Sue was a novice skater.

nullified   Removed the importance of
The penalty nullified the 20-yard gain made by the running back.

objective   A goal
The teacher wrote an objective for each lesson.

oblivious   Unaware and unmindful
Les was half asleep and oblivious to the racket around him.

obscure   Vague, unclear, uncertain
The lawyer quoted an obscure reference.

ominous   Threatening or menacing
There were ominous black storm clouds on the horizon.

palatable Agreeable, acceptable
Sandy's friends tried to make her punishment more palatable.

panorama A comprehensive view or picture
The visitors' center offered a panorama of the canyon below.

pedagogy The science of teaching
Parts of certification tests focus on pedagogy.

perpetuate To continue or cause to be remembered
A plaque was put up to perpetuate the memory of the retiring teacher.

pompous Exaggerated self-importance
Rona acted pompous, but Lynne suspected she was very empty inside.

precarious Uncertain, beyond one's control
A diver sat on a precarious perch on a cliff above the water.

precedent An act or instance that sets the standard
The judge's ruling set a precedent for later cases.

preclude To act to make impossible or impracticable
Beau did not want to preclude any options.

precocious Very early development
Chad was very precocious and ran at six months.

prognosis A forecast or prediction
The stockbroker gave a guarded prognosis for continued growth.

prolific Abundant producer
Isaac Asimov was a prolific science fiction writer.

provoke To stir up or anger
Children banging on the cage would provoke the circus lion to growl.

psychomotor Relates to the motor skill area of learning
I read the Taxonomy of Behavioral
Objectives: Psychomotor Domain.

quagmire Predicament or difficult situation
The regulations were a quagmire of conflicting rules and vague terms.

qualm Feeling of doubt or misgiving
The teacher had not a single qualm about giving the student a low grade.

quandary A dilemma
The absence of the teacher aide left the teacher in a quandary.

quench To put out, satisfy
The glass of water was not enough to quench his thirst.

rancor Bitter continuing resentment
A deep rancor had existed between the two friends since the accident.

rationale The basis or reason for something
The speeder tried to present a rationale to the officer who stopped her.

reciprocal Mutual interchange
Each person got something out of their reciprocal arrangement.

refute To prove false
The lawyer used new evidence to refute claims made by the prosecution.

remedial Designed to compensate for learning deficits
Jim spent one period a day in remedial instruction.

reprove Criticize gently
The teacher would reprove students for chewing gum in class.

repudiate To reject or disown
The senator repudiated membership in an all-male club.

resolve To reach a definite conclusion
A mediator was called in to resolve the situation.

retrospect Contemplation of the past
Ryan noted, in retrospect, that leaving home was his best decision.

revere To hold in the highest regard
Citizens of the town revere their longtime mayor.

sanction To issue authoritative approval or a penalty
The boxing commissioner had to sanction the match.

scrutinize To inspect with great care
You should scrutinize any document before signing it.

siblings Brothers or sisters
The holidays give me the chance to spend time with my siblings.

skeptical Doubting, questioning the validity
The principal was skeptical about the students' reason for being late.

solace Comfort in misfortune
Her friends provided solace in her time of grief.

solitude Being alone
Pat enjoyed her Sunday afternoon moments of solitude.

stagnant Inert, contaminated
In dry weather the lake shrank to a stagnant pool.

stereotype An oversimplified generalized view or belief
We are all guilty of fitting people into stereotypes.

subsidy Financial assistance
Chris received a subsidy from her company so she could attend school.

subterfuge A deceptive strategy
The spy used a subterfuge to gain access to the secret materials.

subtle Faint, not easy to find or understand
Subtle changes in the teller's actions alerted the police to the robbery.

superficial Surface, not profound
The inspector gave the car a quick, superficial inspection.

tacit Not spoken, inferred
They had a tacit agreement.

taxonomy Classification of levels of thinking or organisms
I read each Taxonomy of Educational Objectives.

tenacious Persistent and determined
The police officer was tenacious in pursuit of a criminal.

tentative Unsure, uncertain
The athletic director set up a tentative basketball schedule.

terminate To end, conclude
He wanted to terminate the relationship.

transition Passage from one activity to another
The transition from college student to teacher was not easy.

trepidation Apprehension, state of dread
Erin felt some trepidation about beginning her new job.

trivial Unimportant, ordinary
The seemingly trivial occurrence had taken on added importance.

ubiquitous Everywhere, omnipresent
A walk through the forest invited attacks from the ubiquitous mosquitoes.

ultimatum A final demand
After a trying day, the teacher issued an ultimatum to the class.

usurp To wrongfully and forcefully seize and hold, particularly power
The association vice president tried to usurp the president's power.

vacillate To swing indecisively
He had a tendency to vacillate in his stance on discipline.

valid Logically correct
The math teacher was explaining a valid mathematical proof.

vehement Forceful, passionate
The child had a vehement reaction to the teacher's criticism.

vestige A sign of something no longer there or existing
Old John was the last vestige of the first teachers to work at the school.

vicarious Experience through the activities or feelings of others
He had to experience sports in a vicarious way through his students.

virulent Very poisonous or noxious
The coral snake has a particularly virulent venom.

vital Important and essential
The school secretary was a vital part of the school.

waffle To write or speak in a misleading way
The spokesperson waffled as she tried to explain away the mistake.

wary Watchful, on guard
The soldiers were very wary of any movements across the DMZ.

Xanadu An idyllic, perfect place
All wished for some time in Xanadu.

yearned Longed or hoped for
Liz yearned for a small class.

zeal Diligent devotion to a cause
Ron approached his job with considerable zeal.

Strategies for Taking the Reading Test

This chapter gives an integrated approach to answering literal and critical reading items on the PPST.

The reading test consists of passages followed by multiple-choice questions. You do not have to know what an entire reading passage is about. You just have to know enough to get the answer correct. Less than half, often less than 25 percent, of the information in any passage is needed to answer all the questions.

You do not have to read the passage in detail. In fact, careful, slow reading will almost certainly get you in trouble. Strange as it seems, follow this advice—avoid careful, detailed reading at all costs.

Buried among all the false gold in the passage are a few valuable nuggets. Follow these steps to hit pay dirt and avoid the fool's gold.

READING ABOUT READING

Reading seems to be a natural process. Reading about reading and about steps to taking reading tests can seem contrived and confusing. However, we know that these steps and techniques work. Once you apply the steps to the practice exercises, your reading ability and scores will improve.

FIVE STEPS TO TAKING A READING TEST

During a reading test follow these steps.

1. Skim to find the topic of each paragraph.
2. Read the questions and answers.
3. Eliminate incorrect answers.
4. Scan the details to find the answer.
5. Choose the answer that is absolutely correct.

1. Skim to Find the Topic of Each Paragraph

Your first job is to find the topic of each paragraph. The topic is what a paragraph or passage is about.

The topic of a paragraph is usually found in the first and last sentences. Read the first and last sentences just enough to find the topic. You can write the topic in the margin next to the passage on the PPST. Remember, the PPST test booklet is yours. You can mark it up as much as you like.

Reading Sentences

Every sentence has a subject that tells what the sentence is about. The sentence also has a verb that tells what the subject is doing or links the subject to the complement. The sentence may also contain a complement that receives the action or describes what is being said about the subject. The words underlined in the following examples are the ones you would focus on as you preview.

1. The famous educator <u>John Dewey founded</u> an educational movement called <u>progressive education</u>.
2. Sad to say, we have learned <u>American school children</u> of all ages <u>are poorly nourished</u>.

You may occasionally encounter a paragraph or passage in which the topic can't be summarized from the first and last sentences. This type of paragraph usually contains factual information. If this happens, you will have to read the entire paragraph.

Fact, Opinion, or Fiction

If it is a factual passage, the author will present the fact and support it with details and examples. If the passage presents an opinion, the author will give the opinion and support it with arguments, examples, and other details. Many passages combine fact and opinion. If it is a fiction passage, the author will tell a story with details, descriptions, and examples about people, places, or things.

Once you find the topic, you will probably need more information to answer the questions. But don't worry about this other information and details now. You can go back and find it after you have read the questions.

2. Read the Questions and the Answers

Now read the questions—one at a time. Read the answers for the question you are working on. Be sure that you understand what each question and its answers mean.

Before you answer a question, be sure you know whether it is asking for a fact or an inference. If the question asks for a fact, the correct answer will identify a main idea or supporting detail. We'll discuss more about main ideas and details later. The correct answer may also identify a cause and effect relationship among ideas or be a paraphrase or summary of parts of the passage. Look for these.

If the question asks for an inference, the correct answer will identify the author's purpose, assumptions, or attitude and the difference between fact and the author's opinion. Look for these elements.

3. Eliminate Incorrect Answers

Read the answers and eliminate the ones that you absolutely know are incorrect. Read the answers literally. Look for words such as *always, never, must, all*. If you can find a single exception to this type of sweeping statement, then the answer can't be correct. Eliminate it.

4. Scan the Details to Find the Answer

Once you have eliminated answers, compare the other answers to the passage. When you find the answer that is confirmed by the passage—stop. That is your answer choice. Follow these other suggestions for finding the correct answer.

You will often need to read details to find the main idea of a paragraph. The main idea of a paragraph is what the writer has to say about the topic. Most questions are about the main idea of a paragraph. Scan the details about the main idea until you find the answer. Scanning means skipping over information that does not answer the question.

Look at this paragraph.

> There are many types of boats. Some are very fast while others could sleep a whole platoon of soldiers. I prefer the old putt-putt fishing boat with a ten horsepower motor. That was a boat with a purpose. You didn't scare many people, but the fish were sure worried.

The topic of this paragraph is boats. The main idea is that the writer prefers small fishing boats to other boats.

Unstated Topic and Main Idea

Sometimes the topic and main idea are not stated. Consider this passage.

> The Chinese were the first to use sails thousands of years ago, hundreds of years before sails were used in Europe. The Chinese also used the wheel and the kite long before they were used on the European continent. Experts believe that many other Chinese inventions were used from three hundred to one thousand three hundred years before they were used in Europe.

The topic of this paragraph is inventions. The main idea of the paragraph is that the Chinese invented and used many things hundreds and thousands of years before they appeared in Europe.

Some Answers Are Not Related to the Main Idea

Some answers are not related to the main idea of a paragraph. These questions may be the most difficult to answer. You just have to keep scanning the details until you find the correct answer.

Who Wrote This Answer?

People who write tests go to great lengths to choose a correct answer that cannot be questioned. That is what they get paid for. They are not paid to write answers that have a higher meaning or include great truths.

Test writers want to be asked to write questions and answers again. They want to avoid valid complaints from test takers like you who raise legitimate concerns about their answers.

They usually accomplish this difficult task in one of two ways. They may write answers that are very specific and based directly on the reading. They may also write correct answers that seem very vague.

A Vague Answer Can Be Correct

How can a person write a vague answer that is correct? Think of it this way. If I wrote that a person is 6 feet 5 inches tall, you could get out a tape measure to check my facts. Since I was very specific, you are more likely to be able to prove me wrong.

On the other hand, if I write that the same person is over 6 feet tall you would be hard pressed to find fault with my statement. So my vague statement was hard to argue with. If the person in question is near 6 feet 5 inches tall, then my vague answer is most likely to be the correct one.

Don't choose an answer just because it seems more detailed or specific. A vague answer may just as likely be correct.

5. Choose the Answer That Is Absolutely Correct

Be sure that your choice answers the question. Be sure that your choice is based on the information contained in the paragraph. Don't choose an answer to another question. Don't choose an answer just because it sounds right. Don't choose an answer just because you agree with it.

There is no room on tests like these for answers that are partially wrong. It is not enough for an answer to be 99.9 percent correct. It must be absolutely, incontrovertibly, unquestionably, indisputably, and unarguably correct.

AUTHOR'S PURPOSE

The author's primary purpose explains why the author wrote the passage. The purpose is closely related to the main idea. You might think, "Fine, I know the main idea. But why did the author take the time to write about that main idea? What is the author trying to make me know or feel?"

The author's purpose will be in one of five categories. The categories and their descriptions are given below.

Describe	Present an image of physical reality or a mental image.
Entertain	Amuse, Perform
Inform	Clarify, Explain, State
Narrate	Relate, Tell a story
Persuade	Argue, Convince, Prove

There is no hard and fast rule for identifying the author's purpose. Rely on your informed impression of the passage.

Bias

A statement or passage reveals bias if the author has prejudged or has a predisposition to a doctrine, idea, or practice. Bias means the author is trying to convince or influence the reader through some emotional appeal or slanted writing.

Bias can be positive or negative.

Positive Bias:	She is so lovely, she deserves the very best.
Negative Bias:	She is so horrible, I hope she gets what's coming to her.

Forms of Bias

Biased writing can often be identified by the presence of one or more of the following forms of bias.

Emotional Language	Language that appeals to the reader's emotions, and not to common sense or logic.
	Positive: If I am elected, I will help your family get jobs.
	Negative: If my opponent is elected, your family will lose their jobs.
Inaccurate Information	Language that presents false, inaccurate, or unproved information as though it were factual.
	Positive: My polls indicate that I am very popular.
	Negative: My polls indicate that a lot of people disagree with my opponent.
Name Calling	Language that uses negative, disapproving terms without any factual basis.
	Negative: I'll tell you, my opponent is a real jerk.
Slanted Language	Language that slants the facts or evidence toward the writer's point of view.
	Positive: I am a positive person, looking for the good side of people.
	Negative: My opponent finds fault with everyone and everything.
Stereotyping	Language that indicates that a person is like all the members of a particular group.
	Positive: I belong to the Krepenkle party, the party known for its honesty.
	Negative: My opponent belongs to the Lerplenkle party, the party of increased taxes.

Author's Tone

The author's tone is the author's attitude as reflected in the passage. How do you think the author would sound while speaking? What impression would you form about the speaker's attitude or feeling? The answer to the latter question will usually lead you to the author's tone. A partial list of tone words is given below.

absurd	excited	outraged
amused	formal	outspoken
angry	gentle	pathetic
apathetic	hard	pessimistic
arrogant	impassioned	playful
bitter	indignant	prayerful
cheerful	intense	reverent
comic	intimate	righteous
compassionate	joyous	satirical
complex	loving	sentimental
concerned	malicious	serious
cruel	mocking	solemn
depressed	nostalgic	tragic
distressed	objective	uneasy
evasive	optimistic	vindictive

APPLYING THE STEPS

Let's apply the five steps to this passage and questions.

Many vocational high schools in the United States give off-site work experience to their students. Students usually work in local businesses part of the school day and attend high school the other part. These programs have made American vocational schools world leaders in making job experience available to teenage students.

According to this paragraph, American vocational high schools are world leaders in making job experience available to teenage students because they

(A) have students attend school only part of the day.
(B) were quick to move their students to schools off-site.
(C) require students to work before they can attend the school.
(D) involve their students in cooperative education programs.
(E) involve their students in after-school part time work.

Step 1: Skim to find the topic of each paragraph. Both the first and last sentences tell us that the topic is vocational schools and work experience.

Step 2: Read the questions and answers. Why are American vocational education high schools the world leaders in offering job experience?

Step 3: Eliminate incorrect answers. Answer (C) is obviously wrong. It has to do with work before high school. Answer (B) is also incorrect. This has to do with attending school off-site. This leaves answers (A), (D), and (E).

Step 4: Scan the details to find the answer. Scan the details and find that parts of answer (A) are found in the passage. In answer (D) you have to know that cooperative education is another name for off-site work during school. There is no reference to the after-school work found in answer (E).

Step 5: Choose the answer that is absolutely correct. It is down to answer (A) or answer (D). But answer (A) contains only part of the reason that vocational education high schools have gained such acclaim. Answer (D) is the absolutely correct answer.

Here's how to apply the steps to the following passage.

Problem Solving

Problem solving has become the main focus of mathematics learning. Students learn problem-solving strategies and then apply them to problems. Many tests now focus on problem solving and limit the number of computational problems. The problem-solving movement is traced to George Polya who wrote several problem-solving books for high school teachers.

Problem Solving Strategies

Problem-solving strategies include guess and check, draw a diagram, and make a list. Many of the strategies are taught as skills, which inhibits flexible and creative thinking. Problems in textbooks can also limit the power of the strategies. However, the problem-solving movement will be with us for some time, and a number of the strategies are useful.

Step 1: Skim to find the topic of each paragraph. The topic of the first paragraph is problem solving. You find the topic in both the first and last sentences. Write the topic next to the paragraph. The topic for the second paragraph is problem-solving strategies. Write the topic next to the paragraph.

Now we are ready to look at the questions. If the question is about problem solving "in general" we start looking in the first paragraph for the answer. If the question is about strategies, we start looking in the second paragraph for the answer.

Step 2: Read the questions and answers.

According to this passage, a difficulty with teaching problem-solving strategies is that

(A) the strategies are too difficult for children.
(B) the strategies are taught as skills.
(C) the strategies are in textbooks.
(D) the strategies are part of a movement.
(E) problem solving is for high school teachers.

Step 3: Eliminate incorrect answers. Answer (A) can't be right because difficulty is not mentioned in the passage. Choice (E) can't be correct because it does not mention strategies at all. That leaves (B), (C), and (D) for us to consider.

Step 4: Scan the details to find the answer. The question asks about strategies so we look immediately to the second paragraph for the answer. The correct answer is (B). Choice (C) is not correct because the passage does not mention strategies in textbooks. There is no indication that (D) is correct.

Step 5: Choose the answer that is absolutely correct. The correct choice is (B).

Practice Passage

Apply the five steps to this practice passage. Mark the letter of the correct answer. Follow the directions given below. The answers to these questions are found on pages 170–174. Do not look at the answers until you complete your work.

Read the following passage. After reading the passage, choose the best answer to each question from among the five choices. Answer all the questions following the passage on the basis of what is stated or implied in the passage.

Today's students have hand-held calculators that can graph one or even many equations. Students can even type in several equations and the calculator will "solve" them. This is the best way just to see a plotted graph quickly.

This is the worst way to learn about graphing and equations. The calculator can't tell the students anything about the process of graphing and does not teach them how to plot a graph.

Left to this electronic graphing process, students will not have the hands-on experience needed to see the patterns and symmetry that characterize graphing and equations. They may become too dependent on the calculator and be unable to reason effectively about equations and the process of graphing.

It may be true that graphing and solving equations is taught mechanically in some classrooms. There is also something to be said for these electronic devices, which give students the opportunity to try out several graphs and solutions quickly before deciding on a final solution.

For all their electronic accuracy and patience, these graphing calculators cannot replace the process of graphing and solving equations on your own. For mastery of equations and graphing comes not just from seeing the graph automatically displayed on a screen, but also comes from a hands-on involvement with graphing.

1. The main idea of the passage is that

   (A) a child can be good at graphing equations only through hands-on experience.
   (B) teaching approaches for graphing equations should be improved.
   (C) accuracy and patience are the keys to effective graphing instruction.
   (D) the new graphing calculators have limited ability to teach students about graphing.
   (E) graphing calculators provide one of the best possible ways to practice graphing equations.

2. According to this passage, what negative impact will graphing calculators have on students who use them?

   (A) They will not have experience with four-function calculators.
   (B) They will become too dependent on the calculator.
   (C) They can quickly try out several graphs before coming up with a final answer.
   (D) They will get too much hands-on experience with calculators.
   (E) The teachers will not know how to use the electronic calculator because they use mechanical aids.

3. According to the passage, which of the following is a major drawback of the graphing calculator?

   (A) It graphs many equations with their solutions.
   (B) It does not give students hands-on experience with graphing.
   (C) It does not give students hands-on experience with calculators.
   (D) This electronic method interferes with the mechanical method.
   (E) It does not replace the patient teacher.

4. The passage includes information that would answer which of the following questions?

   (A) What are the shortcomings of graphing and solving equations as it sometimes takes place?
   (B) How many equations can you type into a graphing calculator?
   (C) What hands-on experience should students have as they learn about graphing equations?
   (D) What is the degree of accuracy and speed that can be attained by a graphing calculator?
   (E) What level of ability is needed to show mastery of equations and graphing?

5. The description of a graphing calculator found in this passage tells about which of the following?

   III. The equations that can be graphed
   III. The approximate size of the calculator
   III. The advantages of the graphing calculator

   (A) I only
   (B) II only
   (C) I and II only
   (D) II and III only
   (E) I, II, and III

Practice Passage Explained Answers

Don't read this section until you have completed the practice passage. Here's how to apply the steps.

Step 1: Skim to find the topic of each paragraph. You should have written a topic next to each paragraph. Suggested topics are shown next to the following selection. Your topics don't have to be identical, but they should accurately reflect the paragraph's content.

Graphing Calculators

Today's students have hand-held calculators that can graph one or even many equations. Students can even type in several equations and the calculator will "solve" them. This is the best way to just see a plotted graph quickly.

Problem with Graphing Calculators

This is the worst way to learn about graphing and equations. The calculator can't tell the students anything about the process of graphing and does not teach them how to plot a graph.

Why it's a Problem

Left to this electronic graphing process, students will not have the hands-on experience needed to see the patterns and symmetry that characterize graphing and equations. They may become too dependent on the calculator and be unable to reason effectively about equations and the process of graphing.

It may be true that graphing and solving equations is taught mechanically in some classrooms. There is also something to be said for these electronic devices, which give students the opportunity to try out several graphs and solutions quickly before deciding on a final solution.

Good Points

For all their electronic accuracy and patience, these graphing calculators cannot replace the process of graphing and solving equations on your own. Mastery of equations and graphing comes not just from seeing the graph automatically displayed on a screen, but also from a hands-on involvement with graphing.

Apply Steps 2 through 5 to each of the questions.

1. The main idea of the passage is that

    (A) a student can be good at graphing equations only through hands-on experience.
    (B) teaching approaches for graphing equations should be improved.
    (C) accuracy and patience are the keys to effective graphing instruction.
    (D) the new graphing calculators have limited ability to teach students about graphing.
    (E) graphing calculators provide one of the best possible ways to practice graphing equations.

    Step 2: Read the question and answers. You have to identify the main idea of the passage. This is a very common question on reading tests. Remember that the main idea is what the writer is trying to say or communicate in the passage.

    Step 3: Eliminate incorrect answers. Answers (B) and (C) are not correct. Answer (C) is not at all correct based on the passage. Even though (B) may be true, it does not reflect what the writer is trying to say in this passage. Answer (E) is also not the correct answer. You might be able to imply this answer from the paragraph, but it is not the main idea.

    Step 4: Scan the details to find the answer. As we review the details we see that both answer (A) and answer (D) are stated or implied in the passage. A scan of the details, alone, does not reveal which is the main idea. We must determine that on our own.

    Step 5: Choose the answer that is absolutely correct. Which answer is absolutely correct? The whole passage is about graphing calculators, and they must be an important part of the main idea. The correct answer is (D). The author certainly believes that (A) is true, but uses this point to support the main idea.

2. According to this passage, what negative impact will graphing calculators have on students who use them?

    (A) They will not have experience with four-function calculators.
    (B) They will become too dependent on the calculator.
    (C) They can quickly try out several graphs before coming up with a final answer.
    (D) They will get too much hands-on experience with calculators.
    (E) The teachers will not know how to use the electronic calculator because they use mechanical aids.

Step 2: Read the question and answers. This is a straightforward comprehension question. What negative impact will calculators have on students who use them? The second and third paragraphs have topics related to problems with calculators. We'll probably find the answer there.

Step 3: Eliminate incorrect answers. Answer (E) is obviously incorrect. The question asks about students. This answer is about teachers. Answer (C) is not a negative impact of graphing calculators. Scan the details to find the correct answer from (A), (B), and (D).

Step 4: Scan the details to find the answer. The only detail that matches the question is in paragraph 3. The author says that students may become too dependent on the calculators. That's our answer.

Step 5: Choose the answer that is absolutely correct. Answer (B) is the only correct choice.

3. According to the passage, which of the following is a major drawback of the graphing calculator?

(A) It graphs many equations with their solutions.
(B) It does not give students hands-on experience with graphing.
(C) It does not give students hands-on experience with calculators.
(D) This electronic method interferes with the mechanical method.
(E) It does not replace the patient teacher.

Step 2: Read the question and answers. This is another straightforward comprehension question. This question is somewhat different from Question 2. Notice that the question asks for a drawback of the calculator. It does not ask for something that is wrong with the calculator itself. The topics indicate that we will probably find the answer in paragraph 1 or paragraph 2.

Step 3: Eliminate incorrect answers. Answer (C) is obviously wrong. Graphing calculators do give students hands-on experience with calculators. Be careful! It is easy to mix up (C) with (B). Answer (A) is a strength of the calculator and is also incorrect. Let's move on to the details.

Step 4: Scan the details to find the answer. Choices (B), (D), and (E) remain. The details in paragraph 2 reveal that the correct answer is (B).

Step 5: Choose the answer that is absolutely correct. Answer (B) is the only absolutely correct answer. Notice that answers (B) and (C) are similar. The absolutely correct answer for this question was a possible correct answer for the previous question. Just because an answer seems correct doesn't mean that it is the absolutely correct answer.

4. The passage includes information that would answer which of the following questions?

   (A) What are the shortcomings of teaching about graphing equations as it sometimes takes place?
   (B) How many equations can you type into a graphing calculator?
   (C) What hands-on experience should students have as they learn about graphing equations?
   (D) What is the degree of accuracy and speed that can be attained by a graphing calculator?
   (E) What level of ability is needed to show mastery of equations and graphing?

Step 2: Read the question and answers. This is yet another type of reading comprehension question. You are asked to identify the questions that could be answered from the passage.

Step 3: Eliminate incorrect answers. Choices (B), (D), and (E) are not correct. None of this information is included in the passage. This is not to say that these questions, particularly (E), are not important. Rather it means that the answers to these questions are not found in this passage.

Step 4: Scan the details to find the answer. Both (A) and (C) are discussed in the passage. However, a scan of the details reveals that the answer to (C) is not found in the passage. The passage mentions hands-on experience, but it does not mention what types of hands-on experience students should have. There is an answer for (A). Graphing is taught mechanically in some classrooms.

Step 5: Choose the answer that is absolutely correct. Answer (A) is the absolutely correct answer. This is the only question that can be answered from the passage. The answer is not related to the writer's main idea and this may make it more difficult to answer.

5. The description of a graphing calculator found in this passage tells about which of the following?

   I. The equations that can be graphed
   II. The approximate size of the calculator
   III. The advantages of the graphing calculator

   (A) I only
   (B) II only
   (C) I and II only
   (D) II and III only
   (E) I, II, and III

Step 2: Read the question and answers. This is another classic type of reading comprehension question. You are given several choices. You must decide which combination of these choices is the absolutely correct answer.

Step 3: Eliminate incorrect answers. If you can determine that Statement I, for example, is not addressed in the passage, you can eliminate ALL answer choices that include Statement I.

Step 4: Scan the details to find which of the original three statements is (are) true.

  I. No, there is no description of which equations can be graphed.
 II. Yes, paragraph 1 mentions that the calculators are hand-held.
III. Yes, paragraph 4 mentions the advantages.

Both II and III are correct.

Step 5: Choose the answer that is absolutely correct. Choice (D) is absolutely correct. It lists both II and III.

Targeted Reading Test

This targeted test is designed to help you practice the strategies presented in this chapter. For that reason, questions may have a different emphasis than the actual test, and the actual test will certainly be more complete.

Mark your choice, then check your answers. Use the strategies on pages 161–168.

While becoming a teacher, I spent most of my time with books. I read books about the subjects I would teach in school and books that explained how to teach the subjects. As a new teacher, I relied on books to help my students learn. But I learned, and now the basis for my teaching is to help students apply what they have learned to the real world.

1. Which of the following would most likely be the next line of this passage?

   (A) The world is a dangerous and intimidating place; be wary of it.
   (B) Children should be taught to seek whatever the world has to offer.
   (C) A teacher has to be in the world, not just study about the world.
   (D) But you can't forget about books.
   (E) Teaching is like learning.

2. Which of the following is the underlying moral of this passage?

   (A) Teaching art is very rewarding.
   (B) Children learn a lot from field trips.
   (C) There is much to be said for teachers who think of their students' experiences first.
   (D) Firsthand experiences are important for a teacher's development.
   (E) You never know what you will end up teaching.

The American alligator is found in Florida and Georgia, and has also been reported in other states, including North and South Carolina. Weighing in at more than 400 pounds, the length of an adult alligator is twice that of its tail. Adult alligators eat fish and small mammals while young alligators prefer insects, shrimp, and frogs.

An untrained person may mistake a crocodile for an alligator. Crocodiles are found in the same areas as alligators and both have prominent snouts with many teeth. The crocodile has a long thin snout with teeth in both jaws. The alligator's snout is wider with teeth only in the upper jaw.

3. Which of the following would be a good title for this passage?

(A) Large Reptiles
(B) Eating Habits of Alligators
(C) The American Alligator
(D) How Alligators and Crocodiles Differ
(E) American Alligator: Endangered Species

4. Which of the following would be a way to distinguish an alligator from a crocodile?

(A) Number of teeth
(B) Shape of snout
(C) Habitat
(D) Diet
(E) Mating rituals

5. Which of the following best describes the purpose of the passage?

(A) All animals are noteworthy.
(B) Reptiles are interesting animals.
(C) To educate readers about differences in similar animals.
(D) To describe the life cycle of wetland creatures.
(E) To provide information about the American alligator.

Remove the jack from the trunk. Set the jack under the car. Use the jack to raise the car. Remove the lug nuts. Remove the tire and replace it with the doughnut. Reset the lug nuts loosely and use the jack to lower the chassis to the ground. Tighten the lug nuts once the tire is touching the ground.

6. Which of the following is the main idea of this passage?

(A) Using a jack
(B) Changing a tire on a car
(C) Maintaining a car
(D) Following directions
(E) Caring for a car

Farmers and animals are fighting over rain forests. The farmers are clearing the forests and driving out the animals to make room for crops. If this battle continues, the rain forest will disappear. Both the farmers and the animals will lose, and the soil in the cleared forest will form a hard crust.

Of course, there are global implications as well. Clearing the forests increases the amount of carbon dioxide in the atmosphere. The most promising solution to the problems caused by clearing the rain forests is the education of the local farmers.

7. Which information below is NOT provided in the passage?

(A) Reasons the animals are being run out
(B) Reasons the farmers need more land
(C) Effects of lost rain forests
(D) Ways that people can help globally
(E) Ways that people can help locally

8. What most likely would the opinion of the author be about wildlife conservation?

(A) All animals must fend for themselves.
(B) Damage to the earth affects both people and animals.
(C) Our greatest resource is education.
(D) Testing products on animals is a practice that should be outlawed.
(E) Animals and people should have equal rights.

I love gingerbread cookies, which are flavored with ginger and molasses. I can remember cold winter days when my brother and I huddled around the fire eating gingerbread cookies and sipping warm apple cider. In those days, gingerbread cookies came in many shapes and sizes. When you eat a gingerbread cookie today, you have to bite a "person's" head off.

9. Why did the author of the passage above put quotes around the word *person*?

(A) To emphasize the difference between gingerbread cookies that appear as people rather than windmills
(B) Because gingerbread cookies often don't look like people
(C) To emphasize that this word has a figurative meaning
(D) To emphasize the choice of this word rather than the word *man*
(E) To emphasize how our culture now puts more importance on people than on things

Use this fable attributed to Aesop to answer Questions 10 and 11.

The Frogs Who Wanted a King

The frogs lived a happy life in the pond. They jumped from lily pad to lily pad and sunned themselves without a care. But a few of the frogs were not satisfied with this relaxed and enjoyable life. These frogs thought that they needed a king to rule them. So they sent a note to the god Jupiter requesting that he appoint a king.

Jupiter was amused by this request. In a good-natured response, Jupiter threw a log into the pond, which landed with a big splash. All the frogs jumped to safety. Some time passed and one frog started to approach the log, which lay still in the pond. When nothing happened, the other frogs jumped on the floating giant, treating it with disdain.

The frogs were not satisfied with such a docile king. They sent another note to Jupiter asking for a strong king to rule over them. Jupiter was not amused by this second request and he was tired of the frogs' complaints.

So Jupiter sent a stork. The stork immediately devoured every frog in sight. The few surviving frogs gave Mercury a message to carry to Jupiter pleading for Jupiter to show them mercy.

Jupiter was very cold. He told Mercury to tell the frogs that they were responsible for their own problems. They had asked for a king to rule them and they would have to make the best of it.

10. Which of the following morals fits the passage?

(A) Let well enough alone.
(B) Familiarity breeds contempt.
(C) Slow and steady wins the race.
(D) Liberty is too high a price to pay for revenge.
(E) Misery loves company.

11. Why did the frogs treat the log with contempt?

(A) The log was sent by Jupiter.
(B) The log floated in the pond.
(C) The log was not alive.
(D) The log could not speak.
(E) The log was not assertive.

You may want to go to a park on a virgin prairie in Minnesota. The park borders Canada and is just west of the Mississippi River. The thousands of acres of park land are home to hundreds of species of birds and mammals. In the evening, a sotto wind sweeps across the prairie, creating wave-like ripples in the tall grasses. This prairie park is just one of the wonders you can see when you visit marvelous Minnesota.

12. Where might you find this excerpt?

(A) Cook book
(B) Travel brochure
(C) Hunting magazine
(D) National parks guide
(E) Conservation organization mailing

13. In which part of the United States is this park located?

   (A) Midwest
   (B) Northeast
   (C) Southeast
   (D) Northwest
   (E) Southwest

14. What does the author mean by "virgin prairie"?

   (A) Desolate taiga
   (B) Untouched grasslands
   (C) Wooded plains
   (D) Native American reservation
   (E) Untainted meadows

There was a time in the United States when a married woman was expected to take her husband's last name. Most women still follow this practice, but things are changing. In fact, Hawaii is the only state with a law requiring a woman to take her husband's last name when she marries.

Many women look forward to taking their husband's surname. They may enjoy the bond it establishes with their husband, or want to be identified with their husband's professional status. Other women want to keep their own last name. They may prefer their original last name, or want to maintain their professional identity.

Some women resolve this problem by choosing a last name that hyphenates their surname and their husband's surname. This practice of adopting elements of both surnames is common in other cultures.

15. What would be the best title for this passage?

   (A) Women Have Rights
   (B) Determining a Woman's Name After Marriage
   (C) Determining a Woman's Name After Divorce
   (D) Legal Aspects of Surname Changing
   (E) Hawaii's Domestic Laws

16. What position is the author taking on women's rights?

   (A) For women but against men
   (B) For women and against equality
   (C) For women and for men
   (D) Against women but for men
   (E) Against women and against men

17. The passage would LEAST likely be found in a

   (A) fashion magazine.
   (B) woman's corporate magazine.
   (C) teen magazine aimed at girls.
   (D) fitness magazine.
   (E) bridal magazine.

18. What is the main idea of this passage?

    (A) Women are at the mercy of the law.
    (B) Women in Hawaii have no options.
    (C) Women today have many options related to surnames.
    (D) Children should have the same name as their mother.
    (E) Men have stopped demanding that women change their names.

In recent years, cooperative learning, which involves students in small group activities, has gained popularity as an instructional approach. Cooperative learning provides students with an opportunity to work on projects presented by the teacher. This type of learning emphasizes group goals, cooperative learning, and shared responsibility. All students must contribute in order for the group to be successful.

19. What is the main idea of this passage?

    (A) To show different learning styles
    (B) To examine the best way to teach
    (C) To explain why cooperative learning is the best method for eliminating classrooms
    (D) To illustrate the method of cooperative learning
    (E) To show the role of the teacher in a cooperative learning environment

20. According to this passage what would be a good definition of cooperative learning?

    (A) An instructional arrangement in which children work in small groups in a manner that promotes student responsibility.
    (B) An instructional arrangement in which the teacher pairs two students in a tutor–tutee relationship to promote learning of academic skills or subject content.
    (C) An instructional arrangement consisting of three to seven students that represents a major format for teaching academic skills.
    (D) An instructional arrangement that is appropriate for numerous classroom activities such as show and tell, discussing interesting events, taking a field trip, or watching a movie.
    (E) An instructional arrangement in which the teaching responsibilities are shared.

TARGETED TEST EXPLAINED ANSWERS

1. (**C**) The passage emphasizes the necessary balance of learning from books and learning from experience.

2. (**D**) The passage notes that firsthand experiences are an important part of a teacher's development.

3. (**D**) The passage gives some insight into how these two reptiles are different.

4. **(B)** The passage indicates that the alligator has a wider snout than the crocodile.

5. **(C)** The passage educates readers about differences between these similar animals.

6. **(B)** The passage gives directions for changing a tire on a car.

7. **(D)** The passage mentions global problems but gives no advice on how people can help on a global scale.

8. **(C)** The author concludes that education of local farmers offers the most promising solution. Choice B is incorrect because it is not an opinion about wildlife conservation.

9. **(C)** The quotes indicate that the word *person* is not to be taken literally.

10. **(A)** Things would clearly have been better for the frogs if they had left well enough alone.

11. **(E)** The passage indicates that the frogs were not satisfied with such a docile king.

12. **(B)** This passage has all the flowery and positive wording you would find in a travel guide.

13. **(A)** The passage indicates that the park is near the center of the country around the Mississippi River. *Midwest* is the best of the choices given to describe this area.

14. **(B)** In this context, *virgin* means pristine or untouched. The prairie is grassland.

15. **(B)** The entire passage discusses ways in which a woman can determine her name after marriage.

16. **(C)** The author is objective and takes a balanced view of women and men.

17. **(D)** The passage would be completely out of place in a fitness magazine.

18. **(C)** The passage describes the range of options women have for choosing a surname (last name).

19. **(D)** The passage describes cooperative learning without evaluating its effectiveness.

20. **(A)** This choice best paraphrases the passage's description of cooperative learning. The other choices include information about cooperative learning not found in the passage.

PART III

PRACTICE PPST TESTS WITH EXPLAINED ANSWERS

CHAPTER 6 Practice PPST 1: Computerized Format

TEST INFO BOX

This practice test models the Computerized PPST format, without the pretest multiple-choice items.

Everything here counts toward the scoring. You'll use a pencil to darken the oval directly on the test to record your answer. That simulates using a mouse to select the oval for the correct answer on the actual Computerized PPST. There is no separate answer sheet. You will use a word processor, without the spell checker or the grammar checker, to type your essay.

We leave letters inside the answer ovals on the test so that it is easier to discuss the correct answer you'll find at the end of the test. You won't find those letters on the actual test.

If you have the CD from the book/CD version, you'll be able to get an enhanced sense of what the Computerized PPST is like.

READING	40 items	60 minutes
WRITING MULTIPLE CHOICE	38 items	30 minutes
WRITING ESSAY	1 essay	30 minutes
MATHEMATICS	40 items	60 minutes

Take this test in a realistic, timed setting. Take this practice test after you have completed your review.

The setting will be most realistic if another person times the test and ensures that the test rules are followed exactly. If another person is acting as test supervisor, he or she should review these instructions with you and say "Start" when you should begin a section and "Stop" when time has expired.

Once the test is complete, review the answers and explanations for each item as you correct the test.

Reading Test 1

You should not take this practice test until you have completed Chapter 5 and the targeted test at the end of that chapter.

You have 60 minutes for this test.

Keep the time limit in mind as you work. Answer the easier questions first. Be sure you answer all the questions. There is no penalty for guessing. You may write on the test booklet and mark up the questions.

Each question or statement on the multiple-choice portions of the test has five answer choices. Exactly one of these choices is correct. Mark the oval to show your choice.

Remember that we show the letters in the ovals to make it easier to discuss the correct answers in the explained answers that follow the test. Those letters will not be there on the actual test.

When instructed, turn the page and begin.

READING

40 ITEMS, 60 MINUTES

You will read selections followed by one or more questions with five answer choices. Select the best answer choice based on what the selection states or implies and darken the oval of the correct answer.

1. The computers in the college dormitories are actually more sophisticated than the computers in the college computer labs, and they cost less. It seems that the person who bought the dormitory computers looked around until she found powerful computers at a low price. The person who runs the labs just got the computers offered by the regular supplier.

   The best statement of the main idea of this paragraph is

   Ⓐ it is better to use the computers in the dorms.
   Ⓑ it is better to avoid the computers in the labs.
   Ⓒ the computers in the dorms are always in use so, for most purposes, it is better to use the computers in the labs.
   Ⓓ it is better to shop around before you buy.
   Ⓔ wholesale prices are usually better than retail prices.

   Questions 2–4 are based on this passage.

   Researchers were not sure at first what caused AIDS or how it was transmitted. They did know early on that everyone who developed AIDS died. Then researchers began to understand that the disease is caused by the HIV virus, which could be transmitted through blood and blood products. Even after knowing this, some blood companies resisted testing blood for the HIV virus. Today we know that the HIV virus is transmitted through blood and other bodily fluids. Women may be more susceptible than men, and the prognosis hasn't changed.

2. The main intent of this passage is to

   Ⓐ show that blood companies can't be trusted.
   Ⓑ detail the history of AIDS research.
   Ⓒ detail the causes and consequences of AIDS.
   Ⓓ warn women that they are susceptible to AIDS.
   Ⓔ raise awareness about AIDS.

3. Which of the following questions could be answered from this passage?

   Ⓐ How do intravenous drug users acquire AIDS?
   Ⓑ Is AIDS caused by a germ or a virus?
   Ⓒ Through what mediums is AIDS transmitted?
   Ⓓ How do blood companies test for AIDS?
   Ⓔ What does AIDS mean?

4. Which of the following would be the best concluding summary sentence for this passage?

   Ⓐ AIDS research continues to be underfunded in the United States.
   Ⓑ Sexual activity and intravenous drug use continue to be the two primary ways that AIDS is transmitted.
   Ⓒ People develop AIDS after being HIV positive.
   Ⓓ Our understanding of AIDS has increased significantly over the past several years, but we are no closer to a cure.
   Ⓔ It is better to be transfused with your own blood, if possible.

5. The retired basketball player said that, while modern players were better athletes because there was so much emphasis on youth basketball and increased focus on training, he still believed that the players of his day were better because they were more committed to the game, better understood its nuances, and were more dedicated to team play.

In this passage, the retired basketball player believed that which of the following factors led to today's basketball players being better athletes?

Ⓐ More dedication
Ⓑ Increased salaries
Ⓒ Better nutrition
Ⓓ Youth basketball
Ⓔ More commitment

6. The way I look at it, Robert E. Lee was the worst general in the Civil War—he was the South's commanding general, and the South lost the war.

What assumption does the writer of this statement make?

Ⓐ War is horrible and should not be glorified.
Ⓑ Picket's charge at Gettysburg was a terrible mistake.
Ⓒ A general should be judged by whether he wins or loses.
Ⓓ The South should have won the Civil War.
Ⓔ Slavery is wrong.

7. Advances in astronomy and space exploration during the past twenty-five years have been significant, and we now know more answers to questions about the universe than ever before, but we still cannot answer the ultimate question, "How did our universe originate?"

Which of the following best characterizes the author's view of how the advances in astronomy and space exploration affect our eventual ability to answer the ultimate question?

Ⓐ We now know more answers than ever before.
Ⓑ All the questions have not been answered.
Ⓒ Eventually we will probably find out.
Ⓓ The question can't be answered.
Ⓔ We will have the answer very soon.

Questions 8–12 are based on this passage.

The Board of Adjustment can exempt a person from the requirements of a particular land use ordinance. Several cases have come before the Board concerning three ordinances. One ordinance states that religious and other organizations cannot build places of worship or meeting halls in residential zones. A second ordinance states that any garage must be less than 25 percent of the size of a house on the same lot, while a third ordinance restricts a person's right to convert a one-family house to a two-family house.

It is interesting to note how a person can be in favor of an exemption in one case but opposed to exemption in another. For example, one homeowner applied to build a garage 45 percent of the size of her house but was opposed to a neighbor converting his house from a one-family to a two-family house. This second homeowner was opposed to a church being built in his neighborhood. The woman opposed to his proposal was all for the church construction project.

The pressure on Board of Adjustment members who also live in the community is tremendous. It must sometimes seem to them that any decision is the wrong one. But that is what Board of Adjustments are for, and we can only hope that this example of America in action will best serve the community and those who live there.

8. Which of the following sentences is the author of the passage most likely to DISAGREE with?

   (A) These Boards serve a useful purpose.
   (B) No exemptions should be granted to any zoning ordinance.
   (C) People can be very fickle when it comes to the exemptions they favor.
   (D) Some people may try to influence Board of Adjustment members.
   (E) The garage the woman wanted to build was about twice the allowable size.

9. The author finds people's reactions to exemption requests interesting because

   (A) so many different types of exemptions are applied for.
   (B) a person's reaction is often based on religious principles and beliefs.
   (C) a person can both support and not support requested exemptions.
   (D) people put so much pressure on Board members.
   (E) men usually oppose exemptions sought by women.

10. In which of the following publications would you expect this passage to appear?

    (A) A government textbook
    (B) A local newspaper
    (C) A national newspaper
    (D) A civics textbook
    (E) A newsmagazine

11. According to the author, the actions of a Board of Adjustment

    (A) oppress religious and community groups.
    (B) favor men over women.
    (C) enforce town ordinances.
    (D) are examples of America in action.
    (E) exempt people from property taxes.

12. Which of the following does the passage convey?

    (A) A person should be consistently for or against Board exemptions.
    (B) The Board of Adjustments should act only when all agree.
    (C) People are interested in their own needs when it comes to zoning.
    (D) Board of Adjustments members should not be from town.
    (E) The Board of Adjustments should not approve any of the requests.

13. The college sororities are "interviewed" by students during rush week. Rush week is a time when students get to know about the different sororities and decide which ones they want to join. Each student can pledge only one sorority. Once students have chosen the three they are most interested in, the intrigue begins. The sororities then choose from among the students who have chosen them.

Which of the following strategies will help assure a student that she will be chosen for at least one sorority and preferably get into a sorority she likes?

I Choose at least one sorority she is sure will choose her

II Choose one sorority she wants to get into

III Choose her three favorite sororities

IV Choose three sororities she knows will choose her

(A) I and II
(B) I and III
(C) I only
(D) III only
(E) IV only

14. During a Stage 4 alert, workers in an energy plant must wear protective pants, a protective shirt, and a helmet, except that protective coveralls can be worn in place of protective pants and shirt. When there is a Stage 5 alert, workers must also wear filter masks in addition to the requirements for the Stage 4 alert.

During a Stage 5 alert, which of the following could be worn?

I Pants, shirt, helmet
II Coveralls, helmet, mask
III Coveralls, mask

(A) I only
(B) II only
(C) III only
(D) I and II only
(E) I, II, and III

Questions 15 and 16 are based on this passage.

Using percentages to report growth patterns can be deceptive. If there are 100 new users for a cereal currently used by 100 other people, the growth rate is 100 percent. However if there are 50,000 new users for a cereal currently used by 5,000,000 people, the growth rate is 1 percent. It seems obvious that the growth rate of 1 percent is preferable to the growth rate of 100 percent. So while percentages do provide a useful way to report growth patterns, we must know the initial number the growth percentage is based on before we make any conclusions.

15. According to this passage,

(A) lower growth rates mean higher actual growth.
(B) higher growth rates mean higher actual growth.
(C) the growth rate depends on the starting point.
(D) the growth rate does not depend on the starting point.
(E) a lower starting point means a higher growth rate.

16. Which of the following can be implied from this passage?

(A) Don't believe any advertisements.
(B) Question any percentage growth rate.
(C) Percentages should never be used.
(D) Any growth rate over 50 percent is invalid.
(E) Percentages are deceptive advertising.

17. (1) The science fiction story started with a description of the characters.
    (2) Some of the descriptions were hard for me to understand.
    (3) The book was about time travel in the 22nd century, an interesting subject.
    (4) The authors believed time travel would be possible by then.

In these four sentences, a person describes a science fiction book. Which of the following choices most accurately characterizes these statements made by the person describing the book?

Ⓐ (2) alone states an opinion
Ⓑ (1) and (4) alone state facts
Ⓒ (3) states both facts and opinion
Ⓓ (1), (3), and (4) state facts only
Ⓔ (4) states an opinion

18. The public schools in Hinman have devoted extra resources to mathematics instruction for years. Their programs always reflect the most current thinking about the way mathematics should be taught, and the schools are always equipped with the most recent teaching aids. These extra resources have created a mathematics program that is now copied by other schools throughout America.

The mathematics program at the Hinman schools is copied by other schools because

Ⓐ their programs always reflect the most current thinking about the way mathematics should be taught.
Ⓑ the schools are always equipped with the most recent teaching aids.
Ⓒ the schools use the NCTM standards.
Ⓓ extra resources were devoted to mathematics instruction.
Ⓔ their successful programs were publicized to other schools.

Questions 19–24 apply to this passage.

Computer graphing programs are capable of graphing almost any equations, including advanced equations from calculus. The student just types in the equation and the graph appears on the computer screen. The graphing program can also show the numerical solution for any entered equation. I like having a computer program that performs the mechanical aspects of these difficult calculations. However, these programs do not teach about graphing or mathematics because the computer does not "explain" what is going on. A person could type in an equation, get an answer, and have not the slightest idea what either meant.

Relying on this mindless kind of graphing and calculation, students will be completely unfamiliar with the meaning of the equations they write or the results they get. They will not be able to understand how to create a graph from an equation or to understand the basis for the more complicated calculations.

It may be true that a strictly mechanical approach is used by some teachers. There certainly is a place for students who already understand equations and graphing to have a computer program that relieves the drudgery. But these computer programs should never and can never replace the teacher. Mathematical competence assumes that understanding precedes rote calculation.

19. What is the main idea of this passage?

Ⓐ Mechanical calculation is one part of learning about mathematics.
Ⓑ Teachers should use graphing programs as one part of instruction.
Ⓒ Graphing programs are not effective for initially teaching mathematics.
Ⓓ Students who use these programs won't learn mathematics.
Ⓔ The programs rely too heavily on a student's typing ability.

20. Which of the following questions could be answered from the information in the passage?

    Ⓐ How does the program do integration and differentiation?

    Ⓑ What type of mathematics learning experiences should students have?

    Ⓒ When is it appropriate to use graphing programs?

    Ⓓ Why do schools buy these graphing programs?

    Ⓔ Which graphing program does the author recommend?

21. Which of the following information can be found in the passage?

    I The type of computer that graphs the equation

    II The graphing program's two main outputs

    III How to use the program to teach about mathematics

    Ⓐ I only

    Ⓑ II only

    Ⓒ I and II only

    Ⓓ II and III only

    Ⓔ I, II, and III

22. Which aspect of graphing programs does the author of the passage like?

    Ⓐ That you just have to type in the equation

    Ⓑ That the difficult mechanical operations are performed

    Ⓒ That the calculations and graphing are done very quickly

    Ⓓ That you don't have to know math to use them

    Ⓔ That they can't replace teachers

23. Which of the following could be used in place of the first sentence of the last paragraph?

    Ⓐ It may be true that some strict teachers use a mechanical approach.

    Ⓑ It may be true that some teachers use only a mechanical approach.

    Ⓒ It may be true that a stringently mechanical approach is used by some teachers.

    Ⓓ It may be true that inflexible mechanical approaches are used by some teachers.

    Ⓔ It may be true that the mechanical approach used by some teachers is too rigorous.

24. According to this passage, what could result in students' unfamiliarity with the meaning of equations or results?

    Ⓐ Using a graphing program to display the graph of an equation

    Ⓑ Relying on mindless graphing and calculation

    Ⓒ Strictly mechanical approaches

    Ⓓ Using microcomputers to graph equations and find solutions

    Ⓔ Being able to just type in equations

25. An analysis of models of potential space vehicles prepared by engineers revealed that the parts of the hull of the vehicles that were strongest were the ones that had the most potential for being weak.

    What conclusion can be drawn from the analysis mentioned here?

    Ⓐ The parts of the hull that are potentially strongest do not receive as much attention from engineers as those that are potentially weakest.
    Ⓑ The potentially weaker parts of the hull appear stronger in models than the potentially stronger parts of the hull.
    Ⓒ Being potentially weaker, these parts of the hull appear relatively stronger in a model.
    Ⓓ Potentially weaker parts of the hull have the most potential for being stronger.
    Ⓔ The parts of the hull that are potentially weakest receive less attention from engineers than those parts that are potentially stronger.

    <u>Questions 26 and 27 are based on this passage.</u>

    The growth of the town led to a huge increase in the number of students applying for kindergarten admission. Before this time, students had been admitted to kindergarten even if they were "technically" too young. At first the school administrators considered a testing plan for those applicants too young for regular admission, admitting only those who passed the test. Luckily the administrators submitted a plan that just enforced the official, but previously ignored, birth cut-off date for kindergarten admission. This decision set the stage for fairness throughout the town.

26. What main idea is the author trying to convey?

    Ⓐ Testing of young children doesn't work.
    Ⓑ All children should be treated equally.
    Ⓒ Tests are biased against minority children.
    Ⓓ The testing program would be too expensive.
    Ⓔ Age predicts a child's performance level.

27. Which of the following is the primary problem with this plan for the schools?

    Ⓐ Parents will sue.
    Ⓑ Parents will falsify birth certificates to get their children in school.
    Ⓒ Next year the schools will have to admit a much larger kindergarten group.
    Ⓓ Missing kindergarten because a child is born one day too late doesn't seem fair.
    Ⓔ Parents would not be able to dispute the results of an objective testing plan.

28. A person who is not treated with respect cannot be expected to be a good worker.

    Which of the following can be concluded from this statement?

    Ⓐ A person treated with respect can be expected to be a good worker.
    Ⓑ A person who is expected to be a good worker should be treated with respect.
    Ⓒ A person who cannot be expected to be a good worker is not treated with respect.
    Ⓓ A person not treated with respect can still be expected to be a good worker.
    Ⓔ A person who is not a good worker can't expect to be treated with respect.

Questions 29 and 30 are based on these circumstances.

The state highway department has sets of regulations for the number of lanes a highway can have and how these lanes are to be used. A summary of these regulations follows.

- All highways must be five lanes wide and either three or four of these lanes must be set aside for passenger cars only.
- If four lanes are set aside for passenger cars, then one of these lanes must be set aside for cars with three or more passengers, with a second lane of the four passenger lanes also usable by school vehicles such as buses, vans, and cars.
- If three lanes are set aside for passenger cars, then one of these lanes must be set aside for cars with two or more passengers, except that school buses, vans, and cars may also use this lane.

29. Officials in one county submit a plan for a five-lane highway, with three lanes set aside for passenger cars, and school buses able to use the lane set aside for cars with two or more passengers. Based on their regulations, which of the following is most likely to be the state highway department's response to this plan?

Ⓐ Your plan is approved because you have five lanes with three set aside for passenger cars and one set aside for passenger cars with two or more passengers.

Ⓑ Your plan is approved because you permitted school buses to use the passenger lanes.

Ⓒ Your plan is disapproved because you don't include school vans and school cars among the vehicles that can use the lane for cars with two or more passengers.

Ⓓ Your plan is disapproved because you include school buses in the lane for passenger cars with two or more passengers.

Ⓔ Your plan is disapproved because you set aside only three lanes for passenger cars when it should have been four.

30. County officials send a list of three possible highway plans to the state highway department. Using their regulations, which of the following plans would the state highway department approve?

I 5 lanes—3 for passenger cars, 1 passenger lane for cars with 3 or more passengers, school buses and vans can also use the passenger lane for 3 or more people

II 5 lanes—4 for passenger cars, 1 passenger lane for cars with 3 or more passengers, 1 of the 4 passenger lanes can be used by school buses, vans, and cars

III 5 lanes—3 for passenger cars, 1 passenger lane for cars with 2 or more passengers, school vehicles can also use the passenger lane for 2 or more passengers

Ⓐ I only
Ⓑ II only
Ⓒ III only
Ⓓ I and II only
Ⓔ II and III only

Questions 31–34 are based on this passage.

The choice of educational practices sometimes seems like choosing fashions. Fashion is driven by the whims, tastes, and zeitgeist of the current day. The education system should not be driven by these same forces. But consider, for example, the way mathematics is taught. Three decades ago, teachers were told to use manipulative materials to teach mathematics. In the intervening years, the emphasis was on drill and practice. Now teachers are being told again to use manipulative materials. This cycle is more akin to random acts than to sound professional practice.

31. What does the author most likely mean by the word *zeitgeist* in the second sentence?

Ⓐ Tenor
Ⓑ Emotional feeling
Ⓒ Fabric availability
Ⓓ Teaching methods
Ⓔ Intelligence

32. Which of the following sentences contains an opinion?

    Ⓐ "But consider for example . . ."
    Ⓑ "Three decades ago . . ."
    Ⓒ "In the intervening years . . ."
    Ⓓ "Now teachers are being told . . ."
    Ⓔ "This cycle is more akin . . ."

33. For what reason did the author most likely use the phrase *three decades* in the fifth sentence?

    Ⓐ To represent 30 years
    Ⓑ For emphasis
    Ⓒ To represent 10-year intervals
    Ⓓ To represent the passage of years
    Ⓔ To bring the reader to the current year

34. Which of the following could be substituted for the phrase "random acts" in the last sentence?

    Ⓐ Unsound practice
    Ⓑ A fashion designer's dream
    Ⓒ The movement of hemlines
    Ⓓ A fashion show
    Ⓔ Pressure from mathematics manipulative manufacturers

35. Empty halls and silent walls greeted me. A summer day seemed like a good day for me to take a look at the school in which I would student teach. I tiptoed from door to door looking. Suddenly the custodian appeared behind me and said, "Help you?" "No sir," I said. At that moment, he could have been Aristotle or Plato for all I knew. Things worked out.

    Which of the following best describes the main character in the passage?

    Ⓐ Timid and afraid
    Ⓑ Confident and optimistic
    Ⓒ Pessimistic and unsure
    Ⓓ Curious and respectful
    Ⓔ Careful and quiet

Questions 36–38 are based on the following reading.

I remember my childhood vacations at a bungalow colony near a lake. Always barefoot, my friend and I spent endless hours
Line playing and enjoying our fantasies. We
(5) were pirates, rocket pilots, and detectives. Everyday objects were transformed into swords, ray guns, and two-way wrist radios. With a lake at hand, we swam, floated on our crude rafts made of old
(10) lumber, fished, and fell in. The adult world seemed so meaningless while our world seemed so full. Returning years later I saw the colony for what it was—tattered and torn. The lake was shallow and muddy.
(15) But the tree that had been our lookout was still there. And there was the house where the feared master spy hid from the FBI. There was the site of the launching pad for our imaginary rocket trips. The posts of
(20) the dock we had sailed from many times were still visible. But my fantasy play did not depend on this place. My child-mind would have been a buccaneer wherever it was.

36. Which of the following choices best characterizes this passage?

    Ⓐ An adult describes disappointment at growing up.
    Ⓑ A child describes the adult world through the child's eyes.
    Ⓒ An adult discusses childhood viewed as a child and as an adult.
    Ⓓ An adult discusses the meaning of fantasy play.
    Ⓔ An adult describes a wish to return to childhood.

37. The sentence "The adult world seemed so meaningless while our world seemed so full." on lines (10)–(12) is used primarily to

   Ⓐ emphasize the emptiness of most adult lives.

   Ⓑ provide a transition from describing childhood to describing adulthood.

   Ⓒ show how narcissistic children are.

   Ⓓ describe the difficulty this child had relating to adults.

   Ⓔ emphasize the limited world of the child compared to the more comprehensive world of the adult.

38. Which of the following best characterizes the last sentence in the passage?

   Ⓐ The child would have been rebellious, no matter what.

   Ⓑ Childhood is not a place but a state of mind.

   Ⓒ We conform more as we grow older.

   Ⓓ The writer will always feel rebellious.

   Ⓔ A part of us all stays in childhood.

Questions 39 and 40 apply to this passage.

Sometimes parents are more involved in little league games than their children. I remember seeing a game in which a player's parent came on the field to argue with the umpire. The umpire was not that much older than the player.

Before long, the umpire's mother was on the field. There the two parents stood, toe to toe. The players and the other umpires formed a ring around them and looked on in awe.

Of course, I have never gotten too involved in my children's sports. I have never yelled at an umpire at any of my kid's games. I have never even—well, I didn't mean it.

39. What other "sporting" event is the author trying to recreate in the second paragraph?

   Ⓐ Bullfight

   Ⓑ Wrestling match

   Ⓒ Boxing match

   Ⓓ Football game

   Ⓔ Baseball game

40. The author portrays herself as "innocent" of being too involved in her children's sports. How would you characterize this portrayal?

   Ⓐ False

   Ⓑ A lie

   Ⓒ Tongue in cheek

   Ⓓ Noble

   Ⓔ Self-effacing

Writing Test 1

Take this test in a realistic, timed setting.

You have 30 minutes for this section.

Keep the time limit in mind as you work. Answer the easier questions first. Be sure you answer all the questions. There is no penalty for guessing.

Each question or statement has five answer choices. Exactly one of these choices is correct. Circle your answer choice. Remember, we leave letters there to help show the correct answer in the explained answers that follow the test. Those letters will not be there on the actual test.

When instructed, turn the page and begin.

WRITING

38 ITEMS, 30 MINUTES

USAGE

You will read sentences with four parts underlined and lettered. Determine whether one of the underlined parts contains grammatical, word use, or punctuation errors. If so, circle that part. If there are no errors, circle E.

1. <u>Disgusted by</u> the trash <u>left behind</u> by
   (A)   (B)

   picnickers, the <u>town</u> council passed a law
                   (C)

   <u>requiring convicted litterers</u> to spend five
   (D)

   hours cleaning up the town park. <u>No error</u>.
                                    (E)

2. The teacher <u>was sure</u> that the child's
                (A)

   <u>difficult home</u> life <u>effected</u> her <u>school work</u>.
   (B)   (C)   (D)

   <u>No error</u>.
   (E)

3. It <u>took</u> Ron a long time <u>to realize</u> that
      (A)   (B)

   the <u>townspeople</u> <u>were completely</u> opposed
       (C)   (D)

   to his proposal. <u>No error</u>.
                    (E)

4. A newspaper <u>columnist</u> promised to print
                (A)

   the <u>people who</u> were <u>involved in</u> the secret
       (B)   (C)

   negotiations concerning the <u>sports stadium</u>
                                (D)

   in the next column. <u>No error</u>.
                       (E)

5. The silent <u>halo</u> of a <u>solar eclipse</u>
               (A)   (B)

   <u>could be seen</u> by astronomers across <u>asia</u>.
   (C)   (D)

   <u>No error</u>.
   (E)

6. <u>Also found</u> during the archaeological
   (A)

   dig <u>was</u> a <u>series</u> of animal bone fragments,
       (B)   (C)

   fire signs, and <u>arrow points.</u> <u>No error</u>.
                   (D)   (E)

7. The <u>teacher</u> asked all of <u>her</u> students to
Ⓐ   Ⓑ

bring in <u>they're</u> permission slips <u>to go on</u>
Ⓒ   Ⓓ

the Washington trip. <u>No error.</u>
Ⓔ

8. The <u>plumber</u> <u>did not go to</u> the dripping
Ⓐ   Ⓑ

water <u>than to</u> the place the water
Ⓒ

<u>seemed to be</u> coming from. <u>No error.</u>
Ⓓ   Ⓔ

9. The driver realized that she <u>would either</u>
Ⓐ

have to <u>go completely out of</u> the <u>way</u> or
Ⓑ   Ⓒ

have to wait for the <u>swollen creek</u> to
Ⓓ

subside. <u>No error.</u>
Ⓔ

10. The <u>tracker</u> was so <u>good that</u> he could
Ⓐ   Ⓑ

tell the <u>difference between</u> a hoofprint
Ⓒ

made by a horse with a saddle <u>or</u> a
Ⓓ

hoofprint made by a horse without a

saddle. <u>No error.</u>
Ⓔ

11. The mayor <u>estimated</u> that it <u>would cost</u>
Ⓐ   Ⓑ

$1,200 for each <u>citizen individually</u> to
Ⓒ

repair the storm damage <u>to the town.</u>
Ⓓ

<u>No error.</u>
Ⓔ

12. <u>Sustaining</u> a <u>month-long</u> winning streak
Ⓐ   Ⓑ

in the town baseball A B league, the
young team <u>pressed on</u> with
Ⓒ

<u>unwavering determination.</u> <u>No error.</u>
Ⓓ   Ⓔ

13. The fire chief, <u>like the police chief,</u>
Ⓐ

<u>has so much</u> responsibility, that
Ⓑ

<u>they often have</u> a personal <u>driver.</u>
Ⓒ   Ⓓ

<u>No error.</u>
Ⓔ

14. A talented chef <u>making customers</u> smack
Ⓐ

their lips at her great <u>gustatorial delights,</u>
Ⓑ

the likes of which <u>are not available</u> in any
Ⓒ

<u>ordinary restaurant.</u> <u>No error.</u>
Ⓓ   Ⓔ

15. The fate of small towns in America, which

    were <u>popularized</u> in movies when it seemed
    　　　　(A)

    that everyone came from a small town

    <u>and now</u> face <u>anonymity</u> as
    　(B)　　　　(C)

    cars on highways speed by, <u>is perilous</u>.
    　　　　　　　　　　(D)

    <u>No error</u>.
    　(E)

16. The coach <u>not only</u> <u>works with</u> each
    　　　　(A)　　　(B)

    pitcher and each catcher, but he <u>also has to</u>
    　　　　　　　　　　　　(C)

    change <u>him</u>. <u>No error</u>.
    　　(D)　　(E)

17. When I <u>was a child</u>, a wet washcloth
    　　　　(A)

    was the <u>main method</u> of first <u>aid; it</u>
    　　　(B)　　　　(C)

    reduced swelling, eliminated pain,

    <u>and inflammation was</u> reduced. <u>No error</u>.
    　　　(D)　　　　　　(E)

18. I am going to a <u>World Cup game</u> next
    　　　　　　(A)

    week, and I <u>would be surprised</u> if
    　　　　(B)

    <u>there is even</u> one empty seat
    　(C)

    <u>in the stadium</u>. <u>No error</u>.
    　(D)　　　　(E)

19. It is <u>not uncommon</u> for the claims of land
    　　(A)

    developers to <u>go too</u> far, <u>like</u> the one
    　　　　(B)　　(C)

    reported several years ago in which

    <u>the land was</u> on the side of a sheer cliff.
    　(D)

    <u>No error</u>.
    　(E)

20. <u>During</u> <u>the fall</u>, some fruits are in
    　(A)　　(B)

    <u>so short supply</u> that the prices <u>triple</u>.
    　(C)　　　　　　　　(D)

    <u>No error</u>.
    　(E)

21. The <u>volleyball team</u> won their
    　　(A)

    <u>third consecutive</u> scholastic title,
    　(B)

    <u>both because</u> of their dedication and
    　(C)

    because <u>they are talented</u>. <u>No error</u>.
    　　(D)　　　　　(E)

SENTENCE CORRECTION

You will read sentences with some or all of the sentence underlined, followed by five answer choices. The first answer choice repeats the underlined portion and the other four present possible replacements. Select the answer choice that best represents standard English without altering the meaning of the original sentence. Darken the oval directly on the test.

22. The quality of the parts received in the most recent shipment <u>was inferior to parts in the previous shipments, but still in accordance with</u> manufacturers' specifications.

    (A) was inferior to parts in the previous shipments, but still in accordance with
    (B) were inferior to the previous shipments' parts but still in accordance with
    (C) was the inferior of the previous shipments' parts but still in accordance with
    (D) was inferior to the previous parts' shipments but still not on par with
    (E) was inferior to the previous parts' shipments and the manufacturers' specifications

23. <u>The painful rabies treatment first developed by Pasteur</u> saved the boy's life.

    (A) The painful rabies treatment first developed by Pasteur
    (B) The painful rabies treatment which was first discovered by Pasteur
    (C) Pasteur developed the painful rabies treatment
    (D) First developed by Pasteur the treatment for painful rabies
    (E) The fact that Pasteur developed a rabies treatment

24. By 10:00 A.M. every morning, <u>the delivery service brought important papers to the house in sealed envelopes</u>.

    (A) the delivery service brought important papers to the house in sealed envelopes
    (B) important papers were brought to the house by the delivery service in sealed envelopes
    (C) sealed envelopes were brought to the house by the delivery service with important papers
    (D) the delivery service brought important papers in sealed envelopes to the house
    (E) the deliver service brought sealed envelopes to the house containing important papers

25. The shadows shortened as the sun <u>begun the</u> ascent into the morning sky.

    (A) begun the
    (B) begin the
    (C) began the
    (D) begun that
    (E) begun an

26. Liz and Ann spent all day climbing the mountain, and <u>she was almost</u> too exhausted for the descent.

    (A) she was almost
    (B) they were almost
    (C) they were
    (D) she almost was
    (E) was

27. The embassy announced that at the present time, they could neither confirm <u>nor deny that the ambassador would return home in the event that</u> hostilities broke out.

    (A) nor deny that the ambassador would return home in the event that
    (B) or deny that the ambassador would return home in the event that
    (C) nor deny that the ambassador would return home if
    (D) nor deny that the ambassador would leave
    (E) nor deny that ambassador will return home in the event that

28. Every person <u>has the ultimate capacity to</u> control his or her own destiny.

    (A) has the ultimate capacity to
    (B) ultimately has the capacity to
    (C) has the capacity ultimately to
    (D) can
    (E) could

29. In all likelihood, her mother's absence would be devastating, <u>were it not</u> for the presence of her sister.

    (A) were it not
    (B) it was not
    (C) it were not
    (D) were they not
    (E) was it not

30. She had listened very carefully to all the candidates, and the Independent candidate was the only <u>one who had not said something that did not make sense</u>.

    (A) one who had not said something that did not make sense
    (B) one who did not make sense when he said something
    (C) one who had only said things that made sense
    (D) one to not say something that made sense
    (E) one who never said anything that made no sense

31. The author knew that the book would be finished <u>only by working every day and getting</u> lots of sleep at night.

    (A) only by working every day and getting
    (B) only working every day and getting
    (C) only by working every day and by getting
    (D) only through work and sleep
    (E) only by daily work and by sleepless nights

32. The teacher was sure that Tom's difficult home life affected <u>his school work</u>.

    (A) his school work
    (B) his school's work
    (C) him school work
    (D) his school works
    (E) him school works

33. Small town sheriffs in America, <u>whom were popularized in movies when it seemed that everyone came from a small town</u>, now face anonymity.

    (A) whom were popularized in movies when it seemed that everyone came from a small town
    (B) who were popularized in movies when it seemed that everyone came from a small town
    (C) whom were popularized in movies when it seemed that anyone came from a small town
    (D) whom were popularized in movies when they seemed that everyone came from a small town
    (E) whom were popularized in movies when it seemed that everyone comes from a small town

34. The professor asked the class to consider the development of the human race. She pointed out that, throughout the ages, <u>human beings has learned to communicate by nonverbal means</u>.

   Ⓐ human beings has learned to communicate by nonverbal means
   Ⓑ human beings had learned to communicate by nonverbal means
   Ⓒ human beings has learn to communicate by nonverbal means
   Ⓓ human beings have learn to communicate by nonverbal means
   Ⓔ human beings have learned to communicate by nonverbal means

35. There are a number of specialty business stores. Office World, the office supply store, <u>claimed to be the quintessential supplier of office machines in the United States</u>.

   Ⓐ claimed to be the quintessential supplier of office machines in the United States
   Ⓑ claiming to be the quintessential supplier of office machines in the United States
   Ⓒ claimed to be the quardassential supplier of office machines in the United States
   Ⓓ claims to be the quintessential supplier of office machines in the United States
   Ⓔ has claim to be the quintessential supplier of office machines in the United States

36. The *Hardy Boys* was a book series. <u>As a child he read the *Hardy Boys* series of books and was in awe of the author Franklin Dixon.</u>

   Ⓐ As a child he read the *Hardy Boys* series of books and was in awe of the author Franklin Dixon.
   Ⓑ As a child he read the *Hardy Boys* series of books, but was in awe of the author Franklin Dixon.
   Ⓒ As a child he read the *Hardy Boys* series of books; however he was in awe of the author Franklin Dixon.
   Ⓓ As a child he read the *Hardy Boys* series of books but was also in awe of the author Franklin Dixon.
   Ⓔ As a child he read the *Hardy Boys* series of books; however he was also in awe of the author Franklin Dixon.

37. Bob is deciding which event to compete in. <u>He is a strong swimmer but he is best known for his diving.</u>

   Ⓐ He is a strong swimmer but he is best known for his diving.
   Ⓑ He is a strong swimmer; but, he is best known for his diving.
   Ⓒ He is a strong swimmer, but he is best known for his diving.
   Ⓓ He is a strong swimmer: but he is best known for his diving.
   Ⓔ He is a strong swimmer, but, he is best known for his diving.

38. It was almost time for the test. Vincent and Laura said to <u>their friends "I wonder if we're through studying for the PPST"?</u>

   Ⓐ their friends "I wonder if we're through studying for the PPST"?
   Ⓑ their friends ",I wonder if we're through studying for the PPST"?
   Ⓒ their friends, "I wonder if we're through studying for the PPST"?
   Ⓓ their friends, "I wonder if we're through studying for the PPST?"
   Ⓔ their friends ",I wonder if we're through studying for the PPST?"

Essay Test 1

Take this test in a realistic, timed setting. You should not take this practice test until you have completed Chapter 3 and the targeted test at the end of that chapter.

Write an essay on the topic found on the next page. Write on this topic only. An essay on another topic, no matter how well done, will receive a 0. You have 30 minutes to complete the essay.

Use a word processor to type your essay. You may *not* use the grammar checker or the spell checker.

Once the test is complete, ask an English professor or English teacher to evaluate your essay holistically using the rating scale on page 218.

ESSAY

You have 30 minutes to complete this essay question. Use the lined pages to write a brief essay based on this topic.

To encourage talented people to enter teaching, teachers who score higher on standardized tests should make significantly more money than those teachers who receive lower test scores.

Describe the extent to which you agree or disagree with this statement. Support your response with specific details, examples, and explanations.

_____

_____

_____

_____

_____

_____

_____

_____

_____

_____

_____

Mathematics Test 1

Take this test in a realistic, timed setting. Chapter 4 and the targeted test at the end of that chapter help you prepare for this test.

You have 60 minutes for this test.

Keep this time limit in mind as you work. Answer the easier items first. Be sure you answer all the items. There is no penalty for guessing.

Each item has five answer choices. Exactly one of these choices is correct. Mark the oval to show your choice.

Remember that we show the letters in the ovals to make it easier to discuss the correct answer in the explained answers that follow the test. Those letters will not be there on the actual test.

When instructed, turn the page and begin.

MATHEMATICS

40 ITEMS, 60 MINUTES

Each item below includes five answer choices. Select the best choice for each item and darken the oval to show your choice.

1. **Percent of Freshmen, Sophomores, Juniors, and Seniors at a College**

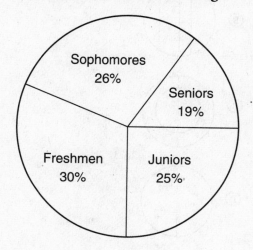

   There are a total of 12,000 students. How many more freshmen are there than seniors?

   Ⓐ 1,320
   Ⓑ 2,280
   Ⓒ 3,000
   Ⓓ 3,120
   Ⓔ 3,600

2. Steve pays $520 a month for rent, and his monthly paycheck after taxes is $1,300. Which computation shows the percent of Steve's paycheck that is used to pay rent?

   Ⓐ $(1300 \div 520) \cdot 100$
   Ⓑ $(520 \div 1300) \cdot 100$
   Ⓒ $(5.2 \cdot 1300) \cdot 100$
   Ⓓ $(13 \cdot 520) \cdot 100$
   Ⓔ $(5.2 \cdot 13) \cdot 100$

3. All of the windows in the house are rectangles. None of the windows in the house are squares.

   Which of the following conclusions in the statements above are true?

   Ⓐ Some of the windows have four sides of equal length.
   Ⓑ None of the windows contain right angles.
   Ⓒ None of the windows are parallelograms.
   Ⓓ None of the windows have four sides of equal length.
   Ⓔ All of the windows contain an acute angle.

4. The area of a square is $4\,\text{in}^2$. There is a larger square made up of 49 of these squares. What is the length of one side of the larger square?

   Ⓐ 7 in
   Ⓑ 14 in
   Ⓒ 28 in
   Ⓓ 56 in
   Ⓔ 112 in

5. Which of the following is written in scientific notation?

   Ⓐ 53794×10
   Ⓑ 5379.4×10
   Ⓒ 537.94×10
   Ⓓ 53.794×10
   Ⓔ 5.3794×10

6.

NUMBER OF AWARDS

Person 1

Person 2

Person 3

Person 4

Person 5

Each 🏆 represents 20 awards

How many more awards did person 5 have than person 3?

(A) 20
(B) 40
(C) 60
(D) 80
(E) 100

7. If 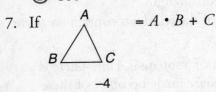 $= A \cdot B + C$

then

(A) −88
(B) −19
(C) −3
(D) 3
(E) 19

8. The following is a list of the ages of ten different people: 53, 27, 65, 21, 7, 16, 70, 41, 57, and 37.

What is the mean age of these people?

(A) 39.4
(B) 40
(C) 65.7
(D) 69
(E) 70.2

9. A pizza has crust all around the edge. Which of the following figures shows a way to cut the pizza into four equal pieces where only two have crust?

(A)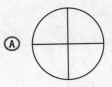

(B)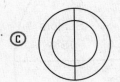

(C)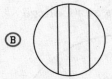

(D)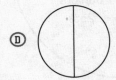

(E)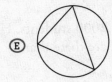

10. What is the area of the circle seen below?

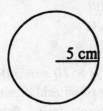

5 cm

(A) 25 cm^2
(B) 10π cm^2
(C) 25π cm^2
(D) 20 cm^2
(E) $166\frac{2}{3}$ π cm^2

11. Frank has 2 dogs and 5 cats. What fraction of these animals are cats?

Ⓐ $\dfrac{2}{5}$

Ⓑ $\dfrac{2}{7}$

Ⓒ $\dfrac{5}{2}$

Ⓓ $\dfrac{5}{7}$

Ⓔ $\dfrac{7}{2}$

12. $\dfrac{4}{9}$ is less than which of the following?

Ⓐ 44%

Ⓑ 0.45

Ⓒ 0.4444

Ⓓ $\dfrac{4}{10}$

Ⓔ 44.4%

13. 0.45 is how many times 45,000?

Ⓐ 0.1

Ⓑ 0.01

Ⓒ 0.001

Ⓓ 0.0001

Ⓔ 0.00001

14. Which of the following shows a line with *x*- and *y*-intercepts equal to 1?

Ⓐ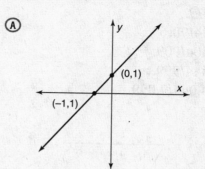

Ⓑ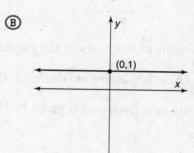

Ⓒ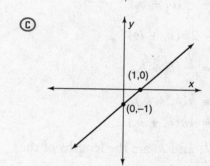

Ⓓ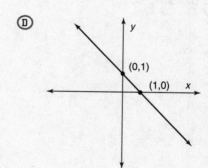

Ⓔ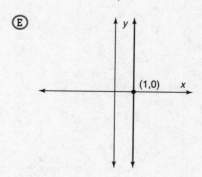

15. All of the following numbers are equal except for

   Ⓐ 4/9.
   Ⓑ 44/90.
   Ⓒ 404/909.
   Ⓓ 444/999.
   Ⓔ 4,044/9,099.

16.

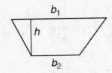

If the lengths of the bases in the trapezoid $(A = \frac{h}{2}(b_1 + b_2))$ above are doubled, the area of the new trapezoid is given by the formula

   Ⓐ $A = \frac{h}{2}(b_1 + b_2)$

   Ⓑ $A = 2h(b_1 + b_2)$

   Ⓒ $A = \frac{h}{4}(b_1 + b_2)$

   Ⓓ $A = h(b_1 + b_2)$

   Ⓔ $A = 4h(b_1 + b_2)$

where b_1 and b_2 are the lengths of the original bases.

17.

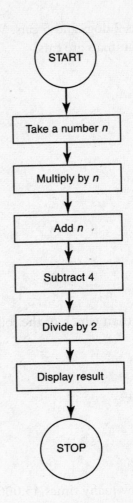

If $n = 5$, what is the result of the computation outlined in the flowchart?

   Ⓐ 12
   Ⓑ 13
   Ⓒ 14
   Ⓓ 15
   Ⓔ 16

18.

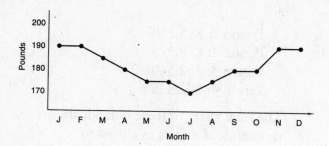

The above line graph displays Jack's weight over a 12-month period. Approximately what percentage of Jack's highest weight is Jack's lowest weight?

ⓐ 97%
ⓑ 94%
ⓒ 91%
ⓓ 89%
ⓔ 85%

19. Alice arrived at work at 7:45 A.M. and left work 11 hours and 15 minutes later. What time did Alice leave work?

ⓐ 8:00 P.M.
ⓑ 7:15 P.M.
ⓒ 7:00 P.M.
ⓓ 6:45 P.M.
ⓔ 6:15 P.M.

20. Which of the following figures could be used to disprove the following statement: "If a quadrilateral has one pair of congruent sides, then it has two pairs of congruent sides"?

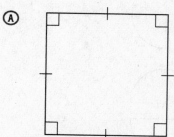

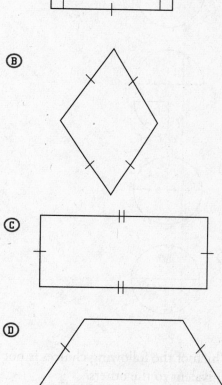

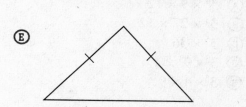

21. The five shapes seen below are made up of identical semicircles and identical quarter-circles. Which of the five shapes has the greatest perimeter?

    Ⓐ

    Ⓑ

    Ⓒ

    Ⓓ

    Ⓔ

22. Which of the following choices is not equivalent to the others?

    Ⓐ $3^4 \times 9 \times 12$
    Ⓑ $3^3 \times 27 \times 12$
    Ⓒ $3^5 \times 36$
    Ⓓ $3^3 \times 9^3 \times 4$
    Ⓔ $3^5 \times 4 \times 9$

23. The salaries of 4 individuals in a company are:

    Person 1: $45,250
    Person 2: $78,375
    Person 3: $52,540
    Person 4: $62,325

    The total salary of these individuals, in thousands of dollars, is closest to

    Ⓐ $237 thousand.
    Ⓑ $238 thousand.
    Ⓒ $239 thousand.
    Ⓓ $240 thousand.
    Ⓔ $241 thousand.

24. Which of the following is true about the graph seen below?

    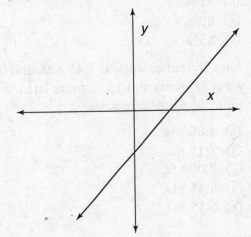

    Ⓐ As x increases, y decreases.
    Ⓑ As x decreases, y does not change.
    Ⓒ As x decreases, y increases.
    Ⓓ As x increases, y increases.
    Ⓔ As x decreases, y decreases.

25. If x is 65% of 400, then what is the value of x?

    Ⓐ 660
    Ⓑ 540
    Ⓒ 260
    Ⓓ 200
    Ⓔ 140

26. What is the average of $\frac{1}{2}$, $\frac{2}{3}$, and $\frac{5}{12}$?

(A) $\frac{19}{12}$

(B) $\frac{19}{24}$

(C) $\frac{19}{36}$

(D) $\frac{19}{44}$

(E) $\frac{19}{52}$

27. In a standard deck of 52 cards, what is the probability of being dealt a king, a queen, or a jack?

(A) $\frac{1}{3}$

(B) $\frac{2}{13}$

(C) $\frac{3}{13}$

(D) $\frac{4}{13}$

(E) $\frac{5}{13}$

28. To find 2.3×10^5 you could multiply 20 by

(A) 15.
(B) 115.
(C) 1,150.
(D) 11,500.
(E) 115,000.

29. A circle can be a part of any of the following except a

(A) circle.
(B) sphere.
(C) cylinder.
(D) cone.
(E) cube.

30. According to the thermometer, what is the temperature?

(A) 80.3°F
(B) 86°F
(C) 80.4°F
(D) 83°F
(E) 80.6°F

31. If $6x + 2y = 10$, which of the following choices are possible values for x and y?

(A) $x = 2$, $y = -1$
(B) $x = 2$, $y = 11$
(C) $x = 3$, $y = 4$
(D) $x = 3$, $y = 14$
(E) $x = 4$, $y = -8$

32. Tickets for a baseball game are $8 each, or 4 tickets for $30. What is the lowest cost for 18 tickets?

(A) $144
(B) $136
(C) $132
(D) $130
(E) $126

33. If $4A + 6 = 2(B - 1)$, then $B = $?

    Ⓐ $2A + 4$
    Ⓑ $8A + 13$
    Ⓒ $2A + 2$
    Ⓓ $4A + 7$
    Ⓔ $4A + 5$

34. Which of the following measurements is not equal to the others?

    Ⓐ 230,000 millimeters
    Ⓑ 0.23 kilometers
    Ⓒ 23 meters
    Ⓓ 23,000 centimeters
    Ⓔ 2.3 hectometers

35. Which of the following choices is a multiple of 7 when 4 is added to it?

    Ⓐ 58
    Ⓑ 114
    Ⓒ 168
    Ⓓ 78
    Ⓔ 101

36. Ryan has gone $3\frac{1}{5}$ miles of his 5-mile run. How many more miles has he left to run?

    Ⓐ A little less than 2 miles
    Ⓑ A little more than 2 miles
    Ⓒ A little less than 3 miles
    Ⓓ A little more than 3 miles
    Ⓔ A little less than 4 miles

37. For every 2 hours that Barbara works she earns $17. How much money will she earn if she works 45 hours?

    Ⓐ $391
    Ⓑ $382.50
    Ⓒ $374
    Ⓓ $365.50
    Ⓔ $357

38. Use the data presented in the pictograph. About how many times greater is the number of computers sold in December than the number of computers sold in January?

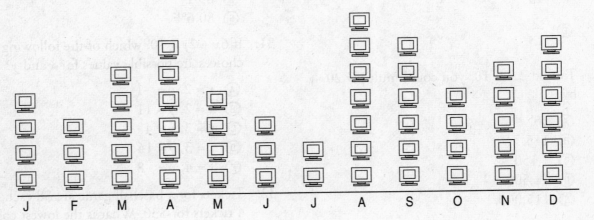

    Ⓐ 1.5
    Ⓑ 2
    Ⓒ 2.5
    Ⓓ 3
    Ⓔ 3.5

39.

Principal Amount	Simple Interest Rate
$1–$5,000	5%
$5,001–$10,000	5.25%
$10,001–$15,000	5.5%
$15,001–$20,000	5.75%
$20,001–$25,000	6%
$25,001 and over	6.25%

The table above shows the interest rate a person will earn based on the principal amount invested. Using the formula $I = P \cdot R \cdot T$, how much interest will a person have earned after 7 years if they invest a principal amount of $20,000?

Ⓐ $1,150
Ⓑ $8,400
Ⓒ $1,200
Ⓓ $8,050
Ⓔ $9,800

40. Which of the following figures has a volume of 72π?

Ⓐ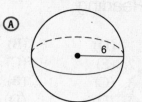

Ⓑ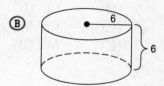

Ⓒ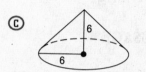

Ⓓ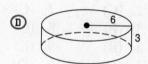

Ⓔ

✓

ANSWERS

Reading

1. **(D)**	8. **(B)**	15. **(C)**	22. **(B)**	29. **(C)**	36. **(C)**
2. **(E)**	9. **(C)**	16. **(B)**	23. **(B)**	30. **(B)**	37. **(B)**
3. **(C)**	10. **(B)**	17. **(C)**	24. **(B)**	31. **(A)**	38. **(B)**
4. **(D)**	11. **(D)**	18. **(D)**	25. **(A)**	32. **(E)**	39. **(C)**
5. **(D)**	12. **(C)**	19. **(C)**	26. **(B)**	33. **(B)**	40. **(C)**
6. **(C)**	13. **(A)**	20. **(C)**	27. **(C)**	34. **(C)**	
7. **(C)**	14. **(B)**	21. **(B)**	28. **(B)**	35. **(D)**	

Writing

USAGE

1. **(E)**	6. **(B)**	11. **(C)**	16. **(E)**	21. **(D)**
2. **(C)**	7. **(C)**	12. **(E)**	17. **(D)**	
3. **(E)**	8. **(C)**	13. **(C)**	18. **(B)**	
4. **(B)**	9. **(E)**	14. **(A)**	19. **(C)**	
5. **(D)**	10. **(D)**	15. **(B)**	20. **(C)**	

SENTENCE CORRECTION

22. **(A)**	26. **(B)**	30. **(C)**	34. **(E)**	38. **(D)**
23. **(A)**	27. **(C)**	31. **(C)**	35. **(D)**	
24. **(D)**	28. **(D)**	32. **(A)**	36. **(A)**	
25. **(C)**	29. **(A)**	33. **(B)**	37. **(C)**	

Mathematics

1. **(A)**	8. **(A)**	15. **(B)**	22. **(D)**	29. **(E)**	36. **(A)**
2. **(B)**	9. **(C)**	16. **(D)**	23. **(B)**	30. **(B)**	37. **(B)**
3. **(D)**	10. **(C)**	17. **(B)**	24. **(D)**	31. **(A)**	38. **(A)**
4. **(B)**	11. **(D)**	18. **(D)**	25. **(C)**	32. **(B)**	39. **(D)**
5. **(E)**	12. **(B)**	19. **(C)**	26. **(C)**	33. **(A)**	40. **(C)**
6. **(C)**	13. **(E)**	20. **(D)**	27. **(C)**	34. **(C)**	
7. **(D)**	14. **(D)**	21. **(B)**	28. **(D)**	35. **(E)**	

Explained Answers

Reading

1. **(D)** The paragraph describes how careful shopping can result in lower prices.

2. **(E)** The author is trying to raise AIDS awareness and not to present any particular fact.

3. **(C)** The passage explains that AIDS is transmitted through blood and other bodily fluids.

4. **(D)** The sentence for this choice best describes the message the author is trying to convey.

5. **(D)** The retired basketball player mentions youth basketball as one of the reasons why today's players were better athletes. The passage also mentions an increased focus on training. However, the question does not ask for all the factors the retired player mentioned.

6. **(C)** This writer believes that generals should be judged by results. Even if you do not agree, that is the view of this writer.

7. **(C)** The author writes that the question still cannot be answered. The author does not say that the question can never be answered.

8. **(B)** The author never questions or attacks Adjustment Boards.

9. **(C)** The passage gives an example of a person who both supported and did not support requested exemptions.

10. **(B)** The author is writing about a local issue.

11. **(D)** In the last paragraph the author uses these words to describe Boards of Adjustment.

12. **(C)** The author gives several examples in which people support or don't support exemptions based on their own needs.

13. **(A)** Strategies I and II, together, assure the student that she will be chosen and give her a chance to get into a sorority she wants.

14. **(B)** List II is the only list that meets all the requirements.

15. **(C)** The rate, alone, does not provide enough information. You must also know the starting point.

16. **(B)** You should question any growth rate when only the percentage is given.

17. **(C)** Choice (C) is correct. A sentence can state both a fact and an opinion. "(2) alone states an opinion" means that it is the only sentence that states an opinion.

18. **(D)** This choice gives the fundamental reason why the schools' programs are copied. The other reasons grow out of the decision to provide extra resources.

19. **(C)** The author objects to using these programs with students who don't know mathematics.

20. **(C)** This is the only question that can be answered from information in the passage. The answer is that it can be used when students already understand equations and graphing.

21. **(B)** Only the information listed next to II can be found in the passage.

22. **(B)** The author mentions liking this aspect in the middle of the first paragraph.

23. **(B)** Choice (B) replicates the intent of the original sentence.

24. **(B)** The author presents this information in the first sentence of the second paragraph.

25. **(A)** This is the only choice that has a plausible explanation of why potentially weaker spots appear stronger.

26. **(B)** The author's view is that all children should be treated the same.

27. **(C)** Choice (C) describes the problem. All the students who might have been admitted early this year will be admitted next year along with the other kindergarten students.

28. **(B)** Only this choice is a logical conclusion.

29. **(C)** When there are three lanes for passenger cars, school buses, school vans, and school cars can all use the lane for cars with two or more passengers.

30. **(B)** Only this choice meets all the rules.

31. **(A)** The context tells us that the answer is the tenor (direction, tendency) of the times.

32. **(E)** Of the listed sentences, only "This cycle is more akin . . ." contains an opinion.

33. **(B)** The author is being a little dramatic to emphasize the length of the time span.

34. **(C)** Hemlines move without apparent reason, which is this author's point about educational practices.

35. **(D)** The character visited the school and so is certainly curious. The character's reaction to the custodian shows respectfulness.

36. **(C)** The author discusses childhood from each of the perspectives described in (C). Choice (D) is incorrect because the meaning of fantasy play is never discussed.

37. **(B)** This sentence juxtaposes adulthood and childhood and provides a transition to discussing adulthood.

38. **(B)** The author says that these childhood experiences would have occurred regardless of the location.

39. **(C)** The description of going toe to toe inside a ring reminds us of a boxing match.

40. **(C)** The author is not lying, but the story is obviously not meant to be taken seriously.

Writing

USAGE

1. **(E)** This sentence does not contain an error.

2. **(C)** The word *effected* is incorrect. It should be replaced by the word *affected*.

3. **(E)** This passage also contains no errors. *Townspeople* is an appropriate word.

4. **(B)** You can't print people. The underlined section should be *names of the people*.

5. **(D)** The word *Asia* is capitalized.

6. **(B)** The correct verb is *were*.

7. **(C)** The contraction *they're* (they are) is used incorrectly. *Their* is the correct word.

8. **(C)** The phrase *than to* is incorrectly used here. *But to* is the correct phrase.

9. **(E)** There are no underlined errors in this sentence.

10. **(D)** The conjunction *or* is incorrectly used here. The correct conjunction is *and*.

11. **(C)** There is no reason to use the word *individually*. Each citizen is an individual. The word *individually* should be removed.

12. **(E)** The passage contains no errors in underlined parts.

13. **(C)** The word *they* creates confusion because it could mean that there is one driver for both of them. A better usage is *each often has*.

14. **(A)** *Making* is the wrong verb. *Made* is the correct choice.

15. **(B)** The words *and now* should read *and which now*, in order to clarify just what faces anonymity.

16. **(E)** This sentence contains no underlined errors.

17. **(D)** This part of the sentence does not follow a parallel development. The correct usage is *reduced inflammation*.

18. **(B)** The correct replacement for *would be surprised* is *will be surprised*.

19. **(C)** The word *like* is incorrectly used here. The correct replacement is *such as*.

20. **(C)** The correct replacement for *so short supply* is *such short supply*.

21. **(D)** These words do not continue a parallel development. The correct replacement is *of their talent*.

SENTENCE CORRECTION

22. **(A)** The underlined portion is appropriate.

23. **(A)** The underlined portion is appropriate.

24. **(D)** The rewording in (D) clarifies that the papers are in sealed envelopes—not in the house.

25. **(C)** This choice is the best wording from among the five choices available.

26. **(B)** This choice creates an agreement in number between nouns and pronoun.

27. **(C)** This choice replaces the wordy *in the event that* with *if*.

28. **(D)** This wordy expression is replaced by *can*.

29. **(A)** The underlined portion is appropriately worded.

30. **(C)** This choice appropriately replaces the double negative underlined in the original sentence.

31. **(C)** Adding the word *by* creates the desired parallel development in the sentence.

32. **(A)** The sentence is correct. The pronoun *his* agrees with the antecedent *Tom*.

33. **(B)** *Who* correctly shows the subjective case.

34. **(E)** *Have learned* indicates this has occurred and may continue.

35. **(D)** *Office World* is singular and takes the singular verb *claims*.

36. **(A)** The sentence is correct. The conjunction *and* shows that the two clauses are equally important.

37. **(C)** Use a comma before the conjunction that joins these two independent clauses. An independent clause can stand on its own as a sentence.

38. **(D)** Punctuation before a quote goes outside the quotation marks, while punctuation following a quote goes inside the quotation marks.

ESSAY

Show your essay to an English professor or teacher for evaluation using this scale.

RATING SCALE

6 This essay is extremely well written. It is the equivalent of an A in-class assignment. The essay addresses the question and provides clear supporting arguments, illustrations, or examples. The paragraphs and sentences are well organized and show a variety of language and syntax. The essay may contain some minor errors.

5 This essay is well written. It is the equivalent of a B+ in-class assignment. The essay addresses the question and provides some supporting arguments, illustrations, or examples. The paragraphs and sentences are fairly well organized and show a variety of language and syntax. The essay may contain some minor mechanical or linguistic errors.

4 This essay is fairly well written. It is the equivalent of a B in-class assignment. The essay adequately addresses the question and provides some supporting arguments, illustrations, or examples for some points. The paragraphs and sentences are acceptably organized and show a variety of language and syntax. The essay may contain mechanical or linguistic errors but is free from an identifiable pattern of errors.

3 This essay may demonstrate some writing ability, but it contains obvious errors. It is the equivalent of a C+ in-class assignment. The essay may not clearly address the question and may not give supporting arguments or details. The essay may show problems in diction including inappropriate word choice. The paragraphs and sentences may not be acceptably developed. There will be an identifiable pattern or grouping of errors.

2 This essay shows only the most limited writing ability. It is the equivalent of a C in-class assignment. It contains serious errors and flaws. This essay may not address the question, it may be poorly organized, or it may provide no supporting arguments or detail. It usually shows serious errors in diction, usage, and mechanics.

1 This essay does not demonstrate minimal writing ability. It is the equivalent of a D or F on an in-class assignment. This essay may contain serious and continuing errors, or it may not be coherent.

Mathematics

1. **(A)** We know from the circle graph that $0.3 \cdot 12{,}000 = 3{,}600$ of the students are freshmen and $0.19 \cdot 12{,}000 = 2{,}280$ are seniors.

   There are $3{,}600 - 2{,}280 = 1{,}320$ more freshmen than seniors.

2. **(B)** To find what percent 520 is of 1,300, divide 520 by 1,300 to get the decimal representation of percent. Then multiply by 100 to get the answer into percent form.

3. **(D)** A is not true because none of the windows are squares. All of the windows are rectangles, so (B), (C), and (E) are not true. Choice (D) meets both of the requirements.

4. **(B)** The larger square has seven of the smaller squares along each side. The area of the smaller square is 4 in^2, so each side of the smaller square is 2 in. The length of one side is $2 \text{ in} \cdot 7 = 14 \text{ in}$.

5. **(E)** 5.3794 is the only number between 1 and 10.

6. **(C)** Person 5 had 3 more awards than person 3. Therefore person 5 had $3 \cdot 20 = 60$ more awards than person 3.

7. **(D)** $A \cdot B + C = -4 \cdot 2 + 11 = -8 + 11 = 3$

8. **(A)** The sum of the ages is 394, and then we divide this number by 10 to get the mean.

9. **(C)** None of the other choices cut into four equal pieces have two pieces containing crust.

10. **(C)** Use the formula for the area of a circle.

    $A = \pi r^2 = \pi \cdot (5 \text{ cm})^2 = 25\pi \text{ cm}^2$

11. **(D)** There are a total of $5 + 2 = 7$ animals, 5 of which are cats. Therefore the answer is $\dfrac{5}{7}$.

12. **(B)** $\dfrac{4}{9} = 0.444\ldots$, which is less than 0.45.

13. **(E)** $45{,}000 \cdot 0.00001 = 0.45$

14. **(D)** $(0, 1)$ shows an x-intercept of 1.

$(1, 0)$ shows a y-intercept of 1.

15. **(B)** The decimal equivalents of each answer choice are

A. $0.\overline{4}$

B. $0.4\overline{8}$

C. $0.\overline{4}$

D. $0.\overline{4}$

E. $0.\overline{4}$

Answer choices (A), (C), (D), and (E) are equal.

16. **(D)** The formula for the area of a trapezoid is $A = \dfrac{h}{2}(b_1 + b_2)$.

However, in the new trapezoid the length of each base is doubled; therefore, the formula is

$$A = \frac{h}{2}(2b_1 + 2b_2) =$$

$$\frac{h}{2} \cdot 2(b_1 + b_2) =$$

$$h(b_1 + b_2)$$

17. **(B)** Follow the steps.

$5 \cdot 5 = 25$

$25 + 5 = 30$

$30 - 4 = 26$

$26 \div 2 = 13$

18. **(D)** Jack's lowest weight is 170 pounds and Jack's highest weight is 190 pounds.

$170 \div 190 \approx 0.89 \approx 89\%$

19. **(C)** 6:45 P.M. is 11 hours after 7:45 A.M.

Add the other 15 minutes to get 7:00 P.M.

20. **(D)** The trapezoid, choice (D), has only one pair of congruent sides.

21. **(B)** Each diameter in choice (B) is part of the perimeter. When answering this question, consider only the perimeter and not any segments within a figure.

22. **(D)** A. $3^4 \times 9 \times 12 = 3^4 \times 9 \times 4 \times 3 =$
$3^5 \times 4 \times 9$
This is choice (E).

  B. $3^3 \times 27 \times 12 = 3^3 \times 9 \times 3 \times 4 \times 3$
$= 3^5 \times 4 \times 9$
This is choice (E).

  C. $3^5 \times 36 = 3^5 \times 4 \times 9$
This is choice (E).

  D. $3^3 \times 9^3 \times 4 = 3^3 \times 3^2 \times 9^2 \times 4 =$
$3^5 \times 4 \times 9^2 \neq 3^5 \times 4 \times 9$
This is NOT choice (E).

23. **(B)** $45{,}250 + 78{,}375 + 52{,}540 + 62{,}325 = 238{,}490 \approx 238{,}000$

24. **(D)** The y-value (vertical axis) moves up as the x-value (horizontal axis) moves right.

25. **(C)** $65\% = 0.65$ $(0.65) \cdot 400 = 260$

26. **(C)** $\dfrac{1}{2} = \dfrac{6}{12}, \dfrac{2}{3} = \dfrac{8}{12}, \dfrac{5}{12}$

$\left(\dfrac{6}{12} + \dfrac{8}{12} + \dfrac{5}{12} \right) \div 3 =$

$\dfrac{19}{12} \div 3 =$

$\dfrac{19}{12} \cdot \dfrac{1}{3} = \dfrac{19}{36}$

27. **(C)** In a standard deck of cards there are 12 "face cards"—4 kings, 4 queens, and 4 jacks out of 52 possible cards.

$P(\text{face card}) = \dfrac{12}{52} = \dfrac{3}{13}$

28. **(D)** $2.3 \times 10^5 = 230{,}000$

$11{,}500 \times 20 = 230{,}000$

29. **(E)**

These figures show the circle in a sphere, a cylinder, and a cone. A cube does not contain a circle.

30. **(B)** Each mark on the scale represents two degrees.

31. **(A)** $6(2) + 2(-1) = 12 - 2 = 10$

32. **(B)** There are 18 tickets and you can buy 16 of the tickets for $120 (4 × $30) and the remaining two tickets at $16.

$120 + $16 = $136

33. **(A)** $\qquad\qquad 4A + 6 = 2(B - 1)$

Divide by 2
on both sides: $\qquad 2A + 3 = B - 1$

Add 1 to both
sides: $\qquad\qquad 2A + 4 = B$

$B = 2A + 4$

34. **(C)** Use this chart

Kilo	Hecto	Deka	Unit	Deci	Centi	Milli
1,000	100	10	1	0.1	0.01	0.001

Given below is each answer choice in meters.

A. 230 meters

B. 230 meters

C. 23 meters

D. 230 meters

E. 230 meters

Choice (C) is not equal to the others.

35. **(E)** $101 + 4 = 105 = 7 \cdot 15$

36. **(A)** $5 - 3\frac{1}{5} = 1\frac{4}{5}$, which is a little less than 2 miles.

37. **(B)** If Barbara earns $17 every 2 hours, she earns $\frac{\$17}{2} = \$8.50$ per hour. In 45 hours she earns $\$8.50 \cdot 45 = \$382.50$.

38. **(A)** There are 4 pictures of computers in January and 6 pictures of computers in December; $\frac{6}{4} = 1.5$. It does not matter how many computers each picture represents, the answer will still be the same.

39. **(D)** The interest rate is based on the principal amount, and does not increase. Since the principal invested is $20,000, the interest rate is 5.75%. The time (T) is 7 years.

$I = \$20,000 \cdot .0575 \cdot 7 = \$8,050$

40. **(C)** A. $V = \frac{4}{3}\pi r^3 = \frac{4}{3}\pi(6)^3 = 288p$

    B. $V = \pi r^2 h = \pi(6)^2(6) = 216\pi$

    C. $V = \frac{1}{3}\pi r^2 h = \frac{1}{3}\pi(6)^2(6) = 72\pi$

    D. $V = \pi r^2 h = \pi(6)^2(3) = 108\pi$

    E. $V = \frac{1}{3}\pi r^2 h = \frac{1}{3}\pi(3)^2(6) = 36\pi$

CHAPTER 7

Practice PPST 2: Paper-Based Format

Practice PPST 2

TEST INFO BOX

This PPST models the paper-based format.

READING	40 items	60 minutes
WRITING MULTIPLE CHOICE	38 items	30 minutes
WRITING ESSAY	1 essay	30 minutes
MATHEMATICS	40 items	60 minutes

Take this test in a realistic, timed setting.

The setting will be most realistic if another person times the test and ensures that the test rules are followed exactly. If another person is acting as test supervisor, he or she should review these instructions with you and say "Start" when you should begin a section and "Stop" when time has expired.

Use the Multiple-Choice Answer Sheet on page 229.

Use a pencil to mark the answer sheet. The actual test will be machine scored, so completely darken in the answer space.

Once the test is complete, review the answers and explanations for each item as you correct the test.

Answer Sheet 2
PRACTICE PPST 2

Reading—60 minutes

1 Ⓐ Ⓑ Ⓒ Ⓓ Ⓔ	11 Ⓐ Ⓑ Ⓒ Ⓓ Ⓔ	21 Ⓐ Ⓑ Ⓒ Ⓓ Ⓔ	31 Ⓐ Ⓑ Ⓒ Ⓓ Ⓔ
2 Ⓐ Ⓑ Ⓒ Ⓓ Ⓔ	12 Ⓐ Ⓑ Ⓒ Ⓓ Ⓔ	22 Ⓐ Ⓑ Ⓒ Ⓓ Ⓔ	32 Ⓐ Ⓑ Ⓒ Ⓓ Ⓔ
3 Ⓐ Ⓑ Ⓒ Ⓓ Ⓔ	13 Ⓐ Ⓑ Ⓒ Ⓓ Ⓔ	23 Ⓐ Ⓑ Ⓒ Ⓓ Ⓔ	33 Ⓐ Ⓑ Ⓒ Ⓓ Ⓔ
4 Ⓐ Ⓑ Ⓒ Ⓓ Ⓔ	14 Ⓐ Ⓑ Ⓒ Ⓓ Ⓔ	24 Ⓐ Ⓑ Ⓒ Ⓓ Ⓔ	34 Ⓐ Ⓑ Ⓒ Ⓓ Ⓔ
5 Ⓐ Ⓑ Ⓒ Ⓓ Ⓔ	15 Ⓐ Ⓑ Ⓒ Ⓓ Ⓔ	25 Ⓐ Ⓑ Ⓒ Ⓓ Ⓔ	35 Ⓐ Ⓑ Ⓒ Ⓓ Ⓔ
6 Ⓐ Ⓑ Ⓒ Ⓓ Ⓔ	16 Ⓐ Ⓑ Ⓒ Ⓓ Ⓔ	26 Ⓐ Ⓑ Ⓒ Ⓓ Ⓔ	36 Ⓐ Ⓑ Ⓒ Ⓓ Ⓔ
7 Ⓐ Ⓑ Ⓒ Ⓓ Ⓔ	17 Ⓐ Ⓑ Ⓒ Ⓓ Ⓔ	27 Ⓐ Ⓑ Ⓒ Ⓓ Ⓔ	37 Ⓐ Ⓑ Ⓒ Ⓓ Ⓔ
8 Ⓐ Ⓑ Ⓒ Ⓓ Ⓔ	18 Ⓐ Ⓑ Ⓒ Ⓓ Ⓔ	28 Ⓐ Ⓑ Ⓒ Ⓓ Ⓔ	38 Ⓐ Ⓑ Ⓒ Ⓓ Ⓔ
9 Ⓐ Ⓑ Ⓒ Ⓓ Ⓔ	19 Ⓐ Ⓑ Ⓒ Ⓓ Ⓔ	29 Ⓐ Ⓑ Ⓒ Ⓓ Ⓔ	39 Ⓐ Ⓑ Ⓒ Ⓓ Ⓔ
10 Ⓐ Ⓑ Ⓒ Ⓓ Ⓔ	20 Ⓐ Ⓑ Ⓒ Ⓓ Ⓔ	30 Ⓐ Ⓑ Ⓒ Ⓓ Ⓔ	40 Ⓐ Ⓑ Ⓒ Ⓓ Ⓔ

Writing—30 minutes

1 Ⓐ Ⓑ Ⓒ Ⓓ Ⓔ	11 Ⓐ Ⓑ Ⓒ Ⓓ Ⓔ	21 Ⓐ Ⓑ Ⓒ Ⓓ Ⓔ	31 Ⓐ Ⓑ Ⓒ Ⓓ Ⓔ
2 Ⓐ Ⓑ Ⓒ Ⓓ Ⓔ	12 Ⓐ Ⓑ Ⓒ Ⓓ Ⓔ	22 Ⓐ Ⓑ Ⓒ Ⓓ Ⓔ	32 Ⓐ Ⓑ Ⓒ Ⓓ Ⓔ
3 Ⓐ Ⓑ Ⓒ Ⓓ Ⓔ	13 Ⓐ Ⓑ Ⓒ Ⓓ Ⓔ	23 Ⓐ Ⓑ Ⓒ Ⓓ Ⓔ	33 Ⓐ Ⓑ Ⓒ Ⓓ Ⓔ
4 Ⓐ Ⓑ Ⓒ Ⓓ Ⓔ	14 Ⓐ Ⓑ Ⓒ Ⓓ Ⓔ	24 Ⓐ Ⓑ Ⓒ Ⓓ Ⓔ	34 Ⓐ Ⓑ Ⓒ Ⓓ Ⓔ
5 Ⓐ Ⓑ Ⓒ Ⓓ Ⓔ	15 Ⓐ Ⓑ Ⓒ Ⓓ Ⓔ	25 Ⓐ Ⓑ Ⓒ Ⓓ Ⓔ	35 Ⓐ Ⓑ Ⓒ Ⓓ Ⓔ
6 Ⓐ Ⓑ Ⓒ Ⓓ Ⓔ	16 Ⓐ Ⓑ Ⓒ Ⓓ Ⓔ	26 Ⓐ Ⓑ Ⓒ Ⓓ Ⓔ	36 Ⓐ Ⓑ Ⓒ Ⓓ Ⓔ
7 Ⓐ Ⓑ Ⓒ Ⓓ Ⓔ	17 Ⓐ Ⓑ Ⓒ Ⓓ Ⓔ	27 Ⓐ Ⓑ Ⓒ Ⓓ Ⓔ	37 Ⓐ Ⓑ Ⓒ Ⓓ Ⓔ
8 Ⓐ Ⓑ Ⓒ Ⓓ Ⓔ	18 Ⓐ Ⓑ Ⓒ Ⓓ Ⓔ	28 Ⓐ Ⓑ Ⓒ Ⓓ Ⓔ	38 Ⓐ Ⓑ Ⓒ Ⓓ Ⓔ
9 Ⓐ Ⓑ Ⓒ Ⓓ Ⓔ	19 Ⓐ Ⓑ Ⓒ Ⓓ Ⓔ	29 Ⓐ Ⓑ Ⓒ Ⓓ Ⓔ	
10 Ⓐ Ⓑ Ⓒ Ⓓ Ⓔ	20 Ⓐ Ⓑ Ⓒ Ⓓ Ⓔ	30 Ⓐ Ⓑ Ⓒ Ⓓ Ⓔ	

Mathematics—60 minutes

1 Ⓐ Ⓑ Ⓒ Ⓓ Ⓔ	11 Ⓐ Ⓑ Ⓒ Ⓓ Ⓔ	21 Ⓐ Ⓑ Ⓒ Ⓓ Ⓔ	31 Ⓐ Ⓑ Ⓒ Ⓓ Ⓔ
2 Ⓐ Ⓑ Ⓒ Ⓓ Ⓔ	12 Ⓐ Ⓑ Ⓒ Ⓓ Ⓔ	22 Ⓐ Ⓑ Ⓒ Ⓓ Ⓔ	32 Ⓐ Ⓑ Ⓒ Ⓓ Ⓔ
3 Ⓐ Ⓑ Ⓒ Ⓓ Ⓔ	13 Ⓐ Ⓑ Ⓒ Ⓓ Ⓔ	23 Ⓐ Ⓑ Ⓒ Ⓓ Ⓔ	33 Ⓐ Ⓑ Ⓒ Ⓓ Ⓔ
4 Ⓐ Ⓑ Ⓒ Ⓓ Ⓔ	14 Ⓐ Ⓑ Ⓒ Ⓓ Ⓔ	24 Ⓐ Ⓑ Ⓒ Ⓓ Ⓔ	34 Ⓐ Ⓑ Ⓒ Ⓓ Ⓔ
5 Ⓐ Ⓑ Ⓒ Ⓓ Ⓔ	15 Ⓐ Ⓑ Ⓒ Ⓓ Ⓔ	25 Ⓐ Ⓑ Ⓒ Ⓓ Ⓔ	35 Ⓐ Ⓑ Ⓒ Ⓓ Ⓔ
6 Ⓐ Ⓑ Ⓒ Ⓓ Ⓔ	16 Ⓐ Ⓑ Ⓒ Ⓓ Ⓔ	26 Ⓐ Ⓑ Ⓒ Ⓓ Ⓔ	36 Ⓐ Ⓑ Ⓒ Ⓓ Ⓔ
7 Ⓐ Ⓑ Ⓒ Ⓓ Ⓔ	17 Ⓐ Ⓑ Ⓒ Ⓓ Ⓔ	27 Ⓐ Ⓑ Ⓒ Ⓓ Ⓔ	37 Ⓐ Ⓑ Ⓒ Ⓓ Ⓔ
8 Ⓐ Ⓑ Ⓒ Ⓓ Ⓔ	18 Ⓐ Ⓑ Ⓒ Ⓓ Ⓔ	28 Ⓐ Ⓑ Ⓒ Ⓓ Ⓔ	38 Ⓐ Ⓑ Ⓒ Ⓓ Ⓔ
9 Ⓐ Ⓑ Ⓒ Ⓓ Ⓔ	19 Ⓐ Ⓑ Ⓒ Ⓓ Ⓔ	29 Ⓐ Ⓑ Ⓒ Ⓓ Ⓔ	39 Ⓐ Ⓑ Ⓒ Ⓓ Ⓔ
10 Ⓐ Ⓑ Ⓒ Ⓓ Ⓔ	20 Ⓐ Ⓑ Ⓒ Ⓓ Ⓔ	30 Ⓐ Ⓑ Ⓒ Ⓓ Ⓔ	40 Ⓐ Ⓑ Ⓒ Ⓓ Ⓔ

Answers on pages 256–262.

Reading Test 2

You should not take this practice test until you have completed practice PPST 1.

The test rules allow you exactly 60 minutes for this test.

Keep the time limit in mind as you work. Answer the easier questions first. Be sure you answer all the questions. There is no penalty for guessing. You may write on the test booklet and mark up the questions.

Each question or statement on the multiple-choice portions of the test has five answer choices. Exactly one of these choices is correct. Mark your choice on the answer sheet provided for this test.

Your score is based on the spaces you fill in on the answer sheet. Make sure that you mark your answer on the answer sheet in the correct space next to the correct question number.

Once the test is complete, review the answers and explanations for each item as you correct the test.

READING

40 ITEMS, 60 MINUTES

You will read selections followed by one or more questions with five answer choices. Select the best answer choice based on what the selection states or implies and mark that letter on the answer sheet.

1. Cellular phones, once used by the very rich, are now available to almost everyone. With one of these phones, you can call just about anywhere from just about anywhere. Since the use of these phones will increase, we need to find legal and effective ways for law enforcement agencies to monitor calls.

   Which of the following choices is the best summary of this passage?

   (A) Criminals are taking advantage of cellular phones to avoid legal wiretaps.
   (B) The ability to use a cellular phone to call from just about anywhere makes it harder to find people who are using the phones.
   (C) The increase in cellular phone use means that we will have to find legal ways to monitor cellular calls.
   (D) Cellular phones are like regular phones with a very long extension cord.
   (E) Since cellular phones are more available to everyone, they are certainly more available to criminals.

2. The moon takes about 28 days to complete a cycle around the earth. Months, 28 days long, grew out of this cycle. Twelve of these months made up a year. But ancient astronomers realized that it took the earth about 365 days to make one revolution of the sun. Extra days were added to some months and the current calendar was born.

   The passage indicates that the current calendar

   (A) describes the moon's movement around the earth.
   (B) is based on the sun's position.
   (C) is based on the earth's rotation and position of the moon.
   (D) combines features of the moon's cycle and the earth's revolution.
   (E) was based on the number 12.

3. Occasionally, college students will confuse correlation with cause and effect. Correlation just describes the degree of relationship between two factors. For example, there is a positive correlation between poor handwriting and intelligence. However, writing more poorly will not make you more intelligent.

The author's main reason for writing this passage is to

(A) explain the difference between correlation and cause and effect.
(B) encourage improved penmanship.
(C) explain how college students can improve their intelligence.
(D) make those with poor penmanship feel more comfortable.
(E) describe a cause-and-effect relationship.

Questions 4–6 are based on this passage.

It is striking how uninformed today's youth are about Acquired Immune Deficiency Syndrome. Because of their youth and ignorance, many young adults engage in high-risk behavior. Many of these young people do not realize that the disease can be contracted through almost any contact with an infected person's blood and bodily fluids. Some do not realize that symptoms of the disease may not appear for 10 years or more. Others do not realize that the danger in sharing needles to inject intravenous drugs comes from the small amounts of another's blood injected during this process. A massive education campaign is needed to fully inform today's youth about AIDS.

4. The main idea of this passage is

(A) previous education campaigns have failed.
(B) AIDS develops from the HIV virus.
(C) the general public is not fully informed about AIDS.
(D) people should not share intravenous needles.
(E) young people are not adequately informed about AIDS.

5. Which of the following is the best summary of the statement about what young people don't realize about how AIDS can be contracted?

(A) The symptoms may not appear for 10 years or more.
(B) AIDS is contracted because of ignorance.
(C) AIDS is contracted from intravenous needles.
(D) AIDS is contracted through contact with infected blood or bodily fluids.
(E) You will not contract AIDS if you know what to avoid.

6. Which of the following best describes how the author views young people and their knowledge of AIDS?

(A) Stupid
(B) Unaware
(C) Dumb
(D) Unintelligible
(E) Reluctant

7. When Lyndon Johnson succeeded John F. Kennedy, he was able to gain congressional approval for programs suggested by Kennedy but never implemented. These programs, called Great Society programs, included low-income housing and project Head Start. To some, this made Johnson a better president.

Based on this statement, Johnson

(A) was a better president than Kennedy.
(B) gained approval for programs proposed by Kennedy.
(C) was a member of a Great Society.
(D) was president before Kennedy.
(E) originally lived in low-income housing.

Practice PPST 2

Questions 8 and 9 are based on this passage.

I think women are discriminated against; however, I think men are discriminated against just as much as women. It's just a different type of discrimination. Consider these two facts: Men die about 6 years earlier than women, and men are the only people who can be drafted into the armed forces. That's discrimination!

8. What is the author's main point in writing this passage?

   (A) Men are discriminated against more than women are.
   (B) Both sexes are discriminated against.
   (C) Women are not discriminated against.
   (D) On average, men die earlier than women.
   (E) Men are not discriminated against.

9. Which of the following could be substituted for the word *drafted* in the next to last sentence?

   (A) Inducted against their will
   (B) Signed up
   (C) Pushed in by society
   (D) Drawn in by peer pressure
   (E) Serve in a foreign country

Questions 10 and 11 are based on this passage.

Alice in Wonderland, written by Charles Dodgson under the pen name Lewis Carroll, is full of symbolism, so much so that a book titled *Understanding Alice* was written containing the original text with marginal notes explaining the symbolic meanings.

10. By symbolism, the author of the passage above meant that much of *Alice in Wonderland*

    (A) was written in a foreign language.
    (B) contained many mathematical symbols.
    (C) contained no pictures.
    (D) had a figurative meaning.
    (E) was set in a special type.

11. What does the author mean by the phrase "marginal notes" found in the last sentence?

    (A) Explanations of the musical meaning of the text
    (B) Notes that may not have been completely correct
    (C) Notes written next to the main text
    (D) Notes written by Carroll but not included in the original book
    (E) An explanation of the text by Alice Liddell, the real Alice

12. Following a concert, a fan asked a popular singer why the songs sounded so different in person than on the recording. The singer responded, "I didn't record my emotions!"

    Which of the following statements is suggested by this passage?

    (A) The singer was probably not in a good mood during that performance.
    (B) The fan was being intrusive, and the performer was "brushing her off."
    (C) The performance was outdoors where sound quality is different.
    (D) The fan didn't realize the controls available for studio recordings.
    (E) The performance may vary depending on the mood of the performer.

Questions 13–18 are based on this passage

Line
(5)

(10)

The War of 1812 is one of the least understood conflicts in American history. However, many events associated with the war are among the best remembered from American History. The war began when the United States invaded British colonies in Canada. The invasion failed, and the United States was quickly put on the defensive. Most Americans are not aware of how the conflict began. During the war, the *USS Constitution* (Old Ironsides) was active against British ships in the Atlantic. Captain William Perry, sailing on Lake Erie, was famous for yelling to his shipmates, "Don't give up the ship." Most Americans remember Perry and his famous plea, but not (15) where or in which war he was engaged.

Most notably, British troops sacked and burned Washington, D.C. during this conflict. Subsequent British attacks on Fort McHenry near Baltimore were repulsed by American forces. It (20) was during one of these battles that Francis Scott Key wrote the "Star Spangled Banner" while a prisoner on a British ship. The "rockets red glare, bombs bursting in air" referred to ordnance used by the Britishto attack the fort. Many Americans (25) mistakenly believe that the "Star Spangled Banner" was written during or shortly after the Revolutionary War.

13. All the following statements can be implied from the passage EXCEPT:

   (A) The British did not start the war.
   (B) Francis Scott Key was not at Fort McHenry when he wrote the "Star Spangled Banner."
   (C) The rockets referred to in the "Star Spangled Banner" were part of a celebration.
   (D) The British army entered Washington, D.C., during the war.
   (E) The nickname for the *USS Constitution* was Old Ironsides.

14. Which of the following words is the most appropriate replacement for "sacked" in line 17?

   (A) Entered
   (B) Ravished
   (C) Invaded
   (D) Enclosed
   (E) Encapsulated

15. Which of the following statements best summarizes the difference referred to in the passage between Perry's involvement in the War of 1812 and the way many Americans remember his involvement?

   (A) Perry was a drafter of the Constitution and later served on the *Constitution* in the Atlantic, although many Americans don't remember that.
   (B) Perry served in the Great Lakes, but many Americans don't remember that.
   (C) Perry served in Washington, D.C., although many Americans don't remember that.
   (D) Perry served on the *Constitution* at Fort McHenry during the writing of the "Star Spangled Banner," although many Americans do not remember that.
   (E) Perry served on the *Constitution* in the Atlantic, but many Americans don't remember that.

16. What can be inferred about Francis Scott Key from lines 21–23 of the passage?

   (A) He was killed in the battle.
   (B) All his papers were confiscated by the British after the battle.
   (C) He was released by or escaped from the British after the battle.
   (D) He returned to Britain where he settled down.
   (E) He was a British spy.

17. Based on the passage, which of the following words best describes the United States' role in the War of 1812?

   (A) Colonizer
   (B) Neutral
   (C) Winner
   (D) Loser
   (E) Aggressor

18. What main point is the author making in this passage?

    (A) The Americans fought the British in the War of 1812.
    (B) The Revolutionary War continued into the 1800s.
    (C) The British renewed the Revolutionary War during the 1800s.
    (D) Many Americans are unaware of events associated with the War of 1812.
    (E) Americans should remember the treachery of the army that invaded Washington during this war.

Questions 19–24 are based on this passage.

Computer-based word processing programs have spelling checkers and even a thesaurus to find synonyms and antonyms for highlighted words. To use the thesaurus, the student just types in the word, and a series of synonyms and antonyms appears on the computer screen. The program can also show recommended spellings for misspelled words. I like having a computer program that performs these mechanical aspects of writing. However, these programs do not teach about spelling or word meanings. A person could type in a word, get a synonym and have not the slightest idea what either meant.

Relying on this mindless way of checking spelling and finding synonyms, students will be completely unfamiliar with the meanings of the words they use. In fact, one of the most common misuses is to include a word that is spelled correctly but used incorrectly in the sentence.

It may be true that a strictly mechanical approach to spelling is used by some teachers. There certainly is a place for students who already understand word meanings to use a computer program that relieves the drudgery of checking spelling and finding synonyms. But these computer programs should never and can never replace the teacher. Understanding words—their uses and meanings—should precede this more mechanistic approach.

19. What is the main idea of this passage?

    (A) Mechanical spell checking is one part of learning about spelling.
    (B) Programs are not effective for initially teaching about spelling and synonyms.
    (C) Teachers should use word processing programs as one part of instruction.
    (D) Students who use these programs won't learn about spelling.
    (E) The programs rely too heavily on a student's typing ability.

20. Which of the following information is found in the passage?

    I. The type of computer that runs the word processor
    II. The two main outputs of spell-checking and thesaurus programs
    III. An explanation of how to use the word-processing program to teach about spelling and synonyms

    (A) I only
    (B) II only
    (C) I and II only
    (D) II and III only
    (E) I, II, and III

21. Which aspect of spell checking and thesaurus programs does the author like?

    (A) That you just have to type in the word
    (B) That the synonyms and alternative spellings are done very quickly
    (C) That the difficult mechanical aspects are performed
    (D) That you don't have to know how to spell to use them
    (E) That they can't replace teachers

22. Which of the following questions could be answered from the information in the passage?

    (A) When is it appropriate to use spell checking and thesaurus programs?
    (B) How does the program come up with recommended spellings?
    (C) What type of spelling learning experiences should students have?
    (D) Why do schools buy these word processing programs?
    (E) Which word program does the author recommend?

23. Which of the following statements could be used in place of the first sentence of the last paragraph?

    (A) It may be true that some strict teachers use a mechanical approach.
    (B) It may be true that a stringently mechanical approach is used by some teachers.
    (C) It may be true that inflexible mechanical approaches are used by some teachers.
    (D) It may be true that the mechanical approach used by some teachers is too rigorous.
    (E) It may be true that some teachers use only a mechanical approach.

24. According to this passage, what could be the result of a student's unfamiliarity with the meanings of words or synonyms?

    (A) Using a program to display the alternative spellings
    (B) Relying on mindless ways of checking spelling and finding synonyms
    (C) Strictly mechanical approaches
    (D) Using microcomputers to find synonyms for highlighted words
    (E) Being able to just type in a word

Questions 25–28 are based on this passage.

As a child he read the *Hardy Boys* series of books and was in awe of the author, Franklin Dixon. As an adult, he read a book entitled the *Ghost of the Hardy Boys*, which revealed that there was no Franklin Dixon and that ghost writers had authored the books. The authors were apparently working for a large publishing syndicate.

25. Which of the following is the likely intent of the author of this passage?

    (A) To describe a book-publishing practice
    (B) To contrast fiction and fact
    (C) To contrast childhood and adulthood
    (D) To correct the record
    (E) To dissuade children from reading the Hardy Boys books

26. Which of the following does the word *syndicate* in the last sentence most likely refer to?

    (A) A business group
    (B) An illegal enterprise
    (C) An illegal activity
    (D) A large building
    (E) A large number of books

27. What does the word *Ghost* in the title of the second mentioned book refer to?

    (A) A person who has died or was dead at the time the book was published
    (B) A person who writes books without credit
    (C) A person who influences the way a book is written
    (D) The mystical images of the mind that affect the way any author writes
    (E) A person who edits a book after the author has submitted it for publication

Practice PPST 2

28. Which of the following would NOT be an acceptable replacement for the word *awe* in the first sentence?

(A) Wonder
(B) Admiration
(C) Esteem
(D) Aplomb
(E) Respect

Questions 29–32 are based on this passage.

The Iroquois nation consisted of five main tribes—Cayuga, Mohawk, Oneida, Onondaga, and Seneca. Called the Five Nations or the League of Five Nations, these tribes occupied much of New York State. Since the tribes were arranged from east to west, the region they occupied was called the long house of the Iroquois.

The Iroquois economy was based mainly on agriculture. The main crop was corn, but they also grew pumpkins, beans, and fruit. The Iroquois used wampum (hollow beads) for money, and records were woven into wampum belts.

The Iroquoian Nation had a remarkable democratic structure, spoke a common Algonquin language, and were adept at fighting. These factors had made the Iroquois a dominant power by the early American colonial period. In the period just before the Revolutionary War, Iroquoian conquest had overcome most other Indian tribes in the northeastern United States as far west as the Mississippi River.

During the Revolutionary War, most Iroquoian tribes sided with the British. At the end of the Revolutionary War the tribes scattered, with some migrating to Canada. Only remnants of the Seneca and Onondaga tribes remained on their tribal lands.

29. Which of these statements best explains why the Iroquois were so successful at conquest?

(A) The Iroquois had the support of the British.
(B) The Iroquois had a cohesive society and were good fighters.
(C) All the other tribes in the area were too weak.
(D) There were five tribes, more than the other Indian nations.
(E) The Iroquois had developed a defensive structure called the long house.

30. Which of the following best describes the geographic location of the five Iroquoian tribes?

(A) The northeastern United States as far west as the Mississippi River
(B) Southern Canada
(C) Cayuga
(D) New York State
(E) The League of Nations

31. Which of the following best describes why the area occupied by the Iroquois was called the long house of the Iroquois?

(A) The tribes were arranged as though they occupied different sections of a long house.
(B) The Iroquois lived in structures called long houses.
(C) The close political ties among tribes made it seem that they were all living in one house.
(D) The Iroquois had expanded their original tribal lands through conquest.
(E) It took weeks to walk the trail connecting all the tribes.

32. According to the passage, which of the following best describes the economic basis for the Iroquoian economy?

    (A) Wampum
    (B) Corn
    (C) Agriculture
    (D) Conquest
    (E) Warfare

Questions 33–38 are based on this passage.

Europeans had started to devote significant resources to medicine when Louis Pasteur was born December 7, 1822. By the time he died in the fall of 1895, he had made enormous contributions to science and founded microbiology. At 32, he was named professor and dean at a French university dedicated to supporting the production of alcoholic beverages. Pasteur immediately began work on yeast and fermentation. He found that he could kill harmful bacteria in the initial brewing process by subjecting the liquid to high temperatures. This finding was extended to milk in the process called pasteurization. This work led him to the conclusion that human disease could be caused by germs. In Pasteur's time, there was a widely held belief that germs were spontaneously generated. Pasteur conducted experiments that proved germs were always introduced and never appeared spontaneously. This result was questioned by other scientists for over a decade. He proved his theory of vaccination and his theory of disease during his work with anthrax, a fatal animal disease. He vaccinated some sheep with weakened anthrax germs and left other sheep unvaccinated. Then he injected all the sheep with a potentially fatal dose of anthrax bacteria. The unvaccinated sheep died while the vaccinated sheep lived. He developed vaccines for many diseases and is best known for his vaccine for rabies. According to some accounts, the rabies vaccine was first tried on a human when a young boy, badly bitten by a rabid dog, arrived at Pasteur's laboratory. The treatment of the boy was successful.

33. What is topic of this passage?

    (A) Microbiology
    (B) Pasteur's scientific discoveries
    (C) Germs and disease
    (D) Science in France
    (E) Louis Pasteur

34. What does the process of pasteurization involve?

    (A) Inoculating
    (B) Experimenting
    (C) Hydrating
    (D) Heating
    (E) Fermenting

35. Which of the following statements could most reasonably be inferred from this passage?

    (A) The myth of spontaneous generation was dispelled immediately following Pasteur's experiments on the subject.
    (B) The pasteurization of milk can aid in the treatment of anthrax.
    (C) Pasteur's discoveries were mainly luck.
    (D) Even scientists don't think scientifically all the time.
    (E) Injecting sheep with fatal doses of anthrax is one way of vaccinating them.

Practice PPST 2

36. Which of the following statements can be implied from this passage?

   (A) That germs do not develop spontaneously was already a widely accepted premise when Pasteur began his scientific work.
   (B) Scientists in European countries had made significant progress on the link between germs and disease when Pasteur was born.
   (C) Europe was ready for scientific research on germs when Pasteur conducted his experiments.
   (D) Most of Pasteur's work was the replication of other work done by French scientists.
   (E) The theory that germs could cause human disease was not yet accepted at the time of Pasteur's death.

37. Which of the following choices best characterizes the reason for Pasteur's early work?

   (A) To cure humans
   (B) To cure animals
   (C) To help the French economy
   (D) To study germs
   (E) To be a professor

38. According to this passage, the rabies vaccine

   (A) was developed after Pasteur had watched a young boy bitten by a rabid dog.
   (B) was developed from the blood of a rabid dog, which had bitten a young boy.
   (C) was developed from the blood of a young boy bitten by a rabid dog.
   (D) was developed in addition to the vaccines for other diseases.
   (E) was developed in his laboratory where a young boy had died of the disease.

Questions 39 and 40 are based on this passage.

I believe that there is extraterrestrial life—probably in some other galaxy. It is particularly human to believe that our solar system is the only one that can support intelligent life. But our solar system is only an infinitesimal dot in the infinity of the cosmos and it is just not believable that there is not life out there—somewhere.

39. What is the author of this passage proposing?

   (A) That there is other life in the universe
   (B) That there is no life on earth
   (C) That humans live on other planets
   (D) That the sun is a very small star
   (E) That we should explore other galaxies

40. The words *infinitesimal* and *infinite* are best characterized by which pair of words below?

   (A) Small and large
   (B) Very small and very large
   (C) Very small and limitless
   (D) Large and limitless
   (E) Small and very large

Writing Test 2

Take this test in a realistic, timed setting. You should not take this practice test until you have completed practice PPST 1.

The test rules allow exactly 30 minutes for this test.

Keep the time limit in mind as you work. Answer the easier questions first. Be sure you answer all the questions. There is no penalty for guessing. You may write on the test booklet and mark up the questions.

Each question or statement has five answer choices. Exactly one of these choices is correct. Mark your choice on the answer sheet provided for this test.

Your score is based on the spaces you fill in on the answer sheet. Make sure that you mark your answer on the answer sheet in the correct space next to the correct question number.

When instructed, turn the page and begin.

WRITING

38 ITEMS, 30 MINUTES

USAGE

You will read sentences with four parts underlined and lettered. Determine whether one of the underlined parts contains grammatical, word use, or punctuation errors. If so, mark the letter of that part on your answer sheet. If there are no errors, mark (E).

1. A professional golfer told the <u>new golfer</u>
    (A)
   that <u>professional instruction</u> or more
    (B)
   practice <u>improve</u> most golfers' <u>scores.</u>
    (C)   (D)
   <u>No error.</u>
    (E)

2. It was <u>difficult for</u> the farmer
    (A)
   <u>to comprehend</u> the unhappiness he
    (B)
   <u>encountered among</u> so many of the rich
    (C)
   <u>produce buyers</u> in the city. <u>No error.</u>
    (D)   (E)

3. No goal is <u>more noble</u>—no feat more
    (A)
   <u>revealing</u>—<u>as the</u> exploration <u>of space</u>.
    (B)   (C)   (D)
   <u>No error.</u>
    (E)

4. The soccer player's <u>slight</u> strain from the
    (A)
   <u>shot</u> on goal led to a <u>pulled</u> muscle,
    (B)   (C)
   <u>resulted</u> in the player's removal from the
    (D)
   game. <u>No error.</u>
    (E)

5. The <u>young college graduate</u> had no family
    (A)
   to help her but <u>she was fortunate</u> to get a
    (B)
   job with a <u>promising school district</u>
    (C)
   <u>superintendent</u> and <u>eventually became a</u>
    (D)   (E)
   <u>superintendent</u> herself. <u>No error.</u>
    (D)   (E)

Practice PPST 2: Paper-Based Format **239**

6. He <u>was concerned</u> about crossing the
          (A)

  bridge, <u>but the officer</u> said <u>that it</u> was
             (B)   (C)

  <u>all right</u> to cross. <u>No error.</u>
   (D)   (E)

7. As the students <u>prepared to take</u> the
             (A)

  test, they <u>came to realize</u> that it was not
           (B)

  only what they knew <u>and also</u> how well
             (C)

  they <u>knew how to</u> take tests. <u>No error.</u>
     (D)   (E)

8. As <u>many</u> as a ton of bananas may have
    (A)

  <u>spoiled</u> when the <u>ship</u> was <u>stuck</u> in the
   (B)   (C)   (D)

  Panama Canal. <u>No error.</u>
            (E)

9. Employment agencies <u>often place</u>
             (A)

  newspaper advertisements <u>when no</u>
              (B)

  jobs <u>exist</u> to get the names of <u>potential</u>
     (C)   (D)

  employees on file. <u>No error.</u>
           (E)

10. Visitors <u>to New York can</u> expect
          (A)

  <u>to encounter people</u>, noise, and
          (B)

  <u>finding themselves in traffic</u> just
         (C)

  <u>about any day of the</u> week. <u>No error,</u>
      (D)   (E)

11. It <u>was obvious</u> to Kim that neither
      (A)

  her family <u>or her friends</u> could
         (B)

  <u>understand why</u> the study <u>of science was</u>
    (C)   (D)

  so important to her. <u>No error.</u>
            (E)

12. While <u>past safaris</u> had entered the jungle
       (A)

  to hunt <u>elephants with rifles</u>, this safari
         (B)

  had only a <u>single armed</u> guard to protect
         (C)

  <u>the tourists as</u> they took photographs.
    (D)

  <u>No errors.</u>
   (E)

13. <u>Buddhism is an</u> interesting <u>religion</u>
    (A)   (B)

    because Confucius <u>was born</u> in India,
                      (C)

    but the religion never <u>gained lasting</u>
                           (D)

    popularity there. <u>No error</u>.
                      (E)

14. John Dewey's <u>progressive</u> philosophy
                 (A)

    <u>influenced</u> thousands of teachers;
    (B)

    however, Dewey was often <u>displeased</u>
                             (C)

    with <u>there</u> teaching methods. <u>No error</u>.
         (D)   (E)

15. <u>While only</u> in the school for <u>a few weeks</u>,
    (A)   (B)

    the gym teacher <u>was starting</u> to
                    (C)

    <u>felt comfortable</u> with the principal.
    (D)

    <u>No error</u>.
    (E)

16. The <u>carnival</u>, which <u>featured</u> a wild
        (A)   (B)

    animal act was due to <u>arrive</u> in town
              (C)   (D)

    next week. <u>No error</u>.
               (E)

17. <u>While</u> the bus <u>driver</u> <u>waited</u>, the motor
    (A)   (B)   (C)

    runs and uses <u>expensive</u> gasoline. <u>No error</u>.
                  (D)   (E)

18. <u>Having needed</u> to eat <u>and earn</u> money,
    (A)   (B)

    the college <u>graduate decided</u> it was <u>time to</u>
                (C)   (D)

    look for a job. <u>No error</u>.
                    (E)

19. The salesman <u>spent the day</u> calling
                 (A)

    contacts <u>with which</u> he had <u>previously had</u>
             (B)   (C)

    <u>business dealings</u>. <u>No error</u>.
    (D)   (E)

20. <u>Thomas, the only player</u> to go
    (A)

    <u>undefeated through</u> the preliminary round,
    (B)

    <u>giving him</u> the highest <u>position for the</u>
    (C)   (D)

    tournament final. <u>No error</u>.
                      (E)

21. Because his <u>father was a wonderful</u>
                (A)

    student, Jim's <u>teachers expected</u> him
                   (B)

    <u>to be a good</u> student just as his sister
    (C)

    Beth <u>did</u>. <u>No error</u>.
         (D)   (E)

SENTENCE CORRECTION

You will read sentences with some or all of the sentence underlined, followed by five answer choices. The first answer choice repeats the underlined portion and the other four present possible replacements. Select the answer choice that best represents standard English without altering the meaning of the original sentence. Mark that letter on the answer sheet.

22. The dean was famous for delivering grand sounding <u>but otherwise unintelligible speeches.</u>

    (A) but otherwise unintelligible speeches.
    (B) but in every other way speeches that could not be intelligible.
    (C) but speeches which were not that intelligent.
    (D) but otherwise speeches that could be understood.
    (E) but speeches that could be unintelligible.

23. <u>The hiker grew tired greater</u> as the day wore on.

    (A) The hiker grew tired greater
    (B) The hiker grew tired more
    (C) The hiker grew greater tired
    (D) The hiker's tired grew greater
    (E) The hiker grew more tired

24. The man knew that <u>to solve the problem now can be easier</u> than putting it off for another day.

    (A) to solve the problem now can be easier
    (B) to solve the problem now is easier
    (C) to solve the problem now can be less difficult
    (D) solving the problem now can be easier
    (E) to try to solve the problem now

25. Lee's <u>mother and father insists that</u> he call if he is going to be out after 8:00 P.M.

    (A) mother and father insists that
    (B) mother and father insist that
    (C) mother and father insists
    (D) mother and father that insist
    (E) mother and father that insists

26. The weather forecaster said that people living near the shore should be prepared <u>in the event that</u> the storm headed for land.

    (A) in the event that
    (B) if the event happened and
    (C) the event
    (D) if
    (E) and

27. After years of observation, the soccer coach concluded that women soccer players were more aggressive than <u>men who played soccer.</u>

    (A) men who played soccer.
    (B) men soccer players.
    (C) soccer playing men.
    (D) those men who played soccer.
    (E) men.

28. The stockbroker advised her client to sell the stock before it <u>could no longer be popular.</u>

    (A) could no longer be popular.
    (B) could be popular no longer.
    (C) may be popular no longer.
    (D) could become unpopular.
    (E) was no longer popular.

29. Bringing in an outside consultant usually means that it will take too long for the consultant to understand what's going on, <u>the functioning of the office will be impaired</u> and, because a new person has been introduced into the company, it will create dissension.

    (A) the functioning of the office will be impaired
    (B) the impairment of office functioning will follow
    (C) caused impairment in office functioning
    (D) office functioning impairment will occur
    (E) it will impair the functioning of the office

30. The primary election was very <u>important because winning could give the candidate a much more</u> clearer mandate.

    (A) important because winning could give the candidate a much more
    (B) important because winning there could give the candidate a much more
    (C) important because a win there could give the candidate a
    (D) important because winning could give the candidate a
    (E) important because a loss there would be devastating

31. She had become a doctor with the noble purpose of saving lives; however, <u>the process of applying for medical benefits and the responsibilities for managing the office had become her primary and overriding concern.</u>

    (A) the process of applying for medical benefits and the responsibilities for managing the office had become her primary and overriding concern.
    (B) applying for medical benefits and managing the office had become her main concerns.
    (C) applying for medical benefits, and the responsibilities for managing the office had become her primary and overriding concern.
    (D) applying for medical benefits and office work had become her main concern.
    (E) she soon found out that being a doctor was not noble.

32. Among the most popular television programs are those that critics classify <u>is soap operas.</u>

    (A) is soap operas.
    (B) are soap operas.
    (C) as soap operas.
    (D) in soap operas.
    (E) with soap operas.

33. If a person <u>has the ability in music</u>, then he should try to develop this ability by taking music lessons.

    (A) has the ability in music
    (B) has musical ability
    (C) can play an instrument
    (D) is a talented musician
    (E) is interested in music

34. <u>The players on the national team were supposed by some of their countrymen to have almost superhuman ability.</u>

    (A) The players on the national team were supposed by some of their countrymen to have almost superhuman ability.
    (B) The players on the national team had superhuman ability, according to some of their countrymen.
    (C) The players in the national team were better at the sport than most of their countryman.
    (D) Suppose the players on the national team were not good enough, thought some of their countrymen.
    (E) Some of their countrymen thought that the players on the national team had almost superhuman ability.

35. Mr. Littler had managed to stay popular with the students, even though any serious breach of discipline <u>inevitably brought</u> them to his office.

    (A) inevitably brought
    (B) brought inevitably
    (C) was inevitable
    (D) considerably brought
    (E) inevitably bring

36. No matter how much she tried, she could never convince her father <u>that he should stop</u> smoking cigarettes.

    (A) that he should stop
    (B) he should stop
    (C) should stop
    (D) to stop
    (E) about stopping

37. The main error <u>of superhighway driving is to forget</u> what the speedometer reads.

    (A) of superhighway driving is to forget
    (B) driving is to forget on superhighways
    (C) is speeding on superhighways
    (D) people make when they drive on superhighways is to forget
    (E) is forgetting on superhighways to drive

38. People who set fires are frequently captured, <u>and it is common</u> at the scene of the crime.

    (A) and it is common
    (B) and common
    (C) in common at the
    (D) and
    (E) commonly

Essay Test 2

Take this test in a realistic, timed setting. You should not take this practice test until you have completed practice PPST 1.

Write an essay on the topic found on the next page. Write on this topic only. An essay written on another topic, no matter how well done, will receive a 0. You have 30 minutes to complete the essay.

Use the space provided to briefly outline your essay and to organize your thoughts before you begin to write. Use this opportunity to demonstrate how well you can write but be sure to write about the topic.

Write your essay on the lined paper provided. Write legibly and do not skip any lines. Your entire essay must fit on these pages.

Once the test is complete, ask an English professor or English teacher to evaluate your essay holistically using the rating scale on page 218.

When instructed, begin.

ESSAY

You have 30 minutes to complete this essay question. Use the lined pages to write a brief essay based on this topic.

A college student who received a poor grade in a class should be able to have any record of the class and the grade removed from a transcript.

Describe the extent to which you agree or disagree with this statement. Support your response with specific details, examples, and explanations. Write a brief outline here.

Mathematics Test 2

Take this test in a realistic, timed setting. You should not take this practice test until you have completed practice PPST 1.

The test rules allow you exactly 60 minutes for this test.

Keep the time limit in mind as you work. Answer the easier items first. Be sure you answer all the items. There is no penalty for guessing. You may write on the test booklet and mark up the items.

Each item has five answer choices. Exactly one of these choices is correct. Mark your choice on the answer sheet provided for this test.

Your score is based on the spaces you fill in on the answer sheet. Make sure that you mark your answer in the correct space next to the correct item number.

When instructed, turn the page and begin.

MATHEMATICS

40 ITEMS, 60 MINUTES

Each item below includes five answer choices. Select the best choice for each item and mark that letter on the answer sheet.

1. A representative of the magazine advertising department is responsible for 9 to 10 full-page ads, 12 to 14 half-page ads, and 15 to 20 quarter-page ads per issue. The minimum and maximum numbers of ads that each representative is responsible for are

   (A) 9 and 20.
   (B) 9 and 15.
   (C) 15 and 20.
   (D) 36 and 44.
   (E) 10 and 20.

2. 7.17 is between

   (A) 7.0 and 7.2.
   (B) 7.02 and 7.10.
   (C) 7.5 and 7.9.
   (D) 7.00 and 7.04.
   (E) 7.012 and 7.102.

3. Which of the following expresses the relationship between x and y shown in the table?

x	y
0	1
3	7
6	13
7	15
9	19

   (A) $y = 3x - 2$
   (B) $y = 2x + 1$
   (C) $y = x + 3$
   (D) $y = 2x - 2$
   (E) $y = 2x + 3$

4. It took Liz 12 hours to travel by train from New York to North Carolina at an average speed of 55 miles per hour. On the return trip from North Carolina to New York, Liz traveled by bus and averaged 45 miles per hour. How many hours did the return trip take?

   (A) $13\frac{2}{3}$
   (B) 14
   (C) $14\frac{2}{3}$
   (D) 15
   (E) 16

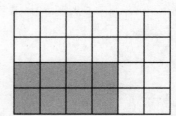

5. In the figure, what percent of the region is shaded?

   (A) $66\frac{2}{3}\%$
   (B) 50%
   (C) 25%
   (D) 60%
   (E) $33\frac{1}{3}\%$

6. 5×10^5 is equal to

   (A) 250
   (B) one-half million
   (C) 5 million
   (D) 50,000
   (E) 0.00005

7. Which of the following could be the length of a couch?

   (A) 75 cm
   (B) 4 meters
   (C) 150 mm
   (D) 1.2 decimeters
   (E) 0.5 kilometers

8. *C* is 5 more than half of *B*. Which of the following expressions states this relationship?

   (A) $C + 5 = B/2$
   (B) $C = \frac{1}{2} B + 5$
   (C) $C + 5 = 2B$
   (D) $C + 5 > B/2$
   (E) $C + 5 < B/2$

9. If your commission for this month is 15% of $500, which of the following commissions is more than yours?

   (A) 20% of $380
   (B) 10% of $500
   (C) 1% of $1,000
   (D) 10% of $750
   (E) 25% of $280

10. Which of these figures has a perimeter measure different from the others?

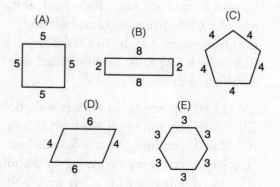

Time	8 A.M.	9 A.M.	10 A.M.	11 A.M.	12 NOON
Temp	50°	55°	60°	60°	70°
Time	1 P.M.	2 P.M.	3 P.M.	4 P.M.	
Temp	75°	80°	70°	65°	
Time	5 P.M.	6 P.M.	7 P.M.	8 P.M.	
Temp	55°	50°	50°	45°	

11. The above table shows the temperature tracked for a 12-hour period of time. Which graph best illustrates this information?

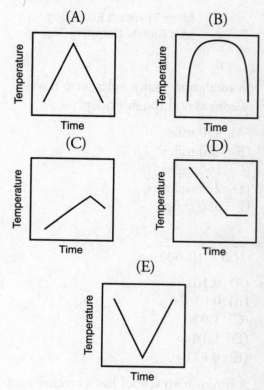

12. A rectangular garden measures 23 feet by 63 feet. What is the greatest number of nonoverlapping 5-foot square plots that can be ruled off in this garden?

   (A) 48
   (B) 57
   (C) 58
   (D) 289
   (E) 290

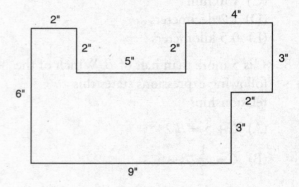

Miles Traveled Each Day
on a Family Camping Trip

13. In total, how many miles were traveled Wednesday through Friday?

   (A) 450 miles
   (B) 400 miles
   (C) 150 miles
   (D) 225 miles
   (E) 350 miles

14. $\dfrac{1}{100} + \dfrac{1}{10,000} =$

   (A) 0.101
   (B) 0.0101
   (C) 1.01
   (D) 1.10
   (E) 0.011

15. A junior high school has a teacher-student ratio of 1 to 15. If there are 43 teachers, how many students are there?

   (A) 645
   (B) 430
   (C) 215
   (D) 630
   (E) 600

Gallons Remaining

16. On the gauge, the arrow points to

   (A) $1\dfrac{1}{2}$

   (B) $1\dfrac{3}{5}$

   (C) 1.5

   (D) $1\dfrac{3}{4}$

   (E) 1.75

17. A floor plan is drawn with a scale of 5 feet per inch. If the diagram represents the floor plan, what is the actual perimeter of the house?

   (A) 38 in
   (B) 38 ft
   (C) 200 ft
   (D) $7\dfrac{2}{5}$ ft
   (E) 190 ft

18. Mary must make tablecloths for 12 banquet tables. She needs a piece of cloth 5 ft. by 8 ft. for each tablecloth. Each cloth must be made from the same bolt and cannot be sewn. Of the five bolts listed here, which one must be eliminated due to insufficient material?

   (A) 25 yd remaining on an 8-ft wide bolt
   (B) 33 yd remaining on a 6-ft wide bolt
   (C) 25 yd remaining on a 5-ft wide bolt
   (D) 20 yd remaining on an 8-ft wide bolt
   (E) 36 yd remaining on a 7-ft wide bolt

19. Blaire bought a pair of shoes at 25 percent off the regular price of $40.00. She had a coupon, which saved her an additional 15 percent off the sale price. What price did she pay for the shoes?

    (A) $24.00
    (B) $15.00
    (C) $25.50
    (D) $11.25
    (E) $27.50

20. Points *L, M, N,* and *O* are on the same line. Which could NOT be values for *LM* and *NO*?

    (A) *LM* = 15; *NO* = 10
    (B) *LM* = 12; *NO* = 9
    (C) *LM* = 3; *NO* = 2
    (D) *LM* = 0.75; *NO* = 0.5
    (E) *LM* = 1; *NO* = $\frac{2}{3}$

21. Store A has DVDs in packs of 3 for $15.60. Store B sells DVDs for $6.00 each. How much is saved (if any) on each DVD if you buy six DVDs from Store A instead of 6 DVDs from Store B?

    (A) $3.40
    (B) $0.80
    (C) $1.80
    (D) $2.40
    (E) There is no saving.

22. Two different whole numbers are multiplied. Which of the following could not result?

    (A) 0
    (B) 1
    (C) 7
    (D) 19
    (E) 319

23. Which of the following does not have the same value as the others?

    (A) (0.9 + 0.2) × 3.2
    (B) (0.9 × 3.2) + (0.2 × 3.2)
    (C) 0.9 + (0.2 × 3.2)
    (D) 3.2 × (0.2 + 0.9)
    (E) 3.2 × (1.1)

24. In the figures, if the first cube represents a weight of 100 grams, which of the other cubes most likely represents 25 grams?

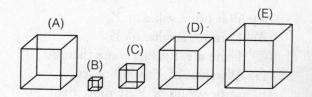

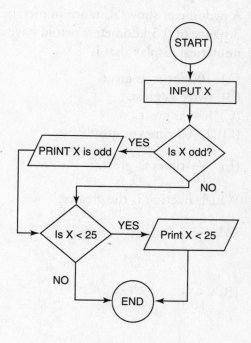

25. One of these numbers was put through the program represented by the flowchart, and nothing was printed. Which number was it?

    (A) 25
    (B) 18
    (C) 13
    (D) 38
    (E) 27

26. A calculator displays a multiple-digit whole number ending in 0. All the following statements must be true about the number EXCEPT:

(A) It is an even number.
(B) It is a multiple of 5.
(C) It is a power of 10.
(D) It is a multiple of 10.
(E) It is the sum of two odd numbers.

27. Some values of Y are more than 50. Which of the following could NOT be true?

(A) 60 is not a value of Y.
(B) 45 is not a value of Y.
(C) There are Y values more than 50.
(D) All values of Y are 50 or less.
(E) Some values of Y are more than 50.

28. A pedometer shows distance in meters. A distance of 0.5 kilometers would have a numerical display that is

(A) 100 times as great.
(B) twice as great.
(C) half as great.
(D) 1,000 times as great.
(E) $\frac{1}{10}$ times as great.

29. Which fraction is the greatest?

(A) $\frac{5}{4}$

(B) $\frac{99}{100}$

(C) $\frac{25}{24}$

(D) $\frac{12}{13}$

(E) $\frac{17}{16}$

30. Two dice are rolled. What is the probability that the sum of the numbers is even?

(A) $\frac{1}{2}$

(B) $\frac{16}{36}$

(C) $\frac{3}{4}$

(D) $\frac{1}{12}$

(E) $\frac{5}{6}$

31. If the product of P and 6 is R, then the product of P and 3 is

(A) $2R$.
(B) $R/2$.
(C) $\frac{1}{2}P$.
(D) $2P$.
(E) $P/6$.

32. The multiplication and division buttons on a calculator are reversed. A person presses

$\boxed{\div}\,\boxed{5}\,\boxed{=}$ and the calculator displays 625.

What answer should have been displayed?

(A) 125
(B) 625
(C) 25
(D) 50
(E) 250

33. If V, l, w, and h are positive numbers and $V = l \times w \times h$, then $l =$

    (A) $\frac{1}{3}\ whv.$

    (B) $\frac{v}{hw}.$

    (C) $\frac{lw}{v}.$

    (D) $vlw.$

    (E) $w(v + h).$

34. If 0.00005 divided by $X = 0.005$, then $X =$

    (A) 0.1.
    (B) 0.01.
    (C) 0.001.
    (D) 0.0001.
    (E) 0.00001.

35. The product of two numbers is 900. One number is tripled. In order for the product to remain the same, the other number must be

    (A) multiplied by 3.

    (B) divided by $\frac{1}{3}$.

    (C) multiplied by $\frac{1}{3}$.

    (D) subtracted from 900.
    (E) quadrupled.

36. Which of the following could be the face of the cross section of a cylinder?

    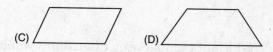

    (A)   (B)   (C)   (D)

    (E)

    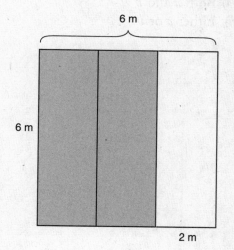

37. What is the area of the shaded portion of the figure?

    (A) 12 m²
    (B) 22 m²
    (C) 20 m²
    (D) 36 m²
    (E) 24 m²

38. Estimate the answer for $124 \times \frac{49}{24}$.

    (A) 200
    (B) 250
    (C) 325
    (D) 500
    (E) 10

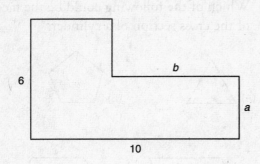

40. Deena finished the school run in 52.8 seconds. Lisa's time was 1.3 seconds faster. What was Lisa's time?

    (A) 51.5 seconds
    (B) 54.1 seconds
    (C) 53.11 seconds
    (D) 65.8 seconds
    (E) 52.93 seconds

39. Which of the following dimensions would be needed to find the area of the figure?

    (A) *a* only
    (B) *b* only
    (C) Neither *a* nor *b*
    (D) Both *a* and *b*
    (E) Either *a* or *b*

Answers

Reading

1. (C)	8. (B)	15. (B)	22. (A)	29. (B)	36. (C)
2. (D)	9. (A)	16. (C)	23. (E)	30. (D)	37. (C)
3. (A)	10. (D)	17. (E)	24. (B)	31. (A)	38. (D)
4. (E)	11. (C)	18. (D)	25. (D)	32. (C)	39. (A)
5. (D)	12. (E)	19. (B)	26. (A)	33. (B)	40. (C)
6. (B)	13. (C)	20. (B)	27. (B)	34. (D)	
7. (B)	14. (B)	21. (C)	28. (D)	35. (D)	

Writing

USAGE

1. (C)	6. (E)	11. (B)	16. (C)	21. (D)
2. (E)	7. (C)	12. (B)	17. (C)	
3. (C)	8. (A)	13. (E)	18. (A)	
4. (D)	9. (E)	14. (D)	19. (B)	
5. (C)	10. (C)	15. (D)	20. (C)	

SENTENCE CORRECTION

22. (A)	26. (D)	30. (D)	34. (E)	38. (E)
23. (E)	27. (B)	31. (B)	35. (A)	
24. (D)	28. (E)	32. (C)	36. (D)	
25. (B)	29. (E)	33. (B)	37. (D)	

Mathematics

1. (D)	8. (B)	15. (A)	22. (B)	29. (A)	36. (E)
2. (A)	9. (A)	16. (B)	23. (C)	30. (A)	37. (E)
3. (B)	10. (E)	17. (E)	24. (C)	31. (B)	38. (B)
4. (C)	11. (A)	18. (C)	25. (D)	32. (C)	39. (D)
5. (E)	12. (A)	19. (C)	26. (C)	33. (B)	40. (A)
6. (B)	13. (A)	20. (B)	27. (D)	34. (B)	
7. (B)	14. (B)	21. (B)	28. (D)	35. (C)	

Explained Answers

Reading

1. **(C)** This choice paraphrases the last sentence of the passage.

2. **(D)** The passage identifies both the moon's cycle and the earth's revolution as factors contributing to the development of the current calendar.

3. **(A)** The author explains the difference with the description and an example.

4. **(E)** The passage is about youth and constantly refers to what they do not know about AIDS.

5. **(D)** This choice paraphrases the third sentence in the paragraph.

6. **(B)** The passage uses many synonyms of this word to describe young people's knowledge of AIDS.

7. **(B)** This choice paraphrases the first sentence in the passage.

8. **(B)** The author says, and then gives an example to show, that men are discriminated against just as much as women.

9. **(A)** Drafted, in the sense used here, means to be inducted into the armed forces against one's will.

10. **(D)** *Alice in Wonderland*, a fanciful story about a young girl's adventures underground, has underlying figurative meanings.

11. **(C)** The content reveals that marginal means the area of a page to the left and right of the text.

12. **(E)** Music is more than notes and varies with the mood of the performer.

13. **(C)** The passage states that rockets refer to ordnance or weapons used by the British.

14. **(B)** *Ravished* is the best choice and describes what happens when a town is sacked.

15. **(B)** The last sentence of the first paragraph says that most Americans remember Perry, but not where he served.

16. **(C)** Francis Scott Key must have been able to distribute his "Star Spangled Banner" in America, so he must have been released by or escaped from the British.

17. **(E)** The second sentence in the paragraph identifies the United States as the aggressor.

18. **(D)** The author signals this main point in the first sentence of the passage.

19. **(B)** The next to the last sentence in the first paragraph indicates that these programs do not teach about spelling or word meanings.

20. **(B)** The type of computer used and teaching methods are not mentioned in the passage.

21. **(C)** The fourth sentence in the first paragraph explains that the author likes having a program to perform the mechanical aspects.

22. **(A)** This question can be answered from information in the passage's last paragraph.

23. **(E)** This choice paraphrases the first sentence in the last paragraph.

24. **(B)** This information is found in the first sentence of the first paragraph.

25. **(D)** The author wants to share what he or she learned about the Hardy Boys books.

26. **(A)** The word *syndicate* can have many meanings. The context reveals that this word *syndicate* means a business group.

27. **(B)** A ghost writer is someone who writes books but does not receive credit.

28. **(D)** Every other choice is an acceptable replacement for the word *awe*.

29. **(B)** The second sentence in the third paragraph supports this choice.

30. **(D)** This information is contained in the first sentence of the first paragraph.

31. **(A)** This choice is supported by the last sentence in the first paragraph.

32. **(C)** The first sentence of the second paragraph provides this information.

33. **(B)** This paragraph is about Pasteur's scientific discoveries and not about Pasteur the person.

34. **(D)** This answer can be found in lines 9–14 of the passage.

35. **(D)** The passage contains examples of scientists who opposed Pasteur's theories even though Pasteur had proven his theories scientifically.

36. **(C)** The first sentence indicates that Europeans had already started to devote resources to medicine when Pasteur was born, and theories about germs existed when Pasteur began his work.

37. **(C)** The passage mentions that his early work was at a university dedicated to supporting an important product of the French economy.

38. **(D)** The third from last sentence in the passage mentions that Pasteur developed vaccines for many diseases.

39. **(A)** This choice paraphrases the first sentence in the paragraph.

40. **(C)** *Infinitesimal* means very small, and *infinite* means without limit.

Writing

USAGE

1. **(C)** This singular verb should end in *s*.

2. **(E)** This sentence contains no errors.

3. **(C)** The phrase *as the* should be replaced by the word *than*.

4. **(D)** *Resulted* should be replaced by *resulting*.

5. **(C)** It is not possible to tell whether the school district or the superintendent is promising.

6. **(E)** This sentence contains no errors.

7. **(C)** Replace *and also* with *but also*.

8. **(A)** Replace *many* with *much*.

9. **(E)** This sentence contains no errors.

10. **(C)** Remove *finding themselves in* to maintain the parallel development of this sentence.

11. **(B)** Replace *or* with *nor.*

12. **(B)** This phrase makes it seem that elephants are armed with rifles.

13. **(E)** This sentence contains no errors.

14. **(D)** Replace *there* with *their*.

15. **(D)** Replace *felt* with *feel*.

16. **(C)** A comma is missing.

17. **(C)** Replace *waited* with *waits*.

18. **(A)** Replace *having needed* with *needing*.

19. **(B)** Replace *which* with *whom*.

20. **(C)** Replace *giving him* with *earned* or *had*.

21. **(D)** Replace *did* with *was*.

SENTENCE CORRECTION

22. **(A)** The underlined portion is acceptable as written.

23. **(E)** Use this replacement for the awkward wording in the original sentence.

24. **(D)** Use this replacement for the awkward wording in the original sentence.

25. **(B)** The plural verb does not end in *s*.

26. **(D)** Use the word *if* in place of the wordy underlined phrase.

27. **(B)** This wording is clearer and more understandable than the original wording in the sentence.

28. **(E)** The correct verb is *was*, rather than *could . . . be*.

29. **(E)** Use this replacement to maintain the parallel structure of the sentence.

30. **(D)** The words *much more* in the original sentence are not needed. Choice (C) is not correct because it unnecessarily changes the sentence.

31. **(B)** Use this more direct wording to replace the underlined portion of the sentence.

32. **(C)** Replace *is* with *as*.

33. **(B)** Use this more direct wording to replace the underlined portion of the sentence.

34. **(E)** Use this more direct wording to replace the underlined portion of the sentence.

35. **(A)** The underlined portion of the sentence is acceptable as written.

36. **(D)** *To stop* is more effective and compact than the original underlined wording.

37. **(D)** While this choice is longer than the underlined wording, it is much easier to understand.

38. **(E)** Use *commonly* to replace the awkward and wordy *and it is common.*

ESSAY

Ask an English professor or teacher to rate your essay using the scale on page 218.

Mathematics

1. **(D)** Add the three smaller numbers and then the three larger numbers to find this answer.

2. **(A)** 7.1_ is always between 7.0 and 7.2

3. **(B)** Multiply x by 2 and then add 1 to find y.

4. **(C)** Multiply 12 times $55 = 660$ to find the total length of the trip. Divide 660 by $45 = 14.66...$ to find the number of hours for the return trip.

5. **(E)** One-third or $33\frac{1}{3}$% of the region is shaded.

6. **(B)** $10^5 \times 100,000$, so $5 \times 100,000 = 500,000$ or $\frac{1}{2}$ million.

7. **(B)** Four meters, or about 12 feet, is the only plausible answer.

8. **(B)** This equation correctly expresses the relationship.

9. **(A)** $0.15 \times 500 = 75$; $0.20 \times 380 = 76$.

10. **(E)** All the other figures have a perimeter of 20 except this hexagon, which has a perimeter of 18.

11. **(A)** This graph best represents the steady movement up and then down of the temperatures.

12. **(A)** $5\overline{)23}$ = 4 R 3; $5\overline{)63}$ = 12 R 3; 4 × 12 = 48.

13. **(A)** Add 225, 75, and 150 to find the answer.

14. **(B)** This is the correct decimal representation for the sum of the fractions.

15. **(A)** Write the proportion $\frac{1}{15} = \frac{43}{x}$, so $x = 645$.

16. **(B)** The gauge is marked in fifths of a gallon.

17. **(E)** Add the perimeters to find the total of 38 inches; 5 × 38 = 190.

18. **(C)** Choice (C) yields a piece 75 feet by 5 feet. Mary needs a piece 96 feet by 5 feet.

19. **(C)** 0.25 × $40 = $10; $40 − $10 = $30; 0.15 × $30 = $4.50; $30 − $4.50 = $25.50.

20. **(B)** The ratio of *LM* to *NO* is 3 : 2. Choice B does not reflect this ratio.

21. **(B)** Three tapes cost $15.60 at Store A and $18.00 at Store B. The saving for all three tapes is $2.40. The saving on one tape is $0.80.

22. **(B)** The product of two whole numbers is 1 only if both whole numbers are 1.

23. **(C)** The value of each of the other choices is 3.52.

24. **(C)** This choice is closest to one-quarter of the first cube.

25. **(D)** The flowchart prints numbers that are odd or less than 25.

26. **(C)** Powers of 10 are 1, 10, 100, 1000. The calculator could be displaying 20, which is not a power of 10.

27. **(D)** If some of the values of *Y* are more than 50, then all of the values of *Y* could not be less than 50.

28. **(D)** The display would show 500, which is 1,000 times (0.5).

29. **(A)** $\frac{5}{4}$ is greater than 1, so (B) and (D) cannot be correct. Cross multiply to see that $\frac{5}{4}$ is greater than choices (C) and (E).

30. **(A)** There are 36 possible outcomes. Half of these outcomes are even and half are odd.

31. **(B)** $6 \cdot P = R$. Divide both sides by 2 to get $3 \cdot P = R/2$.

32. **(C)** Every time the $=$ key is pressed, the calculator multiplies: $125 \times 5 = 625$, which correlates to $125 \div 5 = 25$, the correct answer.

33. **(B)** $V = l \times w \times h$. Divide both sides by $w \times h$ to get $V/w \times h = 1$.

34. **(B)** Dividing by 0.01 is the same as multiplying by 100.

35. **(C)** Multiplying by $\frac{1}{3}$ is the same as dividing by 3.

36. **(E)** Imagine a cylinder with a height equal to its diameter. The vertical cross section of this cylinder is a square.

37. **(E)** The area of the figure is 36 square meters. Two-thirds of the figure is shaded, so $\frac{2}{3} \times 36 = 24$.

38. **(B)** Use 125×2 to estimate. The answer is about 250.

39. **(D)** Both dimensions are needed to find the area of the right-hand rectangle in the figure.

40. **(A)** Faster times are represented by smaller numbers. Subtract 52.8–1.3 to find Lisa's time.

PART IV

PRINCIPLES OF LEARNING
AND TEACHING

CHAPTER 8 Principles of Learning and Teaching Review

TEST INFO BOX

Four Case Histories

3 Short-Answer Questions each   **12 Short-Answer Questions**

Two groups of 12 Multiple-Choice Questions   **24 Multiple-Choice Questions**

Two hours to complete all the questions

You can take the PLT in four areas.

Early Childhood (0521)	**Grades K–6 (0522)**
Grades 5–9 (0523)	**Grades 7–12 (0524)**

The PLT is based on Core Standards 2 through 10 of the Interstate New Teacher Assessment and Support Consortium (INTASC). You can review the INTASC Standards with explanations at *www.ccsso.org/content/pdfs/corestrd.pdf*.

How to Prepare for the PLT

Follow these steps to prepare for the PLT.

Chapter 8: Principles of Learning and Teaching Review

❏ Read the indicated parts of the review.

Chapter 9: Principles of Learning and Teaching Test Strategy and Practice

❏ Review the PLT Test-Taking Strategies on pages 301–303 in Chapter 9.
❏ Read the PLT Practice Scenario on page 303 in Chapter 9.

❏ Complete the PLT Practice Constructed-Response Questions on page 305 in Chapter 9.

❏ Review the Constructed-Response Answers on page 310 in Chapter 9.

❏ Complete the PLT Practice Multiple-Choice Questions on page 317 in Chapter 9.

❏ Review the Multiple-Choice Explained Answers on page 323.

Chapter 10: Principles of Learning and Teaching Practice Test

❏ Complete the PLT Practice Test on page 345.

❏ Review the PLT Practice Test Explained Responses and Answers on page 360.

USING THIS CHAPTER

This chapter helps you review for the Principles of Learning and Teaching Test (PLT).

❏ Read the indicated parts of the review.

REVIEW CHECKLIST

Organizing Content Knowledge for Student Learning

❏ Human Development, page 266
❏ Diversity, page 271

Creating an Environment for Student Learning

❏ Objectives, page 276
❏ Taxonomy of Objectives, page 276
❏ Choosing and Modifying Objectives, page 277
❏ Writing Objectives, page 277
❏ Planning to Teach the Lesson, page 278
❏ Assessment, page 279
❏ Motivation, page 281
❏ Successful Learning, page 282
❏ Classroom Approaches, page 283
❏ Adapting Instruction, page 286
❏ Cultural and Linguistic Diversity, page 287

Teaching for Student Learning

Teacher Professionalism

Principles of Learning and Teaching Review

ORGANIZING CONTENT KNOWLEDGE FOR STUDENT LEARNING

HUMAN DEVELOPMENT

Physical Development

Adequate nutrition in mothers is essential for proper fetal development. Adequate nutrition and exercise are essential for a child's physical growth. Inadequate nutrition can hamper growth and lead to inattentiveness and other problems that interfere with learning.

Alcohol and drug abuse by mothers can cause irreparable brain damage to unborn children. Children of drug-and-alcohol-abusing mothers tend to have lower birth weights. Low birth weight is associated with health, emotional, and learning problems. Alcohol and drug addiction, smoking, stress, and adverse environmental factors are among the other causes of abnormal physical and emotional development.

During the first 12 months after birth, the body weight of infants triples and brain size doubles. Infants crawl by about 7 months, eat with their hands at about 8 months, sit up by about 9 months, stand up by about 11 months, and walk by about 1 year.

From 12–15 months to 2.5 years, children are called toddlers. During this period, children become expert walkers, feed themselves, evidence self control, and spend a great deal of their time playing. This period is characterized by the word *no* and is also when children begin bowel training.

The preschool years span the time from the end of toddlerhood to entry into kindergarten. Children start to look more like adults, with longer legs and a shorter torso. Play continues but becomes more sophisticated.

The elementary school years refer to ages 6–10 in girls but 6–12 years in boys. During this period children enter a period of steady growth. Most children double their body weight and increase their height by one-half. Play continues but involves more sophisticated games and physical activities, often involving groups or teams of other children.

Adolescence begins at about age 10 for girls but at about age 12 for boys. The growth rate spurt begins during this time. Because this period begins earlier for girls than for boys, girls are more mature than boys for a number of years. Sexual and secondary sex characteristics appear during this time. Most adolescents rely heavily on peer group approval and respond to peer pressure.

Behavioral Development

Behaviorism was the first significant theory of development. Behaviorism is concerned with observable, measurable behavior and with those events that stimulate or reinforce the behavior.

Watson

John Watson originated the behaviorist movement during the early 1900s. His theoretical ideas centered around conditioned responses in children. Conditioned response means that a child was "taught" to respond in a particular way to a stimulus that would not naturally elicit that response. Watson's experiment to condition a child to fear a white rat that the child initially liked is most quoted in texts. Many claim that the success of the experiment was overstated.

Pavlov

Many trace the experimental basis for behaviorism to the Russian psychologist Pavlov who, in the 1920s, conducted classical conditioning experiments with dogs. Dogs naturally salivate in an unconditioned response to the unconditioned stimulus of food. Pavlov showed that dogs would salivate in response to any neutral stimulus. The neutral stimulus is called a conditioned stimulus, and the salivation that occurs is called a conditioned response.

Thorndike

Also in the early 1900s Edward Thorndike developed his own form of behaviorism called instrumental conditioning. Thorndike's work with animals led him to two significant conclusions.

- The law of exercise—a conditioned response can be strengthened by repeating the response (practice).

- The law of effect—rewarded responses are strengthened while punished responses are weakened.

Skinner

Skinner was the most influential behaviorist. Skinner referred to his approach as operant conditioning, which studied how voluntary behavior could be shaped. Operant conditioning relies on these basic mechanisms.

- Reward or positive reinforcement—Students are rewarded for repeating desired responses.

- Negative reinforcement—Students escape punishment by repeating desired responses.

- Extinction—Undesired responses are not reinforced.

- Punishment—Undesired responses are punished.

Skinner showed that he could condition very complex behaviors in animals. He believed that students learned when teachers gave immediate positive feedback for a desired behavior and used extinction or punishment for undesirable behaviors.

Congnitive Development

Jean Piaget

Jean Piaget is the most prominent of cognitive psychologists who believe that students develop concepts through a series of stages. Stage theory is currently the most popular form of child development.

According to Piaget, children proceed through a fixed but uneven series of stages of cognitive development. His stages help us understand the general way in which students learn and develop concepts.

Action and logic versus perception are at the center of Piaget's theory. He believed that children learn through an active involvement with their environment. He also believed that students have developed a concept when their logical understanding overcomes their perceptual misunderstanding of the concept.

His conservation experiments explain this last point. In conservation of number, students are shown two matched rows of checkers. The child confirms that there are the same number of checkers in each row. Then one row of checkers is spread out and the child is asked if there are still the same number of checkers. Children who believe there are more checkers in one of the rows do not understand the concept of number because their perception holds sway over their logic.

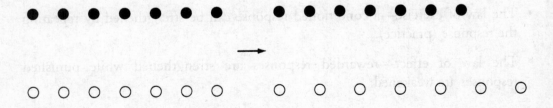

Piaget presents these four stages of cognitive development.

- Sensorimotor (birth to 18 months)—Children exhibit poor verbal and cognitive development. Children develop the idea of object permanence (out of sight not out of mind) during this stage.

- Preoperational (18 months to 7 years)—Children develop language and are able to solve some problems. Students' thinking is egocentric, and they have difficulty developing concepts. For example, students in this stage may not be able to complete the conservation of number task shown above.

- Concrete operational (7–12 years)—Students' thinking becomes operational. This means that concepts become organized and logical, as long as they are working with or around concrete materials or images. During this stage, students master the number conservation and other conservation tasks, but most students do not understand symbolic concepts.

- Formal operational (12+ years)—Children develop and demonstrate concepts without concrete materials or images. In this stage, students think fully in symbolic terms about concepts. Children become able to reason effectively, abstractly, and theoretically. Full development of this stage may depend on the extent to which children have had a full range of active manipulative experiences in the concrete operational stage.

Personality Development

Freud's psychoanalytic theories have profoundly affected modern thought about psychological and personality development. He believed that humans pass through four stages of psychosexual development: oral, anal, phallic, and genital. The personality itself consists of the id, ego, and superego. According to Freud, an integrated personality develops from the gratification experienced at each of these stages.

Psychosocial Development

Eriksen built on Freud's work and partitioned the life span into eight psychosocial stages. An emotional crisis at each stage can lead to a positive or negative result. The result achieved at each stage determines the development pattern for the next stage. Four of these stages fall within the school years.

Stage	Characteristic	Description
Kindergarten	Initiative vs. Guilt	Children accepted and treated warmly tend to feel more comfortable about trying out new ideas. Rejected children tend to become inhibited and guilty.
Elementary grades	Industry vs. Inferiority	Students who are accepted by their peer group and do well in school, and those who believe they are accepted and do well, are more successful than those who do not feel good about themselves.
Grades 6–9	Identity vs. Identity Confusion	Students who establish an identity and a sense of direction and who develop gender, social, and occupational roles experience an easier transition into adulthood than those students who do not establish these roles.
Grades 10–12	Intimacy vs. Isolation	Students who have passed successfully through the other stages will find it easier to establish a relationship with a member of the opposite sex. Those students who are unsuccessful at this stage may face an extremely difficult transition into adult life.

Moral Development

Kohlberg built on Piaget's original work to develop stages of moral development. Kohlberg proposed three levels of moral development with two stages at each level. His stages provide a reasonable approach to understanding moral development. Not everyone moves through all stages.

Preconventional Morality (preschool and primary grades)

Stage 1   Children do not demonstrate a conscience but do react to fear of punishment. Children are very egocentric.

Stage 2   Children still have no clear morality. Children concentrate on their own egocentric needs and let others do the same. Children may not be willing to help others meet their needs even though it would help them meet their own needs.
[Some children and antisocial adults may not pass this stage.]

Conventional Morality (middle grades through high school)

Stage 3   These children want to be good. They associate themselves with parents and other adult authority figures. They show concern for others and evidence a number of virtues and try to live up to expectations.

Stage 4   These children shift from wanting to please authority figures to a more generalized sense of respect for rules and expectations. These children see their responsibility to maintain society through a strict enforcement of society's laws.
[Many adults do not progress beyond this stage of development.]

Postconventional Morality (high school and beyond)

Stage 5   People at this stage differentiate between legality and morality. They have a more flexible view of right and wrong and realize that societal needs often take precedence over individual needs.

Stage 6   Very few people reach this stage. Those at Stage 6 have pure, cosmic understanding of justice and dignity. These principles always take precedence when they conflict with what is considered legal or socially acceptable.

Social Learning Theory

Social learning theory is a fairly new field. Social learning theorists seek to combine behavioral and cognitive learning theories along with other types of learning.

Albert Bandura is the leading social learning theorist. He believes that a great deal of learning can take place through modeling. That is, students often act the way they see others act, or they learn vicariously by observing others. Bandura believes that verbal explanations and reinforcement are also important and that students become socialized through systematic modeling of appropriate behavior. Students can also develop cognitive skills by observing a problem-solving process and learn procedures by observing these procedures in action.

Nature Versus Nurture

The relative effects of nature (heredity and genes) and nurture (environment and experience) on growth and development is still not resolved. Certain traits, sex, eye color, some forms of mental retardation, and susceptibility to some mental illnesses such as schizophrenia are linked to genes and heredity. However, other developmental questions are not clear, and even studies of twins separated at birth has not yielded the kind of conclusive results needed to draw conclusions.

DIVERSITY

Society and Culture

America is a multiethnic and multicultural society. Consequently, the culture of the community and the culture of the school varies widely depending on the school's geographic location, socioeconomic setting, and local norms. To understand schools, we must understand society and culture.

Anthropology and sociology provide a scientific basis for studying society and culture. Anthropology is the formal study of culture and the development of society. Much of the early anthropological work dealt with primitive cultures. However, in recent years anthropologists have turned their attention to communities and schools. Sociology is the study of how people behave in a group. Sociology can help us understand how students behave in school, how teachers function on a faculty, and how citizens interact in the community.

Culture is directly affected by the ethnicity of the community. Each ethnic group brings its own culture, its own language, and its own customs to this country.

Until recently, most immigrant groups have been acculturated. That is, they have largely adopted the dominant language and culture of the United States. Lately there has been a shift toward cultural pluralism in which immigrants maintain their cultural, and occasionally linguistic, identity.

Under cultural pluralism, the challenge is to provide equal educational opportunity while also providing for these cultural differences among students. There is little prospect, however, that non-English speakers will realize their full potential in the United States.

Socioeconomic status has a direct effect on culture and on the schools. As noted earlier, there is a strong correlation between SES and academic achievement. In the United States, groups, communities, and schools are stratified by social class. Social stratification often occurs within schools. Unlike many other countries, individuals are able to move among social classes, usually in an upward direction.

The Family

The family remains the predominant influence in the early lives of children. However, the nature of the American family has changed, and for the worse.

Divorce rates are very high and some say that a majority of Americans under 40 will be divorced. American families are fragmented, with about 30 percent of children living with a step-parent. About one-third of children are raised in one-parent families, and about two-thirds of these children live below the poverty level.

An increasing number of children, called latchkey children, return from school with no parents at home. School programs developed for these students cannot replace effective parenting.

In many respects, the school, social or religious institutions, peer groups, and gangs have replaced parents. This means that parents and families have less influence on children's values and beliefs.

The pressures of economic needs have drastically changed the American family. Less than 10 percent of American families have children, a mother at home, and a father at work. Over 30 percent of married couples have no children, and over 70 percent of mothers with children are working mothers.

Ethnicity

In 2006 the population of the United States was about 74 percent Caucasian, 12 percent African American, 10 percent Hispanic, 3 percent Asian, and 1 percent Native American or Eskimo. Hispanics are the fastest growing ethnic group.

About 13 percent of the families in the United States live below the poverty level. Some 30 percent of African American and Hispanic families do so, and an astonishing 65 percent of Native American families also live below the poverty level.

Hispanics

Hispanics come predominantly from Mexico and from other countries in Central and South America and the Caribbean. Many Mexican American families have been in this country for more than 100 years. Puerto Ricans form another large Hispanic group.

Language is the primary difficulty faced by this ethnic group. About half of the Hispanics in this country speak Spanish as their first language.

The nature of the Hispanic population varies by region. Most Hispanics in California or their forebears are from Mexico. Many Hispanics living in and around New York City are from Puerto Rico or the Dominican Republic, while many Hispanics in Florida trace their ancestry to Cuba.

Hispanic students have more school problems than white students. Hispanics are disproportionately poor and low achieving.

African Americans

African Americans have been in this country for centuries, but they began their lives here as slaves. There is not a recent history of large-scale African immigration to the United States.

Their status as slaves and second-class citizens denied African Americans the education, experience, and self-sufficiency needed for upward social mobility. Even when African Americans developed these qualities, they were frequently discriminated against just because of their race. It took almost 200 years from the founding of this country for the Supreme Court to rule that overt school segregation was unconstitutional. Of course, de facto segregation continues to exist.

Many African Americans have achieved middle class status. However, the overwhelming proportion of poor in urban areas are African Americans. The unemployment rate of young African Americans can be near 50 percent in some areas.

Native Americans

Groups of Eskimos and other Native Americans have lived on the North American continent for over 25,000 years. Most Native Americans living today are ancestors of tribes conquered and put on reservations about 100 years ago.

During this time of conquest, treaties made with tribes were frequently broken. Native Americans lost their lands and their way of life. They were made dependent on the federal government for subsidies and were not able to develop the education, experience, or self-sufficiency needed for upward mobility.

Native Americans have the largest family size and fastest growth rate of any ethnic group. They also have among the highest suicide and alcoholism rates of any ethnic group.

Native Americans are disproportionally poor and disenfranchised. They live in poverty on reservations and are often alienated when they move off reservations to metropolitan areas.

Asian Americans

Asian Americans are predominately Chinese and Japanese together with recent immigrants from Korea and Southeast Asia. Asian Americans represent a countertrend among American minorities. Their achievement and success tend to be above the national average.

Many recent immigrants do not have the educational background of other Asian Americans. They tend to be more ghettoized and to attain a lower SES than other Asian Americans.

However, overall, Asian students perform better on American standardized tests than non-Asian students. This finding holds also for those Asian Americans who immigrated to this country unable to speak, read, or understand English.

Some researchers have said that a particular work ethic currently found in Asian countries together with a strong family structure are responsible for these trends.

Societal Problems

This decade finds our society beset with unprecedented problems of crime and violence, alcohol and drug abuse, sex, AIDS, high dropout rates, and child abuse. Many of these problems can be traced directly to poverty. Schools are a part of society so that they too are affected by these problems.

Crime and Violence

The number of serious crimes in the United States is at the highest level in memory. Students bring guns to school, and large urban areas report dozens of deaths each year from violent acts in school. Murder is the leading cause of death among African American teens. More than 70 percent of those who commit serious crimes are never caught. We live in a society where crime is rampant and crime pays.

Crime in school presents a particular problem for teachers. Some estimate that 3 to 7 percent of all students bring a gun with them to school. Students attack teachers every day in America. While this behavior is not defensible, attention to the principles of classroom management mentioned earlier can help in averting some of these incidents.

Alcohol and Drug Abuse

Alcohol is the most used and abused drug. Even though it is legal, there are serious short- and long-term consequences of alcohol use. Alcoholism is the most widespread drug addiction and untreated alcoholism can lead to death.

Tobacco is the next most widely used and abused substance. Some efforts are being made to declare tobacco a drug. Irrefutable evidence shows that tobacco use is a causative factor in hundreds of thousands of deaths each year.

Other drugs including marijuana, cocaine, heroin, and various drugs in pill form carry with them serious health, addiction, and emotional problems. The widespread illicit availability of these drugs creates additional problems. Many students engage in crimes to get money to pay for drugs. Others may commit crimes while under the influence of drugs. Still others may commit crimes by selling drugs to make money.

More than 90 percent of students have used alcohol by the time they leave high school. About 70 percent of high school graduates have used other illegal drugs. Awareness programs that focus on drug use can have some positive effects. However, most drug and alcohol abuse and addiction has other underlying causes. These causes must be addressed for any program to be effective.

Sex

Many teens and preteens are sexually active. While many of these children profess to know about sex, they do not. It is in this environment that we find increases in teenage pregnancies, abortions, dropouts, and ruined lives. Sex spreads disease. So we also note increases in syphilis, gonorrhea, and other sexually transmitted diseases.

About 10 percent of teenage girls will become pregnant. Teenage pregnancy is the primary reason why girls drop out of high school. These girls seldom receive appropriate help from the child's father and are often destined for a life of poverty and dependence.

AIDS

AIDS stands for Acquired Immune Deficiency Syndrome. AIDS is a breakdown in the body's immune system caused by a virus called HIV. This virus can be detected with blood tests. People with the HIV virus may take 10 years or longer to develop AIDS. Those who develop AIDS die.

The HIV virus is transmitted by infected blood and other bodily fluids. Sexual relations and contact with infected blood, including blood injected with shared hypodermic needles, are all examples of ways that AIDS can be transmitted. Some 2 to 5 percent of the teens in some urban areas may be HIV positive.

Students can try to avoid becoming HIV positive by reducing their risk factors. Abstinence from sex and never injecting drugs will virtually eliminate the likelihood that a teenager will become HIV positive. Less effective measures can be taken to help sexually active students reduce the likelihood of becoming HIV positive. Girls run a higher risk than boys of becoming HIV positive through sexual activity.

Acquiring the HIV virus is associated with drug and alcohol use. Even when students know the risks, and how to avoid them, alcohol and drug use can lower inhibitions and lead to unsafe practices.

Dropouts

About 10 percent of white students, 15 percent of African American students, and 30 percent of Hispanic students drop out of school. Dropout rates are worst in urban areas, with over half the students dropping out of some schools. High school dropouts are usually headed for a life of lower wages and poorer living conditions.

Many of these students feel alienated from society or school and need support or alternative learning environments. Intervention, counseling, and alternative programs such as therapeutic high schools, vocational high schools, and other special learning arrangements can help prevent a student from dropping out.

Child Abuse

Child abuse is the secret destroyer of children's lives. Some estimate that between two and three million children are abused each year. Child abuse is a primary cause of violent youth, runaways, and drug abusers.

Physical and sexual abuse are the most destructive of the abuses heaped upon children. Contrary to popular belief, most child abuse is perpetrated by family members, relatives, and friends. Younger children are often incapable of talking about their abuse and may not reveal it even when asked.

In many states, teachers are required to report suspected child abuse. When child abuse is suspected, a teacher should follow the guidelines given by the school, the district, or the state.

CREATING AN ENVIRONMENT FOR STUDENT LEARNING

Objectives

All useful instruction has some purpose. Planning for instruction begins with choosing an objective that expresses this purpose. Objectives usually refer to outcomes, while goals usually refer to more general purposes of instruction. The terms *aim*, *competency*, *outcome*, and *behavioral objective* are also used to refer to an objective.

Objectives are often established by national or state organizations. The national or state English, mathematics, and science professional organizations may recommend objectives for their subject. The national or state organizations for speech, primary education, elementary education, preschool education, and special education may recommend objectives for specific grades or specialties.

Most school texts contain objectives, usually given for each text unit or lesson. These objectives are also reflected in national, state, and local achievement tests.

School districts usually have their own written objectives. There may be a scope and sequence chart that outlines the objectives for each subject and grade. The district may also have a comprehensive set of objectives for each subject and grade level.

Taxonomy of Objects

Benjamin Bloom and others described three domains of learning: cognitive, affective, and psychomotor. The cognitive domain refers to knowledge, intellectual ability, and the other things we associate with school learning. The affective domain refers to values, interests, attitudes, and the other things we associate with feelings. The psychomotor domain refers to motor skills and other things we associate with movement.

Each domain describes various levels of objectives. The six levels on the cognitive domain, noted below, are most useful in classifying objectives. Students should be exposed to objectives at all levels of the taxonomy.

1. Knowledge—Remembering specifics, recalling terms and theories.

2. Comprehension—Understanding or using an idea but not relating it to other ideas.

3. Application—Using concepts or abstractions in actual situations.

4. Analysis—Breaking down a statement to relate ideas in the statement.

5. Synthesis—Bringing or putting together parts to make a whole or find a pattern.

6. Evaluation—Judging value, comparing work or product to a criteria.

Choosing and Modifying Objectives

Initially, you will identify an objective from one of the sources noted previously. Consider these criteria when choosing and sequencing objectives.

- The objective should meet the overall goals of the school district.

- The objective should be appropriate for the achievement and maturation level of students in the class.

- The objective should be generally accepted by appropriate national, regional, or state professional organizations.

The objective you select may not exactly describe the lesson or unit you are going to teach. Modify the objective to meet your needs. You also may need to select or modify objectives and other plans to meet the needs of diverse student populations.

Your class may be academically diverse. You may teach special-needs students or you may have special-needs students in your class under the inclusion model. When you select and modify objectives for academically diverse students, consider the different achievement levels or learning styles of these students.

Your class may be culturally diverse. When you select and modify objectives for a culturally diverse class, consider the range of experiences and backgrounds found among the class. Do not reduce the difficulty of the objective.

Your class may be linguistically diverse. You may have limited English proficiency (LEP) students in your class. For a linguistically diverse class, take into account the limits that language places on learning. You may have to select or modify objectives to help these students learn English.

Writing Objectives

An objective should answer the question: "What are students expected to do once instruction is complete?" Objectives should not describe what the teacher does during the lesson. Objectives should not be overly specific, involved, or complicated.

Whenever possible, objectives should begin with a verb. Here are some examples.

| Not an objective: | I will teach students how to pronounce words with a silent *e*. |
| | [This is a statement of what the teacher will do.] |

| Not an objective: | While in the reading group, looking at the reading book, students will pronounce words with a silent *e*. |
| | [This statement is overly specific.] |

| Objective: | Sounds out words with a silent *e*. |
| | [This is an objective. It tells what the student is expected to do.] |

| Objective: | States what he or she liked about the trip to the zoo. |

| Objective: | Reads a book from the story shelf. |

| Objective: | Serves a tennis ball successfully twice in a row. |

Do not limit objectives to skills or tiny bits of strictly observable behavior. Specific objectives are not limited objectives. Objectives can include statements that students will appreciate or participate in some activity. Objectives should include integrating subject matter, applying concepts, problem solving, decision making, writing essays, researching projects, preparing reports, exploring, observing, appreciating, experimenting, and constructing and making art work and other projects.

Planning to Teach the Lesson

Once you have decided what to teach, you must plan how to teach it. Consider these factors as you plan the lesson or unit.

- Determine the prerequisite competencies. This is the knowledge and skills students must possess before they can learn the objective. Draw up a plan that ensures students will demonstrate prerequisite competencies before you teach the lesson.

- Determine the resources you need to help students reach the objective. The resources could include books, manipulatives, overhead transparencies, and other materials for you or the students to use. The resources could also include technological resources including computers or computer software and human resources including teacher aides, students, or outside presenters.

- Devise a plan to help students reach the objective. In addition to the factors discussed previously, the plan will usually include motivation and procedures.

Madeline Hunter posited the following important stages for effective lessons.

- Anticipatory set—Something that is said or done to prepare students and focus the students on the lesson.

- Objective and purpose—The teacher should state the objective of the lesson, and the students should be aware of the objective.

- Input—New information is presented during this stage.

- Modeling—The skills or procedures being taught or demonstrated.

- Checking for understanding—Following the instructional components in the previous two stages, the teacher should ensure that students understand the concept before moving to the next phases of the lesson.

- Guided practice—Students are given the opportunity to practice or use the concept or skill with the teacher's guidance.

- Independent practice—Students practice or use the concept on their own.

ASSESSMENT

Assessment Program

Every teacher evaluates instruction. The assessment program and the assessment instruments should measure mastery and understanding of important topics. The assessment program should also be used as a teaching tool. That is, the program should be used to help students learn and to improve instruction. The program should include authentic assessment of students' work as well as teacher-made and standardized tests.

Formative assessment information is usually gathered before or during teaching. Formative information is used to help you prepare appropriate lessons and assist students. Formative evaluations help teachers decide which objectives to teach, which instructional techniques to use, and which special help or services to provide to individual students.

Summative assessment information is usually gathered once instruction is complete. Summative evaluation is used to make judgments about student achievement and the effectiveness of the instructional programs. Summative evaluations lead to grades, to reports about a student's relative level of accomplishment, and to alterations of instructional programs.

Assessment information may be used for both purposes. For example, you may give a test to determine grades for a marking period or unit. You may then use the information from this test to plan further instruction and arrange individual help for students.

You may informally gather formative and summative information. Just walking around the room observing students' work can yield a lot of useful information. You can frequently discern the additional work that students need and identify different levels of student achievement.

Assessment Instruments

Tests have long been used to determine what students have learned and to compare students. Every test is imperfect. Many tests are so imperfect that they are useless. It is important to realize how this imperfection affects test results.

Some students are poor test takers. Every test assumes that the test takers have the opportunity to demonstrate what they know. A student may know something but be unable to demonstrate it on a particular test. We must also consider alternative assessment strategies for these students.

Familiarize yourself with these basic assessment concepts.

- Errors of Measurement—Every test contains errors of measurement. In other words, no one test accurately measures a student's achievement or ability. Carefully designed standardized tests may have measurement errors of 5 percent or 10 percent. Teacher-designed tests typically have large errors of measurement.

    A test result shows that a student falls into a range of scores and not just the single reported score. Focusing on a single score and ignoring the score range is among the most serious of score-reporting errors.

- Reliability—A reliable test is consistent. That is, a reliable test will give similar results when given to the same person in a short time span. You can't count on unreliable tests to give you useful scores. Use only very reliable standardized tests and be very aware of how important reliability is when you make up your own tests.

- Validity—Valid tests measure what they are supposed to measure. There are two important types of validity: content validity and criterion validity.

    A test with high content validity measures the material covered in the curriculum or unit being tested. Tests that lack high content validity are unfair. When you make up a test it should have complete content validity. This does not mean that the test has to be unchallenging. It does mean that the questions should refer to the subject matter covered.

    A test with high criterion validity successfully predicts the ability to do other work. For example a test to be an automobile mechanic with high criterion validity will successfully predict who will be a good mechanic.

Norm-Referenced and Criterion-Referenced Tests

Norm-referenced tests are designed to compare students. Intelligence tests are probably the best-known norm-referenced tests. These tests yield a number that purports to show how one person's intelligence compares to everyone else's. The average IQ score is 100.

Standardized achievement tests yield grade-level equivalent scores. These tests purport to show how student achievement compares to the achievement of all other students of the same grade level.

A fifth grader who earns a grade level equivalent of 5.5 might be thought of as average. A second-grade student with the same grade equivalent score would be thought of as above average. About half of all the students taking these tests will be below average.

Standardized tests also yield percentile scores. Percentile scores are reported as a number from 0 through 100. A percentile of 50 indicates that the student did as well as or better than 50 percent of the students at that grade level who took the test. The higher the percentile, the better the relative performance.

Criterion-referenced tests are designed to determine the degree to which an objective has been reached. Teacher-made tests and tests found in teachers' editions of texts are usually criterion-referenced tests. Criterion-referenced tests have very high content validity.

Authentic Assessment

Standardized and teacher-made tests have significant drawbacks. These types of tests do not evaluate a student's ability to perform a task or demonstrate a skill in a real-life situation. These tests do not evaluate a student's ability to work cooperatively or consistently.

In authentic assessment, students are asked to demonstrate the skill or knowledge in a real-life setting. The teacher and students collaborate in the learning assessment process and discuss how learning is progressing and how to facilitate that learning. The idea is to get an authentic picture of the student's work and progress.

Students have an opportunity to demonstrate what they know or can do in a variety of settings. Students can also demonstrate their ability to work independently or as part of a group.

Portfolio assessment is another name for authentic assessment. Students evaluated through a system of authentic assessment frequently keep a portfolio of their work.

MOTIVATION

Most good lessons begin with a motivation. The motivation interests the learner and focuses their attention on the lesson. It is also important to maintain students' motivation for the duration of the lesson.

The motivation for a lesson may be intrinsic or extrinsic. Intrinsic motivation refers to topics that students like or enjoy. Effective intrinsic motivations are based on a knowledge of what is popular or interesting to students of a particular age.

For example, you might introduce a lesson about the French and Indian War to older students by discussing the book and movie *Last of the Mohicans*. You might introduce a lesson on patterns to young children by picking out patterns in children's clothes. You might introduce a lesson on fractions to middle school students with a discussion about the stock market.

Extrinsic motivation focuses on external rewards for good work or goal attainment. Extrinsic rewards are most successful when used in conjunction with more routine work. Extrinsic motivations may offer an appropriate reward for completing an assignment or for other acceptable performance. Establish rewards for activities that most students can achieve and take care to eliminate unnecessary competition.

For example, you might grant a period of free time to students who successfully complete a routine but necessary assignment. You might offer the whole class a trip or a party when a class project is successfully completed. Special education programs feature token reinforcement in which students receive or lose points or small plastic tokens for appropriate or inappropriate activity.

Motivation needs to be maintained during the lesson itself. Follow these guidelines for teaching lessons in which the students remain motivated. Lessons will be more motivating if you have clear and unambiguous objectives, give the students stimulating tasks at an appropriate level, get and hold the students' attention, and allow students some choices. Students will be most motivated if they like the topic or activities, believe that the lesson has to do with them, believe that they will succeed, and have a positive reaction to your efforts to motivate them.

Individual work gives a further opportunity to use intrinsic motivation. Use the interests and likes of individual students to spark and maintain their motivation.

The extrinsic motivation of praise can be used effectively during a lesson. For praise to be successful, it must be given for a specific accomplishment (including effort) and it must focus on the student's own behavior. It does not compare behavior with other students or establish competitive situations.

SUCCESSFUL LEARNING

Research indicates that the following factors are likely to lead to successful learning.

- Students who are engaged in the learning process tend to be more successful learners, particularly when they are engaged in activities at the appropriate level of difficulty.

- Students learn most successfully when they are being taught or supervised as opposed to working independently.

- Students who are exposed to more material at the appropriate level of difficulty are more successful learners.

- Students are successful learners when their teachers expect them to master the curriculum and use available instructional time for learning activities.

- Students who are in a positive, uncritical classroom environment are more successful learners than students who are in a negative, critical classroom environment. This does not mean that students cannot be corrected or criticized, but that students learn best when the corrections are done positively and when the criticisms are constructive.

- Students generally develop positive attitudes to teachers who appear warm, have a student orientation, praise students, listen to students, accept student ideas, and interact with them.

Classroom Interaction

Flander's Interaction Analysis gives a way to understand how teachers teach. His scheme focuses on the kind of teacher talk and student talk in a classroom. In Flander's work, one of the codes below was assigned to every three seconds of classroom instruction. This kind of frequent coding and the numbers or precise names of the categories are not important. However, the coding system can help you understand how to structure successful learning experiences.

Indirect Teacher Talk

1. Accepts feelings—Teacher acknowledges and accepts students' feelings.

2. Praises and encourages—Teacher praises students' contributions and encourages students to continue their contributions.

3. Accepts or uses students' ideas—Teacher helps students develop their own ideas and uses students' own ideas in the lesson.

4. Asks questions—Teacher asks questions about lesson content or solicits students' opinions. Rhetorical questions and questions not related to the lesson content are not included in this category.

Direct Teacher Talk

5. Lectures, explains, or demonstrates—Teacher presents facts, opinions, or demonstrations related to the lesson topic.

6. Gives directions—Teacher gives directions to which students are expected to comply.

7. Criticizes or justifies authority—Teacher responds negatively to students, criticizes, or justifies authority.

Student Talk

8. Student talk (response)—Student responds to a teacher's question. The correct answer is predictable and anticipated by the teacher.

9. Student talk (initiation)—Student initiates response that is not predictable. The response may follow an open-ended or indirect question from the teacher.

10. Silence or confusion—The classroom is silent or you can't make out what is being said.

CLASSROOM APPROACHES

Effective classrooms are characterized by a variety of teaching approaches. The approaches should be tailored to the ability of the learner and the lesson objectives.

Teacher-Centered Approaches

Teacher-centered approaches are characterized by teacher presentation, a factual question, and a knowledge-based response from the student.

Lecture or Explanation

You can present material through a lecture or an explanation. A lecture is a fairly long verbal presentation of material. Explanation refers to a shorter presentation. Lecture and explanation are efficient ways to present information that must be arranged and structured in a particular way. However, lecture and explanation may place learners in too passive a role.

Lecture and explanation work best under the following circumstances: (1) the lesson begins with a motivation, (2) the teacher maintains eye contact, (3) the teacher supplies accentuating gestures but without extraneous movements, (4) the presentation is limited to about 5–40 minutes depending on the age of the student, and (5) the objective is clear and the presentation is easy to follow and at an appropriate level.

Demonstrations

Demonstrations are lectures or explanations in which you model what you want students to learn. That is, you exhibit a behavior, show a technique, or demonstrate a skill to help students reach the objective. Demonstrations should follow the same general rules as lectures and the actual demonstration should be clear and easy to follow.

Teacher Questions

Teachers frequently ask questions during class. The following guidelines describe successful questions.

- Formulate questions so that they are clear, purposeful, brief, and at an appropriate level for the class.

- Address the vast majority of questions to the entire class. Individually addressed questions are appropriate to prepare "shy" students to answer the question.

- Avoid rhetorical questions.

- Use both higher and lower level questions on Bloom's Taxonomy (knowledge, comprehension, application, analysis, synthesis, evaluation). All types of questions have their place.

- Avoid question-and-answer drills. A consistent pattern of teacher questions that call for responses at the first level of Bloom's Taxonomy is too limiting for most classrooms.

- Pause before you call on a student to answer the question, giving students an opportunity to formulate their responses.

- Call on a wide range of students to answer. Do not pick students just because they are either likely or unlikely to respond correctly.

- Wait 4 or 5 seconds for an answer. Don't cut off students who are struggling with an answer.

- Rephrase a question if it seems unclear or vague.

- Set a target for about 70 percent or so of questions to be answered correctly.

Student-Centered Approaches—Active Learning

In a student-centered or active learning environment, the teacher ceases to be the prime presenter of information. The teacher's questions are more open-ended and indirect. Students will be encouraged to be more active participants in the class. This type of instruction is characterized by student-initiated comments, praise from the teacher, and the teacher's use of students' ideas.

Just because there is student involvement does not mean that the teacher is using a student-centered or active approach. For example, the pattern of questions and answers referred to as drill is not a student-centered approach.

Cooperative Learning

Students involved in cooperative learning work together in groups to learn a concept or skill or to complete a project. Students, in groups of two to six, are assigned or choose a specific learning task or project presented by the teacher. The group consults with the teacher and devises a plan for working together.

Students use many resources, including the teacher, to help and teach one another and to accept responsibilities for tasks as they complete their work. The students summarize their efforts and, typically, make a presentation to the entire class or the teacher.

Cooperative learning is characterized by active learning, full participation, and democracy within a clearly established structure. Cooperative learning also engages students in learning how to establish personal relationships and a cooperative working style.

Inquiry Learning

Inquiry learning uses students' own thought processes to help them learn a concept, solve a problem, or discover a relationship. This kind of instruction has also been referred to as Socratic. Inquiry learning often requires the most structure and preparation by the teacher. The teacher must know that the situation under study will yield useful results.

The teacher begins by explaining inquiry procedures to students, usually through examples. Next the teacher presents the problem to be solved or the situation that will lead to the concept or relationship. Students gather information and ask questions of the teacher to gain additional information. The teacher supports students as they make predictions and provide tentative solutions or results. Once the process is complete, the teacher asks students to think over and describe the process they used to arrive at the solution. This last step is referred to as a metacognition.

Resources for Instruction

You may have to assemble a number of resources for instruction. It often helps to jot down the resources you will need to teach a lesson or a unit. The materials you select should help the students meet the lesson objectives and match the teaching-learning approach you will use. The resources may include textual, manipulative, technological, and human resources.

Be sure to assemble in advance the materials you need to teach a lesson. The materials may include texts, workbooks, teacher-made handouts, or other printed materials. Check the materials to ensure that they are intact and in appropriate condition.

You may use manipulative materials to teach a lesson. Be sure that the materials are assembled and complete. Any laboratory materials should be tested and safe. Be sure that the materials are at an appropriate level for the students.

You may use technological resources, such as a computer, during your lesson. Be sure that the computer will be available during your lesson. Try the computer out and be sure that it is working. Be sure that any software you will use is at an appropriate grade and interest level and matches the objectives of the lesson.

You will frequently use human resources in your lesson. You may decide to cooperatively teach a lesson or unit with another teacher. This approach requires advanced planning and regular communication. You may need to arrange for a guest speaker to speak to the class about a particular topic.

Special education teachers frequently teach in consultative or collaborative roles. That is, they work in classrooms with regular education teachers. In this arrangement, teachers must coordinate their activities and agree on how they will interact during the lesson.

ADAPTING INSTRUCTION

Adapt instruction for the following factors, types of learners, and students.

> Age—Primary students should have more structure, shorter lessons, less explanation, more public praise, more small group and individual instruction, and more experiences with manipulatives and pictures. Older students should have less structure, increasingly longer lessons, more explanation, less public praise, more whole-class instruction, more independent work, and less work with manipulatives.

Academically Diverse

> Aptitude—Students exhibit different abilities to learn. You can provide differentiated assignments to enable students at different aptitude levels to maximize their potential.

> Reading Level—Ensure that a student is capable of understanding the reading material. Do not ask students to learn from material that is too difficult. Identify materials at an appropriate reading level or with an alternative learning mode (tapes, material read to student). Remember that a low reading level does not mean that a student cannot learn a difficult concept.

> Learning Disabled—Learning-disabled students evidence at least a 2-year discrepancy between measures of ability and performance. Learning-disabled students should be given structured, brief assignments, manipulative experiences, and many opportunities for auditory learning.

> Visually Impaired—Place the visually impaired student where he or she can most easily see the instruction. Use large learning aids and large print books. Use a multisensory approach.

> Hearing Impaired—Ensure that students are wearing an appropriate hearing aid. Students with less than 50 percent hearing loss will probably be able to hear you if you stand about 3 to 5 feet away.

Mildly Handicapped—Focus on a few, highly relevant skills, more learning time, and lots of practice. Provide students with concrete experiences. Do not do for students what they can do for themselves, even if it takes these students an extended time.

Gifted—Gifted students have above average ability, creativity, and a high degree of task commitment. Provide these students with enriched or differentiated units. Permit them to test out of required units. Do not isolate these students from the rest of the class.

CULTURAL AND LINGUISTIC DIVERSITY

SES (Socioeconomic Status)—Socioeconomic status and school achievement are highly correlated. Overall, students with higher SES will have higher achievement scores. In America, SES differences are typically associated with differences in race and ethnicity. However, the achievement differences are not caused by and are not a function of these differences in race or ethnicity. Rather, achievement differences are typically caused by differences in home environment, opportunity for enriched experiences, and parental expectations.

Teachers frequently have a higher SES than their students. These students often behave differently than teachers expect. The crushing problems of poor and homeless children may produce an overlay of acting out and attention problems. All this frequently leads the teacher to erroneously conclude that these students are less capable of learning. In turn, the teacher may erroneously lower learning expectations. This leads to lower school performance and a compounding of students' difficulty.

A teacher must consciously and forcibly remind herself or himself that lower SES students are capable learners. These teachers must also actively guard against reducing learning expectations for lower SES students.

There are appropriate ways of adapting instruction for students with different SES levels. For high SES students, minimize competitiveness, provide less structure, and present more material. For low SES students, be more encouraging, guard against feelings of failure or low self-esteem, and provide more structure. Do not lower learning expectations, but do present less material and emphasize mastery of the material.

Culturally Diverse—Almost every class will have students from diverse cultural backgrounds. Use the values embedded in these cultures to motivate individual learners.

Linguistically Diverse—The first language for many students is not English. In addition, a number of American students speak local variants of the English language. Teachers frequently, and erroneously, lower their learning expectations for these students. There are a number of useful strategies for adapting instruction for these students.

A number of students are referred to as Limited English Proficiency (LEP) who need English as a second language (ESL) instruction. Teaching English as a second language can be accomplished in the classroom, but often requires a specialist who works with students in "pull-out programs." When teaching these students, use simpler words and expressions, use context clues to help students identify word meaning, clearly draw students' attention to your speech, and actively involve students in the learning process.

Characteristics of Successful Teachers

In general effective teachers have these general characteristics.

- Accept children within a teacher–student relationship.

- Set firm and clear but flexible limits.

- Enforce rules clearly and consistently.

- Have positive, realistic expectations about students' achievements and adaptations.

- Have clear reasons for expectations about students.

- Practice what they preach (model acceptable behavior).

- Don't take students' actions personally. Students usually misbehave or act out because of who they are, not because of who the teacher is.

TEACHING FOR STUDENT LEARNING

Planning instruction and implementing instruction are intertwined. Many of the points discussed here will have been considered during the planning process.

Classrooms are dynamic places. Students and teachers interact to further a student's learning and development. Follow these guidelines to establish a successful classroom and teach successful lessons.

MANAGING THE INSTRUCTIONAL ENVIRONMENT

Classroom management is a more encompassing idea than discipline or classroom control. Classroom management deals with all the things a classroom teacher can do to help students become productive learners. The best management system for any classroom will establish an effective learning environment with the least restrictions.

Teachers who are proactive and take charge stand the best chance of establishing an effective learning environment. Classroom management is designed to prevent problems, not react to them.

Classroom management begins with understanding the characteristics of students in your class.

Characteristics of Students

We can make some general statements about the students in a class. We know that 3–7 percent of girls and 12–18 percent of boys will have some substantial adjustment problems. Prepare yourself for these predictable sex differences.

Boys are more physically active and younger children have shorter attention spans. Respond to this situation by scheduling activities when students are most likely to be able to complete them.

A teacher's management role is different at different grade levels. Prepare for these predictable differences in student reaction to teacher authority.

In the primary grades, students see teachers as authority figures and respond well to instruction and directions about how they should act in school. In the middle grades, students have learned how to act in school and still react well to the teacher's instruction.

In seventh through tenth grade, students turn to their peer group for leadership and resist the teacher's authority. The teacher must spend more time fostering appropriate behavior among students. By the last two years of high school, students are somewhat less resistant and the teacher's role is more academic.

We know that many adolescents resent being touched and that teachers may anger adolescents by taking something from them. Avoid this problem by not confronting adolescent students.

We know that there will be cultural differences among students. Many minority students, and other students, may be accustomed to harsh, authoritarian treatment. Respond to these students with warmth and acceptance. Many minority students will feel completely out of place in school. These students also need to be treated warmly and with the positive expectation that they will succeed in school.

Many other students may be too distracted to study effectively in school. These students may need quiet places to work and the opportunity to schedule some of their own work time.

Other factors, such as low self-esteem, anxiety, and tension, can also cause students to have difficulty in school.

Classroom Management Techniques

The following guidelines for effective classroom management include techniques for dealing with student misbehavior.

Teacher's Role

Teachers who are good classroom managers understand their dual role as an authority figure and as someone who helps children adapt to school and to life. Teachers are authority figures. Students expect the teacher to be an authority figure and expect teachers to establish a clear and consistent classroom structure.

Teachers must also help students learn how to fit into the classroom and how to get along with others. Teachers fare better in their role as authority figures than they do in this latter role. But teachers who have realistic expectations and know how to respond to problems can have some success.

Establishing an Effective Climate for Management

Classroom Physical Layout

There are several general rules to follow for a successful classroom layout. Set up the initial layout of the room so that you can see the faces of all the students. Rearrange the desks for individual and group work. Ensure that heavily used areas are free of all obstacles. Arrange the room so students do not have to stand in line, by having books and supplies available at several locations.

Classroom Leadership

Research indicates that the following factors are most important in establishing effective classroom leadership. Develop a cohesive class by promoting cooperative experiences and minimizing competition among class members. Identify and gain the confidence of peer leaders, particularly in Grades 7–10. Establish an authoritative, but not authoritarian, leadership style.

Depending on the grade level, set three to six reasonable, adaptable rules that describe the overall nature of acceptable and unacceptable behavior. The expectations that accompany these rules should be stated clearly. The rules should be posted for students to see.

Much of the first two weeks of school should be spent establishing these rules, which may be stated by the teacher and/or developed through class discussion. Once the rules are established and the expectations are understood, the teacher should follow through. Student misbehavior should be handled immediately and appropriately but without causing a confrontation or alienating the student from the class.

Effective classroom managers take steps to ensure that the majority of class time is spent on instruction. They also take steps to ensure that students use their seat work and other inclass study time to complete assignments.

SPECIFIC MANAGEMENT TECHNIQUES

There are some specific management techniques that a teacher can apply to all classes. These techniques are summarized here.

Kounin

Kounin is a well-known expert on classroom management. Research results show that a number of Kounin's management techniques are effective. The following techniques have the most research support.

Kounin noted that teacher with-it-ness is an important aspect of classroom management. In other words, teachers who are constantly monitoring and are aware of what is happening in the classroom are better managers.

Kounin also showed that effective managers' lessons have smoothness and momentum. By this he meant that these lessons are free of teacher behavior that interrupts the flow of activities or slows down lesson pacing.

Finally, Kounin showed that group alerting was an effective technique. In group alerting, the teacher keeps bringing uninvolved students back into the lesson by calling their attention to what is happening and forewarning them of future events.

Canter and Canter

Canter and Canter developed an approach called assertive discipline. Their approach is popular but lacks the research support of the approach recommended by Kounin.

The Canters recommend a direct and assertive approach to problem children. They point out that passive and hostile reactions to student misbehavior are not effective. Among other approaches, they recommend that the teacher and students establish rules and post those rules in the classroom. During each class session, the teacher writes and then marks the names of students who have violated rules. One rule violation in a session requires no action. Two rule violations, and the student meets with the teacher after school. Three violations require a parental visit to the school.

Cueing

Cues are words, gestures, or other signals that alert students to a coming transition or that gain their attention. A cue may be spoken, such as "We'll be leaving for art in about 5 minutes. Take this time to get ready." Another cue might be, "Your group has about 15 minutes to complete your project."

Other cues are nonverbal. You may glance at a student or make eye contact to re-engage them in the lesson. You may raise your arm or hold your hand in a particular way to gain attention. You may flick the classroom lights quickly to indicate that groups should stop working and return to whole-class instruction.

Other Effective Techniques for Maintaining Attention During a Lesson

The techniques listed below have proven effective in classrooms.

- Stand where you can scan and see the entire class.

- Ask questions of the whole class and then call on individuals for a response.

- Involve all students in the question-and-answer sessions and don't call on students just to catch them in a wrong answer or because they will give the correct answer.

- Gain attention through eye contact or a gesture.

- If a comment is required, make it very brief.

- Ensure that the material being taught is at an appropriate level.

- Base seat work or group work on an established system that is monitored closely and positively.

CHANGING BEHAVIOR

Students may act so unacceptably that their behavior must be changed. Here are some suggestions for changing behavior.

Modeling

Students learn how to behave from observing others. In the classroom the teacher is the authority figure and the one whom students may model their behaviors after. The following teacher behaviors can have a positive impact on student behaviors. In general, teachers should act as they expect their students to act.

- Listen carefully to what students say.

- Act after thoughtful consideration, not in anger or on an impulse.

- Treat students with respect.

- Do not be sarcastic or hostile with students.

- Respond to difficulty or criticism calmly. Don't take it personally.

Reinforcement

All teachers use positive reinforcement, whether through grades, praise, tokens, or other means. Teachers also use negative reinforcement by showing students how to avoid an undesirable consequence (poor grade) by doing acceptable work. Negative reinforcement is not punishment.

In the classroom you should increase the duration or quality of the desired behavior before reinforcing. Reach explicit agreements with students about the level of performance that will yield rewards (positive reinforcement). Praise is often an ineffective reinforcer.

Contracts and Logs

You may be able to help children change behavior by using contracts or by asking students to maintain logs. These approaches cause students to think about their behavior and both have been proven effective.

When writing a contract, work with a student to establish desired learning goals or classroom behavior. The contract, signed by the teacher and the student, sets short-term goals for classroom conduct and academic achievement. A teacher may also ask students to maintain a log of their classroom behavior. A brief daily review of the log may improve behavior.

Punishment

Punishment is a temporary measure. It should be administered to improve student performance, not to make the teacher feel better. Limited punishment given for a specific reason when students are emotionally stable can be effective. Other punishments, such as extra work, punishment of the entire class, and corporal punishment, are usually not effective.

Effective punishment should be reasonable, deliberate, and unemotional. The punishment should also be short and somewhat unpleasant. The reason for the punishment should be clear, and the punishment should be accompanied by examples of appropriate behavior.

TEACHING READING AND LANGUAGE ARTS

There are two competing models for reading and language arts instruction—phonics and whole language. The phonics approach is usually associated with drills, a teacher-centered classroom, and direct instruction. The whole language approach is usually associated with holistic teaching, a child-centered classroom, and cooperative learning groups.

Phonics

With the more traditional phonics approach, children learn how to associate letters and groups of letters with sounds. Once students learn to decode the language they learn what the words mean. This phonics approach is usually associated with basal readers. These readers contain basic passages and stories with a carefully controlled vocabulary. Stories taken from literature sources are often changed to conform to the vocabulary reading level desired by those preparing the basal readers. Exercises accompanying basal readers frequently have one narrow correct answer.

Writing instruction in a phonics-based classroom emphasizes correct spelling. Students in these classrooms are expected to master the rules for spelling and grammar before they commit their thoughts to writing.

Whole Language

Children using the whole language approach are often encouraged to decode words from their context. Proponents of the whole language approach point out that children entering school already have a spoken vocabulary of about 10,000 words. The whole language approach is usually associated with books students read outside of school with a more robust and varied vocabulary. Activities in whole language classrooms often include reading real literature and typically have a broader range of responses.

Writing instruction in a whole language-based classroom tolerates incorrect spelling and inappropriate grammatical usage. Students in these classrooms are expected to write thoughtfully and meaningfully with less emphasis on the rules of grammar and spelling.

Middle Ground

We don't want children to pronounce words correctly without knowing their meaning, and we don't want students who can't decode a written word. We do need an approach that fosters both decoding and understanding.

Recent research reports indicate that students learn best when a combination of approaches is used. This seems to be the best advice for the classroom teacher. Teach phonics in a systematic way, but use real stories. Incorporate a combination of narrow questions and questions that call for a broad understanding of the reading material. Ask students to master the rules of grammar and spelling, but encourage early drafts with less emphasis on these rules and more emphasis on meaning.

TEACHER PROFESSIONALISM

THE SCHOOL AND SOCIETY

The School in Society

The school is a part of society. It reflects the society and socializes students. To that end, the schools prepare students to function in society. Students are taught, directly and indirectly, acceptable social values and behavior.

The academic curriculum reflects society's expectations. Students are taught a generally accepted body of knowledge. Students are also prepared for society by being exposed to potential careers as a part of the school curriculum.

Every society has a culture. The culture combines the history of the society and the society's current norms. The culture includes customs, values, ethical and moral structures, religions and beliefs, laws, and a hierarchy of most valued contributions by members of society.

The School as a Society

The school is a society in itself. The school society consists of a complex interrelationship of teachers, students, administrators, parents, and others. Each school has its own character, practices, and informal hierarchy. Generally speaking, new teachers must find a niche in the school's society to be successful. The school has a formal decision-making hierarchy of teachers, supervisors, principals, superintendents, and school boards. The new teacher must usually gain acceptance at each level of this hierarchy to experience success.

Each state in the United States has its own system of education. States are legally responsible for education. Locally elected or appointed school boards usually have the most direct legal impact on the schools. Within state and federal laws, school boards pay for the schools from tax receipts and other funds, hire teachers and administrators, approve curricula, and set school policy.

Many of the decisions made by school boards are affected by the amount of money available to the schools. Generally speaking, wealthier districts have more money to spend on schools. The difference in the funds available may create a difference in the quality of schooling.

LEGAL, LEGISLATIVE, AND POLITICAL INFLUENCES

Who's in Charge of Education

The Constitution of the United States does not assign the responsibility for education to the federal government, leaving this responsibility to each state. The state government, including the governor, the legislature, and the courts have the ultimate responsibility for public education. A state board or commission is usually responsible for the operation of the schools. A state commissioner of education reports to the state board.

The commissioner, in turn, oversees a state education department. The state education department is responsible for the state's daily responsibility for the schools. Other organizations in a state, including regional and county authorities, may have education responsibilities.

Local or regional boards of education are directly responsible for operating schools in their district or town. In more than 80 percent of the cases, these boards are elected. A local or regional superintendent of schools reports to the board and, along with other administrators and support staff, has the daily responsibility for operating the schools.

Building principals report to the superintendent and are responsible for the daily operations of their school building. Teachers have the responsibility for teaching their students and carrying out district and state education policies.

It's the Law

A complex set of federal, state, and local laws govern education. Court cases are changing the interpretation of these laws each day. Here is a brief summary of legal rights as they apply to schools, teachers, and students. This summary should not be used to make any decisions related to school laws. Any specific interest in legal issues should be referred to a competent attorney.

Schools

- Schools may not discriminate against students, teachers, or others because of their race, sex, ethnicity, or religion. "Reverse discrimination" *may* be legal when hiring teachers, but it is not legal when dismissing teachers.

- Prayer is not permitted in schools. In all other ways, schools may not embrace or support religion.

- Schools must make children's school records available to parents and legal guardians.

- Schools may remove books from the school library. However, a book may not be removed from the library just because a school board member or other school official does not agree with its content.

Teachers

- Teachers do not have to provide information unrelated to employment on an employment form or to an interviewer. You do not have to give your age, your marital status, sexual orientation, or any other unrelated information.

- Nontenured teachers usually have very limited rights to reappointment. Generally speaking, schools may not rehire a nontenured teacher for any reason. For example, the schools may simply say that they want to find someone better, that the teacher doesn't fit in, or that they just don't want to renew the contract.

- Teachers cannot be fired for behavior that does not disrupt or interfere with their effectiveness as teachers. However, even personal behavior away from school, which significantly reduces teaching effectiveness, might be grounds for dismissal.

- Pregnant teachers may not be forced to take a maternity leave. Decades ago, pregnant teachers were often forced to resign.

- Teachers may be dismissed or suspended for not doing their job. Any such action must follow a due process procedure.

- Teachers may be sued and be liable for negligence. Successful suits and actions against teachers have occurred when the evidence showed that the teacher could have reasonably foreseen what was going to happen or that the teacher acted differently than a reasonable teacher would have acted in that same situation.

- Teachers have the right to associate freely during off-school hours with whomever they wish. They may belong to any political party, religious group, or other group even if the group is not supported in the community or is disapproved of by board members, administrators, or others.

- Teachers have freedom of speech. Teachers have the same free speech rights as other citizens. They may comment publicly on all issues, including decisions of the school administrators or the school board. However, a teacher may not disclose confidential information or be malicious, and the statements can't interfere with teaching performance. Teachers do not have unlimited academic freedom or freedom of speech in the classroom or elsewhere in the school. Teachers are not permitted to disrupt the school or the school curriculum.

- Corporal punishment is not unconstitutional. However, corporal punishment may be illegal and may only be administered according to the laws of the state. Teachers should never strike children in anger and should administer corporal punishment only as a part of a due process procedure.

Students

- Handicapped students from ages 3 to 21 are entitled to a free and appropriate public education as a matter of federal law. This education should take place in the least restrictive environment available.

- Students have limited freedom of the press. Student newspapers supported by school funds may be reviewed and edited by school officials. However, papers paid for and produced by students off school property may not be censored by school officials.

- Students are entitled to due process. In particular, students have a right to a hearing and an opportunity to present a defense before being suspended. Students who pose a threat to others in the school are not entitled to this due process.

- Students have freedom of speech unless it causes a significant disruption in the school. They may display messages or symbols on their persons, and refuse to participate in the pledge of allegiance. However, they may not use speech considered vulgar or offensive.

HISTORICAL AND PHILOSOPHICAL FOUNDATIONS OF EDUCATION

Development of Formal Education

Education is a fairly recent development. Formal education has existed for only a fraction of the time that humans have been on earth. Many events in the history of education led to the structure of our education system today.

The first formal education probably began about 2000 B.C. in northern Africa and China. It was about 500 B.C. when the formal education that led to our system was instituted in Athens, Greece. Boys were educated in schools, and girls were educated at home.

Three philosopher-intellects of this time—Socrates, Plato, and Aristotle—left an indelible mark on education. Socrates developed the Socratic or inquiry method of teaching. Plato believed that an education should help a person fully develop body and soul. Aristotle introduced a scientific and practical approach to education. Plato and Aristotle both believed in the superiority of the ruling classes and the inferiority of women and slaves.

Formal Roman education began about 50 B.C., after Rome had conquered Greece. The grammiacticus schools, developed in Rome, taught such subjects as Latin, history, mathematics, and music and were like our high schools.

Around 70 A.D. Quintilian wrote a series of twelve books that described current and preferred Roman educational practices. These books may have been the first educational methods and psychology texts.

Education continued to develop and began to bring a unified language and thought throughout the known world. Then the Dark Ages (400 to 1000 A.D.) began. Enormous amounts of learning were lost during this period, and schooling was set back. The revival of learning following the Dark Ages was led by religious leaders such as St. Thomas Aquinas, who devised scholasticism (the formal study of knowledge).

During the Renaissance and the Reformation (1300 to 1700 A.D.), schooling was freed from control by the church. Church groups, particularly the Jesuits and the Christian Brothers, established religious schools.

Beginning around 1700, thought and schooling focused more on reason and logic. During this time, the "common man" in Europe sought a better life and better education. Great educators emerged from this period. Jean Jacques Rousseau, who wrote *Emile* in 1762, held a positive view of children and believed that education should be a natural process. Pestalozzi established schools that incorporated Rousseau's ideas. The schools featured understanding and patience for children and methods that enabled students to develop concepts through manipulative materials.

Herbart was Pestalozzi's student. In the early 1800s, Herbart formalized the approach to education. He presented some steps for teaching including presentation, generalization, and application. These steps bear a remarkable similarity to the stages from the taxonomy of educational objectives presented earlier.

Froebel was another educator influenced by Rousseau and Pestalozzi. Froebel established the first kindergarten with emphasis on social development and learning through experience. Kindergarten means child's garden.

American Education

In the 1600s American children were educated at home by their parents. Later that century, Dame schools began in the East. Classes were offered in a woman's home and often amounted to no more than child care. Secondary education consisted of Latin grammar schools, which provided a classical education.

In the mid-1600s laws were introduced in Massachusetts requiring education. Some localities provided schooling, and this form of local school lasted into the 1800s. Private schools also offered an education during this period. Admission to these schools was limited to those who could afford to pay.

In rural America there were not enough students in one locality to form a school. In these areas schooling was provided by tutors through the 1700s and by itinerant teachers through the 1900s.

English grammar schools and academies began operation as secondary schools during the 1700s. English grammar schools prepared students for careers while academies combined the features of Latin and English grammar schools.

Common schools provided free, public education for all students beginning in the 1800s. About that same time high schools were established to provide free, public secondary education. Junior high schools were introduced in the early 1900s, and middle schools were introduced in the 1950s.

Horn books, the alphabet covered by a transparent horn, were the predominant teaching device of the colonial period. The New England primer was the first substantial text and was used as a reading text until the late 1700s. The American spelling book, written by Noah Webster, contained stories and the alphabet along with lists of spelling words and was the most popular school book in the early 1800s. McGuffey's readers were reading books geared for different grade levels and were the main education materials for Americans from around 1840 to 1920.

American schools from the early 1800s through the early 1900s were based on the teachings of Pestalozzi and Herbart. These schools showed both the compassion suggested by Pestalozzi and the severe formalism based on Herbart's ideas.

Maria Montessori established her school, Casa Bambini, in 1908. She believed that students thrive in an environment that naturally holds their interest and that offers specially prepared materials. Schools following a modified version of her approach are found throughout the United States today.

Around 1900 John Dewey established the first "progressive" school. Progressive schools sought to build a curriculum around the child rather than around the subject matter. Progressive schools were very popular through the 1930s, and the progressive education movement continued into the 1950s.

The essentialist movement has a view opposite to progressivism. Educators associated with this movement favor a teacher-centered classroom. They believe in a more challenging, subject-oriented curriculum, and have a heavy reliance on achievement test results. Most school practices today primarily reflect the essentialist approach.

With the Depression of the 1930s, the federal government took a more active role in the schools. This active role increased through 1960 with programs designed to improve mathematics and science programs to bolster the national defense. In the

1960s and 1970s federal government focused on social issues as they relate to the schools, such as desegregation and equal educational opportunity.

Public Law 94-142 marked the federal government's first direct intervention in school instruction. This law and Public Law 99-457 mandate an appropriate public education in the least restrictive environment for handicapped Americans aged 3–21. Public Law 98-199 mandates transitional services for high school students. The federal government remains a vital force in American education today.

Jerome Bruner, B. F. Skinner, and Jean Piaget had an impact on American schools in the last half of this century.

In the *Process of Education*, Bruner urged the student's active involvement in the learning process. He called for more problem solving and believed that any topic could be taught in some significant way to children of any age.

B. F. Skinner took a different view than Bruner. He thought that material to be learned should be broken down into small manageable steps. Then students should be taught step by step and rewarded for success. Skinner's approach, behaviorism, built on the work of the Russian scientist Pavlov. Token reinforcement is an example of the behaviorist approach. Behaviorism is characterized by many as too limiting and controlling for regular classrooms.

Jean Piaget posited that students go through a series of stages—sensorimotor, pre-operational, concrete operational, and formal operational—as they develop concepts. He believed that students need to work individually, based on their stage of development, and that movement through the stages for a concept could not be accelerated. Piaget's work indicates that more concrete and pictorial materials should be used in the schools and that students should be actively involved in the learning process.

9 Principles of Learning and Teaching Test Strategy and Practice

This chapter contains an overview of Principles of Learning and Teaching (PLT) Test Strategy and Practice, including a practice PLT Case and practice PLT multiple-choice questions. Follow these steps to use this chapter.

USING THIS CHAPTER

- ❏ Review the Test Strategies on pages 301–303.
- ❏ Read the Practice PLT Scenario on page 303.
- ❏ Answer the PLT Constructed-Response Items on page 305 and review the answers.
- ❏ Answer the PLT Multiple-Choice Practice Questions on page 317 and review the answers.

Chapter 8 contains a PLT Review.
Chapter 10 contains a complete PLT Practice Test.

TEST OVERVIEW

The PLT consist of four case histories, each with 3 short-answer items and 24 multiple-choice questions. The multiple-choice questions are unrelated to the case histories. You have 2 hours to complete the test. You have about 25 minutes for each case and a little less than 1 minute for each multiple-choice question. There is enough time to complete the test, but there is no extra time. Be sure to leave enough time to answer all the questions. Do not leave any answers blank.

Test Strategies

MULTIPLE-CHOICE STRATEGIES

You have about 1 minute for each multiple-choice question. There are helpful strategies for responding to the multiple-choice items on pages 57–58. Use these strategies to answer the multiple-choice questions on the test. The multiple-choice items on the PLT are similar to the questions on the Elementary Education: Curriculum, Instruction, and Assessment (0011) on pages 370–398, although the questions on the PLT you take may be at a different grade level.

CONSTRUCTED-RESPONSE STRATEGIES

You have about 25 minutes for each case. That's about 5 minutes to review the case and about 7 minutes to think about and write each constructed response. You will write each constructed-response answer on a special single-page lined sheet provided with the test. Most often you will write 100 to 150 words. Readers are realistic about the length of your response. Try to print your answer; it will be easier to read.

Scoring Criteria

There are four scoring criteria.

- **Understand the case:** Demonstrate that you understand the case as it relates to the question.

- **Complete the response:** Respond to all parts of the question.

- **Provide details:** Support your response with details and examples.

- **Show a knowledge of teaching:** Demonstrate a knowledge of pedagogy—methods, theories, facts—as they relate to the question.

Show that you get the idea.

Answer the question completely and directly.

Don't provide extra or unrelated information.

Show that you know about the case and about pedagogy as they relate to the question.

Support your answer.

A typical PLT constructed-response question asks for TWO of something. It may be TWO strategies, or TWO strengths, or TWO adaptations, or TWO of something else. Be sure to write TWO of whatever the question asks for and then explain why each of the two makes sense.

Here's How They Score You

Two readers, trained to evaluate answers using holistic scoring, will score your response. Holistic scoring means the scorer rates the response based on his or her informed impression, not on a detailed analysis. Each reader rates the response 2, 1, or 0. You have to communicate clearly, but English grammar itself is not evaluated.

2 You will earn a 2 for two clear statements that respond directly to the two points in the question with evident support and an explanation for each statement.

1 You will earn a 1 for one statement that responds directly to one of the two points in the question with evident support and an explanation for the statement. You can also earn a 1 if you provide two statements but one of the statements is deemed unresponsive to the question or if the explanation leaves something to be desired. For example, the question may ask for strategies for teaching two different subjects, but the response gives two strategies for teaching one subject. Or the question may ask for two additional strategies, and the response lists a strategy already mentioned in the case.

0 You will earn a score of 0 if your response does not address the question or if your response is too general or vague. For example, a question may ask for two additional strategies for teaching a lesson, and the response indicates that no additional strategies are necessary.

Most responses rated 2 have about 100 to 150 words. That does not mean that a response this long will always receive a 2. But it does give you some idea about how long your response should be. Most responses rated 1 or 0 are shorter than responses rated 2. But many responses rated 0 or 1 that are off the point may be as long as a response that could be rated a 2.

Use Your Time Wisely

Here is a plan for using your time to respond to each case. The times are recommendations. Monitor your time as you work on this activity to find the appropriate amount of time that you should devote to each step.

Case

Read the questions and skim the case (5 minutes).

- Read the three questions at the end of the case and then read the case.

- Skim the case looking for answers to the questions.

- Make notes on the case.

- Return to the questions.

Questions

1. **Outline a response (2 minutes).** Use this time to think. Read the question carefully to be sure you understand what it asks for. Jot down the two strategies, adaptations, strengths, or ideas called for in the question. Sketch a supporting detail or two under each.

2. **Write your response to each question (4 minutes).** Use this time to write. Write directly and clearly. Print your answer on the response sheet. Plan to write about 100 to 140 words. That's about 25 to 35 words a minute. You can do that. Do not restate the question. Write your response on the sheet provided in the test materials. Responses written in the test booklet or elsewhere outside the response sheet will not be read.

   Follow these steps.

   • **Rewrite the first point from your outline.**

   • **Write a sentence or two with details to support the first point.** The details should support the point. Details tell how or why the point is important. Details can be explanations or examples.

   • **Rewrite the second point from your outline.** Then write at least one other sentence with details.

   • **Write a sentence or two with details to support this point.**

3. **Review (1 minute).** Compare your response to the item to be sure you have responded completely. Delete, add, or change words to clarify your response. Leave time to read your response. Raters understand that your response is a first draft, and they expect to see corrections. Thus, do not spend your time correcting minor grammatical or punctuation errors.

Let's apply these steps to a practice case.

Practice PLT Scenario with Constructed-Response Questions and Explained Answers

What follows is a complete case with three constructed-response questions. Review the questions and the case and then answer the three constructed-response questions. A step-by-step review of how to answer Question 1 and sample constructed-response answers for all three questions follow.

SITUATION

Ms. DelCorso teaches a heterogeneous, self-contained, sixth-grade class of twenty-five students. She is working on her Professional Improvement Plan (PIP), which every teacher in the district prepares each spring. Ms. DelCorso has chosen four students in this class as the basis for her PIP.

The principal will review Ms. DelCorso's PIP, and Ms. DelCorso will reflect on the process and respond.

Ms. DelCorso's First Step Is to Review Her Interactions with the Four Students

Mora is a hearing-impaired student. Mora's IEP requires me to wear a microphone and requires Mora to wear a wireless receiver tuned to the same frequency as my microphone. However, Mora refuses to wear the wireless device during class, and Mora's parents support her decision. Mora can read lips and watches very carefully; however, she misses out on important information in every class because Mora cannot hear me when she is looking at other students in the class.

Peter is a very bright student who is uncomfortable in social situations and something of an outcast among his peers. His test grades and standardized test scores have always been well above average in this class. He is someone who was used to achieving without effort. But lately his test grades have started to fall, and he has not responded to my efforts to help him complete all his homework assignments.

Luke is classified as a Learning Disabled student. He is easily distracted, and he almost never does his homework. He is a poor reader. He is easily frustrated and often abandons a task without giving it his full effort or attention. Luke regains his focus when I intervene and give him specific steps to follow.

Cynthia comes from a family of high achievers. Both of her parents are physicians, and she is driven to achieve beyond what her ability seems to justify. She is a perfectionist who can be very tense and nervous in class, and she works with a professional tutor at home each week. Her focus on schoolwork and her serious demeanor push her to the outer edges of the social group in her class.

Ms. DelCorso's PIP

Mora: Mora needs to use the wireless device to learn effectively in this class. My first step will be to call her parents and tell them that Mora is missing out on too much work because she does not wear the wireless device. I will ask for their support to encourage Mora to use the wireless device, and I will try to make clear how much language she misses each day and that this language deficit will create even more problems in later years. I will also talk to Mora to help her accept the device and point out that it is completely invisible to other students in the class.

Peter: I will bend the rules some to account for Peter's particular personality and learning style. I will provide him with study guides to help structure his homework and other learning activities and to help him review for tests. At the same time, I will open a channel of communication with Peter's parents and enlist them as partners in this effort, particularly to get Peter to do his homework.

Luke: I will establish a learning plan for Luke that requires him to come in on a regular basis to receive help. I will also give him an assignment pad that his parents will have to sign four nights a week. I will also try to motivate him to complete his homework by giving him extra-credit tickets for completed assignments that he can exchange for additional points toward his test grade.

Cynthia: Cynthia concerns me the most because her high expectations and insistence on perfection leave little room for flexibility, which may lead to even more significant problems. I will ask Cynthia to help other students to widen her friendship circle and to remove some of the focus from herself. I will also try to take the pressure off by giving her additional time for tests and other in-class activities.

The Principal's Response

Ms. DelCorso is a truly outstanding teacher, and I am always impressed with her work, as I am with her plan to deal with these four students. However, I recommend that she give further consideration to the following points.

- Parents are very defensive when speaking about their children's deficiencies, and parents are a very powerful force in our school district. We should be very careful about how we approach them, and any suggestions should be carefully considered and presented only after thorough discussion here at the school.

- Luke may benefit from extra-credit points, but how will we deal with the reactions of students and the parents of students who do not receive these points?

- I wonder if it is appropriate for a teacher to engage Cynthia in academic activities that are actually designed to further her social standing.

Ms. DelCorso's Reflection and Reaction

Thank you for your confidence in me, which I certainly have in you as a school administrator. I have reflected on my comments and your response, leading to these reactions.

I appreciate the concern and the delicate nature of dealing with parents, and I will be pleased to discuss my ideas and receive feedback before I engage in parental contact. However, I am very concerned about Mora in particular, and some appropriate action must be taken.

I see that overtly giving Luke extra credit may create problems with other students, and I will explore other ways to reward him when he completes his assignments.

Social activities are an integral part of the classroom environment and, in my opinion, Cynthia badly needs these social contacts to relieve pressure and to enhance her academic performance.

PRACTICE PLT CONSTRUCTED-RESPONSE ITEMS

1. Review Ms. DelCorso's PIP in which she describes her plans for responding to each of four students in her class.

    - Choose TWO students and recommend one additional strategy Ms. DelCorso could have included in her PIP for each of these students.

- Describe each strategy and explain why that strategy would be effective. Base your response on the sound principles of instructional planning.

2. Suppose that Ms. DelCorso and the principal have further discussions about parental involvement.

- Recommend TWO strategies that Ms. DelCorso could use to effectively involve parents in the school.

- Explain how each of the strategies you recommend could improve student learning. Base your answer on sound principles of communication and instructional planning.

3. The Principal's Response and Ms. DelCorso's Reflection and Reaction indicate that Luke needs reinforcement, but it should be done in a way that is unlikely to create problems with other students.

- Describe TWO additional ways in which Luke could be rewarded for completing his assignments.

- Explain why your suggestions will be effective and why they are unlikely to cause problems with other students. Base your answer on sound principles of classroom management and human interaction.

Practice Item 1 Response Sheet

_____

_____

_____

_____

_____

_____

_____

_____

_____

_____

Practice Item 2 Response Sheet

Practice Item 3 Response Sheet

_____

_____

_____

_____

_____

_____

_____

_____

_____

_____

_____

_____

_____

_____

_____

_____

_____

_____

_____

_____

_____

_____

Rated Responses

This section shows you how to apply the steps and gives examples of rated responses for the Practice Case.

Question 1

Review Ms. DelCorso's PIP in which she describes her plans for responding to each of four
students in her class.

- Choose TWO students and recommend one additional strategy Ms. DelCorso could have included in her PIP for each of these students.

- Describe each strategy and explain why that strategy would be effective. Base your answer on sound principles of instructional planning.

Follow these steps.

1. **Think:** I have to choose TWO *different* students. I'll pick Luke and Mora, for example. (You can pick any two students.)

   Then I have to come up with *one* additional PIP strategy for *each* student.

   I have to explain *why*, not how, each strategy will be effective.

2. **Sketch an outline:**

Luke should use a microcomputer.

   Good for LD students.

Mora's parents should come in to see how much she misses.

   Seeing is believing.

---

3. **Write your answer:**

   Review the scored sample responses that follow. A great many other responses could have earned these scores, so concentrate on the general form of each response.

4. **Review your answers to be sure they answer the question:** For this activity, rewrite any of your answers that did not earn a score of 2.

This response would receive a score of 2. It gives one additional strategy for each of two students and explains why the strategies would be effective. This response contains 129 words.

> I can think of something that Ms. DelCorso could have added to her PIP for Luke who is a learning-disabled student. Ms. DelCorso could have added a recommendation that Luke use a microcomputer to research topics on the Internet. Learning-disabled students in particular benefit from using computers to learn because working with a computer helps reduce distractions.
>
> Ms. DelCorso should consider adding this to Mora's PIP. Ms. DelCorso should ask one or both of Mora's parents to come to school and to observe Mora in class without the wireless device. This would let Mora's parents see for themselves how much Mora misses in class, and her parents would be a lot more likely to support Ms. DelCorso as she tries to convince Mora to wear the device.

This response would receive a score of 1. It suggests TWO things that Ms. DelCorso should add to her PIP. But both suggestions are for the same student, and the question asks for a response for TWO different students. This response contains 116 words.

> I can think of something that Ms. DelCorso could have added to her PIP for Luke who is a learning-disabled student. Ms. DelCorso could have added a recommendation that Luke use a microcomputer to research topics on the Internet. Learning-disabled students in particular benefit from using computers to learn because working with a computer helps reduce distractions.
>
> Ms. DelCorso should also consider asking one or both of Luke's parents to come to school and to observe him in class as he works. This would let Luke's parents see for themselves how he works in class and help them understand and support Ms. DelCorso as she tries to help Luke focus on the material at hand and to give it his full attention.

This response would receive a score of 0. It describes a useful process for arriving at a final PIP for Ms. DelCorso's students. However, it does not provide specific recommendations for any of the students. This response contains 97 words.

> There are a number of things Ms. DelCorso could have added to her PIP. The principal suggests some, and I think that it is the process between these two professionals that is important. They should have a meeting to fully discuss additional recommendations and emerge with a consensus that both can support.
>
> Once that process is complete, they should meet with the parents of the students to present their recommendations and receive parental feedback. Following that step, Ms. DelCorso and the principal should develop a final set of recommendations and use these recommendations to help the students.

Question 2

Suppose that Ms. DelCorso and the principal have further discussions about parental involvement.

- Recommend TWO strategies that Ms. DelCorso could use to effectively involve parents in the school.

- Explain how each of the strategies you recommend could improve student learning. Base your answer on sound principles of communication and instructional planning.

This response would receive a score of 2. It provides two useful strategies for involving parents in school, and it explains how each strategy could improve student learning. This response contains 145 words.

It is important to involve parents in school. This may be difficult if both parents work.

Ms. DelCorso could send home a monthly folder of student work. Parents could review the work and teacher's comments then sign the folder and return it to Ms. DelCorso. This strategy could improve student learning because parents will have a good idea of the work their children are doing and the teacher's comments on the work. This will guide them in helping their child with work at home.

Ms. DelCorso could hand out report cards to parents and their children at an after school meeting. This could improve student learning because the teacher can explain the report card and it will be clear to both the parents and the child how things are going and what work needs to be done in the next marking period.

This response would receive a score of 1. It provides two useful strategies that relate to parents. However, only one of the strategies includes an explanation of how to involve parents in the school. This response contains 124 words.

Ms. DelCorso should have a weekly class phone chain. She calls a few parents on the list to update information about classroom activities. These parents then call this information down through the chain. This approach will improve student learning because parents will be up-to-date on the most recent activities and assignments, and they will be able to help their children stay involved in class activities.

Sixth-grade students have lives outside school. They have responsibilities with their parents. Ms. DelCorso should respect a child's parent and family time by not giving assignments and work that unnecessarily interfere with that time. This will help student learning by strengthening the family and by making sure that students have time to complete their work.

This response would receive a score of 0. It provides strong support for the importance of parental involvement and acknowledges that Ms. DelCorso plans to involve parents. However, it does not give any specific approaches for involving parents in the school. This response contains 104 words.

> *Parental involvement is one of just a few things that can make a real difference in school learning for students. So it is clear that involving parents in the school is definitely something that Ms. DelCorso should do.*
>
> *I can see that she already plans to involve parents because she is going to call Mora's parents. That is a good strategy. Ms. DelCorso probably has other ways to involve parents. I can't tell what they are. That is the reason why it is just not possible to make any recommendations without more information. That would not be a responsible approach to a school situation.*

Question 3

The Principal's Response and Ms. DelCorso's reflection indicate that Luke needs reinforcement, but it should be done in a way that is unlikely to create problems with other students.

- Describe TWO additional ways in which Luke could be rewarded for completing his assignments.

- Explain why your suggestions will be effective and why they are unlikely to cause problems with other students. Base your answer on sound principles of classroom management and human interaction.

This response would receive a score of 2. It presents two *additional* ways to reinforce Luke, explains why the suggestions will be effective, and explains why the suggestions are unlikely to cause problems with other students in the class. This response contains 157 words.

The token reinforcement activity the teacher mentioned can be effective, but it is very visible and it might cause problems with other students who will not receive the tickets.

Ms. DelCorso could use social reinforcement. She could praise him for completing his assignments and show that she is very pleased with his work. She could stand near him and react positively while he is completing the assignment. Social reinforcers have been proven effective, and it is unlikely that students will have a problem because these comments and actions are directed just to Luke.

Ms. DelCorso could also schedule a preferred activity for all her students to engage in when their regular assignments are complete. Luke could use the computer following the completion of his assignments. This Premack approach has proven effective in schools, and students will not have a problem with Luke having to complete an undesirable activity before he can participate with them in a desired activity.

This response would receive a score of 1. It describes two useful strategies and explains why each strategy should not cause a problem. However, the first strategy is already mentioned and so it is not an additional strategy. This response contains 129 words.

Giving extra-credit tickets to Luke is a good idea, and it should motivate him to complete his assignments. The teacher can avoid problems with other students by giving the tickets to Luke privately and giving him the reward he gets for accumulating tickets after school when the other students are not around.

Ms. DelCorso could set up some positive consequences when Luke does good work. It could just be a few words or a note sent home to his parents saying that he is doing a good job. These types of positive consequences have been proven to be effective at helping students work better. These types of consequences for Luke should not cause a problem for other students because they will be receiving their own positive consequences as well.

This response would receive a score of 0. It makes some valid points about reinforcement and teaching. However, it does not include any specific recommendations about reinforcement strategies for Luke. This response contains 58 words.

This teacher should not be so concerned with specific types of reinforcement. It is too technical and no one really knows what will work with any given student. Ms. DelCorso should make herself accessible to every one of the students for extra help.

Those are the things to concentrate on if you want to run an effective classroom.

Practice PLT Multiple-Choice Questions with Explained Answers

1. Here is a brief part of a conversation between Alex Whitby, a third-grade teacher, and Marciella Atkins, the school district reading specialist.

   Alex: Thanks for coming by. I wanted to talk to you about one of my students.

   Marciella: Which one?

   Alex: Savaro—he's still having trouble with reading.

   Marciella: I remember Savaro from last year in second grade.

   Alex: I was thinking about more phonics—what do you think?

   Marciella: That's OK—just remember that phonics does not help much. . .

   Which of the following finishes the reading specialist's last sentence?

   (A) to associate sounds with printed letters.
   (B) with reading comprehension.
   (C) to attack new words independently.
   (D) to develop a sight vocabulary.

2. Tara Kirk is concerned about the way she responds to student's questions in science, and she wants to develop a more effective approach. The best advice for Ms. Kirk is to respond in which of the following ways.

   I. Encourage exploration of the answer with activities and materials that stimulate curiosity.
   II. Model good responding skills.
   III. Answer all items as quickly and concisely as possible.
   IV. Include children's questions in evaluation techniques.

   (A) I and II
   (B) III and IV
   (C) I, II, and III
   (D) I, II, and IV

3. Jovina Crockett is planning a lesson to integrate art with haiku, a Japanese poetic form. Which of the following approaches is LEAST likely to meet Ms. Crockett's needs?

   (A) Use the computer as an artistic tool to illustrate the haiku.
   (B) Provide a display of classical Japanese paintings for children to color.
   (C) Provide clay as means to illustrate the haiku.
   (D) Provide paints and brushes for illustrations of the haiku.

4. Sam Meletto, a second-grade teacher, and the principal are discussing Sam's reasons for instituting a whole language program in his classroom. Which among the following is the best reason Sam Meletto could give?

   (A) Whole language instruction is widely accepted.
   (B) It is not necessary to teach word recognition.
   (C) Children comprehend more after using a whole language approach.
   (D) Children have a better attitude toward reading.

5. Jaedo Purmen, a second-grade teacher, says he has found modeling to be an effective form of instruction, meaning that he is most likely to

   (A) show students how to construct replicas of historic buildings.
   (B) respond courteously to students' questions.
   (C) tell students when they have mispronounced a word.
   (D) demonstrate students' inappropriate behavior.

6. Damaris Jones and one of his students are discussing the student's most recent report card. Mr. Jones chooses his words carefully to have the most impact and finally decides on these: "Your grades would have been better if all your homework assignments had been handed in." Which of the following approaches has the teacher decided to use?

   (A) Positive reinforcement
   (B) Reverse psychology
   (C) Threats
   (D) Negative reinforcement

7. Lisa is a student in DeShala Washington's third-grade class. At a parent-teacher conference, Lisa's mother says she has heard about the school using a basal reading program and asks what basal reading programs are NOT good for? Which of the following would be Ms. Washington's best response?

   (A) Teaching and developing skills in a systematic sequential manner
   (B) Meeting individual differences and needs of the child
   (C) Establishing and reinforcing a basic vocabulary
   (D) Providing manuals with detailed outlines for teaching.

8. Elizabeth Milano is an experienced fifth-grade teacher. Ms. Milano notices that one student in her class has particular difficulty when reading problems in the mathematics textbook. In an effort to help this student, it would be most appropriate for Ms. Milano to recognize that this difficulty is most likely the result of

   (A) faulty word identification and recognition.
   (B) inability to locate and retain specific facts.
   (C) deficiencies in basic comprehension abilities.
   (D) inability to adapt to reading needs in this content field.

9. Tom Karel has a number of students in his class who are significantly below grade level in reading. Mr. Karel realizes that he needs to adapt social studies instruction for these students. All of the following options would be appropriate EXCEPT to

   (A) use instructional materials that have a lower reading level.
   (B) use instructional materials with less difficult concepts.
   (C) read information about social studies to the students.
   (D) use recorded tapes that contain social studies information.

10. Frank Rios is a primary teacher who is incorporating authentic assessment in his evaluation techniques. That means that Mr. Rios will

    • (A) collect and evaluate student work.
    (B) use only tests provided by the publisher of the books he uses.
    (C) evaluate students only in real situations outside of school.
    (D) collect evaluative information from other teachers.

11. Renita Lopez is teaching language arts in the upper elementary grades, and she wants to evaluate a student's writing techniques and plan for further writing experiences. Which of the following is the most appropriate choice?

    (A) Administer a standardized grammar test and use the scores as a planning device.
    (B) Use a writing checklist to assess a variety of creative writing samples including writing summaries and samples.
    (C) Have the student prepare a composition on a subject of their choice and holistically evaluate the composition.
    (D) Have the student answer a series of higher-level short-answer questions about a specific writing sample.

12. Sheneoi Goldman is a fifth-grade teacher who conducts science class using the inquiry approach. Which of the following would a person be most likely to observe during Sheneoi Goldman's science class?

    (A) Sheneoi Goldman deliberately does not try out an experiment in advance of the class so that everyone in the class sees the results together for the first time.
    (B) Sheneoi Goldman tells the students to avoid analyzing thought processes and rather to rely on what happens in the experiment.
    (C) Sheneoi Goldman presents a problem for the students to solve or a situation for them to explore.
    (D) Sheneoi Goldman asks students to present a problem for the class to solve or a situation for the class to explore.

Questions 13–16 are based on this situation.

Wayne Yarborough is in his fourth year as a social studies teacher at Roosevelt High School. He is giving some thought to the way he teaches. While teaching a social studies lesson, Mr. Yarborough can get the students' interest, but he is not so good at maintaining that interest. Wayne uses a wide variety of questions as he teaches and is very much interested in changing and reinforcing appropriate student behavior.

13. Mr. Yarborough has the best chance of maintaining student interest in the lesson if

(A) the teacher is animated.
(B) the objectives are clear and unambiguous.
(C) The students understand that what they are learning will help them learn other material later.
(D) there are no choices available to students.

14. When questioning students, which of the following techniques should Mr. Yarborough generally follow?

(A) Make sure students know who will answer a question before it is asked.
(B) Ask questions of the whole class.
(C) Ask questions of students who are not paying attention.
(D) Ask questions of students who usually have the correct answers.

15. Mr. Yarborough knows that modeling is one appropriate way of modifying behavior. Which of the following is an example of a good modeling technique?

(A) Responding courteously to students' questions
(B) Showing students how to construct replicas of historic buildings
(C) Demonstrating students' inappropriate behavior
(D) Stressing the importance of appearance and showing students how to dress

16. Which of the following would be an appropriate way for Mr. Yarborough to reinforce student behavior?

I. Grading on the basis of performance
II. Praising appropriate behavior
III. Ignoring inappropriate behavior

(A) I and II
(B) I and III
(C) II and III
(D) II

17. Chuck Galesky has been teaching a few years but like most newer teachers he still has some problems with discipline. He overhears the assistant principal say, "Chuck should try a more 'with-it' teaching approach to handle his discipline problems," most probably meaning that

    (A) a teacher is always aware of new disciplinary techniques.
    (B) a teacher is always aware of current popular trends among students.
    (C) a teacher is always aware of what is happening in the classroom.
    (D) a teacher is well respected by other teachers.

18. Lisa Germanio has significant discipline problems with her ninth-grade students. However, if Ms. Germanio were teaching high school seniors, she would find that discipline is less difficult because

    (A) it is left to the administration.
    (B) it is the parents' concern.
    (C) students are less resistant.
    (D) teachers are less authoritative.

Questions 19 and 20 are based on this situation.

Ingrid Johanssen is a science teacher who plans to begin the lesson by saying, "OK class, today we're going to learn about photosynthesis." She wants to model photosynthesis for the students and plans to write prerequisite competencies for the lesson on the board. Ms. Johanssen plans to use an inquiry approach and wants to motivate the students as much as possible.

19. Which of the following is the most powerful overall motivation Ms. Johanssen could use in the class?

    (A) Praise
    (B) Grades
    (C) Privileges
    (D) Learning

20. Which of the following best describes a prerequisite competency Ms. Johanssen plans to write on the board?

    (A) The knowledge and skills a teacher must possess to teach an objective
    (B) A subobjective to the main objective of the lesson
    (C) The basis for admitting students when they transfer from another school district
    (D) The knowledge and skills students must possess to learn an objective

21. Which of the following is an appropriate alteration to make in your curriculum to accommodate the needs of recent immigrants in your class?

    (A) Lower the expectations for the group.
    (B) Limit the amount of homework given.
    (C) Teach in the native language.
    (D) Require English proficiency to make progress in school.

22. Stan Heligo is writing objectives based on the Taxonomy of Educational Objectives: Cognitive Domain, which means that he should teach which of these topics to be at the highest level of this taxonomy?

    (A) Evaluating a book
    (B) Understanding a reading passage
    (C) Analyzing a written paragraph
    (D) Applying a mathematics formula to a real situation

23. A teacher using Gardner's multiple intelligences as the basis for instruction is most likely to do which of the following?

    (A) Implement interdisciplinary units
    (B) Help students learn about each of the intelligences
    (C) Eliminate assessments
    (D) Allow students to determine criteria for quality

Base your answers to Questions 24 and 25 on the passage below.

This passage comes from a longer selection about how teachers can use scientifically based research to make decisions about curriculum and instruction.

Education is informed by formal scientific research through the use of archival research-based knowledge such as that found in peer-reviewed educational journals. Preservice teachers are first exposed to the formal scientific research in their university teacher preparation courses (it is hoped), through the instruction received from their professors, and in their course readings (for example, textbooks, journal articles). Practicing teachers continue their exposure to the results of formal scientific research by subscribing to and reading professional journals, by enrolling in graduate programs, and by becoming lifelong learners.

Scientific thinking in practice is what characterizes reflective teachers—those who inquire into their own practice and who examine their own classrooms to find out what works best for them and their students. Being able to access mechanisms that evaluate claims about teaching methods and to recognize scientific research and its findings is especially important for teachers because they are often confronted with the view that "anything goes" in the field of education—that there is no such thing as best practice in education, that there are no ways to verify what works best, that teachers should base their practice on intuition, or that the latest fad must be the best way to teach, please a principal, or address local school reform. The "anything goes" mentality actually represents a threat to the professional autonomy of teachers. It provides a fertile environment for gurus to sell untested educational "remedies" that are not supported by an established research base.

24. In this author's view, which of the following best characterizes a more intuitive approach to identifying effective teaching methods?

- (A) An intuitive approach is a good idea because it gives teachers an opportunity to experiment with a wide array of teaching methods.
- (B) Teaching is an art, not a science, and a teacher must use his or her intuition even if the research seems to indicate that a particular teaching method is better.
- (C) Reflective teaching does not mean intuitive thinking, and an intuitive approach can cause more harm than good.
- (D) A teacher should not use any approach until that approach has been thoroughly validated through extensive study using the scientific method.

25. Which one of the teacher roles mentioned below is the author of this article most likely to favor?

- (A) The teacher should be a researcher who conducts classroom research on the effectiveness of various teaching methods.
- (B) The teacher should be someone who knows how to access and use research information about the best teaching practices.
- (C) The teacher should know how to use statistical tests to confirm that a particular teaching technique is effective.
- (D) The teacher does not have the expertise to engage in classroom research and should rely only on research conducted by professional researchers.

Multiple-Choice Answers

1. **(B)** The reading specialist was most likely going to say that phonics does not address word meaning or reading comprehension. Phonics primarily addresses word recognition and word pronunciation. Each of the remaining choices describes a benefit that can be derived directly from the phonics approach.

2. **(D)** Consider each Roman numeral in turn and then choose your answer.

   I. Correct. It is a good technique to handle a question with encouragement for more explanation.

   II. Correct. It is effective to demonstrate how to respond to questions.

   III. Incorrect. It is generally not a good idea to answer quickly. Ms. Kirk may be able to help the student find the answer for himself or herself.

   IV. Correct. Students' questions often reveal what is most difficult for them to understand, and it is a good technique to include their questions in evaluations.

   I, II, and IV are correct; that's choice (D).

3. **(B)** This is the least effective method because this choice, alone, does NOT integrate haiku with fine arts because only art is displayed. Each of the remaining choices describes an effective way of integrating haiku and art.

4. **(D)** Students develop a better attitude toward reading when they use the real literature found in a whole language approach. (A) It may be reassuring that an approach is widely accepted, but that is never the best reason to use it. (B) Word recognition must always be taught. Students can't read if they can't recognize words. (C) Research does not uniformly support the conclusion that students comprehend better after using a whole language approach. Rather, it seems that a combination of approaches, including aspects of the whole language approach, best develops reading comprehension.

5. **(B)** Modeling means the teacher demonstrates the behavior students should replicate. (A) Classroom modeling does not refer to this hobby. (C) Just telling a student is not modeling. (D) A teacher would not model incorrect behavior for students to copy.

6. **(D)** One example of negative reinforcement is explaining how to improve positive outcomes. (A) Positive reinforcement is praise or a reward for good work (B) Reverse psychology is suggesting the opposite of what you want a student to do. (C) Threats, or bullying, are not appropriate classroom techniques.

7. **(B)** This choice is correct because a basal reading program is not designed to meet the individual needs of students. Note the word NOT in the item. A basal program is typically designed to be used with all the students in a class. A basal program must be supplemented to meet the individual needs of students. The remaining choices describe some of the characteristics of a basal reading program.

8. **(D)** Ms. Milano notices the reading difficulty when the student is reading mathematics problems. This indicates that the difficulty is reading in the context of mathematics, and there is no mention that the reading problem occurs elsewhere. The remaining choices are all potential causes of reading difficulties, but not this reading difficulty, even though they may contribute to the problem in some way.

9. **(B)** Just because a student is below grade level in reading does *not* mean they cannot understand social studies topics that are at grade level or above grade level. Do not adapt instruction to less difficult topics on the basis of a low reading level. Each of the remaining choices represents an acceptable way to adapt social studies instruction for students reading significantly below grade level.

10. **(A)** Authentic assessment means Mr. Rios will observe students as they work or review students' actual work as described in this choice. (B) Mr. Rios would

not use tests as a part of authentic assessment, although he may use them for other purposes in his class. (C) Authentic assessment does not have to be conducted in real-life settings. (D) Mr. Rios would not rely on evaluative information from other teachers as a part of authentic assessment.

11. **(B)** This choice describes the best way to consistently determine a student's writing ability and to prepare for the future. The teacher gathers specific information that can be used for future plans. (A) Standardized grammar tests do not reveal detailed information about a student's writing. (C) Holistic evaluations reflect the evaluator's view of the overall quality of the writing. A holistic evaluation does not yield a specific analysis that can lead to instructional plans. Choice (D) is incorrect because it evaluates reading, not writing.

12. **(C)** This choice describes the essence of the inquiry approach, to solve problems as a way to understand scientific principles. (A) is incorrect because a teacher must have prior experience with an experiment so he or she can guide students. (B) is incorrect because students analyze their thought processes when using the inquiry approach. (D) is incorrect because the inquiry approach is not student-directed.

13. **(B)** Clear and unambiguous objectives are fundamental and crucial to maintaining   interest. There is a difference between students being responsive and students being interested in a lesson. (A) An animated presentation may maintain students' interest in the teacher but not in the lesson at hand unless the teacher has clear objectives in mind. (C) Students are typically not interested in a lesson because it holds the promise of subsequent understanding. (D) Leaving students with no choice does not maintain their interest.

14. **(B)** Mr. Yarborough should address questions to the entire class. This increases the likelihood that students will pay attention and actively think about an answer. (A) This technique focuses on just one student, and only that student will be thinking about an answer to the question. (C) This is a poor questioning technique, although some teachers use it to bring students back into the discussion. (D) This is a poor questioning technique that keeps the majority of students from full participation.

15. **(A)** Modeling means Mr. Yarborough does things in a way he wants his students to copy or emulate. This choice shows that he is engaging in exactly that kind of behavior. (B) This is a different kind of model than the one Mr. Yarborough has in mind. (C) Mr. Yarborough would not model inappropriate behavior to be copied. (D) Talking about the ways things should be or showing people how things should be is not modeling how things should be.

16. **(A)** Consider each Roman numeral in turn.

I. Correct. This is an example of reinforcing behavior.

II. Correct. This is also a way to reinforce student behavior.

III. Incorrect. This is not a way to reinforce behavior but rather a negative reinforcement.

I and II are correct. That's choice (A).

17. **(C)** The answer to this is common sense, but it also fits Kounin's definition of what "with-it" teaching means. (A) Just being aware of techniques does not mean you use them. (B) This choice means "with-it" in one sense, but it does not describe an approach to teaching. (D) The respect from peers described in this choice is not an approach to teaching.

18. **(C)** During the first two years of high school students tend to follow peer leaders. By the last two years of high school, students are more responsive to adult authority. (A) and (B) These choices apply as equally to ninth graders as to seniors. (D) Teachers who are constructively authoritative are usually best at discipline.

19. **(B)** Grades remain the primary motivation for students to do work in school. (A) Praise, (C) privileges, and less so (D) the opportunity to learn all contribute to a student's motivation. But these other choices are only a secondary consideration compared to (B).

20. **(D)** A prerequisite competency refers to some skill or knowledge a *student* must possess to learn a competency. In the sense used here, competency does *not* refer to teachers. (A) A competency refers to what the *student* must learn or do. (B) A prerequisite competency comes before the main objective; it is not a part of the main objective. (C) The term *prerequisite competency* does not apply to admission or transfer requirements.

21. **(B)** Children from immigrant families often do not benefit from extensive homework because there may not be help available from parents. (A) Lowering expectations does not help these students. (C) Teaching in the native language will not help these students who will need to master English to enjoy viable careers. This is different from helping children make the transition from their native language to English, which could be helpful. (D) This requirement is not helpful because English proficiency is beyond the capability of most of these students. However, it may be useful to ask students to *make progress* toward English proficiency.

22. **(A)** Evaluation is at the sixth and highest level of Bloom's cognitive taxonomy. (C) Analysis is at the fourth level, and (D) application is at the third level. (B) Comprehension is at the second level in this hierarchy of learning objectives.

23. **(A)** Gardner's theory supports the use of interdisciplinary units. Gardner's theory holds that students have many intelligences, not just a cognitive

intelligence. Interdisciplinary units promote utilization of these multiple intelligences. (B) Students don't need to know about these intelligences. (C) and (D) There is nothing in Gardner's theory that either supports the elimination of assessments or has students establish the criteria for quality.

24. **(C)** In the last paragraph the author makes this point as intuitive teaching is mentioned as one aspect of the "anything goes" approach. (A) is incorrect because the author indicates that a teacher should not just try out approaches without checking to see if there is approach known to be most effective. (B) This choice states the opposite of the argument the author presents in this article. (D) The author does not go as far as suggesting that no unproven approach should be tried, just that it should not take precedence over proven approaches.

25. **(B)** Throughout the article, the author makes the strongest case for the research-based knowledge found in journals and states that teachers should use that research base. (A) is incorrect because this is not the role the author is most likely to favor, although the article provides support for a teacher's classroom research. (C) The author never indicates that teachers should be statisticians. (D) The author does not go this far and includes support for teachers' classroom research in the article.

Principles of Learning and Teaching Practice Test

PRINCIPLES OF LEARNING AND TEACHING PRACTICE TEST

This full-length PLT has four case histories, each followed by three constructed-response items. There are 24 other discrete multiple-choice items not associated with a case history in two groups of 12. The first case history is early childhood, the second case history is elementary (K–6), the third case history is intermediate (5–9), and the last case history is secondary (7–12).

You can also take this test in computerized form on the CD that accompanies the book.

You should take this practice test after you have completed Chapter 8 and Chapter 9. Take the test in a realistic, timed setting. The setting will be most realistic if another person times the test and ensures that the test rules are followed. If another person acts as test supervisor, they should review these instructions with you and say "START" when you should begin a section and "STOP" when the time has expired.

You have 2 hours to complete the test. Use about 25 minutes for each scenario and the associated constructed-response items. Use the remaining time for the multiple-choice items.

Keep the time limit in mind as you work. There is no penalty for guessing. You may write on the test booklet and mark up the questions.

Each item on the multiple-choice portions of the test has four answer choices. Exactly one of these choices is correct. Mark your choice on the answer sheet provided for this test.

Use a pencil to mark the answer sheet. The actual test will be machine-scored, so completely darken in the answer space. When instructed, turn the page and begin.

PLT Answer Sheets

Remove pages 332–343 to use as your answer sheets.

Scenario 1

1. Write your answer on the sheet provided on page 332, which follows.
2. Write your answer on the sheet provided on page 333, which follows.
3. Write your answer on the sheet provided on page 334, which follows.

Scenario 2

4. Write your answer on the sheet provided on page 335, which follows.
5. Write your answer on the sheet provided on page 336, which follows.
6. Write your answer on the sheet provided on page 337, which follows.

Discrete Multiple-Choice Questions
These questions are not related to any of the scenarios.

7 (A) (B) (C) (D) (E)
8 (A) (B) (C) (D) (E)
9 (A) (B) (C) (D) (E)
10 (A) (B) (C) (D) (E)
11 (A) (B) (C) (D) (E)
12 (A) (B) (C) (D) (E)

13 (A) (B) (C) (D) (E)
14 (A) (B) (C) (D) (E)
15 (A) (B) (C) (D) (E)
16 (A) (B) (C) (D) (E)
17 (A) (B) (C) (D) (E)
18 (A) (B) (C) (D) (E)

Scenario 3

19. Write your answer on the sheet provided on page 338, which follows.
20. Write your answer on the sheet provided on page 339, which follows.
21. Write your answer on the sheet provided on page 340, which follows.

Scenario 4

22. Write your answer on the sheet provided on page 341, which follows.
23. Write your answer on the sheet provided on page 342, which follows.
24. Write your answer on the sheet provided on page 343, which follows.

Discrete Multiple-Choice Questions
These questions are not related to any of the scenarios.

25 (A) (B) (C) (D) (E)
26 (A) (B) (C) (D) (E)
27 (A) (B) (C) (D) (E)
28 (A) (B) (C) (D) (E)
29 (A) (B) (C) (D) (E)
30 (A) (B) (C) (D) (E)

31 (A) (B) (C) (D) (E)
32 (A) (B) (C) (D) (E)
33 (A) (B) (C) (D) (E)
34 (A) (B) (C) (D) (E)
35 (A) (B) (C) (D) (E)
36 (A) (B) (C) (D) (E)

PLT Answer Sheets

SCENARIO 1
CONSTRUCTED-RESPONSE ANSWERS

1. _____

_____

_____

_____

_____

_____

_____

_____

_____

_____

_____

_____

_____

_____

_____

_____

_____

_____

_____

_____

_____

_____

_____

PLT Answer Sheets

2. _____

_____

_____

_____

_____

_____

_____

_____

_____

_____

_____

_____

_____

_____

_____

_____

_____

_____

_____

_____

PLT Answer Sheets

3. _____

_____

_____

_____

_____

_____

_____

_____

_____

_____

_____

_____

_____

_____

_____

_____

_____

_____

_____

_____

_____

_____

PLT Answer Sheets

SCENARIO 2
CONSTRUCTED-RESPONSE ANSWERS

4. _____

_____

_____

_____

_____

_____

_____

_____

_____

_____

_____

_____

_____

_____

_____

_____

_____

_____

PLT Answer Sheets

5. _____

_____

_____

_____

_____

_____

_____

_____

_____

_____

_____

_____

_____

_____

_____

_____

_____

_____

_____

_____

_____

_____

PLT Answer Sheets

6. _____

_____

_____

_____

_____

_____

_____

_____

_____

_____

_____

_____

_____

_____

_____

_____

_____

_____

_____

_____

_____

PLT Answer Sheets

SCENARIO 3
CONSTRUCTED-RESPONSE ANSWERS

19. _____

_____

_____

_____

_____

_____

_____

_____

_____

_____

_____

_____

_____

_____

_____

_____

_____

_____

_____

_____

_____

_____

PLT Answer Sheets

20. _____

_____

_____

_____

_____

_____

_____

_____

_____

_____

_____

_____

_____

_____

_____

_____

_____

PLT Answer Sheets

21. _____

_____

_____

_____

_____

_____

_____

_____

_____

_____

_____

_____

_____

_____

_____

_____

_____

_____

_____

_____

_____

PLT Answer Sheets

SCENARIO 4
CONSTRUCTED-RESPONSE ANSWERS

22. _____

_____

_____

_____

_____

_____

_____

_____

_____

_____

_____

_____

_____

_____

_____

_____

_____

PLT Answer Sheets

23. _____

_____

_____

_____

_____

_____

_____

_____

_____

_____

_____

_____

_____

_____

_____

_____

_____

_____

_____

_____

_____

_____

_____

PLT Answer Sheets

24. _____

_____

_____

_____

_____

_____

_____

_____

_____

_____

_____

_____

_____

_____

_____

_____

_____

_____

Practice PLT Test

SCENARIO 1: K–6 CASE HISTORY

Situation

Ms. Kelly teaches third grade in a K–5 school. This is her fourth year of teaching. "I'm going to get this teaching down—definitely in the next 20 years," is her favorite thing to say to more experienced teachers in the school. She knew it was going to take a long time to become a master teacher, but she had no idea it would take this long. Ms. Kelly emphasizes appropriate classroom behavior.

Document 1: Classroom Behavior Sign

DO UNTO OTHERS AS

YOU

WOULD HAVE THEM DO UNTO

YOU

Document 2: Partial List of Reading Materials and Books

Gladstone's Basal Readers
Gladstone's Reading Workbooks
Gladstone's Phonics Workbooks
26 Fairmount Avenue
Babe, the Gallant Pig
Book of Slime
Dinosaur Bones
The Dog That Stole Home
Encyclopedia Brown and the Case of the Slippery Salamander
Finding Providence
Goin' Someplace Special
How We Crossed the West: The Adventures of Lewis and Clark
I, Amber Brown
In the Time of the Drums
Just Like Mike
Kate Shelley, Bound for Legend
Lizzie Logan, Second Banana
Red-Eyed Tree Frog
So You Want to Be President?
The Truth About Great White Sharks

Document 3: Ms. Kelly's Observations About Students' Reading Performances

Janice: Janice has trouble when she has to sound out new words from the reading book. However, Janice easily remembers new sight words when I present them before she reads the story.

James: James remembers the sound of every letter. He can even sound out blends. But he has difficulty pronouncing new sight words when I present them. James can add quickly and accurately. The unusual thing is that James does not do well when he has word problems to solve.

Elizabeth: Elizabeth has difficulty when she reads stories from the basal text. But give her a book with many pictures at the same reading level as the basal text and she is able to get as much information out of the book as anyone else in the class. I am concerned that Elizabeth is really not able to read many words. Sometimes I think that Elizabeth gets most of her information from pictures. But it doesn't show up on any tests.

Document 4: Portion of the Principal's Notes About Her Last Observation Meeting with Ms. Kelly

I observed the class reading a science-fiction story. Ms. Kelly had a large print version of the book in front of the class. Each student has his or her own version of the book. Some students followed along in their own books, while others followed along on Ms. Kelly's large print book.

The story is about astronauts who land on a friendly planet where they find friendly but impish aliens. In the story, Nayr the alien tries to trick the astronauts away from their spaceship so that Nayr can look inside. As I left Ms. Kelly's classroom, the students were enjoying the story. They read aloud, asked and answered questions, and enjoyed the wonder of this trip to an imaginary planet.

During our meeting Ms. Kelly told me she enjoys hearing her students during choral reading. She said, "There is just something about hearing the sound of all their voices together. And they help one another as they read. I just love it."

Ms. Kelly also told me she is considering implementing a program on reading and mathematics to help her students become more mathematically literate. She also wondered aloud whether to use primarily a whole language approach or primarily a phonics approach in her classroom.

PRACTICE PLT CONSTRUCTED-RESPONSE ITEMS

1. Suppose that Ms. Kelly and the principal are discussing effective classroom management practices.

   • Describe TWO strategies that Ms. Kelly could use for her approach to classroom management described in Document 1.

   • Explain why each of the strategies you recommend would be effective. Base your answer on sound principles of classroom management.

2. Document 2 includes a list of the different types of reading materials used in Ms. Kelly's classroom.

   • Describe TWO approaches that describe how Ms. Kelly could use these resources to establish an effective reading program in her classroom.

   • Explain why each of the approaches you recommend would be effective. Base your answer on sound principles of instructional planning.

3. Document 4, a portion of the principal's observation notes, indicates that Ms. Kelly was considering implementing a plan to integrate reading and mathematics.

   • Recommend TWO ways that Ms. Kelly could implement that plan.

   • Explain why each of the ways you recommend would be effective. Base your answer on sound principles of instructional planning.

SCENARIO 2: 5–9 CASE HISTORY

SITUATION

Ms. Brown has been teaching seventh grade for just one month. It is not unusual for her to work through the weekend preparing lessons. Ms. Brown is concerned about the time it takes for her to teach her lessons and about the interactions she has with certain students and parents. She is gathering information and seeking feedback to help her with these situations.

Ms. Brown's Conversation with a Colleague

Ms. Brown saw a colleague one day when she was shopping in the supermarket. Ms. Brown was pushing around a shopping cart, and in the child's seat Ms. Brown had her plan book.

"What are you doing?" asked the colleague.

"Shopping," said Ms. Brown, "and you never know when you're going to get an idea for a lesson."

"You've got to have some time for yourself," her colleague said.

"Not this year," sighed Ms. Brown.

Supervisor's Summary Report About Ms. Brown

The lessons Ms. Brown prepares are wonderful. I always write complimentary remarks when I return her plans. As I often tell other teachers, Ms. Brown writes the best lesson plans I have ever seen.

Unfortunately, Ms. Brown is frequently unable to finish her lessons. Some beginning teachers prepare more information than they can present. That is not the case with Ms. Brown. It is just that she spends so much time trying to explain everything carefully and in great detail. The students are often not actively involved in the lesson.

When Ms. Brown checks homework assignments, the students act as though it is free time. They talk, take each other's personal property, exchange notes, and just generally make a nuisance of themselves. They should be reviewing their work and correcting mistakes.

Preparing good lessons that are unappreciated by students leaves her frustrated. Ms. Brown has begun to teach in a negative and critical fashion. She has had a few run-ins with parents. They complain that she does not treat their children fairly and that she is too demanding.

Principal's Summary of Some Parent Comments About Ms. Brown

Ms. Sivar is one of the parents who think Ms. Brown is unfair. She told me, "My Tim doesn't finish his tests in Ms. Brown's class because the tests are too long." She added, "It is certainly not because he's fooling around."

Ms. Price, another parent, told me it is unfair for her daughter Estelle to get a B in Ms. Brown's class when all the test grades are A. "So what if she misses a few assignments," she snapped at me.

Mr. Allen told me it was unfair for his son Sam to have to take a test when Sam has been absent the previous day. He was very firm when he told me, "I don't care if Sam knew about the test at the beginning of the week. And I certainly don't care that Ms. Brown sent home a test guide. He wasn't in class the day before, and he shouldn't have to take the test."

Ms. Brown's Comments About Four Students in Her Class

Tommy never brings his book to class, and this is not accidental. Other students come to class without necessary supplies, including a required notebook and something to write with.

Jill almost never pays attention in class, seldom follows directions, and almost never participates in learning activities. At the same time every day, Jill announces that she has to go to the girls' room. I know she doesn't.

Igor always walks in five minutes late. Always! Then he may wander in and out of the class. He deliberately does not copy down the homework assignment. With Igor, it's lots of hard work planning for few results.

Fadia never does any homework and annoys everyone around her. That is why I put her in the back of the class—by herself. Now all Fadia does is read library books or just falls asleep.

Ms. Brown's Discussion with the Guidance Counselor

During a discussion with the guidance counselor, Ms. Brown learned that many of her colleagues had had similar problems with Fadia.

Ms. Brown told the guidance counselor, "I may not be able to get Fadia to do homework. But there is no way that I am going to tolerate her sleeping in my class."

The guidance counselor responded by saying, "I think you should call Fadia's parents to see if they can help with this problem."

PRACTICE PLT CONSTRUCTED-RESPONSE ITEMS

4. The Principal's summary of parental comments about Ms. Brown lists some of the issues parents have with Ms. Brown.

   • Describe TWO approaches that Ms. Brown could take to improve her relationships with parents.

   • Explain why each of the approaches you recommend would effectively improve that communication. Base your answer on sound principles of communication.

5. Ms. Brown's comments about several students and her discussion with the guidance counselor help describe some of the disciplinary issues Fadia has in school.

   • Recommend TWO approaches that Ms. Brown could use to reduce some of Fadia's disciplinary problems.

   • Explain why each of the strategies you recommend would be likely to reduce Fadia's disciplinary problems. Base your answer on sound principles of classroom management and human development.

6. Say that Ms. Brown and her supervisor are discussing the supervisor's summary report about Ms. Brown, with an emphasis on completing each lesson.

   • Describe TWO strategies the supervisor could recommend to Ms. Brown to enable her to complete most of the lessons she teaches.

   • Explain why each of the strategies you recommend would be effective. Base your answer on sound principles of instructional planning and classroom management.

PRACTICE PLT MULTIPLE-CHOICE QUESTIONS

These questions are not related to the scenarios.

7. Teachers on the Carteret Elementary School technology committee are discussing computer use in classrooms. Lee Mombello raises the issue of equity. He says, "In a country where most homes have a computer and the Internet, many of our students have no access to computers outside the school. With this in mind, which of the following choices is the best policy for the committee to establish about the classroom use of computers?

   (A) Special after-school computer clubs should be set up for students who do not have a computer at home.
   (B) Teachers should integrate computers in their teaching whenever possible.
   (C) Each student should be given their own computer to use at school and at home.
   (D) The school should hire a technology specialist who will help teachers integrate computers in their classrooms.

8. Gerard Lancaster is a new teacher who wants to use cooperative learning groups to supplement a teacher-centered approach to social studies instruction. In order to accomplish that task, which of the following should Mr. Lancaster employ when compared to teacher-centered presentations?

   I. More student involvement
  II. More content coverage
 III. More varied outcomes
 IV. More brainstorming

(A) I and II
(B) I, III, and IV
(C) III and IV
(D) II, III, and IV

9. The Carson Hills school district is preparing a pamphlet about effective schools to distribute to teachers. Which of the following choices should be listed as characteristic of effective schools in the pamphlet?

   I. A climate of high expectations
  II. Accountability for student performance
 III. Eliminating standardized tests

(A) I only
(B) I and II
(C) III only
(D) II and III

10. Cindy Weiss is concerned about how she uses class time in her departmentalized fifth-grade English class. She realizes after a year of teaching that she must learn to be an effective classroom manager, which means that she will take steps to ensure that the majority of class time is devoted to

(A) individual work.
(B) on-task activities.
(C) cooperative learning.
(D) lecturing.

Base your answers to Questions 11 and 12 on this situation.

Frank Damico, a special education teacher, is working with Kathy McCoy in Kathy's fifth-grade class that includes mainstreamed students. Mr. Damico and Ms. McCoy have regular meetings with the parents of mainstreamed students in the class.

11. Which of the following best describes Frank Damico's role in the classroom?

(A) Observe the mainstreamed students to identify the out-of-class support they need
(B) Teach the entire class cooperatively with the teacher
(C) Help the mainstreamed students during the teacher's lesson
(D) Observe the nonmainstreamed students to get tips on their successful learning styles to pass on to the special education students.

12. During one meeting a parent expresses extreme anxiety about how her child James is doing in school. The parent is concerned that continued academic problems will make it impossible for him to attend college or to be a success in life. Which of the following choices is the best response for these teachers to give?

    (A) "Don't be concerned; we are confident that James will do fine and be successful."
    (B) "We enjoy working with James, and we have the highest hopes for him."
    (C) "That James is still in a special education setting at this age indicates there are likely some real problems that may or may not be resolved over time."
    (D) "We are sorry you feel that way, but we just cannot discuss these things with parents."

13. Dr. Samson, the school principal, was explaining to a group of beginning teachers that children can learn vicariously, meaning that children can

    (A) learn by doing.
    (B) learn through a wide variety of activities.
    (C) learn if there is a clear structure.
    (D) learn from others' experiences.

14. Stan Powell makes extensive use of portfolio assessment in his anthropology class, and so he knows that the most significant difficulty with portfolio assessment reliability is that

    (A) students put samples of widely different types of work in their portfolios.
    (B) scoring machines don't work reliably with materials in portfolios.
    (C) different teachers place different emphasis on the portfolios when giving grades.
    (D) different teachers assign widely different grades to the same portfolio.

15. Repeated testing of a fourth-grade student in Ray Maw's class reveals an IQ in the 110–115 range, but the student's standardized test scores are two or more years below grade level. Which of the following is the most appropriate interpretation of these test scores?

    (A) The student is a poor test taker.
    (B) The student's achievement and potential match.
    (C) The student is gifted.
    (D) The student has a learning disability.

16. Ezequiel Sanchez administers an end-of-chapter test from the teacher's edition of a language arts text to students in his fourth-grade class. In all likelihood, this is a

    (A) portfolio evaluation.
    (B) standardized test.
    (C) norm-referenced test.
    (D) summative evaluation.

Base your answers to Questions 17 and 18 on these passages.

The following excerpts present opinions about what is good and what is not good about direct instruction.

What's good about direct instruction? Direct Instruction (DI) is the most widely used instructional technique, and for good reason, it works. DI features a research-based curriculum and lessons that have been extensively field-tested and revised. The objective is to develop lessons that students understand the first time the lesson is taught. Each lesson builds on skills fully mastered in the previous lesson. Once a skill has been mastered, students are able to apply the skill to new situations. This emphasis on mastery and application enables the student to learn more complex and more difficult skills. The use of proven lessons lets DI move quickly and efficiently. Students are asked many questions in DI classes, giving them the opportunity for full skill mastery. DI uses achievement grouping for each curricular area to account for achievement differences among students. This grouping enables students to move at their own pace. Students are assessed frequently to facilitate additional help and reteaching. When DI is fully implemented, students in these classes regularly outperform students in other classes regardless of the teaching approach used in the other classes.

What's not good about Direct Instruction? Research shows that Direct Instruction (DI) is great for developing skills. But DI proponents use the research about DI's success in a skills environment to make arguments for its use in all school instruction. That kind of argument just can't be supported. There is no doubt that it is a fantastic approach for teaching early reading. Researchers agree that phonics is the best way to teaching reading, and phonics instruction lends itself to a DI approach. But there is much more to a curriculum than skills, and there is much more to reading than phonics. Once students learn to read, they must explore language, read books on their own, and pursue their own interests. DI is probably the worst way to help students become independent and effective readers. DI might be fine for teaching mathematics skills, but the tightly controlled instruction found in DI is not the best way to help students become effective problem solvers. You get the idea—DI may be fine for narrow skills instruction, but it is not good for instruction that requires higher-order thinking and exploration.

17. The first passage supports which of the following types of student grouping?

   (A) Students should be grouped homogeneously in a way that ensures each student will work with every other student in the class in each curricular area.
   (B) Students should be grouped heterogeneously according to IQ score, and this grouping should be used for each curricular area.
   (C) Students should be grouped homogeneously for each individual curricular area.
   (D) Students should be grouped heterogeneously for each individual curricular area.

18. The second passage argues against using DI throughout the curriculum by making which of the following points?

   (A) DI has been tested only in an environment that supports skills development.

   (B) DI has proven very successful for teaching reading, and reading is an important part of every subject in the school curriculum.

   (C) DI places an emphasis on the mastery and application of school subjects, and these apply across the entire school curriculum.

   (D) DI is still an unproven approach to teaching, and so this approach should definitely not be used throughout the school curriculum.

SCENARIO 3: 7–12 CASE HISTORY

SITUATION

Mr. Hayes worked in industry for years and has been teaching science about three years. He came to the school without formal certification under a plan for bringing experienced scientists into the teaching ranks. Mr. Shifts has been the principal of Everett High School as long as anyone can remember. As usual, this morning finds him out and about the school visiting classes. He is about to drop in on Mr. Hayes, a science teacher in the school. Mr. Shifts had praised Mr. Hayes to the school board as "the kind of person who can help our students learn about science in the world of work." But both he and Mr. Hayes have learned that schools and businesses are not the same. Lots of things that are effective in the workplace simply are not effective in a school.

Preobservation Interaction

The bell rang, and Mr. Shifts stood in the hall as the students streamed by. Things really had not changed since he was a student there. The students dressed differently, but they were really the same. From within the crowds of students he heard calls of "Hey Shifty." That had not changed since he was a student there either.

The last student entered the classroom, leaving the hall desolate again except for the hall monitors seated at each end. Mr. Shifts turned his attention to the classroom. He walked through the door to Mr. Hayes's room, went up to Mr. Hayes, and said, "Morning."

Mr. Hayes groaned. "It's June. I thought I was finished with observations this year."

"Just dropping by," said Mr. Shifts. "Nothing formal, but I'd like to see what's going on with some of the students. What are you teaching today?"

Mr. Hayes smiled a relieved sigh and said, "I'm teaching a lesson on photosynthesis. I am going to model this myself with an experiment in front of the class. I also considered setting up a series of activities and preparing a series of questions that will guide the students through the activities. But this way will be better."

"Great," said Mr. Shifts. "Mind if I stay a bit?"

"You know that you're welcome—always," said Mr. Hayes. Then he thought to himself, "I've got to become an administrator. And am I glad I didn't decide to use that touchy-feely student-based approach to teaching this lesson. These students will be itchy enough on a hot day like this."

Mr. Shift's Observation of Mr. Hayes

Mr. Hayes begins, "OK class, today we're going to learn about photosynthesis. Copy the homework questions from the board while I check the experiment." I think Mr. Hayes hopes the questions will motivate the students to learn about photosynthesis and motivate them to pay attention during the lesson.

Mr. Hayes also tells the students that the class will end with a short quiz on aspects of the subject that he is presenting, apparently to motivate them to pay attention during the lesson.

Mr. Hayes sets up the experiment, moving the apparatus around on his experiment table in front of the class. Some students are not copying the questions. Mr. Hayes notices and urges the students to "get busy." The apparatus consists of a beaker of water with a test tube turned upside down inside it; there is a green plant inside the test tube. A very bright light shines on the beaker and the test tube. The apparatus does seem to hold the attention of many students.

After the students have had enough time to copy the questions, Mr. Hayes begins the lesson and explains the results of the experiment. The test tube started out completely filled with water, but after a while the water was pushed down further in the test tube, which Mr. Hayes explains shows that photosynthesis produces oxygen.

Mr. Hayes is very careful to highlight the key concepts as he conducts the experiment. I can see that the homework questions are all based on the key concepts in the lesson.

Mr. Hayes is demonstrating and explaining important concepts. Most of the students are paying attention, but only a few of them are taking notes.

In my opinion, Mr. Hayes is a good teacher, but he should try using the inquiry approach with these students. I think that many of them would have learned more from what was a very good lesson.

PRACTICE PLT CONSTRUCTED-RESPONSE ITEMS

19. Suppose that Mr. Shifts and Mr. Hayes are discussing Mr. Shift's observation with a focus on how to engage students in note taking during the experiment.

    • Recommend TWO strategies that Mr. Shifts could present to Mr. Hayes to ensure that most of the students take notes during the experiment.

    • Explain why each of the strategies you recommend would be effective. Base your answer on sound principles of instructional planning and classroom management.

20. In the Preobservation interaction, Mr. Hayes indicates he's glad he did not set up a series of student-based activities to complete the lesson.

    • Recommend TWO benefits the students might have derived from a student-based approach.

- Explain why each of these benefits would come from a student-based approach. Base your answer on sound principles of instructional planning and learning theory.

21. The description of the principal includes his opinion that Mr. Hayes's work experience can relate science learning to the world of work.

   - Recommend TWO approaches that Mr. Hayes could use to relate his work experience to learning science in a way that would benefit students.

   - Explain why each of the approaches you recommend would be effective. Base your answer on sound principles of communication and instructional planning.

SCENARIO 4: 4–8 CASE HISTORY

SITUATION

Derek is a student in a mathematics class. Ms. Stendel, Derek's teacher, notices that he has trouble with some relatively simple computation problems. She also notices that Derek is frequently distracted during class. Ms. Stendel is an experienced teacher, and she decides to establish a portfolio of documents about Derek that she can later share with the psychologist and others.

Document 1: Summary of Prior Classroom Notes

Derek's ability test scores and his insights and comments during class reveal that he is unusually intelligent. When I ask him to do something he can complete quickly or to solve a problem mentally, he is amazing. But he gets completely bogged down when we work on projects over several days or when he has to complete a longer project on his own. He often seems distracted and tense in class.

Document 2: Ms. Stendel's Classroom Observation of Derek

I have just given the class a project to work on for thirty minutes that involves solving two mathematics problems. The first problem requires logical thinking, whereas the second problem involves complicated addition, subtraction, multiplication, and division. The students do not have their calculators. Derek is working in a group with four other students. I will observe that group and Derek in particular and record my observations.

The five students are seated around a table, and each student has a copy of the problem to be solved. Derek seems disinterested. But then he starts talking about things unrelated to the problem. He asks other students what they are doing after school. He suggests that the group talk about other things besides the problem in front of them. He brings up a soccer game that will be played on Saturday.

Some of the students seem interested in his distraction, but the group decides to focus on the first problem. Derek is not happy, and he sulks and withdraws from the group and stares at his copy of the problem. The other students are talking about the first problem when Derek interrupts them saying, "I've got it."

He will not tell the other students what his answer is and just continually says "That's wrong" when other students suggest solutions. I cannot tell whether he actually has the answer, but based on my past experiences, I think he probably does. Derek is somewhat more involved in the group now, and the group keeps working, with no help from him, on the first problem. He pushes his chair onto the back two legs and just rocks back and forth saying things like "No—that's not it."

After fifteen minutes the group has not solved the first problem, and Derek will not share the solution he says he has. The group turns their attention to the second problem. Derek demonstrates a new level of confidence and a new level of participation even though he is still ignored by most of the group.

Students have sheets of plain paper, and Derek begins to work on his calculations for the second problem. Derek is right-handed, and I notice that he holds his pencil in an unusual way with his thumb pressing the pencil against his middle finger. There is just enough room for him to touch the pencil with his index finger. He moves the pencil using only his fingers to produce large and often hard-to-read numerals. I can see that the numerals are not aligned well.

I end my observation with everyone in the group doing calculations to solve the second problem. I pick up Derek's work from the table after the group breaks up and have included some of it below for this portfolio.

Document 3: A Sample of Derek's Calculations

$$\begin{array}{r} 1 \\ 174 \\ + 286 \\ \hline 4510 \end{array}$$

$$\begin{array}{r} 31 \\ \times 42 \\ \hline 62 \\ 124 \\ \hline 186 \end{array}$$

$$\begin{array}{r} 121 \ R15 \\ 58 \overline{)7053} \\ \underline{58} \\ 125 \\ \underline{116} \\ 93 \\ \underline{58} \\ 15 \end{array}$$

Document 4: Ms. Stendel's Conversation with Derek After School on the Day of the Observation

Ms. Stendel: Derek, can you stay just a minute?

Derek: OK.

Ms. Stendel: I was watching your group during math today.

Derek: I saw you sitting there.

Ms. Stendel: You seemed to know the answer to that first problem.

Derek: Yes—they're all stupid.

Ms. Stendel: But you would not tell them what your answer was.

Derek: Let them get it.

Ms. Stendel: But it could help them to know what your answer is.

Derek: I don't want to help them. They are very mean to me.

Ms. Stendel: But what if your answer was not correct?

Derek: It was.

Ms. Stendel: Will you tell me what it was.

Derek: I don't remember. Can I go now?

Ms. Stendel: OK, Derek I will see you tomorrow.

PRACTICE PLT CONSTRUCTED-RESPONSE ITEMS

22. Document 2, Ms. Stendel's Classroom Observation of Derek, indicates some of the problems that Derek has with group work.

    - Recommend TWO approaches that may enable Ms. Stendel to effectively involve Derek in cooperative group work.

    - Explain why each of the strategies you recommend would be effective. Base your answer on sound principles of instructional planning and classroom management.

23. Document 3 shows some of Derek's calculations in addition, subtraction, and multiplication, which include some computational errors.

    - Recommend TWO specific techniques Ms. Stendel could use to help Derek with his arithmetic computation.

    - Explain why each of the techniques you recommend would be effective. Base your answer on sound principles of instructional planning and informal assessment.

24. Assume that Ms. Stendel shares the conversation from document 4 with her supervisor.

    - Give TWO recommendations the supervisor might make for effectively dealing with Derek.

    - Explain why each of the approaches you recommend would be effective. Base your answer on sound principles of instructional planning and human development.

PRACTICE PLT MULTIPLE-CHOICE QUESTIONS

These questions are not related to the scenarios.

25. Which of the actions by a teacher is LEAST likely to promote good communication with parents?

    (A) Make phone calls to parents.
    (B) Write personal notes on report cards.
    (C) Initiate a series of home/school letters.
    (D) Meet with groups of parents to discuss individual student achievement.

26. Responsibilities primarily attributed to local school boards include

    I. employing and supervising a superintendent.
    II. assigning teachers and staff to schools and designating their responsibilities.
    III. assigning individual pupils to schools.
    IV. evaluating district goals.

    (A) I, II, and IV
    (B) II and III
    (C) I and IV
    (D) I, III, and IV

27. Frank Carmody usually uses a lecture approach to present his history lessons. Which of the following approaches is most likely to help Mr. Carmody enhance instruction?

    (A) Begin the lesson with a motivation.
    (B) Focus his instruction on the entire class and avoid making eye contact with individual students.
    (C) Walk around the room while he delivers his lecture.
    (D) Choose a topic above the students' ability level.

28. Ms. Johanssen arranges her students in cooperative learning groups to work on photosynthesis, usually meaning that

    (A) Ms. Johanssen cooperates fully with the students.
    (B) Ms. Johanssen gives each group specific instructions on how to proceed.
    (C) a person from each group reports the group's findings.
    (D) each group of students gathers information about photosynthesis from the local Agriculture Department Cooperative Extension.

29. Mr. Rosspaph receives the results of a norm-referenced test indicating that a student has an IQ of 97, leading the teacher to the conclusion that

    (A) the student has below-average intelligence.
    (B) the student's intelligence is in the normal range.
    (C) the student is mildly retarded.
    (D) the standard deviation of the test is 3.

<u>Use this situation to respond to Questions 30–32.</u>

Faith Bisone is teaching a United States history class that is culturally and linguistically diverse. Many of the students in her class have a first language other than English, and many come from homes where English is not spoken. Ms. Bisone knows that the minority students in her class as a whole tend to have lower achievement scores than other students. She wants to familiarize herself with the difficulties these students have and with the teaching approaches that will be effective in her classroom.

30. The data about the achievement of minority students leads Ms. Bisone to the valid conclusion that

    (A) minority students are less capable learners than other students are.
    (B) the parents of minority students care less about their children's education.
    (C) learning expectations should be lowered for minority students.
    (D) minority students have fewer opportunities for enriched learning experiences at home.

31. Which of the following describes an acceptable approach to modifying the objectives or plans for this class?

    (A) Modify the plans to teach history topics about the parents' home countries.
    (B) Modify the objective to adjust its difficulty level.
    (C) Modify the plans to include direct instruction in English.
    (D) Modify the plans to account for the cultural heritage of those in the class.

32. Which of the following is consistent with Ms. Bisone using an ESL approach with a group of Limited English Proficiency students from the class?

    (A) Use context clues to help students identify English words.
    (B) Teach mathematics in the students' first languages.
    (C) Help students learn their native languages.
    (D) Encourage regional and local dialects.

33. When completing an assignment, most successful learning takes place when

    (A) students work independently in school.
    (B) students work supervised by a parent at home.
    (C) students work supervised by the teacher.
    (D) students work on a computer.

34. Ezequiel Sanchez uses a computer-based multimedia encyclopedia as part of his fourth-grade writing program. The multimedia encyclopedia includes hypertext links in most of its articles. To help understand how to use the hypertext links, Mr. Sanchez would best explain that

    (A) the links tie together very (hyper) important ideas in the passage.
    (B) clicking on a link gives additional information.
    (C) the links move or vibrate to draw attention to important ideas.
    (D) clicking on a link with a mouse cursor changes the link's color.

35. Felipe Victorino uses a token economy system to motivate students during a unit in his business class. Which of the following actions is most consistent with Mr. Victorino's approach?

    (A) Mr. Victorino provides token (symbolic) reinforcement for work completed by students as opposed to real or meaningful reinforcement.
    (B) Mr. Victorino distributes subway and bus tokens for reinforcement because this approach was pioneered in urban areas where many students took buses and subways to school.
    (C) Mr. Victorino posts a description of how students can earn points and then exchange a certain number of points for a more tangible reward.
    (D) Mr. Victorino posts a "token of my appreciation list" on the bulletin board and lists the names of students who perform outstanding work.

36. In her 10 years as a superintendent of schools, Dr. Kim Morgan has learned that, generally speaking, class discipline problems are most difficult during

    (A) Grades 2–3.
    (B) Grades 5–6.
    (C) Grades 8–9.
    (D) Grades 11–12.

EXPLAINED RESPONSES AND EXPLAINED ANSWERS

Constructed-Response Items

The essential elements of the responses to each constructed-response item are given below.

Scenario 1

1. You should give TWO strategies Ms. Kelly could use for her approach to classroom management. This item refers to Ms. Kelly's classroom sign, "DO UNTO OTHERS AS YOU WOULD HAVE THEM DO UNTO YOU." Your strategies should directly address that approach.

   Following each strategy, you should give a brief explanation of why the strategy would be successful. That is, you should highlight something about that strategy that will make it successful. That's different from describing how something will be successful, which means describing the impact of the approach in the classroom.

For example, one strategy might be having students meet to agree on the consequences of not following the advice in the sign. You might say the strategy will be effective because it involves the active participation of all the students in the class.

There are many other effective strategies.

2. You should give TWO ways Ms. Kelly should use the resources listed in the case to establish an effective reading program. These materials include both basal readers and children's literature. Your strategies should incorporate both types of reading materials.

   Following each of the ways of using the resources, you should explain why they would be effective. That means you should explain what there is about the approaches that would make them effective, and not about the effect they will have. There are many other effective strategies.

   For example, you could say that you will use the phonics workbook and the basal readers for a phonics-based program and then explain that phonics is the best way to teach students about reading. You could also say that you will use the children's books for a literature-based program.

3. You should give TWO ways that Ms. Kelly can implement a plan to integrate reading and mathematics in her classroom. The question does not specifically refer to the reading materials in Ms. Kelly's class.

   Following each of the ways for integrating reading and mathematics, you should explain why the approach you suggest will be effective. That means what there is about the approach that will make that approach effective.

   For example, you could say that you will teach reading through mathematics word problems and explain that the approach will be effective because improved reading ability will help students become better mathematics problem solvers.

   There are many other effective strategies.

Scenario 2

4. You should give TWO approaches Ms. Brown can take to improve her relationship with parents. All the complaints in the Principal's Summary are about testing and grades. Some of these complaints are bound to be self-serving, but they are still creating problems for Ms. Brown. Other parts of the scenario indicate that Ms. Brown may be trying to do too much, that she has difficulty with classroom discipline, and that she is frustrated and acts in a negative fashion. These problems with students cause them to complain to their parents. This does not seem to be an easy problem to solve.

   Following each of the suggestions for improving relationships with parents, you should explain why it would be effective and what there is about the approach that will make it successful. For example, you could write that Ms. Brown could improve communication with parents through phone calls or through a regular newsletter. You could explain that this approach will be effective because parents respond positively to teachers who reach out to them.

   There are many other effective strategies.

5. You should give TWO approaches that Ms. Brown could take to *reduce some* of Fadia's disciplinary problems. Fadia creates real problems for Ms. Brown, and it seems that Ms. Brown is overwhelmed by other aspects of the classroom. The guidance counselor gives some clear guidance to Ms. Brown when she recommends that Ms. Brown call Fadia's parents, although we do not know what approaches might emerge from that discussion. We know that Fadia's disciplinary problems occur in other classes, not just in this class.

   Following each approach, you should tell why that approach is likely to reduce Fadia's disciplinary problems—what there is about the approach that will reduce some of the problems.

   You might recommend that Ms. Brown structure high-interest activities for Fadia that will lead to her success and explain that this approach will be successful because Fadia will be less likely to bother others if she has work that holds her interest and offers the opportunity for success. A recommendation that Ms. Brown call the parents is not appropriate. This action might lead to an effective strategy for reducing Fadia's disciplinary problems, but it is not an effective strategy in itself. The answer should include only effective strategies.

   There are many other effective strategies.

6. You should give TWO strategies the supervisor could recommend to Ms. Brown to enable her to finish her lessons. The Supervisor's Summary report reveals the supervisor thinks that one reason Ms. Brown's lessons are too long is because she spends too much time on details. The supervisor also mentions that students are not actively involved in the lessons.

   Following each suggestion, you should explain why the strategy will be effective in reducing the length of her lessons—what there is about the strategy that will make it effective.

   You might recommend that Ms. Brown actively involves the students in the lessons, using student feedback to move the lesson along, and explain that this approach is likely to be effective because it may help Ms. Brown stop providing too much detail. A recommendation that Ms. Brown prepare less material is not appropriate because the Supervisor's Summary indicates that Ms. Brown does not prepare more information than she can present.

Multiple-Choice Answers

7. **(B)** This policy statement gives the best guidance to ensure that students have the most opportunities to use computers. (A) and (C) The committee's work is focused on computer use in classrooms, and these policies do not address that area. (D) This policy is not within the committee's control, and it holds little promise of helping because it would require additional approval to implement.

8. **(B)** Consider each Roman numeral in turn.

   I. Correct—Group learning means more student involvement.

   II. Incorrect—Cooperative learning groups do not lead to more content coverage. In fact, teacher-directed lessons would most likely lead to more content coverage.

   III. Correct—The more people involved, the more varied the outcomes.

   IV. Correct—A cooperative learning group means more brainstorming.

   I, III, and IV are correct. That's choice (B).

9. **(B)** Consider each Roman numeral in turn.

   I. Correct—High expectations are a hallmark of effective schools.

   II. Correct—Students do better when teachers and administrators are held accountable for their performances.

   III. Incorrect—Standardized tests are used in effective schools.

   I and II are correct; that's choice (B).

10. **(B)** Spending more time on a task is among a relatively few classroom practices shown to enhance learning. It has a proven and more powerful impact than all the other choices listed. There is room in the classroom for all the other choices. However, if Ms. Weiss had to choose, as you do, she would choose choice (B).

11. **(C)** This choice accurately describes why the special education teacher is in the classroom, to help special education students while the teacher conducts the lesson. (A) Frank Damico's job is to be the support, not to arrange for support. (B) and (C) are incorrect because Mr. Damico's responsibility is not with nonmainstreamed students, although he may spend some time working with these students.

12. **(B)** This is the best response to give a parent. It is positive and truthful, and it neither holds out too much hope nor is too negative. (A) is too positive and unrealistically raises a parent's expectations. (C) is likely the most candidly honest of the four responses. But it is too stark, and it is not the kind of response that should be given at a parent-teacher conference. (D) unnecessarily puts the parent off.

13. **(D)** It's a definition; vicarious learning means that children can learn from others' experiences rather than from direct experience. None of the other choices reflect the definition of vicarious learning.

14. **(D)** Reliability means that the same work consistently receives the same evaluation. Many schools that implemented portfolio assessment had to alter

their policies because different teachers assigned widely different grades to the same portfolio. Clear rubrics or standards have to be established for portfolio assessment to be effective. (A) It is not the diverse group of work students put in portfolios that causes the problem. Rather, it is the way teachers assess these samples. (B) Machines do not typically score the materials in a portfolio. (C) This may be an issue under some circumstances; however, it is not an issue of reliability.

15. **(D)** This is the classic test-based definition of a learning disability—at or above average ability but achievement two or more years below grade level. (A) is incorrect. There is nothing in this record to indicate that the student is a poor test taker, and the IQ score of 110–115 may indicate that the child is not a poor test taker. (B) is incorrect. The student's achievement is well below the student's potential. (C) is incorrect. These IQ test results are not high enough for a gifted classification.

16. **(D)** A summative evaluation assesses what a student has learned about a specific objective or objectives. (A) A portfolio evaluation relies on samples of students' actual work. choices (C) and (D) Standardized tests and norm-referenced tests are essentially the same type of test. These tests have been standardized on a large population of students. End-of-chapter tests are not standardized.

17. **(C)** The first passage supports ability grouping, which means students should be grouped homogeneously by achievement. The passage indicates that there should be a separate grouping for each curricular area. Choices (A) and (D) are incorrect because they call for heterogeneous grouping—grouping not based on achievement. Choice (B) is incorrect because it calls for a single grouping based on ability to be applied to each individual curricular area.

18. **(A)** The main argument against Direct Instruction (DI) in the second passage is that it has been proven effective only for skills instruction. (B) and (C) are incorrect because the answer choices support DI. The support found in choice (C) is from the first passage and not the second passage. (D) is incorrect because the second passage acknowledges that Direct Instruction is a proven form of instruction.

Constructed-Response Items

The essential elements of the response to each item are given below.

Scenario 3

19. You should give two strategies to help ensure that most of Mr. Hayes's students are taking notes during the experiment. Mr. Shift's observation of Mr. Hayes gives most of the information you need to answer this question. Mr.

Hayes spends a lot of time at the beginning of the lesson getting the experiment ready and then demonstrating the experiment.

Following the description of each strategy, you should explain why the strategy would be effective—what there is about the strategy that would make it effective.

You might recommend that Mr. Hayes walk around the room and check on students to be sure they are taking notes and explain that this approach could be successful because students are more likely to take notes if someone is checking on their progress. A recommendation that Mr. Hayes give clear instructions to take notes would not be appropriate because Mr. Hayes gives clear instructions at the beginning of the class to copy questions from the board.

There are many other effective strategies.

20. You should give two examples of benefits that students could have derived from student-based activities in Mr. Hayes's class. Mr. Hayes's lesson was teacher-based and teacher-directed.

Following the description of each benefit, explain why the students would benefit from the activity.

You might recommend the inquiry approach that the principal describes at the end of his observation. In the inquiry approach students observe experiments and draw their own conclusions under the teacher's guidance. You could explain that students would benefit from this approach because they would be actively involved in the lesson.

There are many other effective strategies.

21. You should give two approaches that Mr. Hayes could use to relate his work experience and science in a way that will benefit students. The case history tells us that Mr. Hayes has worked in industry, but it does not tell us what type of industry he worked in. The principal did praise Mr. Hayes as someone who "can help our students learn about science in the world of work."

Following the description of each approach, explain why the approach would benefit students.

You might just say that Mr. Hayes could describe how the science that students were learning was important to the work he did in business and how the students' work in class would help prepare them for a science career. Explain that this approach would be effective because it would give students a real-world basis for studying science.

There are many other effective strategies.

Scenario 4

22. You should give two approaches that Ms. Stendel could use to effectively involve Derek in cooperative group work. Cooperative Learning is a group of students working as a team toward a goal that will be reported, with a focus on individual responsibility, decision making, reflection, and positive interaction. Ms. Stendel's observation of Derek indicates that he is highly intelligent

but uncooperative, although he is more involved when he feels more comfortable and more in control.

Following the description of each approach, explain why this approach would effectively involve Derek in cooperative group work.

You might suggest that Ms. Stendel assign each student in the group a specific responsibility, such as leader, recorder, reporter, questioner, or assessor. Perhaps questioner would be the best role for Derek. Explain that this approach would help to effectively involve Derek in cooperative group work because it would give him a specific task and make him feel more in control of the situation.

There are many other effective strategies.

23. You should give two techniques to help Derek with computation, and the techniques should be specific. The first step is to analyze his errors. Derek has trouble renaming in addition, he adds 6 and 4 to get 10 and just writes the 10 in the sum instead of writing 0 in the ones place and renaming ten ones as one ten. He has trouble aligning the partial products in multiplication. In division he subtracts incorrectly at the last step of the computation.

Following the description of each technique, explain why this technique would effectively help Derek with his arithmetic computation.

You might recommend that Derek do his computation on graph paper, writing digits in each square on the paper. Explain that this approach will help him align digits and at least help him overcome the computational errors he makes by misaligning partial products in multiplication.

There are many other effective strategies.

24. You should give two recommendations that a supervisor might give for effectively dealing with Derek. Derek seems angry, rejected by, and alienated from the other students in the class. He is unwilling to interact with them, let alone cooperate.

Following the description of the recommendation, explain why the strategies you recommend would be effective.

The one thing missing in this report about Derek is any information about his parents or his home life. You might say that the supervisor would recommend that Ms. Stendel involve Derek's parents and explain that this would be effective because parental involvement is known to be effective and because the teachers could learn more about Derek and work with the parents to help him feel less alienated.

There are many other effective strategies.

Multiple-Choice Answers

25. **(D)** This choice identifies the approach that Ms. Zimbui should not use. It is improper to discuss individual student achievement with groups of parents. Even if the parents seem to agree to share the results, the practice can only lead to problems. The remaining choices give examples of ways to promote effective communication with parents.

26. **(C)** In a sense, a school board is responsible for everything in a district, and very little can happen without some sort of approval by the board. In practice the board has a more limited number of primary responsibilities.

    Consider each Roman numeral in turn.

    I. Correct—This is one of the board's most important responsibilities.

    II. Incorrect—This is primarily an administrative responsibility.

    III. Incorrect—The board may make policy about school assignments but very rarely actually assigns a student to a school.

    IV. Correct—This is another of the board's most important responsibilities. The board has a responsibility to ensure that the long-term and short-term goals are being met.

    I and IV are correct. That's choice (C).

27. **(A)** Research shows that starting a lecture with a motivation, compared to the other choices, is the most effective way to enhance instruction. (B) It is good to make eye contact with students during a lecture. (C) Walking around the room, alone, does not enhance instruction. (D) A topic above students' *ability* levels detracts from the effectiveness of a lecture.

28. **(C)** Students in cooperative learning groups devise their own plan and work actively together to gather information. Usually, one member of the group reports the group's findings. (A) This kind of cooperation does not describe cooperative learning groups. (B) The teacher gives cooperative learning groups the topic, but group members themselves devise a working plan. (D) A cooperative learning group may do this, but working with cooperative extensions does not describe cooperative learning groups.

29. **(B)** IQ tests have a mean of 100 and a standard deviation of 10, and IQ scores from 90 to 100 are in the normal range. That means that 97 is in the normal range and that the other choices are incorrect. There is no evidence from this score that this student is mentally retarded.

30. **(D)** Minority students as a whole are *not* less capable than other students, but as a whole they do have fewer opportunities for learning at home, which tends to lower achievement scores. (A) Minority students are not less capable. (B) Parents of minority students are as concerned about their student's education as much as other parents. (C) Ms. Bisone should not lower learning expectations for her students. High expectations lead to more learning.

31. **(D)** The acceptable approach is for Ms. Bisone to modify the plans to account for the cultural heritage of the students in her class. (A) The topics should be those regularly taught in the school's United States history courses. (B) The objective should be at the same difficulty level, although Ms. Bisone

may adapt her teaching approach. (C) It is fine for Ms. Bisone to help her students understand English in the context of learning history, but she should not adapt her objectives to become English objectives.

32. **(A)** Every teacher is a reading teacher. ESL means English as a second language, and LEP means limited English proficiency. Teaching English as a second language includes using context clues to identify words. (B) Teaching mathematics in the first language is an example of bilingual education. (C) Teaching English as a second language does not include instruction in the foreign language. (D) Standard spoken English is the goal, and ESL instruction does not encourage regional or local dialects.

33. **(C)** Students typically learn most when they are supervised by a teacher. Some students may learn most when they work independently, but that is not typical. (B) Some parents are capable of appropriate supervision, but that is not usually the case. (D) Some students may learn most while they complete an appropriate assignment on a computer, but that is not where most successful learning occurs.

34. **(B)** Clicking on a hypertext word reveals a definition or underlying meaning. Hypertext links to word definitions hold tremendous promise for reading instruction. (A) The links do not tie together "hyper" ideas. (C) Links do not usually move or vibrate to draw attention. (D) A link may change color when clicked, but that is to let you know that you have visited that link before.

35. **(C)** A definite reward schedule, some means of giving rewards (points, paper coupons, plastic tokens), and a means of redeeming tokens or points are the essential ingredients of a token economy. (A) The word *token* in this choice means figurative and does not mean a real token to be handed out to children.

36. **(C)** It is during these grades that students turn most to peer groups and are most resistant to authority. The activity that one sees in the early grades and the maturity later in high school typically present fewer discipline problems than choice (C).

PART V

ELEMENTARY EDUCATION INCLUDING FULL-LENGTH PRACTICE TESTS WITH EXPLAINED ANSWERS

Elementary Education: Curriculum, Instruction, and Assessment

---

HOW TO PREPARE FOR THE CURRICULUM, INSTRUCTION, AND ASSESSMENT TEST

This chapter prepares you to take the Elementary Education Curriculum, Instruction, and Assessment test (0011). The chapter gives an overview of each test and full-length practice tests with explained answers.

The Curriculum, Instruction, and Assessment Practice Test begins on page 379.

Preparation Strategies

Other sections in this book will help you prepare for these tests. The PLT Review beginning on page 264 will help you prepare for this test. The Proven Test-Preparation Strategies on page 12 will help you prepare for all the tests. The Multiple-Choice Strategies on page 15 will help you pass the Curriculum, Instruction, and Assessment test.

Elementary Education: Curriculum, Instruction, and Assessment (0011)

OVERVIEW

This 2-hour test has 110 multiple-choice items. Most items relate directly to school settings, while some items are more general. According to ETS, the items are based on the material a new teacher should know. You will encounter items from many grade levels. The items are based on the overall areas of curriculum, instruction, and assessment. The test is also based on the content areas of Reading/Language Arts, Mathematics, Science, Social Studies, Arts (including music) and Physical Education, and General Knowledge items about teaching.

This section includes a full practice test with explained answers.

The test itself is structured in one of two ways: (1) content area organization, or (2) overall area organization.

Overall Area Organization

The items for each overall area are grouped together. The items for the content areas are randomly distributed under each overall area. For example, all the curriculum items are grouped together. The subject area items related to curriculum are arranged in no particular order in the curriculum items.

Content Area Organization

The items for each content area are grouped together. The items for the overall areas are randomly distributed under each content area. For example, all the reading items are grouped together. The curriculum, instruction, and assessment items for reading are arranged in no particular order in the reading items.

Overall Areas

Each overall area below contains questions about each of the six content areas. The following include the topics on which you may be tested in each overall area.

Curriculum

Curriculum questions ask about how each instructional area is organized, as well as how to choose and use the instructional materials and other resources available for teaching the subject. That is, curriculum questions may ask you to communicate why a subject is important to learn, or how subject areas are related, or how to integrate within and across subject areas, or about the textbooks and other materials, including technological resources and software, available for instruction.

Instruction

Instruction questions ask you about specific teaching approaches for a subject area. That is, curriculum questions may ask you to describe how to find out what students know and build on this knowledge, or how to prepare instructional activities that integrate within and across subject areas, or to choose learning and teaching approaches which might include cooperative learning, or how to motivate students to learn.

Assessment

Assessment questions ask you how to devise and implement assessment strategies. That is, assessment questions might ask you about the appropriateness of text-based and other assessment strategies, or about how to use informal assessment techniques, about authentic or portfolio assessment, and appropriate interpretation and reporting of assessment results.

Content Areas

Each content area below contains questions about curriculum, instruction, and assessment. The following include the topics on which you may be tested in each content area.

Reading/Language Arts (35 percent or 38 items)

- The general purpose of teaching reading and language arts, including literacy

- Methodology including readiness, comprehension, word recognition, and teaching techniques

- Strategies for integrating reading, writing, listening, and speaking, children's literature

- Learning theories applied to teaching reading and writing, including constructivism, behaviorism, multiple intelligences, Piaget's stages of cognitive development, and others

- Curriculum, including objectives, overall scope and sequence, and instructional materials

- Assessing and interpreting students' reading and writing development, including teacher-made tests, standardized tests, and authentic (portfolio) assessment

Some test items may ask you to analyze students' work.

Mathematics (20 percent or 22 items)

- The general purpose of teaching mathematics

- Methodology including pre-number activities, problem solving, numeration, operations, algorithms, geometry, estimation, reasonableness of results, probability, elementary statistics, calculators, and computers

- Learning theories applied to teaching mathematics, including constructivism, behaviorism, multiple intelligences, Piaget's stages of cognitive development, and others

- Curriculum including objectives, overall scope and sequence, and instructional materials

- Assessing and interpreting students' mathematics development, including teacher-made tests, standardized tests, and authentic (portfolio) assessment

Some test items may ask you to analyze students' work.

Science (10 percent or 11 items)

- The general purpose of teaching science

- Teaching methodology; observing and describing, formulating and testing hypotheses, experiments, data and data presentation, health and safety

- Learning theories applied to teaching science, including constructivism, behaviorism, multiple intelligences, Piaget's stages of cognitive development, and others

- Curriculum including objectives, overall scope and sequence, and instructional materials

- Assessing and interpreting students' science development, including teacher-made tests, standardized tests, and authentic (portfolio) assessment

Some test items may ask you to analyze students' experiments or experimental results.

Social Studies (10 percent or 11 items)

- The general purpose of teaching social studies

- Teaching methodology; people, social organization, government, economics, communication, transportation, data and data representation, building models, impact of technology, planning and problem solving

- Learning theories applied to teaching, including constructivism, behaviorism, multiple intelligences, Piaget's stages of cognitive development, and others

- Curriculum including objectives, overall scope and sequence, and instructional materials

- Assessing and interpreting students' social studies development, including teacher-made tests, standardized tests, and authentic (portfolio) assessment

Arts (including Music) and Physical Education (10 percent or 11 items)

- The general purpose of teaching the arts, music, and physical education

- Methodology and activities, color, texture, design, rhythm, melody, harmony, timbre, cultural influences, art and music as therapy, creativity, indoor and outdoor safety, activities and games appropriate to developmental level and sports, movement, coordination

- Learning theories applied to teaching the arts, music, and physical education, including constructivism, behaviorism, multiple intelligences, Piaget's stages of cognitive development, and others

- Curriculum including objectives, overall scope and sequence, and instructional materials

- Assessing and interpreting students' art and physical education development, including teacher-made tests, standardized tests, and authentic (portfolio) assessment.

General Curriculum, Instruction, and Assessment (15 percent or 17 items)

- Psychological and social basis for instruction including child development, emotional development, social development, and language development

- Hierarchy of thinking skills and classroom questions

- Classroom organization, management, discipline, and motivation

- Learning theories applied to teaching, including constructivism, behaviorism, multiple intelligences, Piaget's stages of cognitive development, and others

- Curriculum including objectives, overall scope and sequence, and instructional materials

- Assessment and interpretation of students' development, including teacher-made tests, standardized tests, and authentic (portfolio) assessment

- Use and interpretation of assessment of results including fundamental test and measurement concepts

- Relationships with parents and other colleagues

PRACTICE TEST
110 Items, 2 Hours

The items about Curriculum, Instruction, and Assessment are arranged under each content area. The test you take may have items organized by the overall areas of Curriculum, Instruction, and Assessment, with the content items arranged under each of these headings. There are many different versions of this test, and the version you take may have a different emphasis and focus than this practice test.

Take this test in a realistic, timed setting. The setting will be most realistic if another person times the test and ensures that the test rules are followed. If another person is acting as test supervisor, he or she should review these instructions with you and say "START" when you should begin a section, and "STOP" when time is up.

You have 2 hours to complete the test. Keep the time limit in mind as you work. There is no penalty for guessing. You may write on the test and mark up the questions. Each item has four answer choices. Only one of these choices is correct.

Mark your choice on the answer sheet on the next page. Use a pencil to mark the answer. The actual test will be machine scored so completely darken in the answer space. Once the test is complete, correct the answer sheet and review the answer explanations.

When instructed, turn the page and begin.

Answer Sheet

PRACTICE ELEMENTARY EDUCATION

Reading/Language Arts

1 Ⓐ Ⓑ Ⓒ Ⓓ	11 Ⓐ Ⓑ Ⓒ Ⓓ	21 Ⓐ Ⓑ Ⓒ Ⓓ	31 Ⓐ Ⓑ Ⓒ Ⓓ
2 Ⓐ Ⓑ Ⓒ Ⓓ	12 Ⓐ Ⓑ Ⓒ Ⓓ	22 Ⓐ Ⓑ Ⓒ Ⓓ	32 Ⓐ Ⓑ Ⓒ Ⓓ
3 Ⓐ Ⓑ Ⓒ Ⓓ	13 Ⓐ Ⓑ Ⓒ Ⓓ	23 Ⓐ Ⓑ Ⓒ Ⓓ	33 Ⓐ Ⓑ Ⓒ Ⓓ
4 Ⓐ Ⓑ Ⓒ Ⓓ	14 Ⓐ Ⓑ Ⓒ Ⓓ	24 Ⓐ Ⓑ Ⓒ Ⓓ	34 Ⓐ Ⓑ Ⓒ Ⓓ
5 Ⓐ Ⓑ Ⓒ Ⓓ	15 Ⓐ Ⓑ Ⓒ Ⓓ	25 Ⓐ Ⓑ Ⓒ Ⓓ	35 Ⓐ Ⓑ Ⓒ Ⓓ
6 Ⓐ Ⓑ Ⓒ Ⓓ	16 Ⓐ Ⓑ Ⓒ Ⓓ	26 Ⓐ Ⓑ Ⓒ Ⓓ	36 Ⓐ Ⓑ Ⓒ Ⓓ
7 Ⓐ Ⓑ Ⓒ Ⓓ	17 Ⓐ Ⓑ Ⓒ Ⓓ	27 Ⓐ Ⓑ Ⓒ Ⓓ	37 Ⓐ Ⓑ Ⓒ Ⓓ
8 Ⓐ Ⓑ Ⓒ Ⓓ	18 Ⓐ Ⓑ Ⓒ Ⓓ	28 Ⓐ Ⓑ Ⓒ Ⓓ	38 Ⓐ Ⓑ Ⓒ Ⓓ
9 Ⓐ Ⓑ Ⓒ Ⓓ	19 Ⓐ Ⓑ Ⓒ Ⓓ	29 Ⓐ Ⓑ Ⓒ Ⓓ	
10 Ⓐ Ⓑ Ⓒ Ⓓ	20 Ⓐ Ⓑ Ⓒ Ⓓ	30 Ⓐ Ⓑ Ⓒ Ⓓ	

Mathematics

39 Ⓐ Ⓑ Ⓒ Ⓓ	45 Ⓐ Ⓑ Ⓒ Ⓓ	51 Ⓐ Ⓑ Ⓒ Ⓓ	56 Ⓐ Ⓑ Ⓒ Ⓓ
40 Ⓐ Ⓑ Ⓒ Ⓓ	46 Ⓐ Ⓑ Ⓒ Ⓓ	52 Ⓐ Ⓑ Ⓒ Ⓓ	57 Ⓐ Ⓑ Ⓒ Ⓓ
41 Ⓐ Ⓑ Ⓒ Ⓓ	47 Ⓐ Ⓑ Ⓒ Ⓓ	53 Ⓐ Ⓑ Ⓒ Ⓓ	58 Ⓐ Ⓑ Ⓒ Ⓓ
42 Ⓐ Ⓑ Ⓒ Ⓓ	48 Ⓐ Ⓑ Ⓒ Ⓓ	54 Ⓐ Ⓑ Ⓒ Ⓓ	59 Ⓐ Ⓑ Ⓒ Ⓓ
43 Ⓐ Ⓑ Ⓒ Ⓓ	49 Ⓐ Ⓑ Ⓒ Ⓓ	55 Ⓐ Ⓑ Ⓒ Ⓓ	60 Ⓐ Ⓑ Ⓒ Ⓓ
44 Ⓐ Ⓑ Ⓒ Ⓓ	50 Ⓐ Ⓑ Ⓒ Ⓓ		

Science

61 Ⓐ Ⓑ Ⓒ Ⓓ	64 Ⓐ Ⓑ Ⓒ Ⓓ	67 Ⓐ Ⓑ Ⓒ Ⓓ	70 Ⓐ Ⓑ Ⓒ Ⓓ
62 Ⓐ Ⓑ Ⓒ Ⓓ	65 Ⓐ Ⓑ Ⓒ Ⓓ	68 Ⓐ Ⓑ Ⓒ Ⓓ	71 Ⓐ Ⓑ Ⓒ Ⓓ
63 Ⓐ Ⓑ Ⓒ Ⓓ	66 Ⓐ Ⓑ Ⓒ Ⓓ	69 Ⓐ Ⓑ Ⓒ Ⓓ	

Social Studies

72 Ⓐ Ⓑ Ⓒ Ⓓ	75 Ⓐ Ⓑ Ⓒ Ⓓ	78 Ⓐ Ⓑ Ⓒ Ⓓ	81 Ⓐ Ⓑ Ⓒ Ⓓ
73 Ⓐ Ⓑ Ⓒ Ⓓ	76 Ⓐ Ⓑ Ⓒ Ⓓ	79 Ⓐ Ⓑ Ⓒ Ⓓ	82 Ⓐ Ⓑ Ⓒ Ⓓ
74 Ⓐ Ⓑ Ⓒ Ⓓ	77 Ⓐ Ⓑ Ⓒ Ⓓ	80 Ⓐ Ⓑ Ⓒ Ⓓ	

Answer Sheet

PRACTICE ELEMENTARY EDUCATION

Arts and Physical Education

83 (A) (B) (C) (D)   86 (A) (B) (C) (D)   89 (A) (B) (C) (D)   92 (A) (B) (C) (D)
84 (A) (B) (C) (D)   87 (A) (B) (C) (D)   90 (A) (B) (C) (D)   93 (A) (B) (C) (D)
85 (A) (B) (C) (D)   88 (A) (B) (C) (D)   91 (A) (B) (C) (D)

General Knowledge

94 (A) (B) (C) (D)   99 (A) (B) (C) (D)   103 (A) (B) (C) (D)   107 (A) (B) (C) (D)
95 (A) (B) (C) (D)   100 (A) (B) (C) (D)   104 (A) (B) (C) (D)   108 (A) (B) (C) (D)
96 (A) (B) (C) (D)   101 (A) (B) (C) (D)   105 (A) (B) (C) (D)   109 (A) (B) (C) (D)
97 (A) (B) (C) (D)   102 (A) (B) (C) (D)   106 (A) (B) (C) (D)   110 (A) (B) (C) (D)
98 (A) (B) (C) (D)

Elementary Education: Curriculum, Instruction, and Assessment (0011) 110 Items, 2 Hours

READING/LANGUAGE ARTS

38 ITEMS

1. Based on recent findings, which of the following is the best approach to teach reading to young children?

    (A) Sight word programs
    (B) Literature-based programs
    (C) Phonics instruction integrated with literature-based approaches
    (D) Phonics programs

2. Which of the following would be most appropriate for an upper elementary teacher to use to evaluate students' writing techniques and plan for further writing experiences?

    (A) Administer a standardized grammar test and use the scores as a planning device.
    (B) Use a writing checklist to assess a variety of creative writing samples that include writing summaries and samples.
    (C) Have the students prepare a composition on a subject of their choice and holistically evaluate the composition.
    (D) Have the students answer a series of higher-level, short-answer questions about a specific writing sample.

3. Which of the following describes a prerequisite competency in language arts?

    (A) The knowledge and skills a teacher must possess to teach about subject–verb agreement
    (B) A sub-objective to the main objective about subject–verb agreement
    (C) The test for admitting students to language arts classes when they come in from another school
    (D) The knowledge and skills students must possess to learn about subject–verb agreement

4. Lisa writes well, understands verbal directions, but often has trouble understanding written directions. Her difficulty might be related to all of the following EXCEPT

    (A) auditory discrimination.
    (B) visual discrimination.
    (C) sight vocabulary.
    (D) context clues.

5. Which of the following would NOT be supported by a basal reading approach?

    (A) Skills are taught and developed in a systematic sequential manner
    (B) Meeting individual differences and needs of the child
    (C) A basic vocabulary is established and reinforced
    (D) Manuals provide a detailed outline for teaching

6. A student has trouble reading the problems in the mathematics textbook. This difficulty is most likely to be the result of

   (A) faulty word identification and recognition.
   (B) inability to locate and retain specific facts.
   (C) deficiencies in basic comprehension abilities.
   (D) inability to adapt to reading needs in this content field.

7. Which of the following goals would NOT be met through choral reading?

   (A) To help students to feel part of a group
   (B) To appreciate oral reading
   (C) To develop an interest in creative forms of language
   (D) To help students interpret meaning

8. A child has difficulty pronouncing a printed word. The problem may reflect all of the following EXCEPT

   (A) phonetic analysis.
   (B) sight vocabulary.
   (C) language comprehension.
   (D) context analysis.

9. Personal journals should NOT be used as a

   (A) record of feelings.
   (B) way to share thoughts with others.
   (C) means of expressing thought.
   (D) means for writing ideas.

10. Reading books for different grades first appeared in the 1800s as

    (A) *McGuffey's Readers.*
    (B) *The Horn Book.*
    (C) *The New England Primer.*
    (D) *The American Readers.*

11. The most important thing a student can do when writing is to

    (A) decide on the best order for presenting ideas.
    (B) have a clear beginning.
    (C) keep the audience and purpose in mind.
    (D) support the main idea.

12. Which of the following is NOT furthered by a phonics approach?

    (A) Associating sounds with printed letters
    (B) Reading comprehension
    (C) Attacking new words independently
    (D) Developing a sight vocabulary

13. At the beginning of a lesson the teacher says, "OK class, today we're going to learn about reading history." This type of statement is referred to as

    (A) an anticipatory set.
    (B) a motivation.
    (C) an objective.
    (D) an advanced organizer.

14. The second-grade teacher is considering a whole language approach. Which of the following is the best reason to institute the program?

    (A) Whole language instruction is widely accepted.
    (B) It is not necessary to teach word recognition.
    (C) Children comprehend more after using a whole language approach.
    (D) Children have a better attitude toward reading.

15. During a unit on animal stories, sixth-grade students read *Lad a Dog*, by Albert Payson Terhune. The teacher wants to use transactional strategy instruction to help students develop a deeper understanding of the cognitive process involved in understanding Lad's "motivations" as described in the book. Which of the following indicates the teacher is using this approach?

(A) The teacher explicitly explains the processes involved in successful reading comprehension.

(B) The teacher encourages students to explore the processes involved in successful reading comprehension.

(C) The teacher and students cooperate to jointly explore the processes involved in successful reading instruction.

(D) The teacher asks students to explore the processes involved in successful reading comprehension.

16. As a part of a writing program, a teacher uses a computer-based multimedia encyclopedia. The multimedia encyclopedia includes hypertext links in most of its articles. These hypertext links are highlighted words

(A) that link together very (hyper) important ideas in the passage.

(B) linked to underlying meanings.

(C) that move or vibrate to draw attention to important ideas.

(D) that can be clicked with a mouse cursor to change color.

17. A third-grade teacher posts this problem for his students to read critically and to solve.

Charles is traveling on a bus. Charles leaves work at 6:15 P.M. The bus travels 15 minutes on Forest Street, then 20 minutes on Quincy Avenue, then 25 minutes on Chestnut Street. What time does Charles get home?

The most appropriate answer to this problem is

(A) one hour.
(B) you can't tell.
(C) 7:15 P.M.
(D) 1,815 hours.

18. A fourth-grade student hands in a writing assignment containing this sentence.

I are going swimming.

This assignment indicates that the student needs more help with which of the following?

(A) Subject–verb agreement
(B) Pronouns
(C) Sentence fragments
(D) Adjectives and adverbs

19. Your class reads a science fiction story about space travel. Which of the following actions on your part is most likely to help students differentiate between science fact and science fiction?

(A) Guide students to understand that science fiction stories are creative writing and not based on science fact.

(B) Guide students as they identify examples of science fact and science fiction based on the story they just completed.

(C) Ask students to work independently to make their own list of science fact and science fiction.

(D) Ask students to work independently as they identify examples of science fact and science fiction in the story they just completed.

20. Which of the following reading activities would engage a student at the highest level of the *Taxonomy of Educational Objectives: Cognitive Domain*?

    (A) Evaluate a reading passage
    (B) Understand a reading passage
    (C) Analyze a reading passage
    (D) Apply the contents of a reading passage to a real-world situation

21. You have a number of long newspaper articles about whales. Which of the following approaches on your part is most likely to best inform students about the main idea(s) of each article.

    (A) Students work independently and summarize for themselves the main point(s) of each article.
    (B) Students work in cooperative learning groups to summarize and present the main point(s) of each article.
    (C) You present a brief summary of the main point(s) of each article.
    (D) You prepare a brief summary of the main point(s) of each article and distribute them to your students.

22. A young student writes about a sailor on a four-masted schooner. The student's writing contains this sentence.

    He had enuf rope to tie up the boat.

    Which of the actions on the part of the teacher listed below addresses the errors in the sentence?

    (A) Instruction on phonics-based word attack skills
    (B) Instruction on context-based word attack skills
    (C) Instruction on the use of homonyms
    (D) Instruction on variable spelling phonemes

23. A teacher wants to use a token economy system to motivate students during reading. Which of the following actions on the part of the teacher is most consistent with this approach?

    (A) The teacher provides token (symbolic) reinforcement for work completed by students as opposed to real or meaningful reinforcement.
    (B) The teacher distributes subway and bus tokens for reinforcement since this approach was pioneered in urban areas where many students took buses and subways to school.
    (C) The number of points that students can receive is posted and students may exchange a certain number of points for a more tangible reward.
    (D) The teacher posts a "token of my appreciation list" on the bulletin board and lists the names of students who perform outstanding work.

24. A teacher finished a three-day unit on nouns. He wants to be sure students learned the material in the unit. Which of the following assessment techniques would be best for the teacher to use?

    (A) Obtain and have the students complete a standardized assessment.
    (B) Prepare and have the students complete a teacher-made assessment.
    (C) Observe students' writing over the next week.
    (D) Review writing that students have previously completed.

25. A teacher wants to use the Orton-Gillingham approach with a student who is having difficulty reading. The following actions on the part of the teacher are consistent with that approach EXCEPT

    (A) teaching synthetic phonics.
    (B) generally discouraging independent reading.
    (C) emphasizing reading for meaning.
    (D) using a dictionary to learn word pronunciation.

26. A fourth-grade teacher wants to conduct an ongoing assessment of her language arts program. Which one of the following actions on the part of the teacher would NOT indicate that the assessment was underway?

    (A) The teacher walks around the room regularly observing students' writing.
    (B) The teacher asks students to hand in their written work at the end of the day.
    (C) The teacher gives students an in-class composition assignment about the environment.
    (D) The teacher regularly collects performance samples of students' work.

27. Which of the following would be the best opportunity for a formative evaluation of student's writing?

    (A) A discussion with the student
    (B) A portfolio of student's writing samples
    (C) Iowa Test of Basic Skills
    (D) End of unit test

28. You are meeting with the parents of a sixth-grade student to interpret their child's test scores. A standardized reading test shows the student at the 34th percentile in reading. Which of the following is the best explanation of this reading score?

    (A) "This means that your child did better on this test than all but 34 students."
    (B) "This means that your child did better than all but 34 percent of the students who took this test."
    (C) "This means that your child did better than 34 percent of the students who took this test."
    (D) "This means that your child has better reading ability than 34 percent of the students who took this test."

29. Parents of a fourth-grade child are meeting with the teacher to discuss the child's progress in language arts. A standardized English test shows a grade equivalent of 4.3. The average grade equivalent for the fourth grade in that school is 4.4. Which of the following is the best explanation of the child's language arts score?

    (A) "Your child is above average in language arts."
    (B) "Your child's language arts achievement is about average."
    (C) "Your child's language arts achievement is almost at the level of a 4-year-old."
    (D) "Your child's language arts achievement is below average."

30. A teacher is using an ESL approach to teach reading to a group of LEP students. Which of the following actions on the part of the teacher is most consistent with that approach?

   (A) Use context clues to help students identify English words.
   (B) Help students learn to read in the student's native language.
   (C) Translate English reading passages into the student's native language.
   (D) Ask students to bring in original literature in the student's native language.

31. A teacher administers an end of chapter test from the teacher's edition of a language arts text. In all likelihood, this is a

   (A) formative evaluation.
   (B) standardized test.
   (C) norm-referenced test.
   (D) summative evaluation.

32. A fourth-grade teacher keeps a portfolio of written work for a student. In her opinion, the writing samples are well above average for fourth-graders in that school. A standardized language arts test administered last month shows a writing grade equivalent of 3.2. Which of the following is the best description of the child's language arts achievement?

   (A) The child is above average in writing for his grade level.
   (B) The child is below average in writing for his grade level.
   (C) The child needs intensive help in writing at his grade level.
   (D) The child seems to do better when evaluated in real-world settings.

33. A fifth-grade student hands in this writing sample.

   I sat in the audience while my sister play the clarinet. I saw her play while sit there. I guess I will never be a profesional musician.

   The teacher is most likely to help improve this student's writing by providing instruction in which of the following areas?

   (A) Nouns
   (B) Pronouns
   (C) Spelling
   (D) Verbs

34. A teacher wants to use cooperative learning groups for language arts instruction. Which of the following practices is LEAST consistent with this approach to classroom instruction?

   (A) Group members devise a working plan
   (B) Group members are actively involved in learning
   (C) Groups include 10 to 12 members
   (D) The teacher presents the project or topic to be worked on

35. A primary teacher wants to produce the most significant reading benefits for his students. Which of the following actions on the part of the teacher is most likely to create that benefit?

   (A) Providing a literature-rich environment
   (B) Providing effective phonics instruction
   (C) Providing opportunities for oral expression and listening
   (D) Using real literature sources instead of basal texts

36. A classroom teacher is using the whole language approach as a part of reading instruction. The whole language approach is based on the work of which of the following?

    (A) Marie Clay's Reading Recovery
    (B) James Pitman's Initial Teaching Alphabet
    (C) Jean Piaget's developmental levels of learning
    (D) John Dewey's Progressive Education movement

37. Which of the following is the most reasonable explanation of why a child's standardized reading test score is above grade level, but below average for that class?

    (A) The student correctly answered more questions on the first test.
    (B) The class did better on average than the entire group of students who took the test.
    (C) Half of those who take the test are below average.
    (D) The averages are different because the number of students in each group is different.

38. Which of the following is the most appropriate first step to modify plans to meet the needs of a student with a standardized reading score significantly below grade level?

    (A) Modify the plans to account for learning style.
    (B) Modify the plans to account for differences in achievement level.
    (C) Modify the plans to provide peer tutoring.
    (D) Modify the plans to incorporate alternative evaluation techniques.

MATHEMATICS

22 Items

39. These are examples of a student's work.

    $$\begin{array}{c} 86.4 \\ 6\overline{)520} \end{array} \qquad \begin{array}{c} 81.7 \\ 9\overline{)736} \end{array} \qquad \begin{array}{c} 18.6 \\ 8\overline{)150} \end{array}$$

    The student continues to make the same type of error. Which of the following is the student's answer to 124 divided by 5?

    (A) 2.2
    (B) 20.2
    (C) 22.5
    (D) 24.4

40. After examining the diagram of the polygon below the student states that the perimeter is 23 units. Which of the following statements by the teacher is most likely to help the student?

    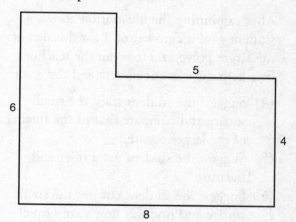

    (A) Check your addition.
    (B) Trace each side of the shape with her finger, stating the length of each side.
    (C) Count the number of sides of the polygon.
    (D) Use a rule for finding perimeter.

41. Which of the following is the best approach to teaching a first lesson on percent to a fourth-grade class?

   (A) A written explanation of what a percent is
   (B) A 100's chart
   (C) Illustrations on the chalkboard
   (D) Manipulative materials

42.

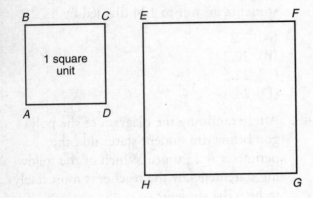

   After examining the illustration above, a student gave an answer of 2 for the area of the larger polygon. How can the teacher best help the student understand the error?

   (A) Suggest the student trace the small square and compare that to the tracing of the larger square.
   (B) Suggest the student get a ruler and measure.
   (C) Suggest the student cut out the small square and find out how many small squares fit inside the large square.
   (D) Suggest the student estimate the increase in distance between *BC* and *EF*.

43. Which of the following is the LEAST appropriate mathematics objective to teach using manipulative materials?

   (A) Adding single-digit numbers
   (B) Solving problems using the strategy "make an organized list"
   (C) Adding double-digit numbers
   (D) Dividing decimals

44. A teacher is planning a middle school mathematics unit. Which of the following would most likely lead to successful learning?

   (A) Students are listening to a lesson at their ability level.
   (B) Students are listening to a lesson and challenged beyond their ability level.
   (C) Students are actively participating in a lesson at their ability level.
   (D) Students are actively participating and challenged beyond their ability level.

45. A student consistently makes addition mistakes such as the one shown below.

$$13 + 9 = 112$$

   Instruction in which of the following areas is most likely to help the student overcome this problem?

   (A) Lining up decimal points
   (B) Place value
   (C) Addition facts
   (D) Writing number sentences

46. A teacher wants to use one of Piaget's conservation tasks to check students' number concept development. Which of the following actions on the part of the teacher represents a conservation task?

   (A) The teacher shows a student a group of attribute shapes. The child can match like shapes.
   (B) The teacher gives a student six-sided number cubes numbered 1–6. The child can place the cubes with the correct number on top when asked by the teacher.
   (C) The teacher shows the student a linear pattern of attribute blocks. The child can successfully duplicate the linear pattern formed by the teacher.
   (D) The teacher shows the student two matched rows of checkers. The child knows the number of checkers has not changed when one of the rows is spread out.

47. Given below is a list of mathematics concepts.

    I Multiplying 4 × 3
    II Solving 3x = 12
    III Joining together 4 groups of 3 blocks
    IV Drawing 3 lines vertically and 4 lines horizontally to create 12 crossing points

    Which of the following best represents the order in which these concepts should be taught?

    (A) III, IV, I, II
    (B) III, I, IV, II, I
    (C) IV, III, II, I
    (D) IV, I, III, II

48. A teacher is considering reviewing arithmetic computation. For which of the following examples does a student need the most in-depth understanding of the relationship among arithmetic operations?

    (A) 7/9 × 1/5 =
    (B) 7/9 + 1/5 =
    (C) 35 ÷ 7 =
    (D) 392 + 26 =

49. A primary objective of a school mathematics program is to use estimation first to be sure a calculation is reasonable. Which of the following instructions to students by a fourth-grade teacher best meets that objective?

    (A) Estimate the answer to 6,294 + 7,892 before you find the answer with a calculator.
    (B) Estimate the answer to 900 ÷ 9 before you find the answer with paper and pencil.
    (C) Estimate the number of beans in the jar before you count them.
    (D) Estimate the distance from your desk to the door before you measure it.

50. A fifth-grade teacher wants to introduce students to the number pi (3.14159 . . .). The teacher plans to use the Internet to research the number. Which of the following actions in the part of the teacher will be LEAST helpful?

    (A) Use a search engine to look up pi.
    (B) Send e-mails to others to find out about pi.
    (C) Type in a web address that seems related to pi.
    (D) Use a chat program to discuss pi with others.

51. A teacher wants to give students experiences making triangles. Which of the following instructional aids will be most helpful?

    (A) String
    (B) Geoboard
    (C) Popsicle sticks
    (D) Ruler and pencil

52. A teacher is helping young students learn about counting. The teacher uses shapes as counters and makes sure students point to a shape each time they say the next numeral. Why is the teacher using this approach?

    (A) The teacher wants to be sure the students are paying attention to what they are doing.
    (B) The teacher wants to be sure students are developing eye-hand coordination.
    (C) The teacher is going to ask the students questions about the shapes once they have finished counting.
    (D) The teacher wants to be sure the students are not just saying counting words.

53. During a second-grade mathematics lesson, the teacher presents this problem.

There are 43 people on the camping trip. If 5 people can fit in a tent, what is the least number of tents needed?

Which of the following is the best strategy for solving this problem?

(A) Guess and check
(B) Interpret the remainder
(C) Make an organized list
(D) Choose the operation

54. A student has difficulty aligning partial products in multiplication as shown below.

$$
\begin{array}{r}
1\ 1\ 9 \\
\times 2\ 5\ 8 \\
\hline
9\ 5\ 2 \\
5\ 1\ 5 \\
2\ 3\ 8 \\
\hline
\end{array}
$$

Which of the following actions is the most appropriate first step for the teacher to take?

(A) Reteach the concept of place value.
(B) Give the student graph paper to write the multiplication problems.
(C) Reteach two-digit multiplication and then return to three-digit multiplication.
(D) Show the child how to write place-holder zeros in blank spaces of the partial products.

55. A primary teacher is about to engage the class in a lesson on adding the value of coins. Which of the following actions on the part of the teacher is most likely to motivate student interest in the lesson?

(A) "Hi everyone—I have some make-believe coins. I'll hold them up and tell you what each coin is worth."
(B) "Here are some make-believe coins. Pretend I am a bank. We'll add as you put the coins in."
(C) "Does anyone know when coins were first used? It is interesting because coins were used a long time ago."
(D) "Before we begin, let me review with you the value of each one of these coins. Knowing the value of the coins is the secret to our lesson today."

56. In a primary grade, each student is given a number line numbered 1 to 30, a group of 30 beans, paper, and pencil. The teacher then gives the students this problem.

There are 7 marbles in each bag, and there are 4 bags in all. Use any of the materials you have to find the total number of marbles in the four bags.

Which of the following learning approaches is most consistent with the teacher's actions?

(A) Problem solving
(B) Constructivist
(C) Modeling
(D) Manipulatives

57. A teacher discusses the results of a mathematics unit test with a student's parents. The student received 85 percent on the test. Which of the following is the best interpretation of this test score?

   (A) This score shows that the child is above average in mathematics.
   (B) This score puts the child at the 85th percentile.
   (C) This score shows that the child did well on this test.
   (D) This score shows that the child needs further review before moving on to the next chapter.

58. Each morning, a teacher presents a mathematics problem for students to solve during the day. Which of the following describes the most effective technique the teacher can use to assess student's solutions?

   (A) Observation
   (B) Standardized test
   (C) Cooperative learning
   (D) Portfolio assessment

59. A sixth-grade teacher notices that the mode of the percent correct on a recent test is 79 percent. This result reveals that

   (A) half of the students scored at or below 79 percent.
   (B) 79 percent was the score that occurred most often.
   (C) half of the students scored at or above 79 percent.
   (D) 79 percent was the average of all the scores.

60. A school district committee wants to formulate a policy for calculator use. Which of the choices below represents the most appropriate policy?

   (A) Calculators should be banned from classrooms until high school.
   (B) Calculators should not be used when the reason for the lesson is to teach computation.
   (C) Calculators should not be used to add, subtract, multiply, or divide. These operations should be completed only by hand.
   (D) Calculators should be used only to check paper and pencil computations.

SCIENCE

11 items

61. A group of advanced fourth-graders had difficulty understanding the resistance (R)–fulcrum (F)–effort (E) characteristics of levers. Which of the following activities would best help students understand these concepts?

   (A) Arrange a variety of levers RFE, FRE, and FER in order so that the students can demonstrate where to place a lever on a fulcrum to reduce or increase effort.
   (B) Have students classify a group of pictorial representations of levers into RFE, FRE, and FER groups.
   (C) Read a textbook description of each type of lever and list examples under each type.
   (D) Chart the resistance and effort levels of different types of levers.

62. When responding to children's science questions, a teacher should do all the following EXCEPT

    (A) encourage exploration of the answer with activities and materials that stimulate curiosity.
    (B) model good responding skills.
    (C) answer all items as quickly and concisely as possible.
    (D) include children's questions in evaluation techniques.

63. All of the following describe how science educators apply Piaget's developmental theory in the science classroom EXCEPT

    (A) using cooperative learning to teach science.
    (B) having an age-appropriate textbook for the class.
    (C) hands-on science experiments.
    (D) organizing results through a systematic thinking process.

64. Young children have many experiences with capacity, including sand and water play. Why do so few children carry over these experiences to understanding volume?

    (A) They have not progressed to that stage
    (B) They usually overfill the containers
    (C) They usually do not have enough variety of containers
    (D) No one told them what they were doing

65. A teacher does an experiment in which a white light is refracted through a prism which splits it into many colors, like the colors of a rainbow. This experiment is best used to demonstrate which of the following concepts?

    (A) The angle of incidence equals the angle of reflection.
    (B) Light rays travel in a straight line.
    (C) White light is formed by a combination of all these colors.
    (D) If all these colors were refracted through a prism, a white light would come out.

66. A fifth-grade teacher conducts a science class using the inquiry approach. Which of the following actions on the part of the teacher is most likely to occur?

    (A) The teacher deliberately does not try out an experiment in advance so the teacher and the children will discover the results together.
    (B) The teacher tells the students to avoid analyzing thought processes, but rather to rely on what happens in the experiment.
    (C) The teacher presents a problem for the students to solve or a situation for them to explore.
    (D) The teacher explains an experiment and the results and then asks students to try the experiment.

67. A teacher plans to give students some activities that will lead the students to discover a science concept. Which of the following best describes this approach to teaching?

    (A) Deductive
    (B) Skill
    (C) Concrete
    (D) Inductive

68. The following is a description of a science activity from a school district manual.

The teacher should have a piece of dense solid material such as lead that weighs about 500 grams and a less dense solid material such as ceramics or rubber that weighs the same. Let students handle the materials. Point out that the objects weigh the same, but are not the same size. Immerse the objects in water so that students can observe that the larger object displaces more water than the smaller object.

This activity is best used to teach which of the following?

(A) Gravity and variable weights
(B) Composition of materials
(C) Density
(D) Geological versus manufactured materials

69.

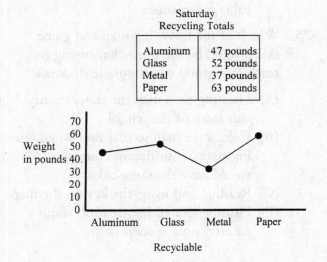

Saturday
Recycling Totals

Aluminum	47 pounds
Glass	52 pounds
Metal	37 pounds
Paper	63 pounds

Students visit the recycling center and gather information about the amount of different recyclables collected during one day. The students organize the information into a table and then sketch the graph, both of which are shown above.

Which of the following comments from the teacher to the students would most help students in future activities?

(A) "You should use a straightedge to draw the lines in your graph."
(B) "You should use a circle graph to show percents of the whole. This table and graph do not show percents of a whole."
(C) "You should use a bar graph when quantities are not related."
(D) "You should use kilograms instead of pounds for science results."

70. A teacher replicates a famous experiment. The teacher has a tennis ball and a plastic ball that weigh about the same, although the plastic ball is larger and has holes. The teacher drops the balls simultaneously from a second-story window to the ground below. After repeated experiments, a student standing on the ground always reports that the tennis ball hits first. The student writes this conclusion.

This experiment does not have the result I expected. These two objects did not fall at the same rate.

Which of the following comments on the part of the teacher is most appropriate?

(A) "Are you sure the balls were dropped at the same time?"
(B) "Did you take into account all variables in the experiment?"
(C) "Wasn't the Leaning Tower of Pisa experiment about falling objects found to be faulty?"
(D) "Did you carefully weigh the two objects?"

71. Students drop a very large grapefruit from five different heights into a large container of sand. The grapefruit is dropped ten times from each height. After each drop the students measure the diameter of the crater formed by the grapefruit. The average, rounded diameter of the crater from each height is shown below.

Height of Drop	Average crater diameter
20 cm	1.6 cm
40 cm	3.2 cm
60 cm	4.8 cm
80 cm	6.4 cm
100 cm	8 cm

The results of this experiment would be most useful for helping students explore which of the following mathematics concepts?

(A) Average
(B) Addition of decimals
(C) Multiplication by a decimal
(D) Decimal representation

SOCIAL STUDIES

11 Items

72. Cooperative learning groups in social studies have the following characteristics when compared to teacher-centered presentations EXCEPT

(A) more student involvement.
(B) more content coverage.
(C) more varied outcomes.
(D) more brainstorming.

73. A multicultural approach to teaching social studies most appropriately includes

(A) a comparison of how different cultures respond to similar issues.
(B) how people from different cultures contribute to world events.
(C) how people around the world have common characteristics.
(D) how events in one part of the globe influence the rest of the world.

74. Which of the following is the most appropriate emphasis for an elementary school social studies program?

(A) Emphasize the learning of cultural facts in order to promote an overall cultural literacy.
(B) Focus on the role of the United States in the contemporary world.
(C) Prepare learners for competent participation in social, political, and economic life.
(D) Avoid students' discussion of divisive, value-laden issues.

75. Which of the following map and globe skills would be the most challenging to teach to a group of fifth-grade students?

(A) Locating on a map the state, county, and town of the school
(B) Coloring a map so that no two adjoining states, counties, or countries would have the same color
(C) Reading and using the key on the map
(D) Plotting factual information about a country on a specific map

76. A teacher wants to adapt social studies instruction for students who are significantly below grade reading level. The following actions on the part of the teacher are appropriate EXCEPT

(A) using instructional materials that have a lower reading level.
(B) using instructional materials with less difficult concepts.
(C) reading information about social studies to the student.
(D) using recorded tapes that contain social studies information.

77.

SCHOOL GRADING RULES	
A	91–100
B	81–90
C	71–80

A teacher constructs his own content-valid multiple-choice test to assess performance on a social studies unit. One student correctly answers 91 percent of the questions, while another student gets 89 percent correct. How confident should the teacher be about assigning grades according to the school grading rules?

(A) Very confident—the teacher should just follow the grading rules
(B) Very confident—the difference between the grades is clear
(C) Somewhat confident—the test is content-valid and probably measures important concepts
(D) Not confident—the errors of measurement in the test could eliminate the meaning of the difference between the scores

78. A teacher is planning to review events in American history. Which of the following is the teacher most likely to cover first?

(A) Writing of the Declaration of Independence
(B) Writing of the Constitution of the United States of America
(C) First Continental Congress
(D) Stamp Act

79. A student gathers information about the amount of money in a state government's seven budget categories. In order to help others understand the relationship among the amounts spent in the budget categories, the student should represent the data graphically as a

(A) flowchart.
(B) circle graph.
(C) bar graph.
(D) line graph.

80. A sixth-grade teacher is going to teach a social studies lesson about cattle trails and railroads after the Civil War. The lesson is based on the map shown below. The teacher is most likely to explain that the Goodnight-Loving Trail turns north after Pecos because

(A) that is the way to Denver.
(B) the cattle drovers did not want to go into Mexico.
(C) of the mountains.
(D) of the Rio Grande River.

81. A teacher is going to conduct a social studies mediated reading thinking activity. Which of the following should the teacher do before reading begins?

    (A) Give students a choice of the material to be read.
    (B) Share responses to the reading with students.
    (C) Predict what might be learned from the reading.
    (D) Focus reading on identified purposes.

82. A teacher carefully planned a lesson on early American settlers and wrote an excellent lesson plan. Once the lesson is underway, the teacher's observation of the students indicates that the plan is clearly not working. The teacher should

    (A) stay with the plan and analyze later why the plan was not successful.
    (B) stay with the plan and discipline any students disrupting the lesson.
    (C) stay with the plan and give other work to those students who can't keep up.
    (D) abandon the plan and try another approach.

ARTS AND PHYSICAL EDUCATION

11 Items

83. A middle grades teacher would like to integrate a lesson on art with haiku. Which of the following LEAST meets the teacher's needs?

    (A) Use the computer as an artistic tool to illustrate the haiku.
    (B) Provide a display of classical Japanese paintings for children to color.
    (C) Provide clay as a means to illustrate their haiku.
    (D) Provide paints and brushes so children can illustrate the haiku.

84. Which of the following should be the main focus for an elementary school art program?

    (A) Help students acquire technical skills in drawing.
    (B) Make sure your students at least have experience coloring, painting, and using clay.
    (C) Help students gain appreciation of art, aesthetics, and human creativity.
    (D) Allow students to illustrate their written work in the way they feel most comfortable.

85. Rhythmic and movement activities are very often a part of today's elementary physical education programs. These activities lay the foundation for future folk and creative dance units. Which of the following is most important when planning for these activities?

    (A) Make sure the music is a lively and catchy tune.
    (B) Make sure you choose partners wisely.
    (C) Make sure you demonstrate each step so that each student can see you.
    (D) Make sure the basic approach is a gradual progression from individual to partner to group activities.

86. A fourth-grade teacher asks students to give their emotional response to a work of art. Which taxonomy of objectives is this lesson related to?

    (A) Psychomotor
    (B) Introspective
    (C) Cognitive
    (D) Affective

87. A teacher is conducting beanbag activities with very young students. These activities can integrate the movement of many body parts. Which of the following beanbag activities is the teacher most likely to do last?

    (A) Adding stunts in place with the beanbag
    (B) Performing locomotor movements with the beanbag
    (C) Tossing to self in place with the beanbag
    (D) Balancing the beanbag on various body parts

88. A teacher wants to assess a student's understanding of an instrumental music lesson while the lesson is underway. Which of the following most accurately characterizes how the assessment should be conducted?

    (A) The teacher should invite students to the teacher's desk to play the instrument.
    (B) The teacher should listen to students play during the lesson.
    (C) The teacher should invite students to the front of the class to play their instrument.
    (D) The teacher should record students' playing to evaluate later.

89. Which of the following is the best example of a teacher's instructional objective for a primary art lesson?

    (A) I will teach students how to create a finger painting.
    (B) I expect 60 percent of my students to complete a finger painting.
    (C) I will gather nontoxic finger paints, finger paint paper, a bowl of water, and a paper towel for each student.
    (D) Students will create a finger painting.

90. During a music lesson, the teacher notices that a child is very anxious about remembering musical notation. Which of the following is NOT an effective way for the teacher to respond to the needs of this child?

    (A) Don't draw attention to the student by providing emotional support.
    (B) Give extra time when practical for the student to learn the notation.
    (C) Reduce the tension with a little humor.
    (D) Don't criticize the student for their lack of progress.

91. A teacher wants to help a student understand the "meaning" of music. The plans call for a lesson on pitch. Which of the following does a student also need to learn to understand what the term "music" means?

    (A) Chord
    (B) Harmony
    (C) Duration
    (D) Timbre

92. Students are frequently active and noisy during physical education lessons, and it can be difficult to maintain discipline. At these times the teacher needs to recall that, above all, students usually expect the teacher to be

    (A) very assertive.
    (B) extremely understanding.
    (C) a tough taskmaster.
    (D) an authority figure.

93. A school's approach to education is built around the progressive schools movement founded by John Dewey. Which of the following is most likely to characterize the school's physical education program?

    (A) The physical education program is conducted in a teacher-centered very friendly classroom.
    (B) The physical education program is based on the future needs of society.
    (C) The physical education program is built around the needs of the child.
    (D) The physical education program is based on team sports and cooperation.

GENERAL KNOWLEDGE

17 Items

94. Economically disadvantaged students, as a whole, tend to have lower achievement than other students, leading educators to the valid conclusion that

    (A) economically disadvantaged students, as a whole, are usually less capable learners than other students.
    (B) minority teachers are more effective with minority students.
    (C) learning expectations should usually be lowered for minority students.
    (D) economically disadvantaged students usually have fewer enriched learning opportunities at home.

95. A principal plans to distribute guidelines for classroom questioning techniques. Which of the following actions on the part of the teacher is generally most appropriate?

    (A) Be sure students know who will answer a question before it is asked.
    (B) Ask questions of the entire class, then call on a student.
    (C) Ask questions of students who are not paying attention.
    (D) Ask questions of students who usually have the correct answers.

96. A new sixth-grade teacher is trying to maintain attention during a lesson. Which of the following actions on the part of the teacher is most likely to be effective?

    (A) The teacher stands where she can see the entire class.
    (B) The teacher limits the number of students who participate in question-and-answer sessions.
    (C) The teacher ensures that the material being taught is very difficult.
    (D) The teacher does not proceed with the lesson if even a single student is not paying attention.

97. Research has shown that modeling can be an effective form of instruction. Which of the following actions on the part of the teacher is an example of appropriate modeling behavior?

    (A) Show students how to construct replicas of historic buildings.
    (B) Respond courteously to student's questions.
    (C) Correct mispronounced words.
    (D) Demonstrate students' inappropriate behavior.

98. A fifth-grade student has been classified as a special education student. The child study team determined that the student is learning disabled. Which of the following choices describes an appropriate placement for that student?

   (A) Place the child in a self-contained class with other learning disabled students and send the student out for music and art specials.
   (B) Place the student in a fifth-grade class with support from a special education teacher.
   (C) Place the student in a self-contained class with other learning disabled students, and send the student to a fifth-grade class for some subjects.
   (D) Place the student in a class that matches his or her reading level, and send the student out of class for other subject instruction as needed.

99. Four influential educators—Froebel, Herbart, Pestalozzi, and Rousseau—were born in the 1700s. Which of the following is an accurate statement about one of these educators?

   (A) Rousseau established the first kindergarten.
   (B) Froebel liberalized schools and called for understanding and patience.
   (C) Herbart formalized schools and called for structure and regularity.
   (D) Pestalozzi established the first Casa Bambini.

100. A teacher and student are discussing the student's most recent report card. The teacher explains that the student's grades would have been better if all homework assignments were handed in. This teacher is using

   (A) punishment.
   (B) reverse psychology.
   (C) threats.
   (D) negative reinforcement.

101. A teacher has a class that is culturally and linguistically diverse. Which of the following actions on the part of the teacher is an appropriate modification of the objectives or plans for this class?

   (A) Modify the objectives to focus more on basic skills.
   (B) Modify the objectives to reduce their difficulty level.
   (C) Modify the plans to teach the class in the foreign language.
   (D) Modify the plans to focus on the cultural heritage of those in the class.

102. A fourth-grade teacher is arranging desks at the beginning of the school year. Which of the following arrangements is LEAST appropriate?

```
(A) X X X          (B) X X X X X
    X X X              X X X X X
    X X X                  T
    X X X
    X X X
      T

(C)   X X          (D) X X X X X
    X     X            X X X
   X       X           X X X X
  X   T   X            X X X
   X       X             T
    X     X
     X X X
    X X X
```

103. A school district is preparing a pamphlet about effective schools. All of the following choices could be listed as characteristics of effective schools EXCEPT

   (A) a climate of high expectations.
   (B) a high proportion of instruction time spent on task.
   (C) accountability for student performance.
   (D) eliminating standardized tests.

104. Effective classroom managers take steps to ensure that the majority of class time is devoted to

    (A) individual work.
    (B) on-task activities.
    (C) cooperative learning.
    (D) lecturing.

105. Which of the following actions on the part of a teacher indicates that the teacher is using authentic assessment?

    (A) The teacher collects and evaluates student work.
    (B) The teacher uses standardized tests.
    (C) The teacher uses only tests that have been authenticated.
    (D) The teacher collects evaluative information from other teachers.

106. A fourth-grade teacher is using a cooperative learning approach. All of the following might occur EXCEPT

    (A) students get help from other students.
    (B) groups of two to six students work together.
    (C) group members consult with the teacher.
    (D) the teacher summarizes students' work.

107. A teacher seeks to use a constructivist approach to teaching. Which of the following actions on the part of the teacher is most consistent with that approach?

    (A) The teacher encourages students to respond quickly and alertly to questions.
    (B) The teacher encourages students to construct complex models of their thought processes.
    (C) The teacher encourages students to elaborate on their initial responses.
    (D) The teacher discourages students from creating metaphors.

108. A teacher using Gardner's multiple intelligences as the basis for instruction is most likely to use which of the following?

    (A) Implement interdisciplinary units.
    (B) Help students learn about each of the intelligences.
    (C) Eliminate assessments.
    (D) Allow students to determine criteria for quality.

109. Comprehensive testing of a fourth-grade student reveals an IQ in the 110–115 range, but standardized test scores are two or more years below grade level. Which of the following is the most appropriate interpretation of these test scores?

    (A) The student is a poor test taker.
    (B) The student's achievement and potential match.
    (C) The student is gifted.
    (D) The student has a learning disability.

110. The most significant difficulty with portfolio assessment is reliability in that

    (A) students put samples of widely different types of work in their portfolio.
    (B) scoring machines don't work reliably with materials in the portfolio.
    (C) different teachers place different emphasis on the portfolios when giving grades.
    (D) different teachers assign widely different grades to the same portfolio.

ANSWERS

Reading/Language Arts

1. **(A)**	8. **(C)**	15. **(C)**	22. **(D)**	29. **(B)**	36. **(A)**
2. **(B)**	9. **(B)**	16. **(B)**	23. **(C)**	30. **(A)**	37. **(B)**
3. **(D)**	10. **(A)**	17. **(B)**	24. **(B)**	31. **(D)**	38. **(D)**
4. **(A)**	11. **(C)**	18. **(A)**	25. **(C)**	32. **(D)**	
5. **(B)**	12. **(B)**	19. **(B)**	26. **(C)**	33. **(D)**	
6. **(D)**	13. **(A)**	20. **(A)**	27. **(B)**	34. **(C)**	
7. **(D)**	14. **(D)**	21. **(B)**	28. **(C)**	35. **(B)**	

Mathematics

39. **(D)**	43. **(D)**	47. **(A)**	51. **(B)**	55. **(B)**	59. **(B)**
40. **(B)**	44. **(C)**	48. **(B)**	52. **(D)**	56. **(B)**	60. **(B)**
41. **(D)**	45. **(B)**	49. **(A)**	53. **(B)**	57. **(C)**	
42. **(C)**	46. **(D)**	50. **(C)**	54. **(B)**	58. **(D)**	

Science

61. **(A)**	63. **(B)**	65. **(D)**	67. **(D)**	69. **(C)**	71. **(C)**
62. **(B)**	64. **(A)**	66. **(C)**	68. **(C)**	70. **(B)**	

Social Studies

72. **(B)**	74. **(C)**	76. **(B)**	78. **(D)**	80. **(C)**	82. **(D)**
73. **(A)**	75. **(D)**	77. **(D)**	79. **(B)**	81. **(D)**	

Arts and Physical Education

83. **(B)**	85. **(D)**	87. **(D)**	89. **(D)**	91. **(C)**	93. **(C)**
84. **(C)**	86. **(D)**	88. **(B)**	90. **(A)**	92. **(D)**	

General Knowledge

94. **(D)**	97. **(B)**	100. **(D)**	103. **(D)**	106. **(D)**	109. **(D)**
95. **(B)**	98. **(B)**	101. **(D)**	104. **(B)**	107. **(C)**	110. **(D)**
96. **(A)**	99. **(C)**	102. **(C)**	105. **(A)**	108. **(A)**	

EXPLAINED ANSWERS

Reading/Language Arts

1. **(D)** Choice (D) is correct. According to experts, the research is overwhelming in support of a phonics program alone as the best approach to teaching reading to young children. Choices (A), (B), and (C) are all incorrect because research indicates that the programs listed, including the blended phonics approaches, are not as effective as phonics alone.

2. **(B)** Choice (B) is correct. A writing checklist is an excellent way to determine a student's writing ability to prepare for further writing experiences. Choice (A) is incorrect. Standardized grammar tests do not reveal a student's writing ability. Choice (C) is incorrect. Holistic evaluations reflect the evaluator's overall view of the quality of the writing. A holistic evaluation does not yield a specific analysis that can lead to instructional plans. Choice (D) is incorrect. This assessment evaluates reading, not writing.

3. **(D)** Choice (D) is correct. A prerequisite competency refers to some skill or ability students must possess in order to learn an objective. That is, learning a prerequisite competency must come before learning the objective. Choice (A) is incorrect. The teacher certainly needs to have the knowledge and skills to teach about subject-verb agreement, but that's not what prerequisite competency means. Choice (B) is incorrect. A subobjective is part of the objective. Learning a sub-objective does not come before learning the objective. Choice (C) is incorrect. A test is not a competency, even though it may assess prerequisite competencies for the listed objective.

4. **(A)** Choice (A) is correct. Note the word EXCEPT in the item. This choice has to do with listening and NOT reading. Difficulty with auditory discrimination does not itself interfere with reading. Early hearing problems can inhibit reading and writing development. However, Lisa writes well and understands verbal directions. Choices (B), (C), and (D) are incorrect. These choices could be the cause of Lisa's trouble understanding written directions. Of course, there are other factors that could cause her difficulty.

5. **(B)** Choice (B) is correct. Note the word NOT in the item. A basal reading program is not designed to meet the individual needs of students. A basal program is designed for all students, typically with all students in the United States. A basal program must be supplemented to meet the individual needs of students. Choices (A), (C), and (D) are incorrect. These choices describe some of the characteristics of a basal reading program.

6. **(D)** Choice (D) is correct. The phrase "most likely" is key to answering this question. It is most likely that this student is having difficulty reading in the context of mathematics. We don't have any other information to base our

decision on. Choices (A), (B), and (C) are incorrect. These choices may be a cause, just not the most likely cause.

7. **(D)** Choice (D) is correct. Note the word NOT in the item. Choral reading is a group of children reading aloud together. This setting does not help students interpret word meaning. Rather, the emphasis is on simultaneous, clear pronunciation. Choices (A), (B), and (C) are incorrect. These choices do describe some of the goals and benefits of choral reading.

8. **(C)** Choice (C) is correct. Note the word EXCEPT in the item. You don't have to understand the meaning of a word to pronounce it. This item points out the important distinction between recognizing a word and knowing what the word means. Word recognition and comprehension are both important parts of reading instruction. Choices (A), (B), and (D) are incorrect. Difficulty with any of these might make it harder for a child to pronounce a word. It is clear how difficulty with phonics, or difficulty with sight vocabulary might lead to the problem. Difficulty with content analysis could also lead to this problem. A young child reads the sentence, "Jamie went to the store." But the child does not remember if the "e" in "went" is pronounced "eh" or "ah." That is, the child is not sure if the word "went" is pronounced "went" or "want." But, the context of the word shows clearly the correct pronunciation is "went."

9. **(B)** Choice (B) is correct. Note the word NOT in the item. Personal journals are just that—personal. These journals are not a way to share thoughts with others. Students should use a different format, such as a response journal, to share their thoughts. Choices (A), (B), and (D) are incorrect. These choices describe appropriate ways of using personal journals.

10. **(A)** Choice (A) is correct. *McGuffey's Readers* were the first schoolbooks written for different grade levels. Choices (B), (C), and (D) are incorrect. The early books in those choices were not the *first* written for different grade levels.

11. **(C)** Choice (C) is correct. The phrase "most important" is key to answering this question. A student must have the audience and purpose in mind before he or she considers the order of presentation, writing a clear beginning, or the main idea. Choices (A), (B), and (D) are incorrect. These are important things for a student to do when writing, but not the most important of the four listed.

12. **(B)** Choice (B) is correct. Note the word NOT in the item. A phonics approach does not address word meaning or reading comprehension. Phonics addresses word recognition and word pronunciation. Educators frequently criticize overreliance on phonics for just this reason. Choices (A), (B), and (D) are incorrect. Each choice describes a benefit that can be derived from the phonics approach.

13. **(A)** Choice (A) is correct. An anticipatory set makes the student aware in advance of the lesson's content. Choice (B) is incorrect. A motivation interests the student in the lesson. Choice (C) is incorrect. An objective specifies what a student is expected to do once instruction is complete. Choice (D) is incorrect. An advanced organizer is an initial overview of the lesson's content.

14. **(D)** Choice (D) is correct. Students develop a better attitude toward reading when they use the real literature found in a whole language approach. Choice (A) is incorrect. It may be reassuring that an approach is widely accepted, but that is never the best reason to use the approach. Choice (B) is incorrect. Word recognition must always be taught. Students can't read if they can't recognize words. Choice (C) is incorrect. Research does not uniformly support the conclusion that students comprehend better after using a whole language approach. It seems that a combination of approaches, including aspects of the whole language approach, best develops reading comprehension.

15. **(C)** Choice (C) is correct. The word "transactional" in the term "transactional strategy instruction" means a give-and-take between students and teachers as they explore the processes involved in successful reading comprehension. Choice (A) is incorrect. This choice describes the direct explanation of cognitive processes. Both the direct explanation approach and the transactional strategy instruction approach hold tremendous promise for reading instruction. Choice (B) and choice (D) are incorrect. They explain neither of these approaches.

16. **(B)** Choice (B) is correct. Clicking on a hypertext word reveals a definition or underlying meaning. Hypertext links to word definitions hold tremendous promise for reading instruction. Choices (A), (C), and (D) are incorrect. The descriptions in these choices have nothing to do with hypertext terms.

17. **(B)** Choice (B) is correct. The problem does not provide enough information to determine what time Charles arrived home. The relationship between reading and mathematics is very important, and this is more a reading problem than a mathematics problem. A child might consider these points as they try to solve the problem. The problem never says that Charles arrived home. Charles left work at 6:15, but we don't know what time he got on the bus. We don't know that the bus is traveling toward his house. Choices (A), (C), and (D) are incorrect. Choice (A) is the sum of the minutes in the problem. Choice (C) is 60 minutes after 6:15. Choice (D) 1815 hours is another way to write 6:15 P.M.

18. **(A)** Choice (A) is correct. The singular subject "I" does not agree with the plural verb "are." Nonagreement of subject and verb should be addressed in the early grades. Choice (B) is incorrect. The use of the pronoun "I" is correct. Choice (C) is incorrect. This sentence contains a subject and a verb.

Fragments are parts of sentences written as though they were sentences. Choice (D) is incorrect. There are no adjectives and no adverbs in this sentence, and none is called for.

19. **(B)** Choice (B) is correct. Guiding students as they work is a very effective strategy for teaching reading. Picking out science fact and science fiction in a space exploration science fiction story is certainly the best kind of guidance among the choices given. Choice (A) is incorrect. Many science fiction stories contain science fact. Choices (C) and (D) are incorrect. Working independently is one of the least effective ways to learn about reading because it lacks interaction with the teacher and with other students.

20. **(A)** Choice (A) is correct. Evaluation is the highest level in Bloom's Taxonomy. Choices (B), (C), and (D) are incorrect. They represent lower levels in the taxonomy.

21. **(B)** Choice (B) is correct. This is exactly the situation in which cooperative learning groups excel. Students learn from interaction in the group, from the presentation made by other groups, and from your reaction and others' reaction to the presentations. Choice (A) is incorrect. Working independently is one of the least effective ways to learn about reading because it lacks interaction with teachers and other students. Choices (C) and (D) are incorrect because the approaches involve direct instruction. A great many reading skills and objectives can best be taught through direct instruction. However, direct instruction is not the best approach for this situation.

22. **(D)** Choice (D) is correct. This student is a phonetic speller. "Enuf" is misspelled, but the student correctly followed phonics rules. This student needs instruction in the alternative spelling used for phonemes (sounds associated with letters and groups of letters). For example, English spelling uses the letters "gh" to represent the "f" sound in "enough." Using many spellings for the same sound can make English a difficult language to learn. Choices (A) and (B) are incorrect. Word attack skills lead to the correct pronunciation of "enuf." Choice (C) is incorrect. "Enough" and "enuf" sound the same, so they are homonyms. However, confusing homonyms is not the problem here.

23. **(C)** Choice (C) is correct. A definite reward schedule, and some means of giving rewards (points, paper coupons, plastic tokens, etc.), and a means of redeeming tokens or points are the essential ingredients of a token economy. Choices (A), (B), and (D) are incorrect. None of these choices bears any resemblance to a token economy.

24. **(B)** Choice (B) is correct. For a brief unit such as this, a teacher-made assessment is almost always the best. There may also be an appropriate assessment available from a text publisher or other source, but this is clearly the best among the choices given. Choice (A) is incorrect. Standardized tests

are used to establish an achievement level, or to compare results between students or groups of students. Standardized tests are not particularly useful for finding out whether or not a student has learned a particular skill or concept. Choice (C) is incorrect. The item states that the teacher wants to know whether the students have learned about nouns before going on. While observing students' written work over a week is an excellent assessment technique, it takes too long to meet the needs of this situation. Choice (D) is incorrect. Reviewing students' previous work, alone, will not help the teacher with this assessment.

25. **(C)** Choice (C) is correct. Note the word EXCEPT in the item. The Orton-Gillingham method does not emphasize reading for meaning. That is not to say that meaning is not important; it's just not an Orton-Gillingham emphasis. Choices (A), (B), and (D) are incorrect. The actions described in these choices are consistent with the Orton-Gillingham approach.

26. **(C)** Choice (C) is correct. Note the word NOT in the item. Note also the word "indicate," which means the incorrect choices do show an ongoing assessment is underway. This choice is correct because an in-class composition does not indicate that an ongoing assessment is underway. Choice (A) is incorrect. Observing students' work while they are writing indicates ongoing assessment is underway. Choice (B) is incorrect. The teacher's review of students' daily work indicates an ongoing assessment is underway. Choice (D) is incorrect. The regular collection of performance samples indicates an ongoing assessment is underway.

27. **(B)** Choice (B) is correct. A formative evaluation helps a teacher plan lessons. Samples of a student's writing best furthers that goal. Choice (A) is incorrect. A discussion with a student may help a teacher, particularly if the discussion follows a review of the student's writing, but a discussion is not the best opportunity for a formative evaluation. Choice (C) is incorrect. The Iowa Test of Basic Skills does not evaluate writing, and it is more useful as a summative evaluation than a formative evaluation. Choice (D) is incorrect. An end of unit test is also more useful as a summative evaluation.

28. **(C)** Choice (C) is correct. This answer correctly describes percentile rank. The 34th percentile means 34 percent of the scores are below that point. The 34th percentile also means that 66 percent of the scores are at or above that point. Choice (A) is incorrect. Percentile rank does not refer directly to the number of students. Choice (B) is incorrect. Another way to word this choice is ". . . did as well as or better than 66 percent of the students who took the test." That wording refers to the 66th percentile. Choice (D) is incorrect. Standardized reading tests measure performance on that test, not overall reading ability. Standardized scores may be a general guide to reading ability. However, an individual student may perform much better, or much worse, on a standardized test than his or her ability indicates.

29. **(B)** Choice (B) is correct. Standardized test scores indicate a range of grade levels, not one single grade level. The teacher's correct response is that the child is about average, meaning about average for that school. The word "about" in the teacher's explanation is important. It shows the teacher understands that reported grade levels are not precise. Choices (A) and (D) are incorrect. The reported grade equivalent is only slightly higher than the baseline 4.0, and in no significant way. If the test were given in the spring, as many are, the grade equivalent would be slightly below the average for all the students who took the test. But whether slightly above, or slightly below, the score indicates a range that is about average. Choice (C) is incorrect. The scores are reported in grade equivalents, not age equivalents.

30. **(A)** Choice (A) is correct. ESL means English as a Second Language. This approach encourages the teaching and use of English. Choices (B), (C), and (D) are incorrect. These choices are not consistent with an ESL approach.

31. **(D)** Choice (D) is correct. A summative evaluation assesses what a student learned about a specific objective or objectives. Choice (A) is incorrect. A formative evaluation helps a teacher plan lessons. Choices (C) and (D) are incorrect. A standardized test and norm-referenced test have been standardized or normed on a large population of students. End of chapter tests are not standardized.

32. **(D)** Choice (D) is correct. The only conclusive information is that the student appears to do better in real-world situations. This just underscores the importance of portfolio assessment. Even though portfolio assessment is often not a reliable indicator, portfolio assessment gives students the opportunity to demonstrate their "real-world" proficiency. Choices (A), (B), and (C) are incorrect. None of these explanations is supported by the reported results.

33. **(D)** Choice (D) is correct. The student's writing contains several verb tense shifts. In the first sentence, "sat" is past tense, while "play" is present tense. In the second sentence, "saw" is past tense, while "sit" is present tense. Choices (A) and (B) are incorrect. The nouns and pronouns are used correctly. Choice (C) is incorrect. The spelling error in the last sentence requires less of the teacher's attention than the tense shift errors.

34. **(C)** Choice (C) is correct. Note the word LEAST in the item. Groups with ten or twelve members are too large for effective interaction. Cooperative learning groups are typically limited to six members. Choices (A), (B), and (D) are incorrect. Each of these choices describes an essential element of cooperative learning groups.

35. **(B)** Choice (B) is correct. Reading is a unique skill, and different from language. Studies show that students benefit most from early, effective phonics instruction. This should not be taken to mean that every phonics program is

effective. Choice (A) is incorrect. This is a good idea, of course, and it would likely improve language development. But it is not a significant factor in reading development, particularly when compared to phonics instruction. Choice (C) is incorrect. Oral expression and effective listening are altogether different from reading. Choice (D) is incorrect. Replacing basal texts with real literature sources can help increase a student's interest in reading. However, this practice does not significantly contribute to reading development.

36. **(A)** Choice (A) is correct. Whole language is a direct descendent of Marie Clay's Reading Recovery programme. The programme was developed in New Zealand and became popular in the 1980s. Choice (B) is incorrect. Pitmans's Initial Teaching Alphabet (ITA) of 45 letters was first used in the early 1960s. Each ITA letter represents a phoneme (sound) in the English language. Choice (C) is incorrect. Piaget and his collaborator Barbel Inhelder posited several stages of child development. They argued that children should not be introduced to concepts until developmentally ready. Piaget made few recommendations about educational practice. Choice (D) is incorrect. Dewey's Progressive Education movement of the early 1900s featured practices similar to many of those found in the whole language approach. However, he did not emphasize using real literature sources and he is not credited with the founding of whole language.

37. **(B)** Choice (B) is correct. The reading grade level is based on the entire national group of students that took the test. In this case, the class as a whole performed better than the student, even though the student performed better than the national average. Choices (A) and (D) are incorrect. These are just meaningless statements about test scores. Choice (C) is incorrect. This statement is generally true. More or less half the students nationally who take a standardized test are below grade level. But this statement does not explain the student's test score situation.

38. **(D)** Choice (D) is correct. Students often perform better on alternative forms of assessment such as informal reading inventories than on standardized reading tests. The first step is to use alternative assessments to ensure that the reading level is actually low, and not just a function of the standardized test. Choice (A) is incorrect. Accounting for learning styles is not the first step, but it can be an effective approach to help students read better. There are many ways to categorize learning style, including multiple intelligences. Choice (B) is incorrect. It is obvious that this is a necessary step if the student is actually reading below grade level. Choice (C) is incorrect. Peer tutoring can be an effective technique, depending on the likelihood that the student will accept help from a classmate.

Mathematics

39. **(D)** Choice (D) is correct. This student divides correctly, but writes the remainder as a decimal. The correct answer to 124 divided by 5 is 24 R 4. Choices (A), (B), and (C) are incorrect. These choices do not show the error pattern.

40. **(B)** Choice (B) is correct. The student failed to include the side that has no indicated length. Tracing each side will eventually lead the student to realize the omission. The length of the missing side is $8 - 5 = 3$, and the correct perimeter is 26 units. Choice (A) is incorrect. The student added correctly, but omitted the length of a side. Choice (C) is incorrect. Counting the sides may help the student realize the length of a side is missing, but choice (B) is most likely to help. Choice (D) is incorrect. The student did use the rule "add the sides to find the perimeter," but omitted the length of a side.

41. **(D)** Choice (D) is correct. It is always best to teach a first lesson with manipulative materials. It is most important that elementary students handle materials during the first stage of the learning process. Choices (A), (B), and (C) are incorrect. In general, the concept should be taught in the following order:
    1. (D)
    2. (B)
    3. (C)
    4. (A)

42. **(C)** Choice (C) is correct. A student is most likely to be helped if he or she actually sees four small squares fit inside the large square. Choice (A) is incorrect. Tracing and comparing might help the student, but choice (C) is the best way. Choice (B) is incorrect. A ruler might help the student calculate the area, but the task here is to help the student see the relationship visually. Choice (D) is incorrect. Estimating the increase in distance might also help the student calculate the area, but choice (C) is best.

43. **(D)** Choice (D) is correct. Note the word LEAST in the item. Dividing decimals is too complex to represent with manipulatives. Choice (A) is incorrect. Counters can help student learn single digit addition. Choice (B) is incorrect. Students might use this strategy to find how many ways to arrange three different shapes in order. Shapes or other objects can be used to represent elements in the list. Choice (C) is incorrect. Tens blocks or bean sticks can help students learn addition of double-digit numbers.

44. **(C)** Choice (C) is correct. Students learn best when the lesson is at their level of *ability*. They become too frustrated when asked to do something they cannot do. While true as a general statement, it may be difficult to accurately determine a student's ability level. Naturally, there is a difference between ability level and achievement level. Students frequently learn

successfully when reasonably challenged beyond their *achievement* level, but not beyond their ability level.

45. **(B)** Choice (B) is correct. This student has trouble with place value. Look below to see the example written vertically. The student adds 9 and 3, for a total of 12 (1 ten and 1 one). But the student writes 12 in the sum, rather than renaming 10 ones as 1 ten.

$$\begin{array}{r} 13 \\ +9 \\ \hline 112 \end{array} \qquad \begin{array}{r} 1 \\ 13 \\ +9 \\ \hline 22 \end{array}$$

Student's error.   **Correct.**

46. **(D)** Choice (D) is correct. This is the classic number conservation task. One matched row of checkers is spread out after a student realizes the original rows contain the same number of checkers. Students who realize the rows still contain the same number of checkers are said to conserve number.

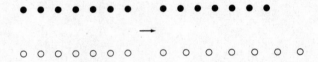

47. **(A)** Choice (A) is correct. Mathematics concepts, in this case multiplication, should be generally taught in this order:
    1. Manipulatives
    2. Visual representation
    3. Symbolic representation

48. **(B)** Choice (B) is correct. These two fractions must share a common denominator before a student can find the sum with the addition algorithm. Finding a common denominator requires a student to think, and then to use multiplication before adding. Choice (A) is incorrect. Multiplying fractions is the only understanding required. The answer is already in the simplest form. Choice (C) is incorrect. A student must know to "invert the divisor" and then multiply. Students do not have to understand the relationship between multiplication and division to complete this task. Choice (D) is incorrect. An understanding of a relationship among arithmetic operations is not required to complete this problem.

49. **(A)** Choice (A) is correct. Students frequently make key entry errors when they use a calculator. A student can tell if the answer is reasonable if he or she estimates before using a calculator. Choice (B) is incorrect. The answer is fairly obvious, and estimation is not nearly as important as choice (A).

Choices (C) and (D) are incorrect. Estimation in these measurement examples will not help ensure that a calculation is reasonable.

50. **(C)** Choice (C) is correct. Note the word LEAST in the item. The least helpful way to find information is to just type in a web address. Frequently, information about a subject is not found at a web address with that name. You also have to enter the correct suffix (.com, .edu, .gov, .net, and so on). Choice (A) is incorrect. Using a search engine is the best way to locate information on the Internet. Choices (B) and (D) are incorrect. These are not the best ways to find information on the Internet, but you may find someone to e-mail, to send messages to, or to chat with in real time.

51. **(B)** Choice (B) is correct. The geoboard is the instructional aid of choice for making triangles and other polygons. The geoboard consists of a board or piece of plastic with nails or pegs evenly spaced horizontally and vertically. Elastic bands are used to form shapes, and the elastic bands can be easily manipulated. Choice (A) is incorrect. You can create triangles with string, but it is very cumbersome. Choice (C) is incorrect. You can create triangles with sticks, but you need glue and it is too time-consuming. The sticks are not easily manipulated. Choice (D) is incorrect. You can create triangles with a ruler and pencil, but the drawn lines can't be manipulated.

52. **(D)** Choice (D) is correct. Just because a student can say counting words in order does not mean the student can count. You may have seen a child correctly count to five as the child counts seven objects. It is the correspondence between the counting words and the objects being counted that is important. Choices (A), (B), and (C) are incorrect. None of these is the reason the teacher is using this approach.

53. **(B)** Choice (B) is correct. In order to solve this problem, the student must interpret the remainder to mean that an extra tent is needed. That is, 9 tents are needed for the camping trip. Choices (A), (C), and (D) are incorrect. None of these strategies are correct.

$$5 \overline{)\begin{array}{l} 8 \text{ R } 3 \\ 43 \end{array}}$$
$$\underline{40}$$
$$3$$

54. **(B)** Choice (B) is correct. This step is first because this student's difficulty is mechanical, not conceptual. The multiplication is completed correctly, and the student tries to put the digits in the correct places. Writing digits in boxes on the graph paper usually solves this problem. Choice (A) is incorrect. Teaching place value is not likely to resolve this difficulty. If the graph paper doesn't help, the next step might be to reteach place value. Choice (C) is incorrect. Reteaching multiplication with fewer digits will not help. This student does not appear to have difficulty with multiplication. Choice (D) is

incorrect. Teaching to use zeros as placeholders may not solve the alignment problem. If the graph paper doesn't work, the next step might be to use zeros as placeholders.

55. **(B)** Choice (B) is correct. This choice draws attention to the coins and actively involves students in the lesson. Choice (A) is incorrect. It sounds interesting, but it does not involve students in the lesson. Choice (C) is incorrect. The question of where coins came from may be interesting to some, but usually not to a class of primary students. Choice (D) is incorrect. This choice is an anticipatory set designed to focus students on the lesson.

56. **(B)** Choice (B) is correct. This is a constructivist approach to teaching. Students are allowed to choose the resource or resources to "construct" their solution to this problem. Choices (A) and (D) are incorrect. True, there is a problem to be solved, and students can use manipulatives; however, problem solving and manipulatives are not general approaches to teaching, and not the most important aspect of this lesson. Choice (C) is incorrect. The teacher does not model a solution to the problem.

57. **(C)** Choice (C) is correct. The test is not standardized, and there is no information about how other students did on the test. The best interpretation among those given that is the student did well. Choice (A) is incorrect. The test is not standardized and there is no comparative information available about the meaning of the score. Choice (B) is incorrect. A score of 85 percent correct does not mean the score is at the 85th percentile. Choice (D) is incorrect. There is nothing about the score to indicate that further review is necessary. A perfect score on an end of chapter test is not required to move on to the next chapter.

58. **(D)** Choice (D) is correct. Students may be working on the problem at different times of the day. The best approach is for students to submit written samples of their solutions for the teacher to review. Choice (A) is incorrect. It will be too difficult to observe all the students as they work on the solution. Choice (B) is incorrect. A standardized test is not appropriate to assess student's solutions to these problems. Choice (C) is incorrect. Cooperative learning is not itself an assessment tool.

59. **(B)** Choice (B) is correct. The mode is the score that occurs most often. Choice (A) is incorrect. This choice describes the median of the scores. Choice (C) is incorrect. This choice also describes the median. Choice (D) is incorrect. This choice describes the average or mean of the scores.

60. **(B)** Choice (B) is correct. This is the most common way to limit the use of calculators. If students are learning a computation method, calculators should not be used. But when students need to compute, particularly to solve problems, the calculator can be used. Students use calculators on many tests, including the PSAT, the SAT, and the ACT. One challenge on these

tests is to determine when a calculator will help, when a calculator may help, and when a calculator will not help, and may even hurt.

Science

61. **(A)** Choice (A) is correct. It is best to help students learn through actual experience. Choices (B), (C), and (D) are incorrect. Each of these choices has value; however, none of them are the best response to this item.

62. **(C)** Choice (C) is correct. Note the word EXCEPT in the item. A teacher should not be quick to answer a question; the teacher may be able to help the student find the answer himself or herself. Choices (A), (B), and (D) are incorrect. These are all appropriate ways of responding to student's science questions.

63. **(B)** Choice (B) is correct. Note the word EXCEPT in the item. This approach does not incorporate Piaget's developmental theory. Piaget emphasizes developmental appropriateness, not age appropriateness. Choices (A), (C), and (D) describe a way to apply Piaget's child development theory.

64. **(A)** Choice (A) is correct. Understanding capacity means understanding that the amount of liquid does not change just because its appearance changes. Volume is a specific measure of how much something holds (2 cubic feet). Students can understand capacity without being ready to understand volume.

65. **(C)** Choice (C) is correct. The prism separates out all the colors that white light consists of. Choices (A) and (B) are incorrect. These choices accurately represent science concepts, but this experiment does not demonstrate either of these concepts. Choice (D) is incorrect because a prism separates colors; it does not combine them.

66. **(C)** Choice (C) is correct. This choice describes the essence of the inquiry approach. Choice (A) is incorrect. A teacher should try out experiments in advance. Choice (B) is incorrect. The inquiry approach encourages analysis of thought processes. Choice (D) is incorrect. The inquiry approach encourages students to conduct experiments and observe results without prior guidance.

67. **(D)** Choice (D) is correct. Inductive teaching helps a student to discover science concepts by leading the student from examples to a generalization. Choice (A) is incorrect. The deductive approach is the opposite of the inductive approach. Deductive teaching leads from rules to examples, and can be effective in many settings. Choices (B) and (C) are incorrect. Neither of these choices describes the inductive approach to teaching.

68. **(C)** Choice (C) is correct. Two objects can weigh the same, but have different densities. The rubber or ceramic solid object is not as dense as the lead solid object. If two solid objects weigh the same, the one that displaces the least water is most dense. Choice (A) is incorrect. The activity does not have to do with gravity. However, the weight of an object does depend on gravity. An object will weigh less on the surface of the moon than on the surface of the earth. However, the mass or amount of the object is the same on earth as it is on the moon. Choices (B) and (D) are incorrect. These answers are not related to the activity.

69. **(C)** Choice (C) is correct. Use a bar graph when quantities are unrelated to one another. A line graph is used when the quantities are related to one another. For example, use a line graph to show temperature change throughout a day, but these quantities in the item are unrelated, and a bar graph is appropriate. Choice (A) is incorrect. The table and graph were made "on site" and their informal appearance is acceptable under those circumstances. Choice (B) is incorrect. This choice correctly describes when to use a circle graph, but a circle graph is not appropriate here. Choice (D) is incorrect. It is fine to use kilograms, but pounds are just as good. The data at the recycling center was probably reported in pounds.

70. **(B)** Choice (B) is correct. The experiment is similar to the Leaning Tower of Pisa experiment that helped establish that all objects fall at the same rate. These objects likely did not land at the same time because air pressure and wind slowed the fall of the plastic ball. The students did not take these variables into account. By the way, the objects don't have to be the same weight to fall at the same rate. For better results, try this experiment with an orange and a grape.

71. **(C)** Choice (C) is correct. Multiply the height of the fall by 0.8 to find the diameter of the crater.

Social Studies

72. **(B)** Choice (B) is correct. Note the word EXCEPT in the item. Cooperative learning groups do not lead to more content coverage. In fact, teacher-directed lessons would most likely to lead to more content coverage. Choices (A), (C), and (D) are incorrect. These choices are characteristics of social studies cooperative learning groups.

73. **(A)** Choice (A) is correct. A multicultural approach to teaching social studies emphasizes the varying experiences across cultures. The intent of a multicultural social studies approach is to help students recognize differences and yet develop a unified bond among the students. Choices (A), (C), and (D) are incorrect. These choices do not characterize a multicultural approach to teaching social studies.

74. **(C)** Choice (C) is correct. This choice represents a consistent emphasis of the National Council for the Social Studies Standards. Choices (A) and (B) are incorrect. These might be teaching goals in a social studies program, but never the overall emphasis of the program. Choice (D) is contrary to the standards.

75. **(D)** Choice (D) is correct. Plotting information on a map is the most complex skill. In fact, it involves many skills including map reading, understanding information to be plotted, devising a plotting key, and others. Choices (A), (B), and (C) are incorrect. These are all useful skills and activities, but none of them are the most challenging skill on the list. It is interesting that every map can be colored with four colors so that no two adjoining areas have the same color.

76. **(B)** Choice (B) is correct. Note the word EXCEPT in the item. Just because a student is below grade level in reading does not mean the student cannot understand on-level or above-level social studies topics. Do not adapt instruction to less difficult topics on the basis of a low reading level. Choices (A), (C), and (D) are all incorrect. Each represents an acceptable way to adapt social studies instruction for students reading significantly below grade level.

77. **(D)** Choice (D) is correct. The teacher should not be confident. Errors of measurement that occur on all teacher-made tests quite likely eliminate any meaning in the difference between these scores. Choice (A) is incorrect. The teacher should not be very confident. Choice (B) is incorrect. The teacher should not be very confident, and the difference between the scores of two percent does not mean much. Choice (C) is incorrect. Content validity means the test actually measures the content in the social studies unit. Content validity does not mean the test is reliable. Reliability loosely means the test consistently yields the same results when given to the same types of students.

78. **(D)** Choice (D) is correct. These events occur over about two decades. The English government instituted the Stamp Act in 1765. The Stamp Act required every legal document (college degrees, licenses, policies, etc.) to carry a tax stamp. Choice (A) is incorrect. The Declaration of Independence was written in 1776. On July 4, 1776, the Continental Congress approved the Declaration of Independence. Choice (B) is incorrect. The United States Constitution was written in 1787. The Constitution was approved by Congress in 1787 and sent to the states for ratification. Delaware was the first state to ratify the Constitution in 1787; Rhode Island was the last in 1790. Choice (C) is incorrect. The First Continental Congress met in 1774, and included representatives from all 13 original colonies except Georgia.

79. **(B)** Choice (B) is correct. A circle graph best displays this type of comparative data. Choice (A) is incorrect. A flowchart shows the steps for completing

a task. Choice (C) is incorrect. A bar graph represents information by the length of a bar. Choice (D) is incorrect. A line graph plots data against two axes. See pages 110–111 in the mathematics review section for examples of these graphs.

80. **(C)** Choice (C) is correct. The map shows the mountains blocking the way west. Choice (A) is incorrect. That is the way to Denver, but the trail continues west after Denver and the trail would not turn north except for the mountains. Choices (B) and (D) are incorrect. Mexico and the Rio Grande River are too far away to cause this turn.

81. **(D)** Choice (D) is correct. The teacher directs a mediated reading thinking activity. Students are asked to read a particular passage for a particular purpose. Choices (A), (B), and (C) are incorrect. These might be appropriate actions by the teacher in other circumstances. However, these choices do not characterize a mediated reading thinking activity.

82. **(D)** Choice (D) is correct. Plans often fail, and for many reasons; it is a reality of teaching, particularly for beginning teachers. The teacher should then try to find alternative ways to teach the lesson. Choices (A), (B), and (C) are incorrect. Don't stick with a failed plan. That's not to say a teacher should abandon a plan at the first sign of trouble. However, let the plan go if it is "clearly not working."

Arts and Physical Education

83. **(B)** Choice (B) is correct. Note the word LEAST in the item. This is the least effective method because this choice, alone, does not integrate haiku with fine arts. Choices (A), (C), and (D) are incorrect. These choices do describe effective ways of integrating haiku and art. Haiku is an Asian poetic form with three lines and a 5-7-5 syllabication pattern

84. **(C)** Choice (C) is correct. This is the most appropriate focus for an elementary school art program. This general focus might include the more specific activities found in the other choices. Choices (A), (B), and (D) are incorrect. While these may be appropriate art activities, none is as an appropriate main focus for an art program as choice C.

85. **(D)** Choice (D) is correct. Contemporary elementary school physical education programs focus on movement activities. This choice describes one of the important aspects of these movement programs. Choices (A), (B), and (C) are incorrect. These approaches may be appropriate in certain circumstances, but none of these choices are the most important when planning this activity.

86. **(D)** Choice (D) is correct. The affective domain presents a taxonomy for feelings and emotions. Choice (A) is incorrect. The psychomotor domain

presents a taxonomy for movement. Choice (B) is incorrect. There is no introspective domain. Choice (C) is incorrect. The cognitive domain presents a taxonomy for cognitive processes.

87. **(D)** Choice (D) is correct. Balancing is the most advanced individual activity given here.

The correct order of these activities is:

1. (C)
2. (A)
3. (B)
4. (D).

88. **(B)** Choice (B) is correct. Listening to students is the best way to find out how they are doing. Choices (A) and (C) are incorrect. These choices interrupt the flow of the lesson and call too much attention to the student. Choice (D) is incorrect. This choice does not permit assessment during the lesson.

89. **(D)** Choice (D) is correct. An objective should describe clearly what the student is expected to do at the completion of instruction. Choices (A) and (B) are incorrect. These choices describe what the teacher will do, not what the student will do. Choice (C) is incorrect. This choice describes what the teacher will do to prepare for the lesson.

90. **(A)** Choice (A) is correct. Note the word NOT in the item. It is fine to provide emotional support even if other students notice. Choices (B), (C), and (D) are incorrect. These are all appropriate ways to respond to the child who is anxious about learning music notation.

91. **(C)** Choice (C) is correct. Music consists of pitch, the actual frequency or sound of a note, and duration. Choice (A) is incorrect. A chord is many different pitches occurring simultaneously. Choice (B) is incorrect. Harmony is a chord with duration. Choice (D) is incorrect. Timbre refers to the unique sound produced by musical instruments; for example, horns (trumpet, trombone) have a similar timbre.

92. **(D)** Choice (D) is correct. Students expect the teacher to be an authority figure. Students may complain, but an authority figure is what students expect and what it is usually best to give them. Choices (A), (B), and (C) are incorrect. Students do not have these general expectations of a teacher, and authority figures do not have to act in one of these ways.

93. **(C)** Choice (C) is correct. Dewey's approach put the child and the child's needs at the center of the curriculum and at the center of the school. Choice (A) is incorrect. Dewey's approach was child centered, not teacher centered. Choice (B) is incorrect. Dewey's approach did not reflect the future needs of

society. Choice (D) is incorrect. Team sports do not necessarily reflect Dewey's philosophy.

General Knowledge

94. **(D)** Choice (D) is correct. Economically disadvantaged students are not less capable, but as a group, economically disadvantaged students do have fewer home learning opportunities, which leads to lower achievement scores. Choices (A), (B), and (C) are false.

95. **(B)** Choice (B) is correct. It is generally most appropriate to address questions to the entire class. This maximizes the number of students who are thinking about the answer. Choices (A), (C), and (D) are incorrect. These choices represent incorrect questioning techniques.

96. **(A)** Choice (A) is correct. The best advice among the four choices is to stand where you can see all the students. Choices (B), (C), and (D) are incorrect. These choices represent inappropriate management techniques.

97. **(B)** Choice (B) is correct. Modeling means demonstrating the behavior students should replicate. Choices (A), (C), and (D) are incorrect. None of these is an example of appropriate modeling behavior.

98. **(B)** Choice (B) is correct. This choice describes the least restrictive environment that meets the child's need for support. Choices (A) and (C) are incorrect. Primary placement in a self-contained special education class is too restrictive. Choice (D) is incorrect. Reading level alone should never be used to place a student.

99. **(C)** Choice (C) is correct. Herbart formalized schools, and much of the formal structure of American schools is due to his influence. Choice (A) is incorrect. Rousseau was a philosopher who advocated liberalizing education and wrote an influential book, *Emile*. Choice (B) is incorrect. Froebel founded the first kindergarten (child's garden). Choice (D) is incorrect. Pestalozzi popularized Rousseau's ideas and called for learning through activity. Maria Montessori established the first Casa Bambini.

100. **(D)** Choice (D) is correct. Negative reinforcement means explaining how to avoid negative consequences. Choice (A) is incorrect. Punishment is negative consequences brought on by inappropriate behavior. Choice (B) is incorrect. Reverse psychology is suggesting the opposite of what you want a student to do. Choice (C) is incorrect. Threats, or bullying, are not appropriate teacher behavior.

101. **(D)** Choice (D) is correct. It is appropriate to alter the objectives or plans to focus on the cultural heritage of those in the class. Choices (A), (B), and (C)

are incorrect. It is not appropriate to adopt these practices in a culturally and linguistically diverse class.

102. **(C)** Choice (C) is correct. This arrangement makes it too difficult for the teacher to see all the students. Having students out of sight, particularly on the first day of class, is not a good idea. Choices (A), (B), and (D) are incorrect. Any of these other chair arrangements is acceptable.

103. **(D)** Choice (D) is correct. Note the word EXCEPT in the item. Standardized tests are used in effective schools. Choices (A), (B), and (C) are incorrect. These choices represent the characteristics of effective schools.

104. **(B)** Choice (B) is correct. More than any of the other factors, research shows that students learn more when they spend more time on task. Choices (A), (C), and (D) are incorrect. These choices can be effective techniques, but are not as important as time on task.

105. **(A)** Choice (A) is correct. Authentic assessment means a teacher observes students as they work or reviews their work product Portfolio assessment is a form of authentic assessment. Choices (B), (C), and (D) are incorrect. These choices do not describe authentic assessment.

106. **(D)** Choice (D) is correct. Note the word EXCEPT in the item. In cooperative learning, students summarize the results of their cooperative work. Choices (A), (B), and (C) are incorrect. All of these choices are characteristics of cooperative learning groups.

107. **(C)** Choice (C) is correct. A constructivist approach encourages students to construct their own understanding of concepts. One way students do this is to build on their initial responses. Choice (A) is not correct. A more reflective approach to questions is in keeping with the constructivist approach. Choice (B) is not correct. This is not the kind of construction that constructivists have in mind. Choice (D) is not correct. The constructivist approach encourages students to create metaphors.

108. **(A)** Choice (A) is correct. Gardner's theory supports the use of interdisciplinary units. Gardner's theory posits that students have many intelligences, not just a cognitive intelligence. Interdisciplinary units promote utilization of these multiple intelligences. Choices (B), (C), and (D) are incorrect. These choices do not reflect Gardner's theory.

109. **(D)** Choice (D) is correct. This is the classic test-based definition of a learning disability—ability at or above average but achievement two or more years below grade level. Choice (A) is incorrect. There is nothing in this record to indicate that the student is a poor test taker, and the IQ score of 110–115 may indicate that the child is not a poor test taker. Choice (B) is incorrect. The student's achievement is well below the student's potential. Choice (C)

is incorrect. These IQ test results are not high enough for a gifted classification.

110. **(D)** Choice (D) is correct. Reliability refers to the same work consistently
receiving the same evaluation. A school that implemented portfolio assessment had to reconsider its decision because different teachers assigned widely
different grades to the same portfolio. Clear rubrics or standards have to be
established in order to reliably evaluate portfolios. Choice (A) is not correct.
It is not the diverse group of work students put in portfolios that causes the
problem; rather, it is the way teacher's assess these samples. Choice (B) is not
correct. Machines do not typically score the materials in a portfolio. Choice
(C) is not correct. The different emphases teachers give to the importance of
a portfolio is not an issue of reliability.

Elementary Education: Content Area Exercises

HOW TO PREPARE FOR THE CONTENT AREA EXERCISES TEST

This chapter prepares you to take the Elementary Education: Content Area Exercises Test (0012). The chapter gives an overview of the test with a full-length practice test and explained answers.

Preparation Strategies

Other sections in the book will help you prepare for this test. The PLT Review beginning on page 264 will also help you prepare for this test. The Proven Test-Preparation Strategies on page 12 and the Essay Strategies and Steps for Writing Passing Essays on page 17 will also help you pass this test.

OVERVIEW

This 2-hour test consists of four constructed-response questions. There is one question from reading and language arts, one from mathematics, one from science or social studies, and one from an integration of these subject areas.

The topics covered correspond to the topics for the Elementary Education: Curriculum, Instruction, and Assessment test described earlier, except that art and physical education are not included.

This section includes a full-length practice test with brief scoring guidelines for Elementary Education: Content Area Exercises.

PRACTICE TEST
Four Questions Requiring Constructed-Response Answers
2 Hours

This test consists of four constructed-response questions. The first question is about teaching reading/language arts. The second question is about teaching mathematics. The third question is about teaching social studies, although it could have been about teaching science. The last question integrates teaching science and teaching language arts (writing), although it could have integrated other areas of teaching. There are many different versions of this test, and the version you take may have a different emphasis and focus than this practice test.

Take this test in a realistic, timed setting. The setting will be most realistic if another person times the test and ensures that the test rules are followed. If another person is acting as test supervisor, he or she should review these instructions with you and say "START" when you should begin a section, and "STOP" when time is up.

You have 2 hours to complete the test. Keep the time limit in mind as you work. Respond directly to the question, and be sure to answer each part of the question. Your response will usually be an essay, although a diagram or a listing of ideas may also be appropriate. Write legibly and clearly, although ETS says grammar and spelling are not included in the evaluation. It's fine to cross out words and rewrite.

Write your answers on the pages provided. Once the test is complete, review the scoring guidelines to evaluate your responses.

When instructed, turn the page and begin.

Elementary Education: Curriculum, Content Area Exercises (0012) Four Questions Requiring Constructed-Response Answers 2 Hours

Question 1

Assume that you are the teacher of a fifth-grade class that is reading books about technology. Your class is going to read a short fiction book titled *The Internet Sleuth Squad*. The book is about a group of middle school students who use futuristic computer technology and the Internet to help people and solve mysteries. The squad members learn about advanced technology and about working together. The squad even has a mascot—Nougat the Net-dog.

You intend to use this book as the basis for a lesson. A brief excerpt from the book that describes the Squad's computer technology, and that introduces the Net-dog, is given below.

> The Sleuth Squad members had tiny computers hidden in special eyeglasses. They could see the display in their glasses, but no one could tell they were looking at the display. The computers were hooked up to the Internet by tiny cellular phones also hidden in the glasses. Sounds came through tiny earplugs in the eyeglass frames. They gave instructions to the computer over a tiny microphone that was also hidden in the glasses. Each Squad member's computer would only respond to that person's voice.

> Two members of the Sleuth Squad were missing. One was a human—and one was not. Then they heard the sound of claws slipping across the kitchen floor. A voice called out, "Nougat—downstairs." The basement door flew open. An energized bundle of sandy fur burst through the open doorway and tumbled down the steps. This canine dynamo jumped from the last step, and Nougat the Net-dog hit the floor running. The most charismatic member of the Squad had arrived.

Each response you write should emphasize the appropriateness of the activities you suggest.

A. Describe *one* prereading activity for your class. Be sure the activity is appropriate for fifth grade and that the activity is related to the topics of technology and working together effectively in *The Internet Sleuth Squad*. Be sure the activity directly addresses these topics and is explained in detail. Be sure also that the activity reflects accepted approaches to reading instruction and child development.

B. Describe *one* instructional approach or technique you would use as students read to fully develop their comprehension. Explain how you would assess the effectiveness of this approach or technique.

C. Devise *one* activity you will use after your students read *The Internet Sleuth Squad* that would continue to develop the topics of technology and working together effectively. Be sure the activity directly addresses these themes and is explained in detail. Be sure also that the activity reflects accepted approaches to reading instruction and child development.

OUTLINE

_____

_____

_____

_____

_____

_____

_____

_____

_____

_____

_____

_____

_____

_____

_____

_____

_____

_____

_____

Question 2

Assume that you are the teacher of a third-grade class. You want to teach subtraction of two-digit numbers with regrouping. As you observe students you notice two distinct developmental levels. Students in the first group do not understand place value, and do not know how to subtract two-digit numbers without regrouping. The second and larger group of students knows about place value and can subtract without renaming. This second group would not benefit from activities needed by the first group:

A. Describe *three* distinct activities to help the first group of students understand the concept of place value through the hundreds place. Give examples of work you expect students to produce during the activities. Explain how you would assess the effectiveness of these activities.

B. Describe *three* distinct activities to help the first group of students add two-digit numbers without renaming and with the recall of single-digit subtraction facts. Give examples of work you expect students to produce during the activities. Be sure to explain how the activities reflect accepted approaches to teaching mathematics.

C. Describe *two* distinct activities for the second group that would solidify what these students know and extend that knowledge. Give examples of work you expect students to produce during the activities. Be sure to explain how the activities reflect accepted approaches to teaching mathematics.

OUTLINE

_____

_____

_____

_____

_____

_____

_____

_____

_____

_____

_____

_____

_____

_____

Question 3

You take your fifth-grade class on a social studies field trip to a restored eighteenth-century village. The village has about two dozen buildings representing the different trades, shops, and houses in the village during the late 1700s. There is an information center that has maps, brochures, and other information about the village. You have a specific objective for the trip—to learn about village government during the 1700s. Before you leave for the trip students will read a story about villages in the 1700s. You are also bringing along one teacher aid or parent for each four students in the class.

A. Describe *two* pretrip activities for your class of fifth-graders related to the topic of village government. Be sure to explain why you choose these activities and describe how the activities will help your students prepare for the trip.

B. Write *two* questions for students to respond to while they are at the village. The questions should ask students to think at the higher levels of Bloom's Taxonomy, and to report what they see and learn at the village. Each question should ask students to write a paragraph response. Be sure the questions directly address the topic of village government. Be sure also to explain how each question fosters thinking at the higher levels of Bloom's Taxonomy, to report what they see, and how it will help students learn more about the topic of village government.

C. Outline a *couple of* additional steps you would take to help guarantee student's safety on the trip and explain why each step is important.

OUTLINE

_____

_____

_____

_____

_____

_____

_____

_____

_____

_____

_____

_____

_____

_____

_____

_____

_____

_____

_____

_____

_____

_____

_____

_____

_____

_____

_____

_____

Question 4

Your fourth-grade class is working on a Living Things chapter in the science book. You want the students to engage in some writing activities about mammals and reptiles to put in their portfolio.

A. Explain the steps you would take to get your students ready for this writing activity. Be sure to include a short explanation of each step.

B. Describe *three* writing activities you would assign students for the mammals and reptiles unit that includes factual and creative writing. Be sure to fully describe each activity and describe how each activity helps students learn about mammals and reptiles.

OUTLINE

_____

_____

_____

_____

_____

_____

_____

_____

_____

_____

_____

_____

_____

EVALUATING ANSWERS

EVALUATORS' GUIDE

Two teachers or teacher educators evaluate your responses on the seven-point scale detailed below. If the evaluators' ratings differ by more than one point, a third reader will evaluate your response. Some things are easy for evaluators to check: It is easy for an evaluator to reduce your score if a question asks for three activities, but you only supply two.

6 All parts are answered correctly, an outstanding grasp of the subject matter is demonstrated, pedagogy and other material is well organized and supports the explanation well with examples and details.

5 All parts are answered correctly, a very good understanding of the subject matter is demonstrated, pedagogy and other material is adequately organized and supports the explanation with examples and details.

4 All significant parts are answered correctly, an adequate, if limited, understanding of the subject matter is demonstrated, pedagogy and other material is adequately organized and supports the explanation with examples and details.

3 Some parts are answered correctly, an understanding of the subject matter is demonstrated, pedagogy and other material, which includes mistakes, is somewhat disorganized and supports the explanation with few examples and details.

2 No parts are answered completely and correctly, a poor understanding of the subject matter is demonstrated, pedagogy and other material is often unclear and supports the explanation with incorrect examples and details.

1 No parts are answered correctly, a very poor understanding of the subject matter is demonstrated, pedagogy and other material is unclear, disorganized, and may not support the explanation with examples and details.

0 The response does not address the questions, or no response is presented.

EXPLAINED ANSWERS

Evaluators are trained how to apply the six-point scoring scale to each section of the test. The brief guidelines below are like the more detailed guidelines these evaluators might be trained to use.

Question 1

This section shows how the evaluators would use their guide to evaluate each section of Question 1.

Score of 5 or 6

A score of 5 or 6 represents well-developed answers, but a score of 5 indicates that the answer is not as clear, as carefully explained, or as complete as a score of 6.

A. Describe *one* prereading activity for your class. Be sure the activity is appropriate for fifth grade and that the activity is related to the topics of technology and working together effectively in *The Internet Sleuth Squad*. Be sure the activity directly addresses these topics and is explained in detail. Be sure also that the activity reflects accepted approaches to reading instruction and child development.

There should be one specific, clearly explained prereading activity. The activity should be an accepted prereading activity such as acquainting children with the story, or a student discussion of what they know about technology or the Internet. The activity should be on grade level. The answer should clearly justify the appropriateness of the activity.

B. Describe *one* instructional approach or technique you would use as students read to fully develop their comprehension. Explain how you would assess the effectiveness of this approach or technique.

This approach or technique should be able to be used as children read. The activity should be an accepted approach or technique to aid reading comprehension, such as discussing and summarizing characters and plot, or predicting outcomes. Reading skill techniques or approaches such as word recognition are not acceptable. The answer should clearly justify the appropriateness of the activity.

C. Devise *one* activity you will use after your students read *The Internet Sleuth Squad* that would continue to develop the topics of technology and working together effectively. Be sure the activity directly addresses these themes and is explained in detail. Be sure also that the activity reflects accepted approaches to reading instruction and child development.

The activity should be based on the technology and working together themes in the story *The Internet Sleuth Squad*. These activities might include suggesting alternate plots and characters, or suggesting how to incorporate technology or working together into students' everyday lives. The answer should clearly justify the appropriateness of the activity.

Score of 4

A score of 4 indicates that all parts of the question are adequately answered. This score may indicate that the activities are not as well focused, or not as well explained or justified as answers that received a score of 5 or 6.

Score of 3

A score of 3 indicates that some but not all parts of the question are adequately answered. This score may indicate that some activities are missing and not at all well focused, or well explained or justified as answers that received a score of 4.

Score of 1 or 2

These scores indicate seriously deficient answers in which no activity is adequately developed and that some or all the activities are inadequately supported.

Score of 0

The answer is blank, on another topic, or the handwriting is illegible.

Question 2

This section shows how the evaluators would use their guide to evaluate each section of Question 2.

Score of 5 or 6

A score of 5 or 6 represents well-developed answers, but a score of 5 indicates that the answer is not as clear, as carefully explained, or as complete as a score of 6.

A. Describe *three* distinct activities to help the first group of students understand the concept of place value through the hundreds place. Give examples of work you expect students to produce during the activities. Explain how you would assess the effectiveness of these activities.

There should be three specific, clearly explained activities for reteaching place value. The activities should be accepted activities such as using bean sticks, using tens blocks, using pennies, nickels, and dimes, or using a place value chart. The activity should be on grade level. The answer should clearly justify the appropriateness of the activity.

B. Describe *three* distinct activities to help the first group of students add two-digit numbers without renaming and with the recall of single-digit subtraction facts. Give examples of work you expect students to produce during the activities. Be sure to explain how the activities reflect accepted approaches to teaching mathematics.

There should be three specific, clearly explained activities for reteaching two-digit addition without renaming using bean sticks, using tens blocks, using pennies, nickels, and dimes, or using a place value chart. One of the activities should focus on recall of single-digit subtraction facts. The answer should clearly justify the appropriateness of the activity.

C. Describe *two* distinct activities for the second group that would solidify what these students know and extend that knowledge. Give examples of work you expect students to produce during the activities. Be sure to explain how the activities reflect accepted approaches to teaching mathematics.

There should be two specific, clearly explained activities for the second group of students about adding two-digit numbers without renaming. The activities might include more difficult subtraction problems (with renaming) or word problems that require addition without renaming. The answer should clearly justify the appropriateness of the activity.

Scores below 5

Refer to the guide for Question 1 on page 433.

Question 3

This section shows how the evaluators would use their guide to evaluate each section of Question 3.

Score of 5 or 6

A score of 5 or 6 represents well-developed answers, but a score of 5 indicates that the answer is not as clear, as carefully explained, or as complete as a score of 6.

A. Describe *two* pretrip activities for your class of fifth-graders related to the topic of village government. Be sure to explain why you decided on these activities and to describe how the activities will help your students prepare for the trip.

There should be two specific, clearly explained activities for students to complete before they take the trip. The activities might include research about the village or village government, questions to ask at the village, or predictions of what they will learn during the trip. The activity should be on grade level. The answer should clearly justify the appropriateness of the activity.

B. Write *two* questions for students to respond to while they are at the village. The questions should ask students to think at the higher levels of Bloom's Taxonomy, to report what they see and learn at the village. Each question should ask students to write a paragraph response. Be sure the questions directly address the topic of village government. Be sure also to explain how each question fosters thinking at the higher levels of Bloom's Taxonomy, to report what they see, and how it will help students learn more about the topic of village government.

There should be two questions. One question should be at the higher levels of Bloom's Taxonomy. The Taxonomy categories are listed here from lowest level to highest level:

1. knowledge
2. comprehension
3. application
4. analysis
5. synthesis
6. evaluation.

An example of an evaluation question is "How effective would the village form of government be in our town?" The other question should ask students to report on some aspect of the village. The answer should clearly explain that a full paragraph response is required to each question, and explain why the question is effective and how the question will help students learn about the village.

C. Outline a *couple of* additional steps you would take to help guarantee students' safety on the trip and explain why each step is important.

There should be two specific, clearly explained steps to help guarantee students' safety on the trip. These steps might include making provisions for students with disabilities or special medical needs, establishing clear rules for student behavior on the trip, and establishing a procedure to ensure that students are with their group when they leave, at the village, and before they return. There are many other possibilities. The answer should clearly explain why each step is important.

Scores below 5

Refer to the guide for Question 1 on page 433.

Question 4

This section shows how the evaluators would use their guide to evaluate each section of Question 4.

Score of 5 or 6

A score of 5 or 6 represents well-developed answers, but a score of 5 indicates that the answer is not as clear, as carefully explained, or as complete as a score of 6.

A. Explain the steps you would take to get your students ready for this writing activity. Be sure to include a short explanation of each step.

The steps might include reading the science text or other sources about mammals and reptiles, discussing ideas with classmates, the teacher, or others, outlining thoughts and ideas, or writing thoughts down on index cards. The steps can be presented in outline form, but each step should be fully explained

B. Describe *three* writing activities you would assign students for the mammals and reptiles unit that includes factual and creative writing. Be sure to fully describe each activity and to describe how each activity helps students learn about mammals and reptiles.

There should be three specific, clearly explained writing activities about mammals and reptiles that may include an essay, a short play, a letter, or a research report. There are many others. The answer should clearly explain how each activity would help students learn more about mammals and reptiles.

Scores below 5

Refer to the guide for Question 1 on page 433.

13 Elementary Education: Content Knowledge

> ## TEST INFO BOX
>
> ### PRAXIS II
>
> ### ELEMENTARY EDUCATION
>
> Read this chapter if you are taking this subject assessment.
>
> Elementary Education: Content Knowledge (0014*)
> 120 multiple-choice items, 2 hours
>
> * Use these ETS codes to identify Elementary Subject Assessments.

HOW TO PREPARE FOR THE CONTENT KNOWLEDGE TEST

This chapter prepares you to take the Elementary Education: Content Knowledge (0014). The chapter gives an overview of this test and a full-length practice test with explained answers for the Content Knowledge Test.

Preparation Strategies

Other sections in this book will help you prepare for these tests. The PLT Review beginning on page 264 will help you prepare for the Curriculum, Instruction, and Assessment test. The Proven Test Preparation Strategies on page 12 will help you prepare for both tests. The Multiple-Choice Strategies on page 15 will help you pass the Curriculum, Instruction, and Assessment test.

ELEMENTARY EDUCATION: CONTENT KNOWLEDGE (0014)

This 2-hour test has 120 multiple-choice items. The test focuses on the knowledge required to be an elementary school teacher. It is based on the content areas of Language Arts, Mathematics, Social Studies, and Science. There are many different versions of this test, and the version you take may have a different emphasis and focus than this practice test.

You may use a basic four-function calculator or a scientific calculator on this test. The calculator must be solar or battery powered. You can't bring a noisy calculator, a calculator with a paper tape, or a pocket organizer.

This book contains a practice test with explained answers.

Content Areas

The following includes the topics on which you may be tested in each content area.

The order of the topics under each content area reflects the importance of those topics on the test.

Reading/Language Arts (25 percent or 30 items)

- Literature

- Reading instruction

- Language in writing

- Communication skills

- Text organization patterns

Mathematics (25 percent or 30 items)

- Number sense and numeration

- Algebraic concepts

- Informal geometry and measurement

- Data organization and interpretation

Social Studies (25 percent or 30 items)

- United States history

- Political science (federal and local government)

- Geography

- Anthropology, sociology, and psychology

- Economics
- World history

Science (25 percent or 30 items)

- Earth science
- Life science
- Physical science
- Science from a personal and social perspective
- Science inquiry
- History of science
- Unifying processes

SUBJECT REVIEW FOR THE ELEMENTARY CONTENT KNOWLEDGE TEST (0014)

There is always a reasonable question about the amount you should review. The idea is to review neither too little nor too much.

Think about the scale score you need to pass and how that translates into the required number correct on the test. A common required scale score for this test is 148 or less, although a few states may require a higher score. That's 148 out of 200, where the lowest possible score is 100.

According to ETS, the first quartile score for this test is 151. That means 75 percent of those who take the test will get a score above 151. Note that 148 is below the first quartile score, which makes it fairly easy to achieve this scale. It's only our estimate, but a scale score of 148 on this test likely means 65 percent or so of the raw score points. If that's right, a raw score of about 80 or more correct out of 120 will earn a scale score of 148 or above. Simply put, if you incorrectly answer one item in three, you will likely earn a scale score of 148.

We have included mathematics, English, vocabulary, and reading reviews in this book that are perfect for this test. We made a decision to provide links to Web-based reviews for the rest of the test. We think you'll like this approach because it will give you more flexibility.

To that end, we scoured the Internet to find the best review sites. Naturally we wanted sites that would provide a useful review, as well as remain active for a long time. Those were our two criteria. A Web site that looked great will not appear here if it seemed bound to disappear. All the links we list were active at press time. Web sites are constantly being added to the Internet and you can always go online and do your own search, but we think the sites mentioned below will serve you well.

For overall subject review, we were frequently drawn to the Wikipedia sites. These sites are under constant review and scrutiny, and because they include many links, you can easily pursue further review, if you choose to. That helps you avoid being trapped in an overwhelming long review. This does not mean all Wikipedia articles are useful, but questionable articles are usually flagged.

You can just go directly to *en.wikipedia.org* and enter your own search terms in the box on the left. But we still list our favorite Wikipedia sites below.

READING/LANGAUGE ARTS

READING

____ Chapter 8 on pages 264–299 contains an extensive vocabulary and reading review.

ENGLISH AND WRITING

____ Chapter 3 on pages 21–72 contains a thorough English and writing review.

READING/LANGUAGE INSTRUCTION

This paper from the National Reading Panel gives an excellent introduction to the fundamental concepts of reading along with a summary of effective reading practices.

____ *www.nichd.nih.gov/publications/nrp/findings.cfm*

"Teaching Reading is Rocket Science" is a practical overview of teaching reading.

____ *www.aft.org/pubs-reports/downloads/teachers/rocketsci.pdf*

LITERATURE

Children's Literature

Comprehensive summary from the University of Connecticut with useful additional links.

____ *www.southernct.edu/%7Ebrownm/300hlit.html*

This detailed Wikipedia article about children's literature includes a chronological list of well-known children's authors and an extensive list of other useful links for further study.

____ *en.wikipedia.org/wiki/Children's_literature*

English Literature

All literature written in English is referred to as English literature.

This Wikipedia article is the most useful concise review of English literature that we have found. It includes many additional links for further study.

____ *en.wikipedia.org/wiki/English_literature*

American Literature

This Wikipedia article is the most useful brief review we found of American literature.

_____ *en.wikipedia.org/wiki/American_literature*

Mathematics

Chapter 4 on pages 73–146 contains a thorough mathematics review with ample practice. You may use a four-function calculator or a scientific calculator during the test, so use the calculator you will bring to the test as you complete the activities in this chapter.

For additional practice, complete the PPST Mathematics tests on page 202 and page 247.

History

UNITED STATES HISTORY

This link from Wikipedia gives an overview of United States history, with many links for further study.

_____ *en.wikipedia.org/wiki/History_of_the_United_States*

This time line of United States history from Wikipedia gives links to specific historical periods beginning in the 1400s.

_____ *en.wikipedia.org/wiki/Timeline_of_United_States_history*

This link-based United States history review gives a fairly thorough overview of United States history and allows you to select the historic periods or events you want to study.

_____ *countrystudies.us/united-states/*

UNITED STATES GEOGRAPHY

This overview of United States geography from Wikipedia provides many links to additional reviews and maps.

_____ *en.wikipedia.org/wiki/Geography_of_the_United_States*

UNITED STATES GOVERNMENT

This United States government overview from Wikipedia gives a thorough overview with links for any additional study you may choose to pursue.

_____ *en.wikipedia.org/wiki/United_States_Government*

WORLD HISTORY

Wikipedia world history overview provides a complete overview with additional links for further study.

_____ *en.wikipedia.org/wiki/History_of_the_world*

Science

We feature these Wikipedia links about life science (biology), earth science, physical science, the history of science, and even for inquiry-based science instruction. All these sites contain many links for further study. Most other online sites typically contain too much information and will not give you the opportunity to limit your study.

EARTH SCIENCE

_____ *en.wikipedia.org/wiki/Earth_science*

LIFE SCIENCE (BIOLOGY)

_____ *en.wikipedia.org/wiki/Biology*

PHYSICAL SCIENCE

_____ *en.wikipedia.org/wiki/Physical_science*

INQUIRY-BASED SCIENCE INSTRUCTION

_____ *en.wikipedia.org/wiki/Inquiry-based_science*

HISTORY OF SCIENCE

_____ *en.wikipedia.org/wiki/History_of_science*

PRACTICE TEST
120 Items, 2 Hours

The items in this practice test are organized by content area: Language Arts, Mathematics, Social Studies, and Science. You may use a basic four-function calculator or a scientific calculator on this test. The calculator must be solar or battery powered. You can't use a noisy calculator, a calculator with a paper tape, or a pocket organizer. There are many different versions of this test, and the version you take may have a different emphasis and focus than this practice test.

Take this test in a realistic, timed setting. The setting will be most realistic if another person times the test and ensures that the test rules are followed. If another person is acting as test supervisor, he or she should review these instructions with you and say "START" when you should begin a section, and "STOP" when time is up.

You have 2 hours to complete the test. Keep the time limit in mind as you work. There is no penalty for guessing. You may write on the test and mark up the questions. Each item has four answer choices. Exactly one of these choices is correct.

Mark your choice on the answer sheet on the next page. Use a pencil to mark the answer sheet. The actual test will be machine scored so completely darken in the answer space. Once the test is complete, correct the answer sheet and review the answer explanations.

When instructed, turn the page and begin.

Answer Sheet

ELEMENTARY EDUCATION PRACTICE TEST

Content Knowledge

Language Arts

1. Ⓐ Ⓑ Ⓒ Ⓓ
2. Ⓐ Ⓑ Ⓒ Ⓓ
3. Ⓐ Ⓑ Ⓒ Ⓓ
4. Ⓐ Ⓑ Ⓒ Ⓓ
5. Ⓐ Ⓑ Ⓒ Ⓓ
6. Ⓐ Ⓑ Ⓒ Ⓓ
7. Ⓐ Ⓑ Ⓒ Ⓓ
8. Ⓐ Ⓑ Ⓒ Ⓓ

9. Ⓐ Ⓑ Ⓒ Ⓓ
10. Ⓐ Ⓑ Ⓒ Ⓓ
11. Ⓐ Ⓑ Ⓒ Ⓓ
12. Ⓐ Ⓑ Ⓒ Ⓓ
13. Ⓐ Ⓑ Ⓒ Ⓓ
14. Ⓐ Ⓑ Ⓒ Ⓓ
15. Ⓐ Ⓑ Ⓒ Ⓓ
16. Ⓐ Ⓑ Ⓒ Ⓓ

17. Ⓐ Ⓑ Ⓒ Ⓓ
18. Ⓐ Ⓑ Ⓒ Ⓓ
19. Ⓐ Ⓑ Ⓒ Ⓓ
20. Ⓐ Ⓑ Ⓒ Ⓓ
21. Ⓐ Ⓑ Ⓒ Ⓓ
22. Ⓐ Ⓑ Ⓒ Ⓓ
23. Ⓐ Ⓑ Ⓒ Ⓓ

24. Ⓐ Ⓑ Ⓒ Ⓓ
25. Ⓐ Ⓑ Ⓒ Ⓓ
26. Ⓐ Ⓑ Ⓒ Ⓓ
27. Ⓐ Ⓑ Ⓒ Ⓓ
28. Ⓐ Ⓑ Ⓒ Ⓓ
29. Ⓐ Ⓑ Ⓒ Ⓓ
30. Ⓐ Ⓑ Ⓒ Ⓓ

Mathematics

31. Ⓐ Ⓑ Ⓒ Ⓓ
32. Ⓐ Ⓑ Ⓒ Ⓓ
33. Ⓐ Ⓑ Ⓒ Ⓓ
34. Ⓐ Ⓑ Ⓒ Ⓓ
35. Ⓐ Ⓑ Ⓒ Ⓓ
36. Ⓐ Ⓑ Ⓒ Ⓓ
37. Ⓐ Ⓑ Ⓒ Ⓓ
38. Ⓐ Ⓑ Ⓒ Ⓓ

39. Ⓐ Ⓑ Ⓒ Ⓓ
40. Ⓐ Ⓑ Ⓒ Ⓓ
41. Ⓐ Ⓑ Ⓒ Ⓓ
42. Ⓐ Ⓑ Ⓒ Ⓓ
43. Ⓐ Ⓑ Ⓒ Ⓓ
44. Ⓐ Ⓑ Ⓒ Ⓓ
45. Ⓐ Ⓑ Ⓒ Ⓓ
46. Ⓐ Ⓑ Ⓒ Ⓓ

47. Ⓐ Ⓑ Ⓒ Ⓓ
48. Ⓐ Ⓑ Ⓒ Ⓓ
49. Ⓐ Ⓑ Ⓒ Ⓓ
50. Ⓐ Ⓑ Ⓒ Ⓓ
51. Ⓐ Ⓑ Ⓒ Ⓓ
52. Ⓐ Ⓑ Ⓒ Ⓓ
53. Ⓐ Ⓑ Ⓒ Ⓓ

54. Ⓐ Ⓑ Ⓒ Ⓓ
55. Ⓐ Ⓑ Ⓒ Ⓓ
56. Ⓐ Ⓑ Ⓒ Ⓓ
57. Ⓐ Ⓑ Ⓒ Ⓓ
58. Ⓐ Ⓑ Ⓒ Ⓓ
59. Ⓐ Ⓑ Ⓒ Ⓓ
60. Ⓐ Ⓑ Ⓒ Ⓓ

Social Studies

61. Ⓐ Ⓑ Ⓒ Ⓓ
62. Ⓐ Ⓑ Ⓒ Ⓓ
63. Ⓐ Ⓑ Ⓒ Ⓓ
64. Ⓐ Ⓑ Ⓒ Ⓓ
65. Ⓐ Ⓑ Ⓒ Ⓓ
66. Ⓐ Ⓑ Ⓒ Ⓓ
67. Ⓐ Ⓑ Ⓒ Ⓓ
68. Ⓐ Ⓑ Ⓒ Ⓓ

69. Ⓐ Ⓑ Ⓒ Ⓓ
70. Ⓐ Ⓑ Ⓒ Ⓓ
71. Ⓐ Ⓑ Ⓒ Ⓓ
72. Ⓐ Ⓑ Ⓒ Ⓓ
73. Ⓐ Ⓑ Ⓒ Ⓓ
74. Ⓐ Ⓑ Ⓒ Ⓓ
75. Ⓐ Ⓑ Ⓒ Ⓓ
76. Ⓐ Ⓑ Ⓒ Ⓓ

77. Ⓐ Ⓑ Ⓒ Ⓓ
78. Ⓐ Ⓑ Ⓒ Ⓓ
79. Ⓐ Ⓑ Ⓒ Ⓓ
80. Ⓐ Ⓑ Ⓒ Ⓓ
81. Ⓐ Ⓑ Ⓒ Ⓓ
82. Ⓐ Ⓑ Ⓒ Ⓓ
83. Ⓐ Ⓑ Ⓒ Ⓓ

84. Ⓐ Ⓑ Ⓒ Ⓓ
85. Ⓐ Ⓑ Ⓒ Ⓓ
86. Ⓐ Ⓑ Ⓒ Ⓓ
87. Ⓐ Ⓑ Ⓒ Ⓓ
88. Ⓐ Ⓑ Ⓒ Ⓓ
89. Ⓐ Ⓑ Ⓒ Ⓓ
90. Ⓐ Ⓑ Ⓒ Ⓓ

Answer Sheet

ELEMENTARY EDUCATION PRACTICE TEST

Science

91 Ⓐ Ⓑ Ⓒ Ⓓ	99 Ⓐ Ⓑ Ⓒ Ⓓ	107 Ⓐ Ⓑ Ⓒ Ⓓ	114 Ⓐ Ⓑ Ⓒ Ⓓ
92 Ⓐ Ⓑ Ⓒ Ⓓ	100 Ⓐ Ⓑ Ⓒ Ⓓ	108 Ⓐ Ⓑ Ⓒ Ⓓ	115 Ⓐ Ⓑ Ⓒ Ⓓ
93 Ⓐ Ⓑ Ⓒ Ⓓ	101 Ⓐ Ⓑ Ⓒ Ⓓ	109 Ⓐ Ⓑ Ⓒ Ⓓ	116 Ⓐ Ⓑ Ⓒ Ⓓ
94 Ⓐ Ⓑ Ⓒ Ⓓ	102 Ⓐ Ⓑ Ⓒ Ⓓ	110 Ⓐ Ⓑ Ⓒ Ⓓ	117 Ⓐ Ⓑ Ⓒ Ⓓ
95 Ⓐ Ⓑ Ⓒ Ⓓ	103 Ⓐ Ⓑ Ⓒ Ⓓ	111 Ⓐ Ⓑ Ⓒ Ⓓ	118 Ⓐ Ⓑ Ⓒ Ⓓ
96 Ⓐ Ⓑ Ⓒ Ⓓ	104 Ⓐ Ⓑ Ⓒ Ⓓ	112 Ⓐ Ⓑ Ⓒ Ⓓ	119 Ⓐ Ⓑ Ⓒ Ⓓ
97 Ⓐ Ⓑ Ⓒ Ⓓ	105 Ⓐ Ⓑ Ⓒ Ⓓ	113 Ⓐ Ⓑ Ⓒ Ⓓ	120 Ⓐ Ⓑ Ⓒ Ⓓ
98 Ⓐ Ⓑ Ⓒ Ⓓ	106 Ⓐ Ⓑ Ⓒ Ⓓ		

LANGUAGE ARTS

30 ITEMS

Questions 1–3 refer to the following poem.

> My love falls on silence nigh
> I am alone in knowing the good-bye
> For while a lost love has its day
> A love unknown is a sadder way

1. The word *nigh* in line 1 means

   (A) clear.
   (B) complete.
   (C) near.
   (D) not.

2. This passage describes

   (A) loving someone and being rebuffed.
   (B) being loved by someone you do not love.
   (C) loving someone who loves another person.
   (D) loving someone without acknowledgment.

3. The subject and the verb in line 2 are

   (A) I . . . am.
   (B) I . . . alone.
   (C) I . . . knowing.
   (D) alone . . . knowing.

---

4. Literature written specifically for children did not appear until the

   (A) 1500s.
   (B) 1600s.
   (C) 1700s.
   (D) 1800s.

5. *Peter Piper picked a peck of pickled peppers.*

   The sentence above is an example of

   (A) alliteration.
   (B) euphemism.
   (C) hyperbole.
   (D) metaphor.

6. *The Odyssey* is best categorized as

   (A) an epic.
   (B) a lyric.
   (C) a novel.
   (D) a romance.

7. I grew up in Kearny, New Jersey, now known as Soccer Town, USA. I played football in high school and barely knew that the soccer team existed. However, a look back at my high school yearbook revealed that the soccer team won the state championship. We had a 0.500 season.

   Which of these techniques is used by the author of this passage?

   (A) Exposition
   (B) Reflection
   (C) Argumentation
   (D) Narration

8. Which of the following words or word pairs would NOT be used to coordinate sentence elements?

   (A) And
   (B) Either or
   (C) But
   (D) When

9.

> ah autumn coolness
> hand in hand paring away

   Which of the following could be the third line in the haiku poem above?

   (A) in the wetness
   (B) branches and leaves
   (C) eggplants cucumbers
   (D) til the end of day

10. The word *paring* in the poem in question 9 means

    (A) putting together.
    (B) doubling up.
    (C) cutting off.
    (D) planting fruit.

11. The root *frac* in the word *fraction* means

    (A) break.
    (B) eighths.
    (C) part.
    (D) piece.

12. In which sentence is the underlined word used correctly?

    (A) The rider grabbed the horse's <u>reign</u>.
    (B) The teacher had just begun her <u>lessen</u>.
    (C) The dog's collar showed <u>its</u> address.
    (D) The road offered a steep <u>assent</u> to the plateau.

13. Which of the following shows the correct syllables for *simultaneous*?

    (A) simul ta neous
    (B) sim ul ta neous
    (C) si mul ta ne ous
    (D) sim ul ta ne ous

14. Empty halls and silent walls greeted me. A summer day seemed like a good time for me to take a look at the school in which I would student teach. I tiptoed from classroom door to classroom door—looking. Suddenly the custodian appeared behind me and said, "Help you?" "No sir," I said. At that moment he may have been Plato or Homer for all I knew.

    Which of the following best describes the main character in the paragraph above?

    (A) Timid and afraid
    (B) Confident and optimistic
    (C) Pessimistic and unsure
    (D) Curious and respectful

15. The storm moved slowly through the day
    Like a huge car wash for the earth

    What figure of speech is represented in the second line of this passage?

    (A) Simile
    (B) Metaphor
    (C) Euphemism
    (D) Onomatopoeia

16. The speaker described her teen years and spoke about the arguments she had with her brothers and sisters. Then the speaker told the audience that she and her siblings were now the best of friends.

    This account of the speaker's presentation best characterizes

    (A) argumentation.
    (B) exposition.
    (C) narration.
    (D) propaganda.

Question 17 refers to the following passage.

In response to my opponent's question about my record on environmental issues, I want to say that the real problem in this election is not my record. Rather the problem is the influence of my opponent's rich friends in the record industry. I hope you will turn your back on his rich supporters and vote for me.

17. What type of rhetorical argument does this passage reflect?

    (A) Narration
    (B) Reflection
    (C) Argumentation
    (D) Exposition

18. Which of the following is the most accurate statement about children's literature?

    (A) The *Wizard of Oz* was among the first books written specifically for children.
    (B) *Robinson Crusoe* was really written for adults, not children.
    (C) Most children's literature through about 1890 conveyed a religious or moral theme.
    (D) Washington Irving wrote *Last of the Mohicans.*

19. The stories of *King Arthur and the Knights of the Round Table* originated between about 1000 A.D. and 1200 A.D. To which genre of literature do these stories belong?

    (A) Poetry
    (B) Epic
    (C) Lyric
    (D) Romance

Questions 20–22 refer to the following poem.

The Sullen Sky
I see the sullen sky;
Dark, foreboding sky.
Swept by dank and dripping clouds;
Like ominous shrouds.

A sky should be bright,
Or clear and crisp at night.
But it hasn't been that way;
Oh, a dungenous day.

That has been my life,
And that has been my strife.
I wish the clouds would leave;
Ah, a sweet reprieve.

20. The last two lines in the first stanza reflect which of the following?

    (A) Simile
    (B) Hyperbole
    (C) Metaphor
    (D) Euphemism

21. What main literary technique does the author use to convey the poem's message?

    (A) Morphology
    (B) Alliteration
    (C) Allegory
    (D) Personification

22. The author wants to use a line that reflects onomatopoeia. Which of the following lines could be used?

    (A) Soggy, slippery, sad
    (B) Drip, drip, drip
    (C) Like being at the bottom of a lake
    (D) The rain, the pain, explain

23. You ain't going to no party.

    Which of the following statements most accurately describes this quote?

    (A) The quote effectively communicates in function and structure.
    (B) The quote effectively communicates in function but not structure.
    (C) The quote effectively communicates in structure but not function.
    (D) The quote effectively communicates in neither function nor structure.

24. Which of the following examples does NOT point out the difficulty of using the 26-letter alphabet to represent spoken English?

    (A) "Live and on stage, the rock group Phish"
    (B) "The new tuf truck line from Tough Trucks"
    (C) "'I' before 'e' except after 'c' and when sounded as 'a' in neighbor and weigh."
    (D) "It's a terrrr-iffic day here at the car wash."

25. The Newbery Award and Caldecott Medal are given annually to the best American books for young people. Which type of book receives which recognition?

    (A) Newbery, elementary grade book; Caldecott, young adult book
    (B) Newbery, young adult book; Caldecott, elementary grade book
    (C) Newbery, children's book; Caldecott, picture book
    (D) Newbery, picture book; Caldecott, children's book

26. Which sentence below is incorrect?

    (A) The dinner tastes good.
    (B) The dinner tastes badly.
    (C) The chef cooked badly.
    (D) The chef cooked well.

27. Which alphabet does the English language use?

    (A) French
    (B) Greek
    (C) Latin
    (D) Persian

28. Which sentence below is correct?

    (A) The cowboy reigned in his horse to accept a cup of water.
    (B) The cowboy led his horse and spoke of times passed.
    (C) The cowboy gave his assent to their request for a ride.
    (D) The cowboy only wanted peace on they're section of the plains.

29. What does *ante* in the word *antebellum* mean?

    (A) Before
    (B) Against
    (C) After
    (D) During

30. What statement best characterizes how poems have developed since ancient times?

    (A) From figurative meaning to literal meaning
    (B) From rhymed to unrhymed verse
    (C) From high regard to ill repute
    (D) From the rhythm of music to a linguistic cadence

MATHEMATICS

30 ITEMS

31. If the original price is $83.00, what would be the sale price if the sale took off 35%?

    (A) $136.25
    (B) $53.25
    (C) $53.95
    (D) $41.50

32. What percent of 125 is 105?

    (A) 84%
    (B) 0.84%
    (C) 119%
    (D) 1.19%

33. $(5^3)^4 =$

    (A) 125^7
    (B) 5^{12}
    (C) 5^7
    (D) 5^1

34. $8/25 =$

    (A) 0.32%
    (B) 8%
    (C) 32%
    (D) 3.25%

35. Ms. Stendel's class is forming groups. When they form groups of 2, 3, or 4 students, there is never anyone left over. How many are in the class?

    (A) 24
    (B) 25
    (C) 21
    (D) 30

36. A number divided by 0.01 equals 1,000. What is the number?

    (A) 0.01
    (B) 0.1
    (C) 1.0
    (D) 10

37. Which of the following fractions has the least value?

    (A) $\dfrac{46}{30}$

    (B) $\dfrac{241}{159}$

    (C) $\dfrac{240}{97}$

    (D) $\dfrac{195}{97}$

38. The length of a road was measured in kilometers. The length measured in meters would be

    (A) one thousand times as much.
    (B) one hundred times as much.
    (C) one-tenth as much.
    (D) one-hundredth as much.

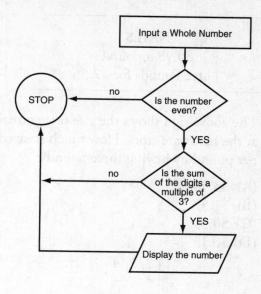

39. Use the steps in the above flowchart. The number displayed will always be

    (A) a factor of 6.
    (B) a factor of 2.
    (C) a factor of 3.
    (D) divisible by 6.

40. It took the oil truck 3 hours to fill the empty oil tank pumping at 100 gallons an hour. How long will it take another oil truck to fill the same empty tank pumping 80 gallons an hour?

    (A) $2\dfrac{2}{5}$ hours

    (B) $3\dfrac{2}{5}$ hours

    (C) $3\dfrac{3}{8}$ hours

    (D) $3\dfrac{3}{4}$ hours

41. On a map, 2 centimeters represents 300 kilometers. A road is 3,000 kilometers long.

    How long will it be on the map?

    (A) 10 cm
    (B) 20 cm
    (C) 150 cm
    (D) 300 cm

NAILS
$0.98 a pound
Three Pounds for $2.55

---

42. The above sign shows the sale price of nails at the hardware store. How much is saved per pound by buying three pounds?

    (A) $3.53
    (B) $1.57
    (C) $0.39
    (D) $0.13

$$
\begin{array}{c|l}
1 & 2, 2, 4 \\
2 & \\
3 & 4, 7 \\
4 & 1
\end{array}
$$

43. The numbers represented on this stem and leaf chart are

    (A) 12, 14, 20, 34, 37, 41.
    (B) 8 ones, 0 twos, 11 threes, 1 four.
    (C) 1,224, 2, 347, 41.
    (D) 12, 12, 14, 34, 37, 41.

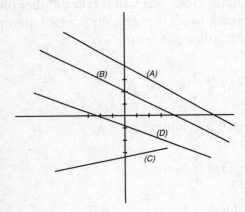

44. In the above graph, which line passes through the point (−2, 3)?

    (A) Point *A*
    (B) Point *B*
    (C) Point *C*
    (D) Point *D*

45. Which of the following measures could NOT be the height of a real building?

    (A) 0.3 kilometers
    (B) 60,000 millimeters
    (C) 23 centimeters
    (D) 29 meters

x	y
0	2
4	14
7	23
9	29

46. Which of the following equations shows the relationship between x and y in the table?

    (A) $y = x + 2$
    (B) $y = 2x + 6$
    (C) $y = 2x + 2$
    (D) $y = 3x + 2$

47. Which of these events has a probability of $\dfrac{1}{8}$?

    (A) Flipping a head on a penny after flipping two tails
    (B) Picking a red sock out of a drawer with four red socks and four black socks
    (C) Picking two red socks out of a drawer with 16 red socks
    (D) Flipping three pennies and getting all heads

48. On the above scale, the arrow points to which weight?

    (A) 957
    (B) 960
    (C) 983
    (D) 990

49. Which of the following would be an estimate of the answer to 0.004913 × 0.04108?

   (A) 0.02
   (B) 0.002
   (C) 0.0002
   (D) 0.00002

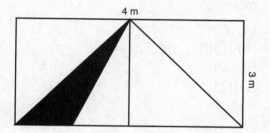

50. In the diagram above, what is the area of the shaded region?

   (A) 1 m²
   (B) 1.5 m²
   (C) 2 m²
   (D) 2.5 m²

MOST POPULAR BABY NAMES IN ONE TOWN

	Girls		Boys	
1980	2000		1980	2000
Michele	Lisa		Michael	William
Jennifer	Alexandra		Steven	Dylan
Lisa	Michelle		Joseph	Michael
Stephanie	Jillian		Peter	Gregory
Christine	Jennifer		Robert	
Alexandra				

   I 60 percent of the names popular in 1980 were also popular in 2000.

   II William was not popular in 1980.

   III 40 percent of the names popular in 2000 were not popular in 1980.

   IV Lisa and Michele accounted for 40 percent of all the popular names in 1980.

51. Which of the following choices includes all the correct statements about the preceding popular name table?

   (A) I and II
   (B) I only
   (C) II, III, and IV
   (D) II only

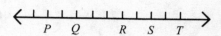

52. The number line above shows the relationship of points *P*, *Q*, *R*, *S*, and *T*. The product of *Q* and *R* is 1.00. What do we know about the points on the number line?

   (A) Points *Q* and *R* are less than 1.
   (B) Only Point *Q* is less than 0.
   (C) Point *Q* is more than 2.
   (D) The product of *P* and *Q* is less than 1.

53. Some birds in the zoo weigh 10 pounds or less. Which of the following is consistent with this statement?

   (A) All birds weigh less than 10 pounds.
   (B) There are some 100-pound birds.
   (C) There is a 5-pound bird.
   (D) There may be some birds who weigh more than 10 pounds.

54. The electrician has a 50 foot long roll of electrical wire. The electrician uses 9 feet 8 inches of the wire. How much of the wire is left?

   (A) 41 ft 4 in
   (B) 41 ft 2 in
   (C) 40 ft 4 in
   (D) 40 ft 2 in

55. In which of the following choices is the answer closest to 30 × 0.02?

   (A) 0.1 + 0.2 × 0.2
   (B) 0.5 × (0.4 + 0.8)
   (C) (0.9 − 0.3) × 2.0 − 1.0
   (D) 0.6 × 1.0 − 1.0

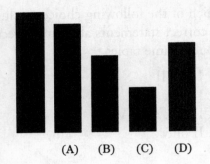

(A) (B) (C) (D)

56. The first rectangle above represents 400 square meters. Which of the other rectangles most likely represents 300 square meters?

57. A rectangle has an area of 56.7 cm² and a width of 3 cm. What is the perimeter of the rectangle?

   (A) 170.1 cm
   (B) 113.4 cm
   (C) 43.8 cm
   (D) 18.9 cm

58. 0.1 + 0.001 =

   (A) $\dfrac{11}{100}$

   (B) $\dfrac{1,001}{10,000}$

   (C) $\dfrac{101}{1,000}$

   (D) $\dfrac{11}{1,000}$

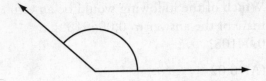

59. A protractor is used to measure the above angle. What is the approximate angle measure?

   (A) 60°
   (B) 130°
   (C) 45°
   (D) 240°

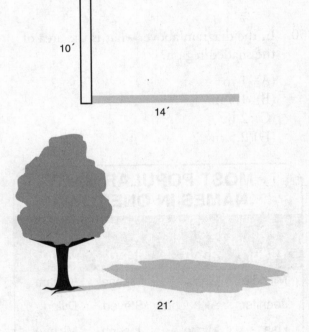

60. About how tall is the above tree?

   (A) 25 ft
   (B) 15 ft
   (C) 17 ft
   (D) 29 ft

SOCIAL STUDIES

30 ITEMS

Use this map for Questions 61–64.

Official Languages of South American Countries

61. The non-Spanish languages spoken in western South America result from

   (A) early Incan influence.
   (B) the primitive nature of the countries.
   (C) immigration by Mayan Indians.
   (D) proximity to Central America.

62. What accounts for the use of Italian as an official language in southeastern South America?

   (A) The voyages of Christopher Columbus
   (B) The exploration of the Americas by Amerigo Vespucci
   (C) Italian and German immigration following World War II
   (D) Italian and German immigration in the eighteenth century

63. The only French-speaking South American nation was the site of

   (A) the French Government in exile during World War II.
   (B) the "Jonestown Massacre" in 1978.
   (C) the revolt of the Foreign Legion during the Algerian crisis.
   (D) the French penal colony Devil's Island.

64. According to the map, about what percent of South American countries have Spanish as an official language?

   (A) 80%
   (B) 70%
   (C) 60%
   (D) 40%

65. In the United States, the Senate and the House of Representatives combine to form

    (A) the Legislature.
    (B) the Parliament.
    (C) the Congress.
    (D) the judiciary.

66. The way in which humans learn to live in different habitats is called

    (A) acculturation.
    (B) adaptation.
    (C) climatization.
    (D) imprinting.

67. Which of the following is an example of a reproof?

    (A) Her mother touched her shoulder to remind her to be quiet.
    (B) The teacher asked her to do proof again.
    (C) She read the book again to make sure she understood it.
    (D) The coach yelled at her for being out of position on the field.

68. Which of the following shows the correct order of the listed events in United States history?

    I Reconstruction
    II Sherman's March to the Sea
    III Surrender at Appomattox Courthouse
    IV Approval of the XIII Amendment

    (A) I, II, III, IV
    (B) II, III, I, IV
    (C) II, I, III, IV
    (D) IV, II, III, I

69. Which of the following would you turn to for a primary source of information about World War II?

    (A) The film *The Longest Day*
    (B) A handwritten log by the Captain of the *Lusitania*
    (C) An essay on war by George Sherman
    (D) Letters written by an Italian soldier fighting in North Africa to his sister in Sicily

Use this map to answer Questions 70 and 71.

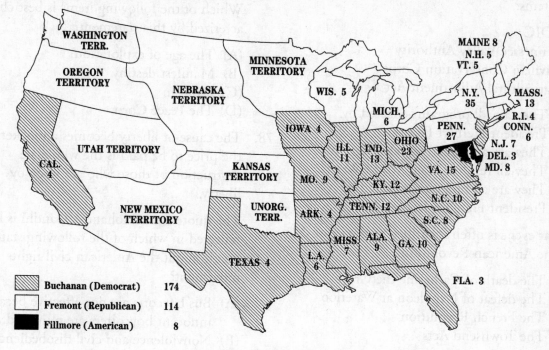

[Election of 1856]

Buchanan (Democrat)	174
Fremont (Republican)	114
Fillmore (American)	8

70. The numbers in each state on this map show

(A) the number of counties in each state.
(B) the number of representatives from each state.
(C) the electoral votes in each state.
(D) the number of representatives won by the victorious party in each state.

71. What conclusion might you reasonably draw from this map?

(A) Were it not for Texas and California, Fremont would have won the election.
(B) Buchanan supported the rebel cause.
(C) Fremont was favored by the northernmost states.
(D) Fremont was favored by the states that fought on the Union side in the Civil War.

72. Which of the following is the best definition of representative democracy?

(A) Political and social equality exist in spirit and in practice.
(B) The various states have rights and power not expressly assigned to the national government.
(C) The populace of individual regions elect those who will represent them.
(D) A set of checks and balances exists among the legislative, judicial, and executive branches of government.

73. Which of the following best describes the Rorschach test?

(A) Visual perception test
(B) Projective test
(C) Intelligence test
(D) Achievement test

74. What is the connection among the following items?

    - FDIC
    - Tennessee Valley Authority
    - Civilian Conservation Corps
    - Agricultural Adjustment Act

    (A) They are all programs enacted by President Herbert Hoover.
    (B) They are all federal works programs.
    (C) They all resulted from World War II.
    (D) They are all programs enacted by President Franklin Roosevelt.

75. What event is often identified as the cause of the American Revolution?

    (A) The death of Catherine the Great
    (B) The defeat of Napoleon at Waterloo
    (C) The French Revolution
    (D) The Townsend Acts

76. All the following happened in full or part as a result of World War I EXCEPT

    (A) World War II.
    (B) the Depression.
    (C) the growth of the Nazi Party.
    (D) the Yalta Agreement.

77. Go west young man.

    Which of the following items is best characterized by this statement?

    (A) The age of exploration
    (B) Manifest destiny
    (C) Zionism
    (D) The Peace Corps

78. The cause of liberty becomes a mockery if the price to be paid is the wholesale destruction of those who are to enjoy liberty.

    The quote from Mohandas Gandhi is best reflected in which of the following statements about the American civil rights movement?

    (A) Bus boycotts are not effective because innocent boycotters are punished.
    (B) Nonviolence and civil disobedience are the best approaches to protest.
    (C) Desegregation laws were a direct result of freedom marches.
    (D) America will never be free as long as minorities are oppressed.

Questions 79–81 are based on this map.

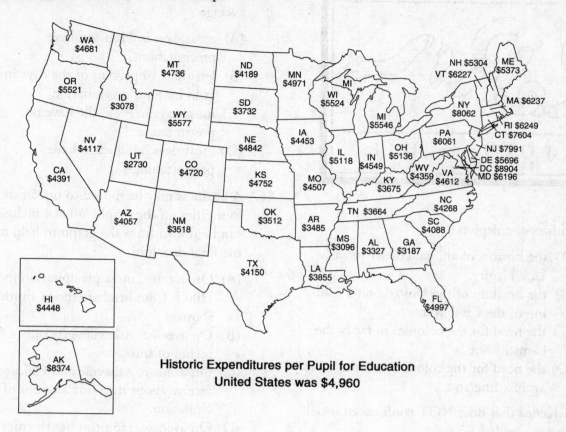

Historic Expenditures per Pupil for Education
United States was $4,960

79. You can deduce from the map that teachers' salaries are probably lowest in

    (A) Georgia, Alabama, and Idaho.
    (B) South Dakota, Tennessee, and Oklahoma.
    (C) Kentucky, Louisiana, and New Mexico.
    (D) Florida, Hawaii, and Iowa.

80. You can deduce from the map that school taxes are probably highest in

    (A) the southeastern states.
    (B) the northeastern states.
    (C) the northwestern states.
    (D) the southwestern states.

81. Based on the information on this map, which of these states would be in the second quartile of per pupil expenditures?

    (A) Alaska
    (B) Alabama
    (C) Idaho
    (D) Arizona

82. According to the law of supply and demand,

    (A) decreased supply results in increased prices.
    (B) increased prices result in increased demand.
    (C) increased supply results in decreased demand.
    (D) decreased demand results in increased prices.

JOIN, or DIE.

83. This poster depicts

    (A) the horrors of animal cruelty in early U.S. history.

    (B) the breakup of the United States leading to the Civil War.

    (C) the need for the colonies to ratify the Constitution.

    (D) the need for the colonies to unite against England.

84. Behavior that does NOT conform to social norms is called

    (A) idiosyncratic.

    (B) deviant.

    (C) phobic.

    (D) psychotic.

Use this graph to answer Questions 85 and 86.

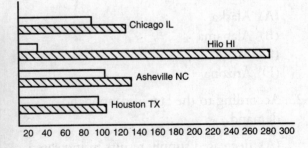

Clear Days
Days with Precipitation

[Average Clear Day and Days with Precipitation]

85. A correct interpretation of this graph is, on average,

    (A) most days in Houston have precipitation.

    (B) less than 10 percent of the days in Hilo have no precipitation.

    (C) most days in Asheville have no precipitation.

    (D) most days in Chicago have precipitation.

86. A business may be moved to one of the four cities on the graph. What conclusion can be drawn from the graph to help make the final decision?

    (A) On average, most precipitation in Hilo is from brief afternoon thundershowers.

    (B) On average, Asheville gets only a few inches of snow.

    (C) On average, Asheville and Chicago receive about the same amount of precipitation.

    (D) On average, Houston has the most days without precipitation.

87. What action by the states is needed to amend the Constitution of the United States?

    (A) None, the Constitution is a federal document.

    (B) Congress must ratify amendments submitted by the states.

    (C) Two-thirds of the states may agree to amend the Constitution.

    (D) Three-quarters of the states must ratify amendments approved by Congress.

Use this information to answer Questions 88 and 89.

Amendments to the Constitution

Amendment N
Section 1—Neither Slavery, nor involuntary servitude, except as a punishment for crime whereof the party shall have been duly convicted, shall exist within the United States, or any place subject to their jurisdiction.
Section 2—Congress shall have power to enforce this article by appropriate legislation.

Amendment O
Section 1—The right of citizens of the United States to vote shall not be denied or abridged by the United States or by any State on account of race, color or previous condition of servitude.
Section 2—The Congress shall have power to enforce this article by appropriate legislation.

Amendment P
The Congress shall have power to lay and collect taxes on incomes, from whatever source derived, without apportionment among the several States, and without regard to any census or enumeration.

88. In what years did Amendments N and O take effect?

   (A) 1865, 1970
   (B) 1870, 1965
   (C) 1870, 1865
   (D) 1865, 1870

89. What prompted approval of Amendment P?

   (A) The IRS was challenged in court.
   (B) Washington, D.C., residents had been exempted from paying income taxes.
   (C) Southern states objected to paying taxes to the federal government.
   (D) The Supreme Court had ruled the income tax unconstitutional.

90. Approximately when was the world population 2 billion?

   (A) 1780
   (B) 1830
   (C) 1880
   (D) 1930

SCIENCE

30 ITEMS

91. Radioactive materials release particles because of

   (A) their environment.
   (B) their place in the periodic table.
   (C) their nuclear make-up.
   (D) the instability of the outer shell electrons.

92. In the formula $E = MC^2$ the C represents

   (A) energy.
   (B) mass.
   (C) velocity.
   (D) the speed of light.

93. A person is markedly overweight as a result of a glandular disorder. What gland would this refer to?

   (A) Adrenal gland
   (B) Pituitary gland
   (C) Pancreas
   (D) Thyroid gland

94. You are floating on a lake in a boat about 100 yards from the shore. You can hear someone talking at the shoreline. What is the best way to explain this phenomenon?

   (A) Sound travels faster through air.
   (B) Sound travels faster through water.
   (C) Sound traveled from the shore because of the materials the boat was constructed of.
   (D) An echo causes the sound to be heard.

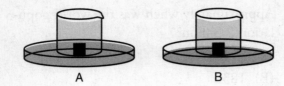

A   B

95. Identical beakers (above) were filled with water. The overflow was caused by the different solid objects placed in the beakers. The size of the objects cannot be determined. What is the most likely explanation of the differing amounts of overflow?

(A) The object in beaker A is heavier.
(B) The object in beaker B is heavier.
(C) The object in beaker A has more mass.
(D) The object in beaker B has more mass.

96. What type of rock, millions of years from now, would most likely be formed from current animal remains?

(A) Conglomerate
(B) Sedimentary
(C) Igneous
(D) Metamorphic

97. Which of the following contributes to the idea that DDT is not biodegradable?

(A) Insects and animals other than pests are poisoned by DDT.
(B) DDT is found in the carcasses of life forms.
(C) DDT is used as a pesticide in orchards.
(D) DDT has been found in river banks.

98. Which diagram shows object ● to have the most potential energy?

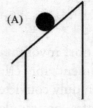
(A)

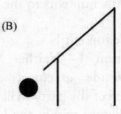
(B)

(C)

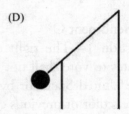
(D)

99. All the following examples represent potential energy EXCEPT

(A) gasoline in a car's motor.
(B) a sled at the top of a hill.
(C) carbonated water in a sealed bottle.
(D) a moving pendulum.

100. Which of the following represents the correct sequence of events that occurs during photosynthesis?

I CO_2 and water are broken down.
II Carbohydrates are formed.
III Sunlight is absorbed by chlorophyll.
IV Plant emits O_2.

(A) I, II, III, IV
(B) I, III, II, IV
(C) III, I, II, IV
(D) II, IV, I, III

101. The destruction of the South American rain forests directly influences all the following EXCEPT

(A) animal habitats.
(B) rare plant species.
(C) climate shifts.
(D) reproduction of natural resources.

102. There are 12 electrons in an element with a neutral charge. How many protons does it have?

    (A) 3
    (B) 4
    (C) 6
    (D) 12

103. The half-life of uranium is 82 years. Approximately how much of a mass of uranium would remain after 330 years?

    (A) $\dfrac{1}{2}$

    (B) $\dfrac{1}{4}$

    (C) $\dfrac{1}{8}$

    (D) $\dfrac{1}{16}$

RECYCLING RATE BY CITY
(PER HUNDRED THOUSAND POUNDS PER YEAR FROM 2003–2008)

	2003	2004	2005	2006	2007	2008
Chicago, Illinois	*	52	67	120	302	485
St. Louis, Missouri	20	80	175	360	420	650
Seattle, Washington	15	70	98	136	243	358
San Francisco, California	*	23	75	124	285	402
New York, New York	*	10	56	250	370	590
Miami, Florida	*	25	98	145	290	370

* The recycling rate is less than one per hundred thousand pounds.

104. Which of the following statements is supported by the data given in the above table?

    (A) St. Louis increased the capabilities of its recycling plants by 50 percent during the years 2005 and 2006.
    (B) Since 2006 the recycling rate increased significantly in each city.
    (C) People living in Miami are not recycling as they should be.
    (D) The population of all these cities has increased significantly since 2006.

105. Meiosis always involves

    (A) cells making carbon copies of themselves.
    (B) the formation of zygotes.
    (C) the creation of cells equal to all others in terms of DNA.
    (D) the formation of gametes.

106. All the following statements about AIDS are true EXCEPT

(A) intravenous drug use increases the risk of AIDS.
(B) women are less likely than men to acquire AIDS.
(C) hemophiliacs are at risk because of blood transfusions.
(D) AIDS can be considered a sexually transmitted disease.

107. When ironing clothes, the heat is transferred from the iron to the clothes by

(A) convection.
(B) acceleration.
(C) radiation.
(D) conduction.

108. You take an ecology course at a college. Which of the following best describes the subject matter of a college ecology course?

(A) The topography of earth
(B) The solar system
(C) The relationships between organisms and their habitat
(D) Earth's atmosphere

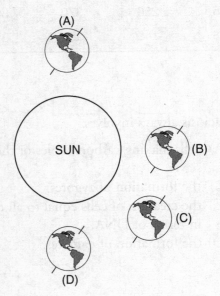

109. Which diagram above shows earth's position at the beginning of summer in the southern hemisphere?

110. The rate of work is measured as

(A) ohms.
(B) volts.
(C) amperes.
(D) foot-pounds.

111. Which would NOT be found in our solar system?

(A) Asteroid
(B) Star
(C) Galaxy
(D) Moon

112. The two cats are the parents of these three kittens. How can this happen?

(A) Both parents have recessive white genes.
(B) One parent has a recessive white gene.
(C) Both parents have a dominant white gene.
(D) One parent has a dominant black gene.

AVERAGE OUNCES GAINED PER ANIMAL		
Week #	HF1	HF2
1	4	9
2	3	4
3	2	3
4	1	2
5	1	2
6	1	1

113. An experiment is set up to determine the effects of a new hamster food HF2 as compared to the effects of a current hamster food HF1. Each group receives the same quantity of food and the same attention. From the above data choose the best conclusion for the experiment.

(A) HF2 group gained more weight.
(B) HF1 group lived longer.
(C) HF2 group got more protein.
(D) HF1 group got better nutrition.

114. What appropriate criticism might a scientist have of this experiment?

(A) Averages should not be used in this type of experiment.
(B) The null hypothesis is not stated in the appropriate form.
(C) Hamsters are not found as pets in enough homes for the experiment to be widely applicable.
(D) The experiment does not describe sufficient controls to be valid.

115. Which diagram could result in a solar eclipse?

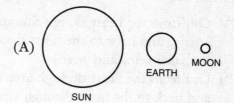

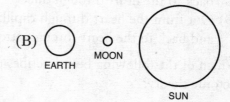

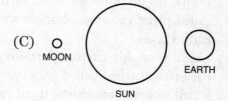

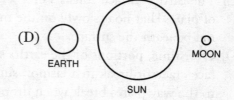

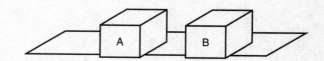

116. Two blocks that weigh the same amount are set on a flat, frictionless surface. What happens when block A is pushed into block B such that both blocks remain on the frictionless surface?

(A) Both blocks stop.
(B) Block A touches block B, and they separate.
(C) Block A touches block B, and they stay together.
(D) Block A stops, and block B keeps moving.

117. Which of the following paths best describes how blood circulates in the human body?

    (A) Out from the heart along veins and arteries and back to the heart through the same veins and arteries

    (B) Out from the heart through arteries and back to the heart through veins

    (C) Out from the heart along veins and back to the heart through ducts

    (D) Out from the heart through capillaries and back to the heart through arteries

118. Which of the following best describes plate tectonic theory?

    (A) Molten material from within the earth pushes up on portions of the earth called plates causing volcanoes and earthquakes.

    (B) Certain roughly circular portions of the earth's surface called plates are subjected to pressure causing them to turn left or right causing earthquakes.

    (C) The earth's surface consists of a series of plates that float slowly on the material beneath the surface.

    (D) Over time, portions of the earth's surface crack or break in a fashion similar to the way plates break when dropped.

119. A scientist cuts in half a just fallen hailstone and finds a series of rings much like tree rings. What could be found from counting the approximate number of rings?

    (A) How long the hailstone has been in the atmosphere

    (B) How long the hailstone was in space before falling to earth

    (C) How many miles from the surface the hailstone fell

    (D) How many times the hailstone has been blown from a lower to higher altitude

120. A person throws a black cloth over a pile of snow to make the snow melt faster. Why is that?

    (A) Cloth will make snow melt faster.

    (B) The black material absorbs more sunlight and more heat.

    (C) The black material holds the heat in.

    (D) The black cloth reflects light better and so absorbs more heat.

ANSWERS

Language Arts

1. (C)	6. (A)	11. (A)	16. (C)	21. (C)	26. (B)
2. (D)	7. (D)	12. (C)	17. (C)	22. (B)	27. (C)
3. (A)	8. (D)	13. (C)	18. (B)	23. (B)	28. (C)
4. (C)	9. (C)	14. (D)	19. (D)	24. (D)	29. (A)
5. (A)	10. (C)	15. (A)	20. (A)	25. (C)	30. (D)

Mathematics

31. (C)	36. (D)	41. (B)	46. (D)	51. (D)	56. (D)
32. (A)	37. (B)	42. (D)	47. (D)	52. (D)	57. (C)
33. (B)	38. (A)	43. (D)	48. (D)	53. (D)	58. (C)
34. (C)	39. (D)	44. (B)	49. (C)	54. (C)	59. (B)
35. (A)	40. (D)	45. (C)	50. (B)	55. (B)	60. (B)

Social Studies

61. (A)	66. (B)	71. (C)	76. (B)	81. (D)	86. (D)
62. (D)	67. (A)	72. (C)	77. (B)	82. (A)	87. (D)
63. (D)	68. (B)	73. (B)	78. (B)	83. (D)	88. (D)
64. (C)	69. (D)	74. (D)	79. (A)	84. (B)	89. (D)
65. (C)	70. (C)	75. (D)	80. (B)	85. (C)	90. (D)

Science

91. (D)	96. (B)	101. (C)	106. (B)	111. (C)	116. (B)
92. (D)	97. (B)	102. (D)	107. (D)	112. (A)	117. (B)
93. (B)	98. (C)	103. (D)	108. (C)	113. (A)	118. (C)
94. (D)	99. (D)	104. (B)	109. (B)	114. (D)	119. (D)
95. (C)	100. (B)	105. (B)	110. (D)	115. (B)	120. (B)

EXPLAINED ANSWERS

Language Arts

1. **(C)** The word *nigh* means near in space or time.

2. **(D)** The passage tells us that love falls on silence and that love unknown is sad, leading to the conclusion that the passage is about loving without acknowledgment.

3. **(A)** *I* is the subject; *am* is the verb. *Alone* is not a verb, and *knowing* is a part of the prepositional phrase.

4. **(C)** The first books written for children appeared during the 1700s. Books such as *Gulliver's Travels* were adult books that appealed to some children.

5. **(A)** Alliteration refers to the repetition of an initial consonant in nearby words.

6. **(A)** *The Odyssey* is an epic, a very long narrative with great scope.

7. **(D)** The author is narrating, or telling a story, about a part of his life.

8. **(D)** The word *when* is used to subordinate sentence elements. All of the other choices are used to coordinate sentence elements.

9. **(C)** Haiku follows a 5-7-5 syllabic scheme with no rhyming. Choice (C) alone meets these criteria.

10. **(C)** The word *paring* means to cut off. Do not confuse this word with its homonym *pairing*.

11. **(A)** The word *fraction* developed from the root *frac*, which means breaking something into pieces.

12. **(C)** This sentence correctly uses the possessive form of *its*. The other underlined words are homonyms (words that sound the same but are spelled differently) of the correct word.

13. **(C)** This is the correct syllabication for *simultaneous*.

14. **(D)** The character visited the school and is certainly curious. The character's response to the custodian shows respect.

15. **(A)** A simile compares two different things, usually using the words *like* or *as*. A metaphor does not use the words *like* or *as*.

16. **(C)** The speaker is telling a story about her life.

17. **(C)** The speaker is clearly trying to convince the audience of his or her position and uses several rhetorical devices to that end.

18. **(B)** *Robinson Crusoe* was written for adults. The *Wizard of Oz* was written in this century. Most children's literature conveyed a religious or moral theme through about the 1700s, and James Fenimore Cooper wrote the *Last of the Mohicans*.

19. **(D)** The King Arthur legends showing brave men, defenseless women, and stories of love are the classic romance. The epic and the lyric appeared much earlier.

20. **(A)** The last two lines in the first stanza compare clouds to shrouds. We know that the figure of speech must be a metaphor or simile. The poem uses the word *like*, so the figure of speech is a simile.

21. **(C)** Allegory means that a work represents some other idea and is not to be taken literally.

22. **(B)** Onomatopoeia uses words to represent sounds.

23. **(B)** Language has two main aspects—function and structure. Language function refers to the ability to communicate. Language structure refers to the way words are used in a language. The structure of the quote is inappropriate; however, we know what it means.

24. **(D)** Choices (A), (B), and (C) point out the kind of spelling difficulties regularly encountered in the English language. Choice (D) does not have such a problem but emphasizes the *r* sound by repeating the letters a number of times.

25. **(C)** Choice (C) is correct.

26. **(B)** This sentence uses the adverb *badly* to modify the noun *dinner*. Choice (A) correctly uses the adjective *good*. Choices (C) and (D) correctly use the adverbs *badly* and *well*.

27. **(C)** Choice (C) is correct.

28. **(C)** Other choices contain "classic" word usage errors. These errors: (A) *reigned* instead of *reined* (B) *passed* instead of *past*, and (D) *they're* instead of *their*.

29. **(A)** *Ante* means before. *Anti* means against, and *post* means after.

30. **(D)** Poems were originally sung. Over time, the melody of the song was replaced with a word cadence.

Mathematics

31. **(C)** Use formula a% of b is c.

    $35\% \times \$83.00 \quad = ?$
    $.35 \times \$83 \qquad = \$29.05$
    $\$83 - \$29.05 \quad = \$53.95$

32. **(A)** $84\% = 0.84 \quad 0.84 \times 125 = 105$

33. **(B)** $(5^3)^4 = (5^{3\times4}) = 5^{12}$

34. **(C)** $\dfrac{8}{25} = \dfrac{32}{100} = 0.32 = 32\%$

35. **(A)** This is the only number in the answer choice divisible by 2, 3, and 4.

36. **(D)** You can approach the problem this way. $0.01 = \dfrac{1}{100}$ Dividing by

    $\dfrac{1}{100}$ is the same as multiplying by 100. $100 \times 10 = 1,000$. That is the

    answer. You could set it up as an equation.

    $X \div 0.01 = 1,000 \qquad X \cdot 100 = 1,000$
    $X = 10$

37. **(B)** Begin by looking quickly at all the fractions. Choice (C) is too high, more than 2—so is choice (D). Eliminate these. The only ones left are (A) and (B). Cross multiply to see which is greater. The smaller cross product is over the smaller fraction.

    $$7314 \qquad 7230$$

    $$\dfrac{46}{30} \quad \cancel{X} \quad \dfrac{241}{159}$$

38. **(A)** There are 1,000 meters in a kilometer. So a road one kilometer long would be 1,000 meters long.

39. **(D)** To be displayed a number must be divisible by both 2 and 3. This is the divisibility test for 6.

40. **(D)** There are two steps to this one. First multiply 3 and 100 to find out that there are 300 gallons in the tank. Then divide 300 by 80 to get 3.75 or $3\frac{3}{4}$ hours.

41. **(B)** 300 km × 10 = 3,000 km. 2 cm = 300 km, so 20 cm = 3,000 miles. You could solve it as a proportion: 2/300 = x/3000, 300x = 6000, x = 20.

42. **(D)** Three single pounds costs $2.94. $2.94 − $2.55 = $.39. Divide by 3. That's $0.13 a pound.

43. **(D)** The digits to the left of the line represent tens, the digits to the right of the line represent ones.

44. **(B)** Only one passes through point (−2, 3).

45. **(C)** 23 centimeters should jump right out at you. All the others work out to a reasonable height for some real building.

46. **(D)** Each one of these equations works for one pair of numbers in the table. But the only equation that works for all of them is $3x + 2$.

47. **(D)** There are eight possible combinations of heads and tails when you flip three coins. All heads (H H H) is one of those possibilities.

48. **(D)** The correct answer is 990. The arrow is halfway between 980 and 1,000.

49. **(C)** Round the numbers to 0.04 and 0.005. Multiply to get .0002.

50. **(B)** The entire region has an area of 12 sq. m. One-eighth of the region is shaded. $\frac{1}{8} \times 12 = 1.5$.

51. **(D)** Any statements about all the names must take into account both girls' and boys' names.

52. **(D)** Eliminate some choices. Choice (A) can't be correct because the product is not less than 1. Choice (B) can't be correct because Point Q is not less than zero. Choice (C) can't be correct because Point R would have to be less than Point Q to get a product of 1. That leaves answer (D). This is the correct answer because if the product of two different numbers is 1, then one of the numbers must be greater than 1 and the other must be less than 1. So Q must be less than 1, as is P, which we can tell is a positive number because it is greater than zero.

53. **(D)** Choice (C) is not correct because we cannot know that there is a bird of that specific weight.

54. **(C)** Remember that there are 12 inches in a foot.

$$
\begin{array}{r}
50 \text{ ft} = 49 \text{ ft } 12 \text{ in} \\
-\ 9 \text{ ft } 8 \text{ in} \\
\hline
40 \text{ ft } 4 \text{ in}
\end{array}
$$

55. **(B)** $30 \times 0.02 = 0.6$. Remember to use order of operations as you calculate the answers. Answer (B) says find 0.5 or half of 1.2. That's what you are looking for.

56. **(D)** That rectangle is about three-quarters the size of the first rectangle.

57. **(C)** First divide the area by the width to find the length of the rectangle. $56.7 \div 3 = 18.9$. Then add the lengths and the widths to find the perimeter $3 + 3 + 18.9 + 18.9 = 43.8$ cm.

58. **(C)** $0.1 + 0.001 = \dfrac{1}{10} + \dfrac{1}{1,000}$

$$
= \frac{100}{1,000} \div \frac{1}{1,000} = \frac{101}{1,000}
$$

59. **(B)** The angle measure is between 90° and 180°, but it is less than 135°.

60. **(B)** Set up a proportion $\dfrac{10}{14} = \dfrac{x}{21}$

Cross multiply $14x = 210$
The tree is about 15 ft tall $x = 15$

Social Studies

61. **(A)** The Incas had an early culture in this region.

62. **(D)** This part of South America, particularly Argentina, experienced significant European immigration.

63. **(D)** The French penal colony of Devil's Island was located off the coast of French Guyana.

64. **(C)** Eight of thirteen South American countries have Spanish as an official language. That's about 60 percent.

65. **(C)** These two legislative bodies combine to form the Congress.

66. **(B)** Adaptation is correct. Acculturation refers to adopting a culture, and climatization refers to adapting to a particular climate.

67. **(A)** A reproof is a very mild reprimand.

68. **(B)** Sherman's march to the sea occurred during the Civil War and was followed by Lee's surrender to Grant at Appomattox Courthouse, Virginia. Reconstruction and the XIII amendment followed the war.

69. **(D)** Choices (B), (C), and (D) are all primary sources. Only (D) refers to World War II.

70. **(C)** The map's caption reveals this information.

71. **(C)** Refer to the map, which shows that Fremont won most northern states.

72. **(C)** Representative democracy means that people elect others to represent them.

73. **(B)** This ink blot test permits the testee to "project" his or her personality.

74. **(D)** These are just a few of the measures FDR implemented during the Depression.

75. **(D)** These taxation acts moved many colonists to revolution.

76. **(B)** The Depression occurred some 15 to 20 years after World War I.

77. **(B)** The manifest destiny of the United States was to stretch from ocean to ocean.

78. **(B)** Gandhi believed in and "popularized" non-violence.

79. **(A)** These states have the lowest per pupil expenditures.

80. **(B)** These states, as a group, have the highest per pupil expenditures.

81. **(D)** The second quartile is the second quarter of ranked per pupil expenditures. Arizona is in the top of the second quartile.

82. **(A)** The law of supply and demand describes the relationship between the availability and cost of goods.

83. **(D)** This famous poster reflects the sentiment "United we stand, divided we fall."

84. **(B)** Deviant is the correct response. The behaviors described in choices (A), (C), and (D) are not necessarily nonconforming—nor are they illegal behaviors.

85. **(C)** On average, Asheville has 235 days without precipitation. Note that the graph does not show days which are cloudy but have no precipitation.

86. **(D)** On average, Houston has 259 days without precipitation. Notice that this question is different from the previous one because it asks for the one city that has the most days without precipitation.

87. **(D)** Three-quarters of the states must ratify any amendment passed by Congress.

88. **(D)** Both of these amendments followed the Civil War. Amendment N was designed to abolish slavery. Amendment O was designed to prevent racial discrimination by the states.

89. **(D)** Yes, at one time the Supreme Court had ruled that income taxes were unconstitutional, and the amendment was needed to rectify this situation.

90. **(D)** World population reached 2 billion in about 1930. Today, world population is about 7 billion.

Science

91. **(D)** The instability of this outer shell permits radioactive particles to be released.

92. **(D)** The speed of light is represented by *C* in this formula, which is Einstein's relativity equation.

93. **(B)** This gland produces the growth hormone.

94. **(D)** Echos frequently appear to enhance sound production around bodies of water.

95. **(C)** More mass means that there is more of the object.

96. **(B)** Sedimentary rocks are generally nearest the surface and contain the remains of living things.

97. **(B)** Even living things are not able to "break down" DDT.

98. **(C)** The ball at the top of the ramp has the most potential for creating energy.

99. **(D)** The pendulum represents kinetic energy—energy in use.

100. **(B)** This is the correct sequence.

101. **(C)** Even the vastness of the rain forests cannot profoundly affect the way in which climatic shifts occur.

102. **(D)** Elements with neutral charges have a balance of electrons (negative charge) and protons (positive charge).

103. **(D)** Multiply $\frac{1}{2}$ four times:

$$\frac{1}{2} \times \frac{1}{2} \times \frac{1}{2} \times \frac{1}{2} = \frac{1}{16}.$$

104. **(B)** This statement is the only one supported by the data.

105. **(B)** Zygote formation is a fundamental step in meiosis.

106. **(B)** In fact, women may be more likely to be infected by the HIV virus when exposed to it.

107. **(D)** Conduction means heat transfer by physical contact.

108. **(C)** This is the definition of ecology.

109. **(B)** The sun is facing directly at the southern hemisphere at this position.

110. **(D)** Foot-pound is the amount of work it takes to move 1 pound 1 foot.

111. **(C)** Our solar system is part of a galaxy. The sun is a star.

112. **(A)** The effects of a recessive gene may not appear in parents but may appear in one of their offspring.

113. **(A)** This is the only conclusion supported by the data.

114. **(D)** The experiment does not describe how experimenters ensured that the HF2 group received no special attention, nor does it describe any other controls.

115. **(B)** In a solar eclipse, the moon blocks the sun's light from reaching earth.

116. **(B)** The force of the blocks coming together will cause them to separate.

117. **(B)** Arteries carry blood away from the heart, and veins bring the blood back to the heart.

118. **(C)** Plate tectonic theory shows that all parts of the earth's surface are slowly moving.

119. **(D)** A new layer of water is added at lower levels and frozen when the stone is blown to an upper level.

120. **(B)** Dark material absorbs more heat than light material.

Elementary Education: Curriculum, Instruction, and Assessment (K–5) (0016)

HOW TO PREPARE FOR THE CURRICULUM, INSTRUCTION, AND ASSESSMENT TEST (K–5)

This 2-hour test has 120 multiple-choice items. This test focuses on kindergarten through fifth grade. Most items relate directly to subject matter taught in schools, while some items are more general. According to ETS, the items are based on the material a new teacher should know. They are based on the overall areas of curriculum, instruction, and assessment. The test is also based on the content areas of Reading/Language Arts, Mathematics, Science, Social Studies, Arts and Physical Education, and General Knowledge items about teaching.

Overall Areas

Curriculum

Curriculum questions are about how each instructional area is organized, as well as how to choose and use the instructional materials and other resources available for teaching the subject. That is, curriculum questions may ask you to communicate why a subject is important to learn, or how subject areas are related, or how to integrate within and across subject areas, or about the textbooks and other materials, including technological resources and software, available for instruction.

Instruction

Instruction questions ask about specific teaching approaches for a subject area. That is, curriculum questions may ask you to describe how to find out what students know and build on this knowledge, or how to prepare instructional activities that integrate within and across subject areas, or to choose learning and teaching approaches that might include cooperative learning, or how to motivate students to learn.

Assessment

Assessment questions ask you how to devise and implement assessment strategies. These assessment questions might ask you about the appropriateness of text-based and other assessment strategies, or about how to use informal assessment techniques, about authentic or portfolio assessment, and appropriate interpretation and reporting of assessment results.

Content Areas

Each content area below contains questions about curriculum, instruction, and assessment. The following include the topics on which you may be tested in each content area.

Reading/Language Arts (35 percent or 42 items)

- The general purpose of teaching reading and language arts, including literacy

- Methodology including readiness, comprehension, word recognition, and teaching techniques

- Strategies for integrating reading, writing, listening, and speaking, children's literature

- Learning theories applied to teaching reading and writing, including constructivism, behaviorism, multiple intelligences, Piaget's stages of cognitive development, and others

- Curriculum, including objectives, overall scope and sequence, and instructional materials

- Assessing and interpreting students' reading and writing development, including teacher-made tests, standardized tests, and authentic (portfolio) assessment

Some test items may ask you to analyze students' work.

Mathematics (20 percent or 24 items)

- The general purpose of teaching mathematics

- Methodology including prenumber activities, problem solving, numeration, operations, algorithms, geometry, estimation, reasonableness of results, probability, elementary statistics, calculators, and computers

- Learning theories applied to teaching mathematics, including constructivism, behaviorism, multiple intelligences, Piaget's stages of cognitive development, and others

- Curriculum including objectives, overall scope and sequence, and instructional materials

- Assessing and interpreting students' mathematics development, including teacher-made tests, standardized tests, and authentic (portfolio) assessment

Some test items may ask you to analyze students' work.

Science (10 percent or 12 items)

- The general purpose of teaching science

- Teaching methodology; observing and describing, formulating and testing hypotheses, experiments, data and data presentation, health and safety

- Learning theories applied to teaching science, including constructivism, behaviorism, multiple intelligences, Piaget's stages of cognitive development, and others

- Curriculum including objectives, overall scope and sequence, and instructional materials

- Assessing and interpreting students' science development, including teacher-made tests, standardized tests, and authentic (portfolio) assessment

Some test items may ask you to analyze students' experiments or experimental results.

Social Studies (10 percent or 12 items)

- The general purpose of teaching social studies

- Teaching methodology; people, social organization, government, economics, communication, transportation, data and data representation, building models, impact of technology, planning and problem solving

- Learning theories applied to teaching, including constructivism, behaviorism, multiple intelligences, Piaget's stages of cognitive development, and others

- Curriculum including objectives, overall scope and sequence, and instructional materials

- Assessing and interpreting students' social studies development, including teacher-made tests, standardized tests, and authentic (portfolio) assessment

Arts (including music) and Physical Education (10 percent or 12 items)

- The general purpose of teaching the arts, music, and physical education

- Methodology and activities, color, texture, design, rhythm, melody, harmony, timbre, cultural influences, art and music as therapy, creativity, indoor and outdoor safety, activities and games appropriate to developmental level and sports, movement, coordination

- Learning theories applied to teaching the arts, music, and physical education, including constructivism, behaviorism, multiple intelligences, Piaget's stages of cognitive development, and others

- Curriculum including objectives, overall scope and sequence, and instructional materials

- Assessing and interpreting students' art and physical education development, including teacher-made tests, standardized tests, and authentic (portfolio) assessment

General Curriculum, Instruction, and Assessment (15 percent or 18 items)

- Psychological and social basis for instruction including child development, emotional development, social development, and language development

- Hierarchy of thinking skills and classroom questions

- Classroom organization, management, discipline, and motivation

- Learning theories applied to teaching, including constructivism, behaviorism, multiple intelligences, Piaget's stages of cognitive development, and others.

- Curriculum including objectives, overall scope and sequence, and instructional materials

- Assessing and interpreting students' development, including teacher-made tests, standardized tests, and authentic (portfolio) assessment

- Use and interpret assessment results including fundamental test and measurement concepts

- Relationships with parents and other colleagues

Practice Test Items

The practice test for Elementary Education: Content Knowledge on page 444 provides excellent practice items for this test.

PART VI

PARAPRO ASSESSMENT OVERVIEW

14 ParaPro Assessment Overview

TEST INFO BOX

Registration and Other Test Information—*www.ets.org/parapro*

2½ hours (150 minutes)

Reading	30 Multiple-Choice Items 25 items count toward scoring
Mathematics	30 Multiple-Choice Items 25 items count toward scoring
Writing	30 Multiple-Choice Items 25 items count toward scoring

TEST ADMINISTRATION

The ParaPro Assessment is administered as both a paper-based and an Internet-based test. The test has an identical format for each administration type.

Paper-based test administrations are given at test centers. Internet-based test administrations are typically given through participating school districts.

TEST SCORING

The ParaPro Assessment consists of 90 multiple-choice items. Test scoring is based on 75 predetermined items, but you will not know in advance which items they are.

ParaPro test scores are reported on a scale of 420 to 480. Each state or school has its own passing score, and most required passing scores are from 455 to 465. That usually means that about 45 to 54 correct answers (60 percent to 72 percent) will earn a passing score.

Use these equivalencies to estimate your scale score.

Correct Out of 75	Scale Score
21	430
26	435
31	440
40	450
45	455
50	460
54	465

HOW TO PREPARE FOR THE PARAPRO ASSESSMENT

There is a complete preparation for the ParaPro Assessment, which is very similar to preparation for the Preprofessional Skills Test (PPST).

Follow these steps.

Review

Strategies

❑ Review the Test-Preparation Strategies on pages 10–19.

❑ Review the Multiple-Choice Test-Taking Strategies on pages 15 and 16. Do not review the Essay Strategies.

Writing

❑ Complete the Targeted Writing Test, Part A, on pages 63–72.

❑ Complete the indicated part of the English Review on pages 22–60.

You will find two PPST Writing tests on pages 194–200 and 237–255 with explained answers. You can use these tests for extra English practice items, although there are question types on the ParaPro Assessment that do not appear on these tests.

Mathematics

❑ Complete the indicated part of the Mathematics Review on pages 73–124. You do not have to complete the Problem-Solving Review on pages 112–121.

❑ Complete the Targeted Mathematics Test on page 125 and review the answers.

There are two PPST Mathematics Tests on pages 202–212 and 247–255 with explained answers. You can use these tests for extra mathematics practice, although some of the questions are harder than the questions on the ParaPro Assessment.

Reading

❑ Complete the Reading Strategies on pages 161–172.

❑ Take and correct the Targeted Reading Test on page 174 and review the answers.

There are two PPST Reading Tests on pages 183–193 and 227–236 with explained answers. You can use these tests for extra reading practice, although some of the questions may be harder than the questions on the ParaPro Assessment.

❑ Sample Items.

Review the sample ParaPro items on the following pages. You'll find a complete practice test on the CD that comes with the book/CD edition.

Answer Sheet

PARAPRO ASSESSMENT SAMPLE ITEMS

1 Ⓐ Ⓑ Ⓒ Ⓓ 6 Ⓐ Ⓑ Ⓒ Ⓓ 11 Ⓐ Ⓑ Ⓒ Ⓓ 16 Ⓐ Ⓑ Ⓒ Ⓓ
2 Ⓐ Ⓑ Ⓒ Ⓓ 7 Ⓐ Ⓑ Ⓒ Ⓓ 12 Ⓐ Ⓑ Ⓒ Ⓓ 17 Ⓐ Ⓑ Ⓒ Ⓓ
3 Ⓐ Ⓑ Ⓒ Ⓓ 8 Ⓐ Ⓑ Ⓒ Ⓓ 13 Ⓐ Ⓑ Ⓒ Ⓓ 18 Ⓐ Ⓑ Ⓒ Ⓓ
4 Ⓐ Ⓑ Ⓒ Ⓓ 9 Ⓐ Ⓑ Ⓒ Ⓓ 14 Ⓐ Ⓑ Ⓒ Ⓓ 19 Ⓐ Ⓑ Ⓒ Ⓓ
5 Ⓐ Ⓑ Ⓒ Ⓓ 10 Ⓐ Ⓑ Ⓒ Ⓓ 15 Ⓐ Ⓑ Ⓒ Ⓓ 20 Ⓐ Ⓑ Ⓒ Ⓓ

ParaPro Assessment Sample Items

1. Lyndon Johnson was born in a farmhouse in central Texas in 1908. He grew up in poverty and had to work his way through college. He was elected to the United States House of Representatives in 1937 and served in the United States Navy during World War II. Following 12 years in the House of Representatives, he was elected to the United States Senate, where he became the youngest person chosen by any party to be its Senate leader.

The main idea of this passage is that

(A) Lyndon Johnson spent a number of years in government.
(B) Lyndon Johnson was successful because of his years spent in Texas.
(C) Lyndon Johnson rose from poverty to achieve the presidency.
(D) Lyndon Johnson was the youngest person to be chosen Senate leader.

Use this table of contents to answer Questions 2 and 3.

Earth and Space Science

Table of Contents

2. On which page would a person start to look for information about Mars?

(A) 1
(B) 3
(C) 12
(D) 34

3. On which page would a person be most likely to find a discussion of how water can erode the earth?

(A) 54
(B) 55
(C) 56
(D) 58

4. A student wants to use a word in place of *right* in this sentence. "You are *right* to want to keep your place in the movie line." The student uses a thesaurus to find four possible replacements for the word. Which of the replacements is correct?

(A) Accurate
(B) Correct
(C) Honorable
(D) Real

Use this passage to answer Question 5.

Music consists of pitch, the actual sound of a note, and duration, how long the note lasts. Three different tones occurring together are called chords. Harmony is chords with duration. Pitches separated by specific intervals are called a scale. Most music is based on the scale found on a piano's white keys.

5. A student reading this paragraph has trouble understanding the meaning of the word *scale*. Which of the following could a paraprofessional say to best help the student understand the meaning of the word?

(A) "Reread the earlier parts of the paragraph for clues about the meaning of pitch and harmony."
(B) "Read the rest of the passage to get more information about scales."
(C) "Think of some everyday examples of scales."
(D) "Take your time, relax, and sound the word out."

6. $40 = 50\%$ of $\square$

A student needs help answering the question shown above. Which of the following is the best help a paraprofessional could offer to help the student find the answer?

(A) Fifty times one hundred equals what?
(B) Fifty percent is what part of 100%?
(C) Fifty percent of what number equals forty?
(D) What number would make this equation correct?

7.
$$\xleftarrow{\qquad} \overset{-4 \quad -3 \quad -2 \quad -1 \quad 0 \quad +1 \quad +2 \quad +3 \quad +4}{\xrightarrow{\quad\quad}}$$

Where is $-9/4$ found on the number line above?

(A) To the right of +1
(B) Between 0 and 2
(C) Between 0 and −2
(D) To the left of −2

8. The circle graph below shows the percent distribution of eye colors among students in a class. If there are 30 students in the class, how many have blue eyes?

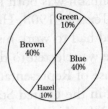

(A) 8
(B) 12
(C) 18
(D) 24

9. At the park, a train ride costs $1.25 and a horse ride costs $2.75. What is the cost of three train rides and four horse rides?

A paraprofessional is helping students write the correct expression to solve this word problem. Which of the following is the correct expression?

(A) 3 + 4 ($1.25 + $2.75)
(B) 3($1.25) + 4($2.75)
(C) 3 + $1.25 + 4 + $2.75
(D) 7($1.25 + $2.75)

10.

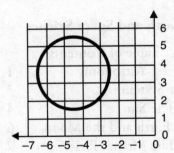

In the grid above, which point listed below is inside the circle?

(A) (−2, 3)
(B) (3, −2)
(C) (−4, 2)
(D) (2, −4)

11. At one school, 1/3 of the students ride to school in a car, whereas 1/2 of the students take the bus. What fraction of students at the school ride in a car or take the bus to school?

    (A) 1/6
    (B) 1/5
    (C) 2/5
    (D) 5/6

12. The list of numbers below shows a pattern. Each number is double the previous number. If things continue the same way, what will the sixth number be?

    2   4   8

    (A) 12
    (B) 24
    (C) 64
    (D) 128

Choose the underlined part that contains an error.

13. The tugboat <u>strains against</u> the <u>ship, revved</u>

          (A)   (B)

    up its engines, <u>and was able to</u> <u>maneuver</u>

                   (C)   (D)

    the ship into the middle of the channel.

14. A newspaper columnist <u>promised</u> <u>to print</u>

                     (A)   (B)

    the story about the <u>secret negotiations</u>

                   (C)

    concerning the sports stadium in <u>their</u> next

                      (C)

    column.

15. The <u>incredible</u> <u>intense</u> seminar held all

        (A)   (B)

    <u>the participants</u> in a <u>hypnotic</u> trance.

        (C)   (D)

Choose the correct answer.

16. The developmental psychology of Jean Piaget still has an impact in schools, particularly on the education of young children.

    What is the subject of the sentence above?

    (A) Developmental psychology
    (B) Jean Piaget
    (C) Developmental psychology of Jean Piaget
    (D) Schools

17. It was not that long ago that glaciers covered much of the United States, leaving behind evidence of their visit as glacial moraines.

    What is the simple predicate in the sentence above?

    (A) Covered
    (B) Leaving
    (C) Was
    (D) Visit

18. As James looks over his essay, he realizes that sentences are out of order. What should he do to improve the sentence order?

    (A) Move sentence (1) after sentence (2).
    (B) Move sentence (2) after sentence (3).
    (C) Move sentence (3) after sentence (4).
    (D) Move sentence (4) after sentence (5).

Use this outline to answer Questions 19 and 20.

The team captain was working on a letter to the team. The first draft of the outline for this letter is shown below.

A Letter to the Team

I. Team spirit
  A. Work together.
    1. Cooperate rather than compete.
    2. Put aside personal feelings.
  B. Support each other.
    1. Make positive comments.
    2. Don't be too critical.
    3. Make useful suggestions.
II. Team goals
  A. Have a successful season.
    1. Success is an attitude.
    2. Get our fans behind this.
  B. Win one game at a time.
    1. _____
    2. Forget any losses.
III. Team plays
  A. Play book.
    1. Don't lose it.
    2. Memorize the plays.
  B. _____
    1. Practice makes perfect.
    2. Review play execution.

19. Entry II.B.1. in the outline can't be read. Which of the following is the most likely entry for this line?

(A) Involve players' families.
(B) Get teachers involved.
(C) Focus on player commitment.
(D) Focus on today.

20. Which of the following is the best entry for III.B.?

(A) Play design
(B) Play evaluation
(C) Play practice
(D) Play distribution

EXPLAINED ANSWERS

1. **(C)** This paragraph describes how Lyndon Johnson rose from poverty to the presidency. (A) is incorrect because, while the passage mentions his years in government, the main idea of the entire paragraph is (C) and is reflected in the topic sentence.

2. **(C)** The discussion of Planets and Asteroids begins on page 12. Mars is a planet, and page 12 is the page on which a person would start to look for information.

3. **(B)** Page 55 includes the discussion of external geological processes. Water erosion occurs on the surface of the earth, and so it is an external geological process.

4. **(B)** The context of the word *right* indicates that it means correct. A person is correct to want to keep his or her place in the movie line.

5. **(B)** If the student reads the rest of the passage, he or she will see a further explanation of a scale, which could help the student understand what a scale is.

6. **(C)** A student who thinks "fifty percent of what number is 40" can see that fifty percent of <u>80</u> is 40. The missing number is 80.

   The student could solve the equation:
   $40 = 50\%$ of $\square$

   $40 = \dfrac{1}{2}x$

   $40 \times 2 = \dfrac{1}{2} \times 2x$

   $80 = x$

7. **(D)** $-\dfrac{9}{4} = -2\,\dfrac{1}{4}$, which is just to the left of –2.

   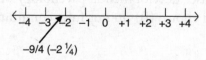

8. **(B)** Follow these steps to find the answer.
   The graph shows that 40% of the students have blue eyes.
   $40\% = 0.4$
   $0.4 \times 30 = 12$

9. **(B)** The equation and an explanation are shown below.

   $$3 \quad (\$1.25) \quad + \quad 4 \quad (\$2.75)$$

   Number of × Cost of a + Number of × Cost of a
   train rides   train ride   horse rides   horse ride

10. **(C)** Point *B* and point *D* have a positive *x* value, and these points are to the right of 0 on the *x*-axis. These points are not on the grid. As shown below, point *A* and point *C* are on the grid, and only point *C* is inside the circle.

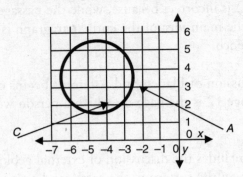

11. **(D)** This problem asks you to add $\frac{1}{3}$ and $\frac{1}{2}$.

That will show the fraction of students who either ride in a car or take the bus to school, combined.

$$\frac{1}{3} + \frac{1}{2} = \frac{2}{6} + \frac{3}{6} = \frac{5}{6}$$

12. **(C)** Continue the doubling pattern. The sixth number is 64.

$$2 \quad 4 \quad 8 \quad 16 \quad 32 \quad \underline{64}$$

13. **(A)** The verb tense of *strains* is incorrect. Replace the present tense *strains* with the past tense *strained* to agree with the other verbs *revved* and *was*.

14. **(D)** The pronoun *their* does not agree with antecedent *columnist*. Replace *their* with *his* or *her*.

15. **(A)** Replace *incredible* with the adverb *incredibly* to modify the adjective *intense*.

16. **(C)** The entire phrase "developmental psychology of Jean Piaget" is the subject. Choice (A) and choice (B) do not fully communicate what the sentence is about.

17. **(A)** Notice first that *glaciers* is the subject of the sentence and that the verb *covered* describes what the glaciers did.

18. **(B)** The *It* in sentence 2 has nothing to refer to until you reverse the positions of sentence 1 and sentence 2.

19. **(D)** Of all the suggested entries, the advice to "Focus on today" fits best with the entry "Win one game at a time."

20. **(C)** The choice "Play practice" makes the most sense when compared to the entries that appear in III.B.1. and III.B.2.

PART VII

OVERVIEW OF SELECTED SUBJECT ASSESSMENTS WITH SAMPLE QUESTIONS

Assessments in Biology and General Science, Early Childhood Education, English, French, and Fundamental Subjects: Content Knowledge

CHAPTER 15

TEST INFO BOX

Read this chapter if you are taking a Praxis II Subject Assessment or Specialty Area Test in one or more of these areas.

PREPARATION TIPS

Read the following Introduction. Then go over Preparation Tips at the beginning of each section you review. Read the test descriptions and take the practice test questions for the tests you have to take.

INTRODUCTION

This chapter reviews Subject Assessments in the areas listed above. Most of the tests are multiple choice, but a number of the Subject Assessments require a constructed-response, short-essay, answer. Each state has its own testing requirements. Check with the state certification office to confirm the requirements. The phone numbers for state certification offices are given also in Chapter 17.

Biology and General Science

TEST INFO BOX

Read this section if you are taking one of these tests.

Biology: Content Knowledge—Part 1 (0231)
75 multiple-choice questions, 1 hour

Biology: Content Knowledge—Part 2 (0232)
75 multiple-choice questions, 1 hour

Biology: Content Essays (0233)
3 short-essay questions, 1 hour

Biology: Pedagogy (0234)
1 essay question, 1 hour

Biology: Content Knowledge (0235)
150 multiple-choice questions, 2 hours

Biology and General Science (0030)
160 multiple-choice questions, 2 hours

General Science: Content Knowledge—Part 1 (0431)
60 multiple-choice questions, 1 hour

General Science: Content Knowledge—Part 2 (0432)
60 multiple-choice questions, 1 hour

General Science: Content Essays (0433)
3 short-essay questions, 1 hour

General Science: Content Knowledge (0435)
120 multiple-choice questions, 2 hours

PREPARATION TIPS

Chapter 2, "Test Preparation and Test-Taking Strategies," will help you prepare for the multiple-choice tests as well as the Content Essays and the Pedagogy test.

Use the following test description(s) as a study guide. They provide important information about test content, format, and scoring. Complete and score the practice test questions to get a sense and feel for the type of questions you will encounter.

The practice questions do not represent the full range of questions on a test. The answers to all practice questions are at the end of the chapter.

TEST DESCRIPTIONS

Biology (0230)

This 2-hour test has 150 multiple-choice questions covering the following areas:

- *Animals, Fungi, and Protists (30 percent).* Classification, growth, and development of these creatures

- *History and Methodology of Science and Society (10 percent).* Issues related to the history and methodology of science, including the environment and the integration of science and technology

- *Prokaryotes and Eukaryotes (23 percent).* Development of these primitive cellular creatures and the function of cells including respiration, genes, and viruses

- *Evolution (18 percent).* Origin, development, and adaptation of life forms

- *Ecology (19 percent).* Development and survival of communities and populations, ecosystems

Biology: Content Knowledge—Part 1 (0231)

This 1-hour test has 75 multiple-choice questions at a beginning level.

- *Diversity of Living Things (26 percent).* Classification and characteristics of the five kingdoms; plant anatomy, adaptation, and reproduction (fertilization and zygotes); photosynthesis (include C_3 and C_4 as nutrients); animal classification and evolution; body systems including circulation, excretion, and immunity; and growth and reproduction including gametogenesis and embryogenesis

- *Principles of Science (17 percent).* History of science including scientific methods and skills; measuring, collecting, displaying, analyzing, and interpreting data; experiments, laboratories, and field activities

- *Molecular and Cellular Biology (16 percent).* Molecules, chemical structure, cells, respiration, and photosynthesis; characteristics of prokaryotic and eukaryotic cells; proteins, genes, viruses, DNA, and cancer

- *Genetics and Evolution (15 percent).* Genes, genetic disorders, Mendel's laws, and probability and environmental influences

- *Ecology (13 percent).* Populations, communities, and ecosystems

- *Science and Technology (13 percent).* Resource management and ethical questions of genetic engineering

Biology: Content Knowledge—Part 2 (0232)

This 1-hour test has 75 multiple-choice questions at a more advanced level.

- *Diversity of Living Things (37 percent).* Classification and characteristics of the five kingdoms; plant anatomy, adaptation, and reproduction (fertilization and zygotes); photosynthesis (include C_3 and C_4 as nutrients); animal classification and evolution; body systems including circulation, excretion, and immunity; growth and reproduction including gametogenesis and embryogenesis

- *Molecular and Cellular Biology (21 percent).* Molecules, chemical structure, cells, respiration, and photosynthesis; characteristics of prokaryotic and eukaryotic cells; proteins, genes, viruses, DNA, enzymes, and cancer; meiosis, mitosis, and cytokinesis

- *Genetics and Evolution (24 percent).* Genes, genetic disorders, Mendel's laws, and probability and environmental influences

- *Ecology (18 percent).* Populations, communities, and ecosystems

Biology: Content Essays (0233)

This 1-hour test includes three short-essay questions; one from cellular and molecular biology, one from genetics and evolution, and one from organic biology and ecology. The content of these questions is the same as that covered from these three areas on Biology: Content Knowledge, Part 1.

Biology: Pedagogy (0234)

The 1-hour test includes one three-part essay question and measures your knowledge of high school biology planning and pedagogy. The test consists of a passage of about 100 to 200 words about biology and is drawn from the subject matter covered on Biology: Content Knowledge, Part 1.

You are asked to: (1) identify learning objectives for a lesson based on the passage, (2) describe learning strategies to help students learn the concept, and (3) outline assessment techniques to determine if students have achieved the objectives.

Biology: Content Knowledge (0235)

This 2-hour test has 150 multiple-choice questions based on the combined topics from tests (0231) and (0232).

Biology and General Science (0030)

This two-hour test has 160 multiple-choice questions covering the following areas:

- *History and Methodology of Science and Society (10 percent).* Issues related to the history and methodology of science, including the environment and the integration of science and technology

- *Prokaryotes and Eukaryotes (15 percent).* Development of these primitive cellular creatures and the function of cells including respiration, genes, and viruses

- *Animals, Fungi, and Protists (20 percent).* Classification, growth, and development of these creatures

- *Evolution (12 percent).* Origin, development, and adaptation of life forms

- *Ecology (13 percent).* Development and survival of communities and populations, ecosystems

- *Chemistry (10 percent).* Structure and states of matter, laboratory work and safety, environment

- *Physics (10 percent).* Physics of heat, light, magnetism, atomic reactions, waves, and environment

- *Astronomy, Geology, Meteorology, and Oceanography (10 percent).* Relevant areas of these sciences

General Science (0430)

This 2-hour test includes 120 multiple-choice questions.

- *Biology (25 percent).* Classification, cells and cell functions, organs and organ systems, photosynthesis, respiration, genetics, evolution and ecology, and metric and English measurements

- *Chemistry (25 percent).* Periodic table, formulas, acids and bases, periodicity, oxidation and chemical bonding, mixtures, compounds, solutions, laboratory procedures, and customary and metric measurement

- *Physics (25 percent).* Physics of heat, light, sound, optics, and atomic reactions; waves; and environment

- *Astronomy, Geology, Meteorology, and Oceanography (25 percent).* Fundamental concepts in these areas

General Science: Content Knowledge—Part 1 (0431)

This 1-hour test has 60 multiple-choice questions at a beginning level.

- *Methods, Laboratory Procedures, Data, and Measurement (23 percent).* Scientific methods and laws, lab procedures, metric system, data presentation, analysis, and interpretation

- *Science Principles (23 percent).* Matter, mass and energy, heat and thermodynamics, atomic structure, nuclear transformations, and radiation

- *Life Science (22 percent).* Cells' features and reproduction, genetics, DNA, Mendel's laws, evolution, and diversity

- *Astronomy, Geology, Meteorology, Oceanography, Technology, and Society (32 percent).* Fundamental concepts in these areas

General Science: Content Knowledge—Part 2 (0432)

This 1-hour test has 60 multiple-choice questions at a more advanced level.

- *Physics (27 percent).* Motion (circular, projectile, and straight line), Newton's laws, Archimedes principle, work and energy, and laws of conservation; types and effects of electricity and magnetism; types of waves, including sound and light waves, reflection, and refraction

- *Chemistry (27 percent).* Periodic table, bonding (mole and chemical), inorganic compounds; molecular and kinetic theories and gas laws; chemical reactions, effects of temperature, etc., on reactions; and types of solutions and solvents, acids, bases, and salts

- *Life Science (18 percent).* Cells and cell structure; genetics, and evolution; plants and animals including physiology and reproduction; and ecology including populations, biomes, and communities

- *Geology, Meteorology, Oceanography, Technology, and Society (28 percent).* Rocks and minerals, tectonics, and weathering; geological dating and earth history; ocean currents, tides, and waves; and atmosphere, solar radiation, precipitation, climate, pressure systems, and weather maps

General Science: Content Essays (0433)

This 1-hour test includes three short-essay questions from the content of General Science: Content Knowledge Test, Parts 1 and 2. Check back to these test descriptions for a quick review of this subject matter. Most questions fall into one of the following categories.

Questions about data analysis and scientific investigations ask you to design simple experiments, analyze data, or describe how to investigate and learn about a scientific concept. Questions about concepts, models, and patterns ask you to write about major scientific concepts, to describe how scientists use models, or to identify and describe scientific patterns in the real world. Questions about science and technology ask you to describe the way science and technology affect society and to demonstrate an understanding of these concepts.

General Science: Content Knowledge (0435)

This 2-hour test has 120 multiple-choice questions based on the combined topics from tests (0431) and (0432).

PRACTICE QUESTIONS

On the Web

Additional test questions are available free at the ETS Web site. Visit the Tests at a Glance portion of the Praxis Web site at *www.ets.org/praxis/prxtest.html* and click on the title of the test you are preparing for.

Biology

Biology and General Science

Choose the correct answer.

1. All the following are probable results from large-scale deforestation of tropical rain forests EXCEPT

   (A) increased erosion by waterways flowing through the region.
   (B) an increase of CO_2 in the atmosphere.
   (C) a decline in the amount of oxygen in the atmosphere.
   (D) flourishing of rare species in the region.

2. Which of the following is an example of an annelid?

   (A) Bee
   (B) Lichen
   (C) Fungus
   (D) Leech

3. Acid rain, resulting in depletion of organisms in Canadian and North Eastern American lakes, is caused primarily by

   (A) lowered water levels.
   (B) garbage dumping.
   (C) emissions from power stations.
   (D) nuclear waste.

4. Lunar phases are primarily a result of

   (A) distance of moon to sun.
   (B) position of the earth and moon relative to the sun.
   (C) rotation of solar system around sun.
   (D) distance between earth and sun.

5. What determines the type of an atom?

   (A) The number of ions
   (B) The number of quarks
   (C) The number of protons
   (D) The sum of number of protons and number of electrons

Questions 6 and 7

Match one of the following items with the example of that group of compounds.

   (A) Steroid
   (B) Acid
   (C) Carbohydrate
   (D) Platelet

6. Cholesterol

7. Glycogen

8. Select the item that best completes the analogy: oxidation : reduction : :

   (A) gravity : weightlessness.
   (B) anode : cathode.
   (C) photosynthesis : sunlight.
   (D) electrode : laser.

9. Car A weighs 2,000 kg and is moving 40 m/s. Car B weighs 4,000 kg and is moving 20 m/s. Which of the following answers is the best description of the momentum and kinetic energy of the cars?

   (A) The cars have the same kinetic energy and momentum because the product of their weight times their speed are the same.
   (B) The momentum is the same, but A has greater kinetic energy because speed is a squared variable in the formula of kinetic energy.
   (C) There is not enough information to make a determination about kinetic energy, but the momentum is the same.
   (D) There is too little information to make a determination about kinetic energy, but the momentum of car A is greater, as indicated by its increased speed.

10. The Galapagos finch is a good example of adaptive radiation because

    (A) it lives in an environment very close to the equator.
    (B) it is very nonselective in mating.
    (C) it shares its living environment peacefully with many different genus of animals.
    (D) many different species arose from a single ancestral type.

Biology: Content Knowledge—Parts 1 and 2

Choose the correct answer.

11. Where is blood pressure highest in the human circulatory system?

    (A) Ventricles
    (B) Atriums
    (C) Arteries
    (D) Veins

12. The following are examples of the first trophic level EXCEPT

    (A) bushes.
    (B) dead grass.
    (C) mushrooms.
    (D) flowers.

13. Two parents with brown eyes have a son with blue eyes. What is the most likely explanation?

    (A) Blue eyes are the dominant trait.
    (B) A mutation occurred in the genes of the child.
    (C) Blue eyes are a recessive trait.
    (D) The gene for blue eyes is located in the X chromosome.

14. The process by which cells make exact copies of themselves is called

    (A) meiosis.
    (B) mitosis.
    (C) gene splitting.
    (D) photosynthesis.

15. Which of the following kingdoms consist of one-celled living things?

    (A) Moneran
    (B) Fungi
    (C) Plantae
    (D) Animalie

16. The process of homeostasis

    (A) breaks down food to usable forms.
    (B) maintains the cell's equilibrium.
    (C) creates more cells.
    (D) creates useful substances.

17. All the following are part of the endocrine system EXCEPT

    (A) ovaries.
    (B) pituitary gland.
    (C) adrenal glands.
    (D) lymphocytes.

18. Which of the following includes interdependent life forms and supports life through food, atmosphere, energy, and water?

    (A) Ecosystem
    (B) Biosphere
    (C) Food web
    (D) Biome

General Science

General Science: Content Knowledge

Choose the correct answer.

19. During which period of the Cenozoic era did the land bridge between North America and Europe disappear?

    (A) Quaternary
    (B) Tertiary
    (C) Jurassic
    (D) Permian

20. Which of the following statements does NOT summarize one of Newton's laws of motion?

    (A) What goes up, must come down.
    (B) A body at rest stays at rest, and a body at motion stays in motion, unless acted upon by an outside force.
    (C) Force = Mass × Acceleration.
    (D) For every action, there's an equal and opposite reaction.

21. If the half-life of element X is 3,000 years, it will have decreased to $\frac{1}{8}$ of its original potency after

    (A) 12,000 years.
    (B) 4,500 years.
    (C) 6,000 years.
    (D) 9,000 years.

22. Two cars are connected by a cable. If the first pulls in one direction at 4,500 newtons (N), and the other pulls in the opposite direction with a force of 3,000 N, what is the magnitude of the resultant force?

    (A) 7,500 N
    (B) 4,500 N
    (C) 1,500 N
    (D) 3,000 N

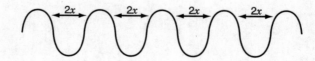

23. The wavelength of the microwave diagrammed above is

    (A) 4x.
    (B) 8x.
    (C) 2x.
    (D) 6x.

24. All the following are the same EXCEPT

    (A) absolute zero.
    (B) zero degrees Celsius.
    (C) −273°C.
    (D) −460°F.

25. If a person strikes two objects together, the sound will travel most quickly

    (A) if the objects are struck in an open field.
    (B) if the objects are struck under water.
    (C) if the objects are struck in a cave.
    (D) if the objects are struck inside a building.

26. All the following are parts of the muscular system EXCEPT

    (A) tendons.
    (B) cardiac muscles.
    (C) skeletal muscles.
    (D) cartilage.

27. Which earth sphere includes the rigid crust and upper mantle?

    (A) Outer core
    (B) Lithosphere
    (C) Asthenosphere
    (D) Inner core

Biology: Content Essays

Select one current theory of evolution. Explain how this theory differs from the more or less "smooth" evolutionary process described by Darwin.

Biology: Pedagogy

Explain how you would teach a week-long unit on the ecology of the salt marsh. Your unit should include objectives, procedures, and methods, including laboratory experiences that you would use to help students learn the material and methods for assessing student learning.

> Consider this comment.

The universe we live in is a vast and mysterious place. We have developed telescopes which can detect a large number of galaxies. But this is not very helpful. How can we decipher anything about our world through looking at stars so very far away? Can we tell anything even from the stars we can see in our own galaxy, the Milky Way? I would say that these distant galaxies and solar systems can give us few clues to our own planet.

How would you respond to this comment? Discuss what is uninformed or incorrect, using appropriate examples.

Early Childhood Education

TEST INFO BOX

Read this section if you are taking this test.

❑ **Early Childhood Education (0020)**
  120 multiple-choice questions, 2 hours

PREPARATION TIPS

The questions on the Elementary Education: Curriculum, Instruction, and Assessment Practice Test (0011) in Chapter 11 on pages 370–418 provide a useful practice test for the Early Childhood Education Test. Questions on that test are somewhat more focused on older children than the Early Childhood Education Test, but the questions have the same general focus.

Chapter 2, "Test-Preparation and Test-Taking Strategies," will help you prepare for this test.

The items on this test measure your understanding of topics related to children aged three to eight, although some items may deal with children who are somewhat older or somewhat younger. Visit the Web site of the National Association for the Education of Young Children at *www.naeyc.org*. This site includes links to NAEYC standards and certification resources.

Use the following test descriptions as a study guide. They provide important information about test content, format, and scoring. Complete and score the practice test questions to get a feel for the type of questions you will encounter. The practice questions do not represent the full range of questions on a test. The answers to all practice questions are at the end of the chapter.

The sections of the PLT Review on pages 264–299 related to young children may help you prepare for this test. The items on the Targeted Principles of Learning Test may give you additional practice with the types of question you will encounter on this test.

TEST DESCRIPTION

The 120 multiple-choice items on this test cover the following areas:

The Growth, Development, and Learning of Young Children
Factors Influencing Individual Growth and Development
Applications of Development and Curriculum Theory
Planning and Implementing Curriculum
Evaluating and Reporting Student Progress and the Effectiveness of Instruction
Understanding Professional and Legal Responsibilities

PRACTICE QUESTIONS

On the Web

Additional test questions sold in book form are available free at the ETS Web site. Visit the Tests at a Glance portion of the Praxis Web site at *www.ets.org/praxis/prxtest.html* and click on **0020 Early Childhood Education**.

EARLY CHILDHOOD EDUCATION

Choose the correct answer.

1. Which of the following statements most accurately describes Maria Montessori's beliefs about school environment?

   (A) Students should use commonly available materials during instruction.
   (B) Students do best in an environment that naturally holds their interest.
   (C) Students do best when they learn outdoors with natural experiences.
   (D) Students should learn concepts and not depend on manipulative materials.
   (E) Students should have their own private areas into which neither the teacher nor other children can enter.

Subject Assessments

2. Here is brief part of a conversation between Alex Whitby, a third-grade teacher, and Marciella Atkins, the school district reading specialist.

Alex: Thanks for coming by. I wanted to talk to you about one of my students.

Marciella: Which one?

Alex: Savaro—he's still having trouble with reading.

Marciella: I remember Savaro from last year in second grade.

Alex: I was thinking about more phonics—what do you think?

Marciella: That's OK—just remember that phonics does not help much . . .

Which of the following finishes the reading specialist's last sentence?

(A) in associating sounds with printed letters.
(B) with early childhood reading.
(C) with reading comprehension.
(D) in attacking new words independently.
(E) in developing a sight vocabulary.

3. A primary-grade teacher is working in a school where most of the students are economically disadvantaged. The teacher knows that these economically disadvantaged students, as a whole, tend to have lower reading achievement than other students, leading the teacher to which of the following understandings that will enable him to help his students.

(A) Economically disadvantaged students, as a whole, are usually less capable learners than other students.
(B) Minority teachers are more effective with minority students.
(C) Learning expectations should usually be lowered for minority students.
(D) The parents of economically disadvantaged students do not read at home.
(E) Economically disadvantaged students usually have fewer enriched learning opportunities at home.

4. A second-grade teacher and a principal are discussing the teacher's reasons for instituting a whole language program in his classroom. Which of the following is the best reason the teacher could give?

(A) Whole language instruction is widely accepted.
(B) It is not necessary to teach word recognition.
(C) Children comprehend more after using a whole language approach.
(D) Children have a better attitude toward reading.
(E) Whole language is better for helping students sound out words.

5. A kindergarten teacher says she has found modeling to be an effective form of instruction, meaning that she is most likely to

    (A) show students how to work with clay.
    (B) respond courteously to students' questions.
    (C) tell a student when the student has mispronounced a word.
    (D) demonstrate students' inappropriate behavior.
    (E) ask students to show other students how to act.

6. A teacher realizes that his class is culturally and linguistically diverse. Which of the following actions by the teacher would be the most appropriate modification of the objectives or plans to meet the needs of this class?

    (A) Modify objectives to focus more on basic skills.
    (B) Modify objectives to reduce their difficulty level.
    (C) Modify plans to teach the class in the foreign language.
    (D) Modify plans to focus on the cultural heritage of those in the class.
    (E) Modify plans to include instruction about other countries.

7. A preschool teacher is incorporating authentic assessment in his evaluation techniques. That means that the teacher will

    (A) collect and evaluate student work.
    (B) use only tests provided by the publisher of the books he uses.
    (C) evaluate students only in real situations outside school.
    (D) collect evaluative information from other teachers.
    (E) ask students to help one another as they work.

8. Betty Ann DelCorso is helping her first-grade students learn about counting. She uses shapes as counters and makes sure that students point to a shape each time they say the next counting word. Which of the following is the most likely reason why she uses this approach?

    (A) Ms. DelCorso wants to be sure the students are paying attention to what they are doing.
    (B) Ms. DelCorso wants to be sure the students are developing eye-hand coordination.
    (C) Ms. DelCorso is going to ask the students questions about the shapes once they have finished counting.
    (D) Ms. DelCorso wants to help the children learn the names of the shapes.
    (E) Ms. DelCorso wants to be sure the students are not just saying counting words.

9. Eileen, a primary-grade student, wrote the following sentence about a sailor on an old-time sailing boat.

He had enuf rope.

Which of the actions listed below would best address the problem in this sentence?

(A) Instruction on phonics-based word attack skills
(B) Instruction on context-based word attack skills
(C) Instruction on the use of homonyms
(D) Instruction on variable spelling phonemes
(E) Instruction on word meaning

10. Which of the following is the best example of instruction using Gardner's multiple intelligences as the basis for instruction?

(A) Implement interdisciplinary units.
(B) Help students learn about each of the intelligences.
(C) Eliminate assessments.
(D) Allow students to determine criteria for quality.
(E) Match instruction to a student's intelligence.

11. Elma, a second-grade student, has difficulty pronouncing some printed words. The problem may reflect all of the following EXCEPT

(A) phonetic analysis.
(B) sight vocabulary.
(C) language comprehension.
(D) context analysis.
(E) phoneme recognition.

12. An aide has been assigned to a preschool class because there are more students in the class than the district usually allows. Which of the following represents the LEAST appropriate instructional duties for the teacher to assign to the aide?

(A) Help preschool children dress themselves.
(B) Duplicate instructional worksheets.
(C) Read to small groups of students.
(D) Help manage difficult children.
(E) Take a student to a special class.

English

TEST INFO BOX

Read this section if you are taking one of these tests.

English Language, Literature, and Composition

Content Knowledge (0041)
150 multiple-choice questions, 2 hours

Essays (0042)
2 essay questions, 2 hours

Pedagogy (0043)
2 essay questions, 1 hour

PREPARATION TIPS

Chapter 2, "Test-Preparation and Test-Taking Strategies," will help you prepare for the multiple-choice tests, as well as for the Essay and Pedagogy tests.

Use the following test description(s) as a study guide. They provide important information about test content, format, and scoring. Complete and score the practice test questions to get a feel for the type of questions you will encounter. The practice questions do not represent the full range of questions on a test. The answers to all practice questions are at the end of the chapter.

TEST DESCRIPTIONS

English Language, Literature, and Composition: Content Knowledge (0041)

This 2-hour test has 150 multiple-choice questions.

- *Literature (25 percent) [American (15 percent), British and Others (10 percent).]* Literature including American cultural and feminist literature, adolescent literature

- *Literary Forms and Devices (20 percent).* Analysis and interpretation of literature including figurative language, cultural and historical perspectives, critical and literary forms

- *Linguistics and Language (25 percent).* Language history, development, and acquisition; dictionary use, grammar, syntax, semantics, and dialects

- *Rhetoric and Composition (30 percent).* Process and assessment of writing; argumentation, usage, conventions, exposition, and narration

English Language, Literature, and Composition: Essays (0042)

This 2-hour test has two essay questions, each 1 hour long.

The interpretation question either presents a literary selection and asks for an analysis or presents two passages and asks for an analysis and comparison. The position question asks you to present and defend a position on issues associated with the study of English; it may ask a question directly or present a passage to react to.

English Language, Literature, and Composition: Pedagogy (0043)

This 1-hour test has two essay questions, one 40 minutes long and one 20 minutes long.

The first question gives a passage and asks you to describe learning activities that will help students understand the passage and present an assessment plan for determining to what extent students have learned the objective. Your response is also evaluated for English content.

The second question gives a piece of student composition and asks you to write a note to the student about the strengths and weaknesses that you note in the sample and make recommendations for revisions. Your writing is also evaluated for how appropriately it communicates with the students.

PRACTICE TESTS

On the Web

Additional test questions are available free at the ETS Web site. Visit the Tests at a Glance portion of the Praxis Web site at *www.ets.org/praxis/prxtest.html* and click on the title of the test you are preparing for.

English Language and Literature

Choose the correct answer.

1. The first American to make a living as a writer, and the disputed "father" of American literature, is

   (A) Samuel Clemens.
   (B) James Fenimore Cooper.
   (C) Mark Twain.
   (D) Washington Irving.

2. What action was Charles Dickens considering in the aftermath of the death of Little Nell in his work *The Old Curiosity Shop?*

    (A) Adopting a child
    (B) Bringing Nell back to life
    (C) Living incognito
    (D) Writing columns reminding the outraged populace that Little Nell was a fictional character

3. Which of the following best describes the most significant common feature of *1984* and *Pilgrims Progress?*

    (A) Both were originally written in German.
    (B) Each title has a religious meaning.
    (C) Each title reflects its author's childhood.
    (D) Both are allegorical.

4. The 19th century poet whose work presented episodes of the Arthurian legends, is

    (A) William Makepeace Thackery.
    (B) James Thomson.
    (C) Dylan Thomas.
    (D) Alfred, Lord Tennyson.

5. When Miguel de Cervantes writes of Don Quixote's exploits as a latter-day knight errant, Cervantes was

    (A) providing a metaphor for life.
    (B) satirizing romantic novels.
    (C) describing pastoral scenes.
    (D) responding to popular demand.

6. "and now begins the search"

    Which of the following best describes the versification of the poetic line above?

    (A) Iambic pentameter
    (B) Iambic trimeter
    (C) Trochaic tetrameter
    (D) Trochaic hexameter

Questions 7 and 8

Choices (A)–(D) list fallacious forms of argument often used to support a point. Read the passages and identify the fallacious argument each reflects.

7. The infomercial hostess announces that "every person who participated in our skin care program now has beautiful skin." She then goes on to say that "this shows that if you want to have beautiful skin, you need to participate in our program."

(A) Using the converse
(B) Begging the question
(C) Non sequitur
(D) False analogy

8. A parent at a meeting says, "There is research to show that students who read more do better in school. So I propose that we require all the students in our schools to read one book every week."

(A) Using the converse
(B) Begging the question
(C) Non sequitur
(D) False analogy

9. According to Chomsky, transformational grammar indicates that

(A) words precede thoughts.
(B) grammar must be learned.
(C) grammar is innate.
(D) ontology recapitulates philology.

10. I grew up in Kearny, New Jersey, now known as Soccer Town, USA. I played football in high school and barely knew that the soccer team existed. However, a look back at my high school yearbook revealed that the soccer team won the state championship and we had a .500 season. So much for awareness.

Which of the following techniques is used by the author of the passage?

(A) Exposition
(B) Reflection
(C) Argumentation
(D) Narration

Language, Literature, and Composition: Content Knowledge

Choose the correct answer.

11. Robert Frost's poems were a revolutionary departure from the poetry of the time because they

    (A) were less grand and pretentious.
    (B) were unrhymed.
    (C) were more pastoral.
    (D) were not written in couplets.

12. Which of the following statements best describes the common element or feature of *Three Soldiers* by Dos Pasos and e e cummings' *The Enormous Room?*

    (A) Both authors turned to poetry.
    (B) Both are set during World War I.
    (C) Both are metaphorical.
    (D) Both were based on works by F. Scott Fitzgerald.

13. The 19th century pre-Raphaelite writers were motivated by the reaction

    (A) to the French Revolution.
    (B) to the writings of Ralph Waldo Emerson.
    (C) against the Church of England.
    (D) against Victorian materialism.

14. Which of the following would be most likely to occur in concrete poetry?

    (A) d l r o w d r a w k c a b a n i e v i l e w
    (B) the world is backward and it's tough
    (C) the world's a wall—that's all
    (D) hard, tough, backward, rancid—world

15. In Swift's *Gulliver's Travels*, horses take on human characteristics in a literary technique called

    (A) transubstantiation.
    (B) onomatopoeia.
    (C) alliteration.
    (D) anthropomorphism.

16. Which work by an American writer described passive resistance, his reaction against paying a tax to support an American foreign war?

    (A) Whitman's *Leaves of Grass*
    (B) Emerson's *Nature*
    (C) Thoreau's "Civil Disobedience"
    (D) Douglass' *My Bondage and My Freedom*

For Questions 17 and 18 use the following options.

    (A) *The Odyssey*, Homer
    (B) *Sonnets From the Portuguese*, Elizabeth Barrett Browning
    (C) *Sir Gwain and the Green Knight*, Anon.
    (D) *Gulliver's Travels*, Swift

17. Which of these works is best described as a romance?

18. Which of these works is best described as an epic?

For Questions 19 and 20 use the following poem.

    [1] The rain falls against the window
    [2] with a monotonous drip-drip-drip.
    [3] Outside, the bugs pass away by
    [4] the thousands as they are swept away
    [5] down the yawning storm drain.
    [6] It seems to me that this is the
    [7] worst storm in the history of the world.
    [8] This storm moves slowly through the day
    [9] Like a huge carwash for the earth.

19. What figure of speech is represented in line [2]?

    (A) Simile
    (B) Metaphor
    (C) Euphemism
    (D) Onomatopoeia

20. What figure of speech is represented in line [9]?

    (A) Simile
    (B) Metaphor
    (C) Euphemism
    (D) Onomatopoeia

English Language, Literature, and Composition: Essays

Read the following excerpt from *Uncle Tom's Cabin.* Write an essay on a separate sheet of paper describing the images of slavery and the attitudes toward slaves that the writing portrays. Describe the style and the techniques used by Harriet Beecher Stowe to convey these images. Be sure to support any points you make with specific references to the work cited here.

Eliza, a runaway slave, made her desperate retreat across the river just in the dusk of twilight. The gray mist of evening, rising slowly from the river, enveloped her as she disappeared up the bank, and the swollen current and floundering masses of ice presented a hopeless barrier between her and her pursuer. Haley, the pursuer, therefore slowly and discontentedly returned to the little tavern, to ponder further what was to be done. Haley sat him down to meditate on the instability of human hopes and happiness in general.

"What did I want with the little cuss, now," he said to himself, "that I should have got myself treed like a coon, as I am, this yer say?"

He was startled by the loud and dissonant voice of a man who was apparently dismounting at the door. He hurried to the window.

"By the land! if this yer an't the nearest, now, to what I've heard folks call Providence," said Haley, "I do b'lieve that ar's Tom Loker."

Haley hastened out. Standing by the bar, in the corner of the room, was a brawny, muscular man, full six feet in height and broad in proportion. In the head and face every organ and lineament expressive of brutal and unhesitating violence was in a state of the highest possible development. Indeed, could our readers fancy a bull-dog come into man's estate, and walking about in a hat and coat, they would have no unapt idea of the general style and effect of his physique. He was accompanied by a traveling companion, in many respects an exact contrast to himself. The large man poured out a big tumbler half full of raw spirits, and gulped it down without a word. The little man stood tiptoe, and putting his head first to one side and then to the other, and snuffing considerately in the directions of the various bottles, ordered at last a mint julep, in a thin and quivering voice, and with an air of great circumspection.

"Wall, now, who'd a thought this yer luck 'ad come to me? Why, Loker, how are ye?" said Haley, coming forward, and extending his hand to the big man.

"The devil" was the civil reply. "What brought you here, Haley?"

The mousing man, who bore the name of Marks, instantly stopped his sipping . . .

English Language, Literature, and Composition: Pedagogy

You are teaching a unit on early American literature to a twelfth-grade class with average ability. The unit will include a lesson on the work of Washington Irving. An excerpt from Irving's *The Legend of Sleepy Hollow* is given here.

Review the excerpt.

On the next page, write an objective for the lesson on Washington Irving.

Describe the methods and procedures you would use to help your students reach this objective, including references to the excerpt cited here.

Explain how you would assess students' mastery of the objective.

About two hundred yards from the tree a small brook crossed the road and ran into a marshy and thickly wooded glen, known by the name of Wiley's swamp. A few rough logs, laid side by side, served for a bridge over this stream. On that side of the road where the brook entered the wood, a group of oaks and chestnuts, matted thick with wild grapevines, threw a cavernous gloom over it. To pass this bridge was the severest trial. It was at this identical spot that the unfortunate André was captured, and under the covert of those chestnuts and vines were the sturdy yeomen concealed who surprised him. This has ever since been considered a haunted stream, and fearful are the feelings of the schoolboy who has to pass it alone after dark.

As he approached the stream his heart began to thump; he summoned up, however, all his resolution, gave his horse half a score of kicks in the ribs, and attempted to dash briskly across the bridge; but instead of starting forward, the perverse old animal made a lateral movement and ran broadside against the fence. Ichabod, whose fears increased with the delay, jerked the reins on the other side, and kicked lustily with the contrary foot; it was all in vain; his steed started, it is true, but it was only to plunge to the opposite side of the road into a thicket of brambles and alder bushes. The schoolmaster now bestowed both whip and heel upon the starveling ribs of old Gunpowder, who dashed forward, snuffling and snorting, but came to a stand just by the bridge with a suddenness that had nearly sent his rider sprawling over his head. Just at this moment a plashy tramp by the side of the bridge caught the sensitive ear of Ichabod. In the dark shadow of the grove, on the margin of the brook, he beheld something huge, misshapen, black and towering. It stirred not, but seemed gathered up in the gloom, like some gigantic monster ready to spring upon the traveler.

French

PREPARATION TIPS

Chapter 2, "Test-Preparation and Test-Taking Strategies," will help you prepare for the multiple-choice tests and the essays.

Use the following test description(s) as a study guide. They provide important information about test content, format, and scoring. Complete and score the practice test questions to get a feel for the type of questions you will encounter. The practice questions do not represent the full range of questions on a test. The answers to all practice questions are at the end of the chapter.

TEST DESCRIPTIONS

French: Productive Language Skills (0171)

This 1-hour test is partitioned into two 30-minute sections. The test consists of three written and nine spoken exercises. Spoken responses are recorded on tape, and you are given several warm-up exercises before beginning the scored section.

- *Spoken* (All responses are in French). Read a 150-word passage with the correct pronunciation; answer written questions to describe a picture; tell a story based on a picture; role-play a response to a situation described in English; give instructions based on a picture; describe a situation presented in English; defend a statement printed in English; deliver a brief talk based on a situation printed in English; paraphrase a spoken French passage

- *Written.* Write questions you would ask during an interview; write a brief passage describing a set of pictures; write a short letter.

French: Content Knowledge (0173)

The 2-hour test has 120 multiple-choice questions partitioned into four sections. The questions consist of recorded and written questions in French and written English questions.

- *Interpretive Listening in French (27 percent).* Multiple-choice questions in French about recorded French passages

- *Reading in French and English (Grammatical Accuracy) (28 percent).* Multiple-choice questions in spoken and written French

- *French Language Structure and Expression (26 percent).* Questions about French passages

- *Cultural Perspectives in French and English (19 percent).* Questions in French and English about the history, cultural background, and literature of French-speaking parts of the world

PRACTICE QUESTIONS

On the Web

Additional test questions are available free at the ETS Web site. Visit the Tests at a Glance portion of the Praxis Web site at *www.ets.org/praxis/prxtest.html* and click on the title of the test you are preparing for.

French

> Choose the correct answer.

1. (You hear)

   Nous allons à la plage ou aux montagnes?

   (You read)

   (A) Je crois que cette idée est excellente.
   (B) J'aime les vacances.
   (C) Je préfère toujours un séjour à la mer.
   (D) Je ne peux pas; j'ai perdu les gants.

The following dialogue relates to Questions 2 and 3.

(You hear)

(Homme) Pour combien de temps devons-nous attendre les enfants?

(Femme) Ils ont dit qûils viendraient ici à six heures et il est six heures et demil maintenant.

(Homme) La circulation est horrible à cette heure.

(Femme) Qu'est-ce qu'on peut faire? Il faut les attendre.

(You read)

2. Il est certain

   (A) que les parents n'ont pas de patience.
   (B) que les enfants ne retourneront pas.
   (C) que les parents vont attendre leurs fils.
   (D) qu'il va pleuvoir.

3. Depuis combien de temps les parents attendent-ils leurs enfants?

   (A) Dix minutes
   (B) Vingt minutes
   (C) Trente minutes
   (D) Soixante minutes

Use the following text to answer Questions 4 and 5.

Jacqueline était très contente parce que ses enfants allaient retourner à la maison pour célébrer son anniversaire. Son fils venait en avion de Los Angeles où il travaille dans un h'pital. Sa fille la plus âgée habitait près de la ville de New York où elle est professeur à l'université. Cette fille voyageait en voiture avec ses deux enfants. Sa fille la moins âgée est étudiante à l'université d'Arizona. Jacqueline lui avait envoyé un billet d'avion pour qu'elle puisse assister à sa fête.

4. Qui va célébrer une fête d'anniversaire?

   (A) Le fils
   (B) La fille
   (C) La soeur
   (D) La mère

5. Il est probable que le fils de Jacqueline que

   (A) pilote.
   (B) boulanger.
   (C) médecin.
   (D) avocat.

6. S'il a le temps, Michel nous _____ visite.

   (A) rend
   (B) rende
   (C) rendra
   (D) rendrait

7. Nous avons fait une promenade parce qu'il _____ beau.

   (A) fait
   (B) faisait
   (C) a fait
   (D) fera

Use the following conversation to answer Questions 8 and 9.

   Paul: Avec _____ (8) _____ es-tu sortie hier soir.

   Sylvie: _____ (9) _____ sortie avec mon frère.

8. (A) qui
   (B) que
   (C) quoi
   (D) lequel

9. (A) J'ai
   (B) J'avais
   (C) Je suis
   (D) J'étais

10. Which of the following verbs has a similar pattern as *sortir* in the formation of the present indicative tense?

    (A) Finir
    (B) Voir
    (C) Avoir
    (D) Courir

11. Liaison occurs in all of the following EXCEPT

    (A) les haches.
    (B) les herbes.
    (C) les hôtels.
    (D) les heures.

12. An important French poet of the Renaissance was

    (A) Michel de Montaigne.
    (B) Pierre Corneille.
    (C) Jean-Jacques Rousseau.
    (D) Pierre de Ronsard.

Read the following paragraph. It contains errors in written French. Underline each error and write the correct replacement in the space above.

Line 1: L' été passée mon amie Francoise

Line 2: a visité la France. Elle a partie

Line 3: août 10. Ce voyage était un cadeau

Line 4: d'anniversaire de ses parents parce

Line 5: qu'elle était vingt et un ans. L'été

Line 6: prochain elle veut aller à Espagne.

French: Productive Language Skills

Study the following pictures. You will then have two minutes to speak and record your explanation in French of how to open a soft drink can and pour out the soda.

Fundamental Subjects: Content Knowledge

TEST INFO BOX

Read this section if you are taking this test.

❏ **Fundamental Subjects: Content Knowledge**
   100 multiple-choice questions, nonprogrammable calculator allowed, 2 hours

PREPARATION TIPS

The 120 questions on the Elementary Education: Content Knowledge (0014) in Chapter 13 on pages 438–477 provide an excellent practice test for Fundamental Subjects: Content Knowledge, although the precise topics covered on that test may vary somewhat from those Fundamental Subjects test.

Chapter 2, "Test-Preparation and Test-Taking Strategies," on page 11 will help you prepare for this Test. Chapter 4, "Mathematics," on page 73, will help you prepare for the mathematics portion of this test.

Use the following test descriptions as a study guide. They provide important information about test content, format, and scoring. Complete and score the practice test questions to get a feel for the type of questions you will encounter. The practice questions do not represent the full range of questions on a test. The answers to all practice questions are at the end of the chapter.

TEST DESCRIPTION

The 100 multiple-choice items on this test cover the following areas. The percentages reflect the approximate number of questions drawn from each.

English Language Arts (25 percent)

- Reading/literature

- Literary methods and effects

- Reading and communication skills

Mathematics (25 percent)

- Number sense and algebra

- Geometry and measurement

- Data analysis and probability

Citizenship and Social Sciences (25 percent)

- Historical continuity and change
- People, places, and geographic regions
- Civics and government
- Scarcity and economic choice

Science (25 percent)

- Nature and history of science
- Basic principles and fundamentals of science
- Science, technology, and social perspectives

PRACTICE QUESTIONS

On the Web

Additional test questions are available free at the ETS Web site. Visit the Tests at a Glance portion of the Praxis Web site at *www.ets.org/praxis/prxtest.html* and click on **30511 Fundamental Subjects: Content Knowledge.**

English Language Arts

<u>Base your responses to Questions 1 and 2 on this story.</u>

A fox was strolling through a vineyard and after a while he came upon a bunch of grapes. The grapes had just ripened, but they were hanging high up on the vine. It was a hot summer day, and the fox wanted to get the grapes to drink a little grape juice.

The fox ran and jumped to reach the grapes but could not reach them. Then the fox went a great distance from the grapes and ran as fast as possible and jumped as high as he could. He still could not reach the grapes. For over an hour, the fox ran and jumped but had no luck. The fox was never able to reach the grapes and had to give up. The fox walked away, sullenly proclaiming, "Those grapes were probably sour."

1. The structure of this story indicates that

   (A) it is a legend.
   (B) it is a fable.
   (C) it is a lyric.
   (D) it is a satire.

2. The point made by this story is that

   (A) height makes right.
   (B) the longer the run, the shorter the triumph.
   (C) it is easy to despise what you cannot get.
   (D) the fox would have done better by trying to solve the problem in another more clever way.

Use the poem "The Sullen Sky" to answer Questions 3 and 4.

The Sullen Sky

I see the sullen sky
Dark foreboding sky
Swept by dank and dripping clouds
Like ominous shrouds

A sky should be bright
Or clear and crisp at night
But it hasn't been that way
Oh dungenous day

That has been my life
And that has been my strife
I wish the clouds would leave
Ah, a sweet reprieve

3. Which of the following best describes the author's message?

   (A) The author's life is particularly impacted by rainy, cloudy days.
   (B) The author wants people to be free of worry.
   (C) The author is hoping life will get better.
   (D) The author lives on the coast where it is often rainy and cloudy.

4. What main literary technique does the author use to convey the poem's message?

   (A) Morphology
   (B) Alliteration
   (C) Allegory
   (D) Personification

Use this passage to answer Questions 5 and 6.

> I remember my childhood vacations at a bungalow colony near a lake. Always barefoot, my friend Eddie and I spent endless hours playing and enjoying our fantasies. We were pirates, rocket pilots, and detectives.
> *Line* Everyday objects were transformed into swords, ray guns, and two-way wrist
> *(5)* radios. With a lake at hand, we swam, floated on our crude rafts made of old lumber, fished, and fell in. The adult world seemed so empty while our world seemed so full. Returning years later I saw the colony for what it was—tattered and torn. The lake was shallow and muddy. But the tree that had been our lookout was still there. And there was the house where the
> *(10)* feared master spy hid from the FBI. And there was the launching pad for our imaginary rocket trips. The posts of the dock we used to sail from were still visible. But my fantasy play did not depend on this place. My child-mind would have been a buccaneer wherever it was.

5. Which of the following best characterizes this passage?

   (A) An adult describes disappointment at growing up.
   (B) A child describes the adult world through the child's eyes.
   (C) An adult discusses childhood viewed as an adult and as a child.
   (D) An adult describes the meaning of fantasy play.

6. The sentence "The adult world seemed so meaningless while our world seemed so full" on lines (6) through (7) is used primarily to

   (A) emphasize the emptiness of most adult lives when compared to the lives of children.
   (B) provide a transition from describing childhood to describing adulthood.
   (C) show how narcissistic children are.
   (D) describe the difficulty this child obviously had trying to relate to adults.

Use this passage to answer Question 7.

The computers in the college dormitories are actually more sophisticated than the computers in the college computer labs, and they cost less. It seems that the person who bought the dormitory computers looked around until she found powerful computers at a low price. The person who runs the labs just got the computers offered by the regular supplier.

7. The best statement of the main idea of this paragraph is that

   (A) it is better to use the computers in the dorms.
   (B) the computers in the dorms are always in use, so, for most purposes it is better to use the computers in the labs.
   (C) it is better to shop around before you buy.
   (D) wholesale prices are usually better than retail prices.

Use this passage to answer Question 8.

In England during the late 1800s, Charles Dodgson, writing as Lewis Carroll, penned several versions of *Alice's Adventures Underground*. The book is known to us as *Alice in Wonderland*. The story was originally written for a young child, Alice Liddell. The story was written to entertain Alice, but it was more than just a children's tale because of the symbolic meaning that was reflected in the traits of the story's characters.

8. The passage refers to the symbolism found in *Alice in Wonderland*, meaning that the story

   (A) was written in a foreign language.
   (B) contained many mathematical symbols.
   (C) contained no pictures.
   (D) has a figurative meaning.

Use this poem to answer Questions 9 and 10.

Solitude
by Ella Wheeler Wilcox

Laugh, and the world laughs with you;
        Weep, and you weep alone.
For the sad old earth must borrow it's mirth,
        But has trouble enough of it's own.
Sing, and the hills will answer;
        Sigh, it is lost on the air.
The echoes bound to a joyful sound,
        But shrink from voicing care.
Rejoice, and men will seek you;
        Grieve, and they turn and go.
They want full measure of all your pleasure,
        But they do not need your woe.
Be glad, and your friends are many;
        Be sad, and you lose them all.
There are none to decline your nectared wine,
        But alone you must drink life's gall.
Feast, and your halls are crowded;
        Fast, and the world goes by.
Succeed and give, and it helps you live,
        But no man can help you die.
There is room in the halls of pleasure
        For a long and lordly train,
But one by one we must all file on
        Through the narrow aisles of pain.

9. The style in this poem is best described as

   (A) analytical.
   (B) sentimental.
   (C) repetitive.
   (D) free verse.

10. Ms. Wilcox likely choose the title "Solitude" because

    (A) she wrote her poetry in solitude.
    (B) a person needs solitude to make appropriate life choices.
    (C) it is what the poem shows you how to avoid.
    (D) as the poem indicates, reflection is the path to happiness and acceptance.

Mathematics

11. An even number has two different prime factors. Which of the following could be the product of those factors?

    (A) 6
    (B) 12
    (C) 36
    (D) 48

12. Two types of elevators travel up and down inside a very tall building. One elevator starts at the first floor and stops every x floors. Another elevator starts at the first floor and stops every y floors. Which of the following is the best way to find at which floors both elevators stop?

    (A) Find the common multiples of x and the multiples of y.
    (B) Find the common factors of x and y.
    (C) Find the prime factors of x and y.
    (D) Find the divisors of x and y.

13. A school received $5,300 to use for eight different activities. A total of 91 percent of the money was allocated for seven of the activities, with the remainder used for a school trip. How much money was used for the school trip?

    (A) $477
    (B) $663
    (C) $757
    (D) $4,293

14. A landscaper recommended a mix of 3 1/2 pounds of rye grass seed and 3/4 pound of blue grass seed. If the lawn needs 5 1/4 pounds of rye grass seed, how many pounds of blue grass seed is needed?

    (A) 3/8 lb
    (B) 1 1/8 lb
    (C) 1 1/2 lb
    (D) 4 1/3 lb

Use this chart to answer Question 15.

Diameter	Circumference
2	6.28
3	9.42
4	12.56
5	15.70

15. The table above shows the diameter and circumference of several circles. Which of the graphs below best represents this data?

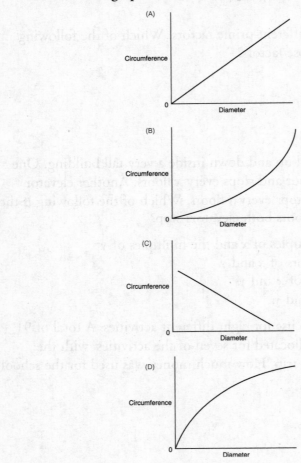

16. Cubes one centimeter on a side are used to form a square pyramidal shape. The bottom square of the pyramid measures six cubes on a side. The top of the pyramid shape has a single centimeter cube. How many centimeter cubes are used to make the pyramid?

(A) 81
(B) 91
(C) 100
(D) 216

Use this coordinate grid to answer Question 17.

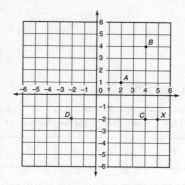

17. Point *X* is on a line with a slope of –1, meaning that which of the other points is also on that line?

(A) *A*

(B) *B*

(C) *C*

(D) *D*

Use this diagram to answer Question 18.

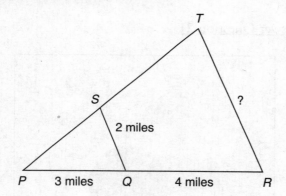

18. In the diagram, $\overline{SQ}$ is parallel to $\overline{TR}$. How long is $\overline{TR}$?

(A) $1.\overline{5}$

(B) 2.3

(C) $2.\overline{6}$

(D) 5

19. The area of a garden is 12 square yards. How many square feet is that?

    (A) 36 ft²
    (B) 72 ft²
    (C) 108 ft²
    (D) 120 ft²

Use this table to answer the question below.

January	February	March	April	May	June	July	August	September	October	November	December
3	7	6	4	8	7	8	6	4	3	2	2

20. The table above shows the amount of precipitation each month, to the nearest inch. What is the median of these precipitation amounts?

    (A) 3
    (B) 4
    (C) 5
    (D) 6

Citizenship and Social Science

Use this map to answer Question 21.

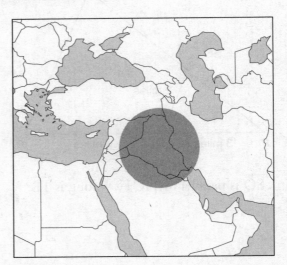

21. The shaded area on the map shown above best represents the location of which of the following ancient civilizations?

    (A) Egypt New Kingdom
    (B) Hellenistic Greece
    (C) Kush Kingdom
    (D) Mesopotamia

22. When Christopher Columbus sailed, he

   (A) never returned to Europe from his explorations.
   (B) first established a settlement in what is now the state of North Carolina.
   (C) never reached the mainland of North America.
   (D) first established a settlement in what is now the state of Virginia.

Use this excerpt from the Constitution of Article II, Section 1 to answer Question 23.

Article. II.

[Section 1.] The executive Power shall be vested in a President of the United States of America. He shall hold his Office during the Term of four Years, and, together with the Vice President, chosen for the same Term, be elected, as follows:

Each State shall appoint, in such Manner as the Legislature thereof may direct, a Number of Electors, equal to the whole Number of Senators and Representatives to which the State may be entitled in the Congress: but no Senator or Representative or Person holding an Office of Trust or Profit under the United States, shall be appointed an Elector.

23. What is the impact of Article II, Section 1, on the election of the President of the United States of America?

   (A) The President of the United States is elected directly by the people of the United States.
   (B) The President of the United States is elected by a majority of the states.
   (C) The President of the United States can be elected by less than a majority of the voters.
   (D) The number of presidential electors is equal to the number of representatives.

24. The Declaration of Independence featured six self-evident truths, including

   (A) the right of the people to alter or abolish a destructive government.
   (B) equality of all who were not slaves.
   (C) freedom of religion, speech, press, assembly, and petition.
   (D) the right to bear arms.

Use this map to answer Question 25.

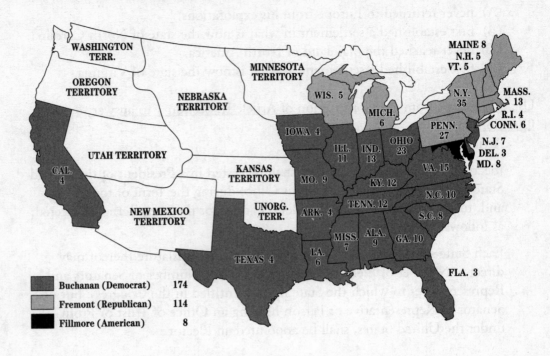

1856 Election Map

25. Which of the following conclusions can reasonably be drawn from the map above?

    (A) Were it not for Texas and California, Fremont would have won the election.

    (B) Buchanan was a strong supporter of the rebel cause.

    (C) Fremont was favored by those living in the northernmost states

    (D) Fremont was favored by the states that fought for the Union in the Civil War.

26. In understanding the impact of the Civil War on all Americans, it is worth noting that

    (A) more than six million prisoners were held in northern and southern camps.

    (B) the entire towns of Gettysburg and Atlanta were devastated and their entire populations were killed.

    (C) just as many men as women were killed during the war.

    (D) one in every thirty Americans was killed or wounded.

27. The Jim Crow South emerged following Reconstruction in part because of

    (A) the Supreme Court's decision in the *Amistad* Case that freed the slaves held on the ship.
    (B) the Supreme Court's decision in *Plessy v. Ferguson* that ruled separate but equal accommodations were legal.
    (C) the Supreme Court's decision in *Marbury v. Madison* that established the Court's right to rule that federal actions were unconstitutional.
    (D) the Supreme Court's decision in *Brown v. Board of Education* that essentially overturned the *Plessy v. Ferguson* ruling.

Use this map to answer Question 28.

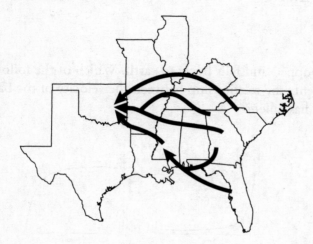

28. The map above best shows what events between the Revolutionary and Civil Wars?

    (A) The migration of settlers from the East Coast toward California
    (B) The forced removal of Native Americans to Oklahoma
    (C) The establishment of railroads from the East to the Midwest
    (D) The first wagon train trails to jumping-off points in the Midwest.

29. After the slave ship *Amistad* was seized by the American Coast Guard in 1839,

    (A) the Supreme Court ruled that the Africans aboard the ship were the property of their owners.
    (B) authorities learned that slaves aboard had revolted, killing several crew members.
    (C) the current president Van Buren and the past president Adams sided with the slave owners.
    (D) the Africans from the ship were given land to settle on in upstate New York.

30. Which of the following shows the correct order of listed events in United States history?

    I. Reconstruction
    II. Sherman's march to the sea
    III. Surrender at the Appomattox Courthouse
    IV. Approval of the XIII Amendment to the Constitution of the United States

    (A) I, II, III, IV
    (B) II, III, IV, I
    (C) II, I, III, IV
    (D) IV, II, III, I

Science

31. A ball is dropped and falls freely to earth. Which of the following graphs best represents the relationship between the velocity of the ball compared to the time it has fallen?

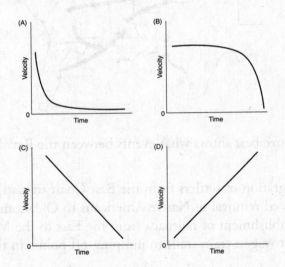

32. A green plant is placed in a terrarium and subjected to continuous light and to watering. Which of the following can we be sure will happen as a result of photosynthesis?

    (A) The plant will produce oxygen.
    (B) The plant will produce carbon dioxide.
    (C) The plant will produce water.
    (D) The plant will produce carbon monoxide.

Use this diagram to answer Question 33.

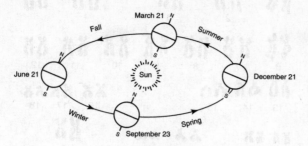

Seasons in the Southern Hemisphere

33. The diagram above demonstrates that seasons on earth are due to

    (A) the earth's rotation.
    (B) the distance from the earth to the sun.
    (C) the earth's tilt.
    (D) the earth's revolution.

34. When describing the mass of an object, it is most appropriate to say that

    (A) the mass of an object cannot change.
    (B) the weight of an object is proportional to its mass.
    (C) if two objects have the same specific gravity, they have the same mass.
    (D) an object with a given mass always weighs the same.

35. When a white light is refracted through a prism, it can split into many colors, like the colors of a rainbow, showing that

    (A) the colors appear only when light is refracted through a triangular object.
    (B) the prism has a colored filter that separates out these colors.
    (C) white light is formed by a combination of all these colors.
    (D) if all these colors were refracted through a prism, a white light would come out.

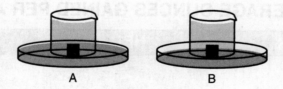

A   B

36. Identical beakers above each contain the same amount of water. The different solid objects placed in the beakers cause the overflow. The objects weigh exactly the same amount. What is the most likely explanation for the differing amounts of overflow?

    (A) The object in beaker A has more mass.
    (B) The object in beaker B is denser.
    (C) The object in beaker A is denser.
    (D) The object in beaker B has more mass.

37. What conclusion could you reach about the person whose chromosomes are shown above?

   (A) The person is a man.
   (B) The person is a woman.
   (C) The person has an abnormal gene.
   (D) The person has more genes than are usually found in humans.

38. Which of the following represents the correct sequence of events that happen during photosynthesis?

   I. CO_2 and water are broken down.
   II. Carbohydrates are formed.
   III. Sunlight is absorbed by chlorophyll.
   IV. A plant emits O_2.
   (A) I, II, III, IV
   (B) I, III, II, IV
   (C) III, I, II, IV
   (D) II, IV, I, III

Use this table to answer Question 39.

AVERAGE OUNCES GAINED PER ANIMAL		
Week	HF1	HF2
1	4	9
2	3	4
3	2	3
4	1	2
5	1	2
6	1	1

39. An experiment is set up to determine the effects of a new hamster food HF2 compared to the effects of a current hamster food HF1. Each group receives the same quantity of food and the same attention. From the data in the table, choose the best conclusion for the experiment.

    (A) The HF2 group gained more weight.
    (B) The HF1 group lived longer.
    (C) The HF2 group obtained more protein.
    (D) The HF1 group received better nutrition.

40. A scientist working in the Sierra Nevada comes across some hail that has just fallen. The scientist cuts a piece of hail in half and finds a series of rings much like tree rings. What information could the scientist obtain from the approximate number of rings?

    (A) How long the hailstone had been in the atmosphere
    (B) How long the hailstone was in space before falling to earth
    (C) How many miles above the surface of the earth the hailstone was before it began to fall
    (D) How many times the hailstone was blown from a lower to a higher altitude

ANSWERS

BIOLOGY AND GENERAL SCIENCE

Biology
Biology and General Science

1. **(D)** 2. **(D)** 3. **(C)** 4. **(B)** 5. **(C)** 6. **(A)** 7. **(C)**
8. **(B)** 9. **(C)** 10. **(D)**

Biology: Content Knowledge—Parts 1 and 2

11. **(C)** 12. **(C)** 13. **(C)** 14. **(B)** 15. **(A)** 16. **(B)** 17. **(D)**
18. **(A)**

General Science
General Science: Content Knowledge—Parts 1 and 2

19. **(B)** 20. **(A)** 21. **(D)** 22. **(C)** 23. **(C)** 24. **(B)** 25. **(A)**
26. **(D)** 27. **(B)**

Biology: Content Essays
Biology: Pedagogy

GENERAL SCIENCE: CONTENT ESSAYS

Show your written work to a qualified professor or teacher and ask that person to rate your responses.

EARLY CHILDHOOD EDUCATION

1. **(D)** 2. **(C)** 3. **(E)** 4. **(D)** 5. **(B)** 6. **(D)**
7. **(A)** 8. **(E)** 9. **(D)** 10. **(A)** 11. **(C)** 12. **(B)**

ENGLISH

English Language and Literature

1. **(D)** 2. **(B)** 3. **(D)** 4. **(D)** 5. **(B)** 6. **(B)** 7. **(A)**
8. **(C)** 9. **(C)** 10. **(D)**

Language, Literature, and Composition: Content Knowledge

11. **(A)** 12. **(B)** 13. **(D)** 14. **(A)** 15. **(D)** 16. **(C)** 17. **(C)**
18. **(A)** 19. **(D)** 20. **(A)**

English Language, Literature, and Composition: Essays
English Language, Literature, and Composition: Pedagogy

Show your written work to a qualified professor or teacher and ask that person to rate your responses.

FRENCH

French

1. **(C)** 2. **(C)** 3. **(C)** 4. **(D)** 5. **(C)** 6. **(C)**
7. **(B)** 8. **(A)** 9. **(C)** 10. **(D)** 11. **(A)** 12. **(D)**

ERROR ANALYSIS

Line	Error	Correction
13	passée	passé
14	a	est
15	août 10	le 10 août
16	no error	
17	était	avait
18	à	en

French: Productive Language Skills

Ask a professor or a teacher of French to listen to your recording and evaluate it.

FUNDAMENTAL SUBJECTS: CONTENT KNOWLEDGE

1. **(B)**   2. **(C)**   3. **(C)**   4. **(C)**   5. **(C)**   6. **(B)**   7. **(C)**
8. **(D)**   9. **(B)**   10. **(C)**   11. **(A)**   12. **(A)**   13. **(A)**   14. **(A)**
15. **(A)**   16. **(B)**   17. **(A)**   18. **(C)**   19. **(C)**   20. **(C)**   21. **(D)**
22. **(C)**   23. **(C)**   24. **(A)**   25. **(C)**   26. **(D)**   27. **(B)**   28. **(B)**
29. **(B)**   30. **(B)**   31. **(D)**   32. **(A)**   33. **(C)**   34. **(B)**   35. **(C)**
36. **(B)**   37. **(B)**   38. **(B)**   39. **(A)**   40. **(D)**

CHAPTER 16

Assessments in Mathematics, Social Studies, Spanish, Special Education, and Education of Exceptional Students

PREPARATION TIPS

Read the following Introduction. Then go over Preparation Tips at the beginning of each section you review. Read the test descriptions and take the practice test questions for the tests you have to take.

INTRODUCTION

This chapter reviews Subject Assessments and Specialty Area Tests in the areas listed above. Most of the tests are multiple choice, but a number of the Subject Assessments require a constructed-response, short-essay, answer. Each state has its own testing requirements. Check with the state certification office to confirm the requirements. The phone numbers for state certification offices are given also in Chapter 17.

Mathematics

TEST INFO BOX

Read this section if you are taking one of these tests.

Mathematics Content Knowledge (0061)
50 multiple-choice questions, graphing calculator required, 2 hours

Mathematics: Proofs, Models, and Problems—Part 1 (0063)
4 basic—1 proof, 1 model, 2 problems, graphing calculator required, 1 hour

Mathematics Pedagogy (0065)
3 essay questions, calculators prohibited, 1 hour

PREPARATION TIPS

Chapter 2, "Test-Preparation and Test-Taking Strategies," will help you prepare for the multiple-choice tests.

Use the following test description(s) as a study guide. They provide important information about test content, format, and scoring. Complete and score the practice test questions to get a feel for the type of questions you will encounter. The practice questions do not represent the full range of questions on a test. The answers to all practice questions are at the end of the chapter.

TEST DESCRIPTIONS

Mathematics Content Knowledge (0061)

The 50 multiple-choice items on this test cover the following areas. The percentages reflect the approximate number of questions drawn from each area. These questions are typically more difficult than the ones found on the older specialty area test and may require the use of a scientific calculator.

- *Arithmetic, Algebra, Geometry, Trigonometry, and Analytic Geometry (34 percent)*

  Number systems including complex numbers, properties, elementary groups, factors, multiples, and primes; ratio, proportion, percent and elementary statistics, measures of central tendency, and the binomial theorem; evaluate expressions, formulas, and equations; graph and solve equations, inequalities, and systems of equations and inequalities; show geometric representations of algebraic principles; solve problems using two- and three-dimensional geometric figures and their parts; quadrilaterals and their relationships; perimeter, area, and volume of two- and three-dimensional figures; problem solving using the properties of geometric figures including triangles, polygons, circles, and the Pythagorean theorem; motion geometry and problem solving using motion geometry; construction of geometric figures with a straight edge and compass; the six trigonometric ratios in degrees and radians including period, amplitude, phase, displacement, and asymptotes, as well as special angles, identities, and applications and the trigonometric form of complex numbers; trigonometric functions of $x/2$, $2x$, $x + y$, and $x - y$ including applications; solve equations and inequalities involving trigonometric functions; polar coordinates and rectangular coordinates including dual representation of a point; the equations of lines and planes; distance in two- and three-dimensional space; conics, representing with graphs and equations.

- *Functions, Their Graphs, and Calculus (24 percent)*

Functions, mapping, and graphs; graph equations and find equations for graphs; the range, domain, intercepts, asymptotes, and other properties of functions; into and onto functions and inverses; use of functions, composite functions, and inverse functions to solve problems; limits including establishing if limits exist and finding limits, properties of limits, and limits of sequences and elementary infinite series; continuity and differentiability including identifying continuous functions; relate derivative, limit and slope of a function; differentiate and integrate including numerical approximations, improper integrals, and the process of integration; functions including maxima, minima, and problem solving; l'Hopital's rule, mean value theorem, and the fundamental theorem of calculus; tests for convergence and divergence.

- *Probability and Statistics, Discrete Mathematics, Linear Algebra, Computer Science, Reasoning, and Modeling (42 percent)*

Organize and graph data; discrete probability and outcomes; discrete probability problems and problems involving the binomial distribution; calculation and application measures of central tendency and deviation; probability distributions including normal and chi-square; identification of a valid test to accept or reject a hypothesis; sets and operations on sets; logic including symbolic logic and diagrams; permutations and combinations; other number bases; linear programs; properties of binary operations including reflexive, symmetric, and transitive; recursive and closed form of functions; operations with scalars, vectors, and matrices; matrices including inverses, linear transformations, and linear equations; function of hardware and software; computer programs written in a logical code but not a knowledge of any programming language; model real world or abstract situations; estimating answers and awareness of the reasonableness of results; determination and use of problem-solving strategies; axioms and axiomatic systems; mathematical improbability or impossibility such as, until recently, the four-color theorem and trisecting an angle.

Mathematics Proofs, Models, and Problems—Part 1 (0063 and 0064)

This 1-hour short-answer test examines your knowledge on the preceding topics. You are asked to demonstrate your knowledge of mathematics and not just pick the correct answer from among a list of choices. The test requires a graphing calculator.

This is a basic mathematics test devoted to algebra, analytic geometry, functions and their graphs, discrete probability and statistics, and discrete mathematics.

It has four exercises including a proof, a model, and two problems.

Mathematics Pedagogy (0065)

The 1-hour test includes three essay questions and measures your knowledge of high school mathematics planning and pedagogy. Calculators are prohibited.

The areas covered on this test include mathematics scope, mathematics performance and achievement assessment, sequence and curricular materials, prerequisite skills or competencies, problem-solving strategies, remediation, teaching strategies and teaching materials, classroom management, and teaching to various socioeconomic, cultural, ethnic, and gender groups.

PRACTICE QUESTIONS

On the Web

Additional test questions are available free at the ETS Web site. Visit the Tests at a Glance portion of the Praxis Web site at *www.ets.org/praxis/prxtest.html* and click on the title of the test you are preparing for.

Mathematics

Choose the correct answer.

1. An integer n is divisible by both 2 and 3. This means that there is some integer x such that

   (A) $x/n = 6$.
   (B) $x/n = 3$.
   (C) $(n)(2) = x$.
   (D) $(x)(6) = n$.

2. A student hands in this work to show the steps used to solve the following equation. At which step did the student make an error?

$$-4x < x + 6$$

(A) $-4x - x < x - x + 6$
(B) $-5x < 6$
(C) $-5x/5 < 6/5$
(D) $x < -6/5$

3. A square located on the Cartesian plane is rotated 180° around the origin. The same result could be accomplished by

(A) flipping the square about the *x*-axis.
(B) flipping the square about the *y*-axis.
(C) flipping the square about the square's own diagonal.
(D) flipping the square about the *y*-axis and then the *x*-axis.

4. The sum of $1 + 3 + 5 + 7 + \ldots + (2n - 1)$ equals

(A) $(2n - 1)(2n + 1)$.
(B) $n(2n - 1)$.
(C) n^2.
(D) $(n - 1)^2$.

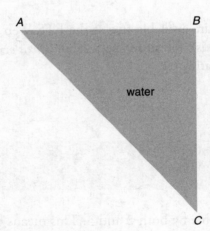

5. Engineers want to build a bridge from point *A* to point *C* above. Angle *B* is a right angle; the length of $\overline{AB}$ is 2.5 kilometers; the length of $\overline{CB}$ is 4.5 kilometers. What angle measure will the engineers use for angle *A*?

(A) 60°
(B) 29°
(C) 56°
(D) 61°

6. Experience shows that there is an even chance that an individual tire on a car will blow out during a race. Using this information, what is the probability that *no* tire will blow out?

   (A) 1
   (B) 0
   (C) $\frac{1}{16}$
   (D) $\frac{1}{8}$

7. There is an Abelian group *F* with an operation $\odot$. If *x*, *y*, and *z* are elements of *F*, which of the following is true for this group, but NOT true for a non-Abelian group?

   (A) $x \odot y$ is an element of *F*.
   (B) $x \odot (y \odot z)$ is an element of *F*.
   (C) $x \odot (y \odot z) = (x \odot y) \odot z$.
   (D) $(y \odot z) = (z \odot y)$.

8. Which of the following best describes the mapping of even integers to all integers under the operation of multiplication?

   (A) 1 to 1
   (B) Into
   (C) Onto
   (D) Monotonic

9. A bowling ball with diameter of 1 foot rotates 30 times along the ball return. About how far did the bowling ball travel?

   (A) About 82 ft
   (B) About 48 ft
   (C) About 30 ft
   (D) About 94 ft

10. Which of the following would most mathematics educators credit with establishing problem-solving strategies?

    (A) Jean Piaget
    (B) Seymour Papert
    (C) Zoltan Dienes
    (D) George Polya

11. A 6 foot tall person casts an 11.4 foot long shadow and a nearby pole casts a 28.5 foot long shadow. How tall is the pole?

    (A) 16 ft
    (B) 13.1 ft
    (C) 16.2 ft
    (D) 15 ft

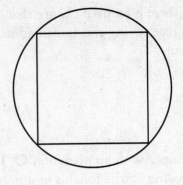

12. As shown above, a square with an area of 16 cm² is inscribed in a circle. What is the approximate area of the circle?

(A) 25.12 cm²
(B) 48.16 cm²
(C) 12.56 cm²
(D) 16.83 cm²

13. A line segment on the Cartesian plane is 5 units long and has an endpoint at (6, 4). Which of the following could be the other endpoint?

(A) (6, 10)
(B) (11, 3)
(C) (10, 1)
(D) (8, 2)

14. Which of the following is strictly increasing?

(A) $\int\limits^{12} (x+1)^2 - 4$

(B) $\int\limits^{+2} (x+1)^2 - 4$

(C) $\int\limits^{-3} (x+1)^2 - 4$

(D) $\int\limits_0^1 (x+1)^2 - 4$

15. [0 - 1 - 2 - 3 - 4 - 5 - 6 - 7]

     A game piece is placed on the 3. A fair coin is flipped. The piece moves one space left with every head and one space right with every tail. What is the probability that the piece will reach 0 *before* it reaches 7?

     (A) $\dfrac{3}{10}$

     (B) $\dfrac{3}{4}$

     (C) $\dfrac{4}{7}$

     (D) $\dfrac{2}{3}$

16. $A = \{A, B, C\}$ $B = \{w, x, y, z\}$

     Set *C* will consist of two elements from *A* and two elements from *B*. In how many different ways can *C* be constructed?

     (A) 12
     (B) 4
     (C) 18
     (D) 8

17. Review this program.

     [1] Input any number *X*
     [2] If *X* ≥ 1 then go to Step [5]
     [3] Print [enter another number]
     [4] Go to Step [1]
     [5] Add *X* and 1 − *X*

     The result of Step 5 is always

     (A) *X*.
     (B) 1.
     (C) X^2.
     (D) 1/*X*.

18. An ice cream store has 23 different flavors of ice cream. In how many different ways can you select flavors to put into a milkshake, including no flavor at all?

     (A) 2^{23}
     (B) 23!
     (C) $23 \cdot 23$
     (D) 23^{23}

Mathematics: Proofs Models, and Problem—Part 1

1. A rectangle 20 cm long and 10 cm wide is drawn on a piece of paper. A toothpick 5 cm long is dropped randomly so that at least a part of it is inside the rectangle. What is the probability that the toothpick will touch the boundary of the rectangle?

2. A topological graph consisting of dots and connecting segments is drawn on a piece of paper. Explain how to determine whether or not the graph can be drawn in one continuous motion without retracing. Give examples.

3. Give an example of two isomorphic Abelian groups. Explain why these structures are groups and demonstrate the isomorphism of the groups.

Mathematics: Pedagogy

Explain how you would present a first lesson on the Pythagorean theorem to a class of middle school students. Your plan should include a motivation, the steps and procedures you would follow to help students learn, practice exercises, and assessment techniques.

Social Studies

TEST INFO BOX

Read this section if you are taking one of these tests.

Social Studies

Content Knowledge (0181)
   130 multiple-choice questions, 2 hours

Analytical Essays (0082)
   2 essay questions, 1 hour

Interpretation of Materials (0083)
   5 two-part essay questions, 1 hour

Pedagogy (0084)
   2 five-part case study essay questions, 1 hour

Interpretation and Analysis
   5 short-answer questions and 2 essay questions, 2 hours

PREPARATION TIPS

Chapter 2, "Test-Preparation and Test-Taking Strategies," will help you prepare for the multiple-choice tests and essay items.

Use the following test description(s) as a study guide. They provide important information about test content, format, and scoring. Complete and score the practice test questions to get a feel for the type of questions you will encounter. The practice questions do not represent the full range of questions on a test. The answers to all practice questions are at the end of the chapter.

Social Studies: Content Knowledge (0081)

This 2-hour test has 130 multiple-choice questions in the following areas.

- *United States History (22 percent)*—Native Americans, American settlement and colonies and the Revolution, early Republic, Western settlement and the new nation, slavery and the Civil War, modern America, progressivism and the World Wars, new deal, space age, the United States since 1980, and North American geography

- *World History (22 percent)*—prehistory, Greek civilization, Roman civilization, Persian civilization, Chinese civilization, South America including Mayan and Incan people and culture, European and Japanese feudalism, Islamic people and culture, Renaissance, Reformation, exploration, colonization and European imperialism, industrialization, and the world since 1900

- *Government (16 percent)*—Constitution, governments (federal, state, and local), elections and the electoral college, and other political systems

- *Behavioral Science (10 percent)*—human growth and development, group behavior, personality, and cognitive development and perception; social groups, organizations and movements, the family and its impact on society, relations among different races, and ethnic and gender groups; development of human culture and organizations, rituals, and family

- *Geography (15 percent)*—reading and interpreting maps, continental features, climate and weather, and human geography

- *Economics (15 percent)*—macro- and microeconomics, fiscal and monetary policy, foreign trade, opportunity cost, balance of payments, budget deficits, and other current issues

Social Studies: Analytical Essays (0082)

This 1-hour test has two interdisciplinary essay questions.

The question asks you to interpret and analyze issues. Each question will draw on at least two of the fields covered in the Content Knowledge test. One question will be about United States issues and the other will be about world issues. One question will incorporate a graphic aid such as a map or diagram and one question will normally be about American, Latin American, African, Asian, or Oceanic culture.

Social Studies: Interpretation of Materials (0083)

This 1-hour test has five two-part essay questions, which are responses to social studies materials. These questions may ask you to respond to a chart, graph, map, quote, or excerpt. There is one question each from United States history, world history, government, economics, and geography. The subject matter for these questions is the same as that for the Content Knowledge test. At least one question will deal with cultural diversity.

Social Studies: Pedagogy (0084)

This 1-hour test has five two-part essay questions about two case studies.

The first question gives you a choice between a United States history or a world history topic and asks you to plan a 2-week unit for that topic. You must complete the following five steps, but you do not write an entire unit.

- Identify the key unit topic and explain why it is key (10 percent).
- Identify two other key topics (5 percent).
- Identify a key social studies concept and explain why it is important (10 percent).
- Present an analogy or metaphor that helps students understand the key concept (15 percent).
- Write two challenging discussion questions to help students understand the concept (10 percent).

The second question gives you a choice among units in geography, economics, or government and asks you to plan a single class lesson. You must complete the following five steps, but you do not present a complete plan.

- Identify the key unit topic and explain why it is key (10 percent).
- Write an objective for the lesson plan (10 percent).
- Explain how you would teach the lesson (15 percent).
- Present an essay question to assess students' mastery of the objective (5 percent).
- Describe an alternative, nonexamination, assessment question (10 percent).

PRACTICE QUESTIONS

On the Web

Additional test questions are available free at the ETS Web site. Visit the Tests at a Glance portion of the Praxis Web site at *www.ets.org/praxis/prxtest.html* and click on the title of the test you are preparing for.

Social Studies

Choose the correct answer.

1. Which of the following best describes European colonization of the Western Hemisphere?

   (A) There was no organized civilization in the Western Hemisphere until European colonization.
   (B) Columbus was the first explorer to reach North America.
   (C) Spain was the only country to explore the Western Hemisphere before 1600.
   (D) A number of expeditions visited North America prior to 1500, and they encountered advanced Native American cultures.

2. The Fourth Amendment of the United States Constitution guarantees what right(s)?

   (A) Freedom of religion, speech, press, assembly, and petition
   (B) Warrants and probable cause are needed for search and seizure
   (C) Right to a jury trial
   (D) Rights not spelled out are retained by the people

3. Which war was triggered by an incident involving the Battleship *Maine*?

   (A) Spanish-American War
   (B) World War II
   (C) World War I
   (D) French and Indian War

4. Which of the following best describes the Buddhist religion or its founder?

   (A) Buddha, its founder, was a Chinese philosopher born around 550 B.C. whose thoughts largely concerned conformity and respectful behavior.
   (B) Buddhism is a "sect" that does not believe in a human soul and worships animals.
   (C) Buddha, its founder, was an Indian who preached nirvana and emphasized rejection of worldly and material concerns.
   (D) Buddhism developed in India where its followers worship many gods including Brahma, Vishnu, and Shiva.

5. All the following statements are true about the American Civil War EXCEPT

   (A) in 1862 Lincoln issued the Emancipation Proclamation, freeing slaves in Confederate States.
   (B) General Lee surrendered to General Grant at Appomattox Court House, Virginia.
   (C) the South dominated the early battles of the war.
   (D) the English and French lent support to the South, in hopes of later gaining colonies in a weaker, disunified America.

6. The Nineteenth Amendment, which passed in 1920, guaranteed

   (A) equality of women and men.
   (B) a woman's right to citizenship.
   (C) a woman's right to consume liquor.
   (D) a woman's right to vote.

7. Which of the following statements best describes Japanese society prior to 1900?

   (A) The Japanese were a largely nomadic people.
   (B) From around 1150 A.D. on, the Shoguns, not emperors, headed Japan's government system.
   (C) Christianity became the dominant religion early in Japan's history, when introduced there by Marco Polo.
   (D) The Ming dynasty ruled for almost 300 years, from the 1300s to the mid 1600s.

8. Most anthropologists would agree that the three primary determinants of culture are

   (A) food, energy, and technology.
   (B) religion, government, and science.
   (C) family, economy, and government.
   (D) technology, government, and economy.

9. Which would the psychologist Kohlberg most likely give as the reason for the conventional morality of an adolescent female?

   (A) Duty to other living beings due to social contract
   (B) Fear of punishment
   (C) Approval of others
   (D) Consideration of higher principles

10. What historic decisions were made at the Yalta conference?

   (A) World War II Allies planned the D-Day invasions.
   (B) World War II "war criminals" were tried in an international court resulting in the death sentence for many Nazi leaders.
   (C) The Japanese officially surrendered, ending World War II.
   (D) Churchill, Roosevelt, and Stalin made agreements about the partition of post-war Europe and Germany.

11. What was the basic tenent of supply-side economics, expounded during the Reagan administration?

    (A) Manufacturers should increase supplies, thus lowering prices and stimulating the economy.
    (B) Tax cuts would result in more investment and, in turn, investments would create more jobs.
    (C) Increased taxes would allow an increase in federal programs, supplying Americans with much-needed goods and services.
    (D) Tax increases should be used to subsidize industry.

12. Aristophanes, Euripides, and Sophocles all had WHAT in common?

    (A) All were Greek philosophers during the Classic Age.
    (B) All were characters in the Greek tragedies in the Classic Age.
    (C) All were Greek authors of works written in the Classic Age.
    (D) All were Greek tutors of the conqueror Alexander the Great.

13. Most historians would agree that the event that marked the beginning of the Reformation occurred

    (A) when Mary I of England (Bloody Mary) killed many Protestants during her reign.
    (B) in Italy during the time of the Renaissance.
    (C) when Puritans sailed for the New World and established Protestant colonies.
    (D) when Martin Luther nailed his 95 theses to a church door in Germany.

14. All these countries were members of the Quadruple Alliance, which finally defeated Napoleon at Waterloo, EXCEPT

    (A) Italy.
    (B) England.
    (C) Russia.
    (D) Prussia.

15. Which of the following defines a tax rate that increases as income increases?

    (A) Retroactive
    (B) Proportional
    (C) Progressive
    (D) Income-neutral

16. Which social philosophers would most likely have agreed with the statement "government exists as a contract between the governor and the governed"?

    (A) Marx and Lenin
    (B) Kant and Keirkegaard
    (C) Socrates and Plato
    (D) Hobbes and Locke

17. All the following authors are considered part of the "Romantic" movement in literature EXCEPT

   (A) Emerson.
   (B) Pound.
   (C) Dostoyevsky.
   (D) Byron.

18. On the world map below, which area was NOT part of the British Empire prior to World War II?

   (A) 1
   (B) 2
   (C) 3
   (D) 4

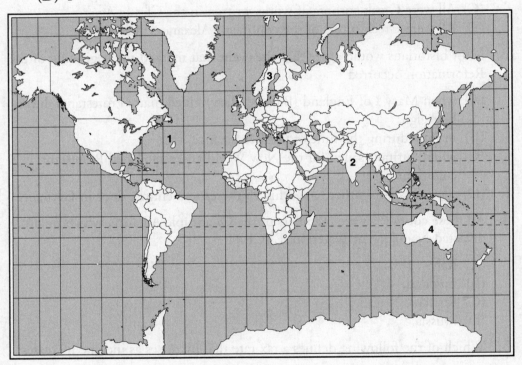

19. Which of the following is the most accurate interpretation of how Copernicus portrayed the universe?

   (A) The sun, earth, and moon are surrounded by other planets.
   (B) The earth is surrounded by many stars (including the sun).
   (C) The earth is surrounded by other planets.
   (D) All planets revolve around the sun.

20. The Third Estate and Committee of Public Safety are associated with what conflict?

   (A) The Russian Revolution
   (B) The French Revolution
   (C) The English Civil War
   (D) The 100 Years War

21. Which term was defined by Aristotle as "government by a few?"

    (A) Aristocracy
    (B) Democracy
    (C) Republicanism
    (D) Monarchy

22. Which of the following is the task of a physical anthropologist?

    (A) Investigating the social systems of the people of biblical times
    (B) Tracing the roots and beginnings of the English language
    (C) Investigating the ancient temples of Egypt
    (D) Investigating links between chimpanzees and human beings

23. All the following were New Deal plans under FDR EXCEPT

    (A) Civilian Conservation Corps.
    (B) Securities and Exchange Commission.
    (C) Federal Income Tax.
    (D) Tennessee Valley Authority.

24. What was the cause of the Chinese–British Opium War?

    (A) The Chinese resisted importation of opium into China.
    (B) The British resisted importation of opium into Britain.
    (C) The British resisted exportation of opium from Britain.
    (D) The Chinese resisted tax on opium imported into China.

25. Which of the following is one of the "self-evident truths" found in the Declaration of Independence?

    (A) Freedom of religion
    (B) Right to bear arms
    (C) Rights of government come from the governed
    (D) Secure domestic tranquillity

Social Studies: Analytical Essays

Drawing on your knowledge of economics and the political air of the times, explain the impact of the Sugar Act, Quartering Act, and Stamp Act on the events leading up to the American Revolutionary War. In addition, explain how reactions to these and other similar Acts, which led to the Revolution, affected the way the United States government was structured after the Revolutionary War.

Social Studies: Pedagogy

Course: United States History
Unit: Civil War

Course: European History
Unit: Renaissance

Select one of the two options. Assume that you are in the process of creating a 10-day unit of study. Answer the questions to help explain how you would teach the unit.

1. Identify a major topic essential for teaching the unit.

2. Identify two other important topics to be included in the unit.

3. Distinguish one important social studies concept that should be included in this unit and that is fundamental to one or more of the subject matter topics you identified in Questions 1 and 2.

4. Use an analogy or historical parallel that would help you explain the concept to students.

5. Present for class discussion two questions that would help bring out the important topics about the concept you have identified. Both questions should ask for more than mere facts. They should encourage thinking that incorporates many disciplines of social studies and historical concepts.

Social Studies: Interpretation of Materials

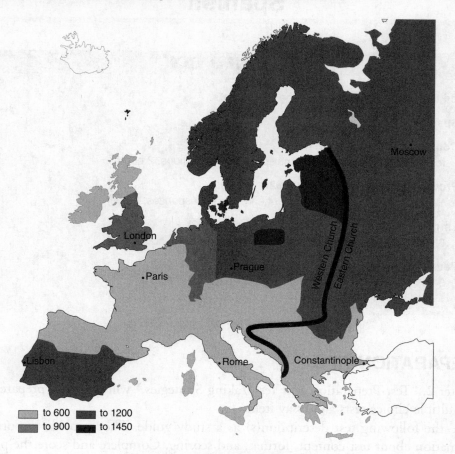

Christianity in Europe and Asia to 1450

Legend:
- to 600
- to 900
- to 1200
- to 1450

1. Describe the map and what it indicates about trends in religion between 500 A.D. and 1500 A.D.

2. Based on your knowledge of Middle Eastern and European history, describe the events and factors that contributed to the distribution of Christianity during this time.

3. "It is the power to regulate; that is, to prescribe the rule by which commerce is to be governed . . . if it is interstate commerce that feels the pinch, it does not matter how local the operation which applies the squeeze . . ."

   Briefly explain the principle of government expounded by the quotation, including its possible basis in the United States Constitution.

Subject Assessments

Spanish

TEST INFO BOX

Read this section if you are taking these tests.

Spanish:

Content Knowledge (0191)
 four timed sections with 140 multiple-choice questions, 2 hours

Productive Language Skills (0192)
 12 exercises, 9 spoken and 3 written Spanish responses, 1 hour

Linguistic, Literary, and Cultural Analysis (0193)
 3 essay questions with written Spanish responses, 1 hour

Pedagogy (0194)
 3 essay questions with written Spanish responses, 1 hour

PREPARATION TIPS

Chapter 2, "Test-Preparation and Test-Taking Strategies," will help you prepare for the multiple-choice tests and essay items.

Use the following test description(s) as a study guide. They provide important information about test content, format, and scoring. Complete and score the practice test questions to get a feel for the type of questions you will encounter. The practice questions do not represent the full range of questions on a test. The answers to all practice questions are at the end of the chapter.

TEST DESCRIPTIONS

Spanish: Content Knowledge (0191)

The 2-hour test has 140 multiple-choice questions in four separately timed sections. The questions consist of recorded and written questions in Spanish and written English questions about teaching Spanish and Spanish culture.

- *Listening in Spanish (28 percent)*—answer multiple-choice questions in Spanish about recorded Spanish passages

- *Reading in Spanish (25 percent)*—answer multiple-choice questions in Spanish about written Spanish passages

- *Spanish Language Structure and Expression (29 percent)*—identify errors from recorded Spanish speech, identify errors from written passages, and select correct passage for passages with missing elements

- *Spanish Culture Questions in English and Spanish (19 percent)*—answer questions about historical and cultural background and sociolinguistics of culture of Spanish-speaking parts of the world (Questions are roughly evenly divided between Spanish and English.)

Spanish: Productive Language Skills (0192)

This 1-hour test is partitioned into two 30-minute sections. The test consists of three written and nine spoken exercises. Spoken responses are recorded on tape, and you are given several warm-up exercises before beginning the scored section.

- *Spoken* (all responses are in Spanish). Read a 150-word passage with correct pronunciation; answer written questions to describe a picture; tell a story based on a picture; role-play a response to a situation described in English; give instructions based on a picture; describe a situation presented in English; defend a statement printed in English; deliver a brief talk based on a situation printed in English; paraphrase a spoken Spanish passage

- *Written.* Write questions you would ask during an interview; write a brief passage describing a set of pictures; write a short letter

Spanish: Linguistic, Literary, and Cultural Analysis (0193)

This 1-hour test is partitioned into three timed sections. The three short-essay questions call for written Spanish responses. The first section asks you to find and fix written Spanish passages, the second section asks you to analyze a literary or cultural passage, and the third section asks you to write about your understanding of Spanish culture and attitudes.

- *Error Analysis (38 percent—10 minutes).* Find and correct ten errors in two Spanish passages. Errors include grammatical mistakes, poor language choice and language register errors.

- *Literary and Cultural Analysis (31 percent—35 minutes).* Read a Spanish literary passage and write an essay 150 words or longer. Your essay should discuss the Spanish culture and history reflected in the passage and the way the writer uses literary devices and language to present the main theme.

- *Spanish Culture and Attitudes (31 percent—15 minutes).* Write an essay of 100 words or more. The essay should describe Spanish culture and institutions and explain how these differ from American culture and institutions.

Spanish: Pedagogy (0194)

This 1-hour test includes three short essays in Spanish. One essay is devoted to planning; you will be asked to describe how lesson plans can be developed and about the school Spanish curriculum. The second question is devoted to teaching; you will be asked about teaching approaches and strategies appropriate for effective Spanish instruction. The final question is about assessment; you will have an opportunity to describe how to conduct an effective assessment program and how to rate and evaluate curricular materials.

PRACTICE QUESTIONS

On the Web

Additional test questions are available free at the ETS Web site. Visit the Tests at a Glance portion of the Praxis Web site at *www.ets.org/praxis/prxtest.html* and click on the title of the test you are preparing for.

Spanish

Choose the correct answer.

(You hear)

1. ¿Vamos a la playa o a las montañas?

(You read)

(A) No puedo. Perdí mis zapatos.
(B) Prefiero el ambiente de la costa del mar.
(C) Me gustan las montañas.
(D) Creo que esta idea es excellente.

Use this dialogue to answer Questions 2 and 3.

(You hear)

(Hombre)   ¿Por cuánto tiempo tenemos que esperar a nuestros hijos para que lleguen a casa?

(Mujer)   Dijeron que llegarían el aeropuerto a las seis y que nos avisarían por teléfono a esa hora.

(Hombre)   Talvez haya mucho tráfico.

(Mujer)   Bien. Vamos a esperar un poco más.

(You read)

2. Es seguro que

(A) los padres tienen poca paciencia.
(B) los hijos no volverán.
(C) va a llover.
(D) los padres van a atender a sus niños.

3. ¿Qué decidieron hacer los padres?

   (A) Ir a buscar a los hijos.
   (B) Llamar a los hijos desde el aeropuerto.
   (C) Esperar a los hijos en la casa.
   (D) Esperar un poco mas en el aeropuerto.

Use the following text to answer Questions 4 and 5.

   Patricia estaba muy alegre porque sus hijos iban a regresar a casa para celebrar su cumpleaños. Un hijo venía en avión de Los Angeles donde trabaja de programador de computadoras. Su hija mayor vivía cerca de la ciudad de Nueva York donde era profesora en la universidad. Esta hija viajaba en coche con sus dos hijos, los solos nietos de Patricia. Su hija menor es una estudiante universitaria en Arizona. Patricia le había mandado un billete de avión para que ella pudiera asistir a su fiesta.

4. ¿La última linea de la selección se refiere a la fiesta de quién?

   (A) La madre
   (B) El nieto
   (C) La hija
   (D) El hijo

5. ¿Donde viven los hijos de Patricia?

   (A) Viven en Los Angeles y en Nueva York.
   (B) Viven en Los Angeles pero estudian en Arizona.
   (C) Viven en ciudades diferentes.
   (D) Viven en Arizona pero trabajan en Los Angeles.

6. Las escuelas y clubes deportivos participan en el fútbol con grande entusiasmo. ¿Qué revisión es necesaria en esta oracíon?

   (A) Cambiar *deportivos* a *deportivas*.
   (B) Cambiar *participan* a *participen*.
   (C) Cambiar *en el fútbol* a *por el fútbol*.
   (D) Cambiar *con grande entusiasmo* a *con gran entusiasmo*.

7. Si yo _____ bastante dinero, iré a España este verano.

   (A) tengo
   (B) tenga
   (C) tuve
   (D) tendré

Use the following sentence to answer Questions 8 and 9.

Mi hogar est _____ (8) _____ en un barrio nuevo de la ciudad que es conocido (9) _____ sus buenas escuelas.

8. (A) situando
   (B) situado
   (C) situada
   (D) situar

9. (A) de
   (B) por
   (C) para
   (D) con

10. Which underlined word is an error?

    Al profesor <u>les</u> <u>quedan</u> sólo diez

            (A) (B)

    <u>exámenes</u> a <u>corregir</u>.

      (C)   (D)

11. Which of the following has the same pattern in the formation of the conditional as *salir*?

    (A) Abrir
    (B) Pedir
    (C) Venir
    (D) Oír

12. Which of the following words contains three syllables?

    (A) Veinte
    (B) Traigo
    (C) Treinta
    (D) Leía

13. In his novel *The Sun Also Rises* Ernest Hemingway popularized the annual Spanish custom of

    (A) spear fishing off the coast of Majorca.
    (B) the running of the bulls in Pamplona.
    (C) wine tasting in Madrid.
    (D) pilgrimaging to El Jardín Botánico.

Spanish: Content Knowledge

Choose the correct answer.

14. (You hear)

    Carlos, me prometiste que me ayudarás con la tarea de español pero no lo hiciste. ¿Qué te pasó?

    (You hear again)

    Carlos, me prometiste que me ayudarás con la tarea de español pero no lo hiciste. ¿Qué te pasó?

    Identify the error in the sentence.

    (A) Ayudarás
    (B) Prometiste
    (C) Hiciste
    (D) Pasó

<u>Use this passage to answer Questions 15–17.</u>

(2) Juan y su amigo Raúl llegan al cine hace media hora. (3) Esperan que tienen todavía entradas disponibles. (4) La última vez que fueron todas los billetes estaban vendidas.

15. Identify the error in sentence 2.

    (A) Su amigo
    (B) Llegan
    (C) Hace
    (D) Media hora

16. In sentence 3, the word *tienen* is used incorrectly. Which of the following is correct in the context of the passage?

    (A) Tendrán
    (B) Tendrían
    (C) Tengan
    (D) Tuvieran

17. Identify the error in sentence 4.

    (A) Lack of agreement between subject and verb
    (B) Lack of agreement between noun and adjective
    (C) Incorrect verb tense
    (D) Incorrect word order

Read the following paragraph. It contains errors in written Spanish. Underline each error and write the correct replacement in the space above. If there is no error, write No Error. There may be more than one error.

18. Diego entró en la sala de su apartamento

19. por mirar la televisión. Estas programas

20. de juegos son sus favoritas. También

21. se pasa el día leyendo y telefoneando

22. sus amigos. Se quedó en caso todo el día

23. sin saliendo.

Spanish: Productive Language Skills

Study the pictures. Then you have 2 minutes to speak and record your explanation in Spanish of how to open a soft drink can and pour out the soda.

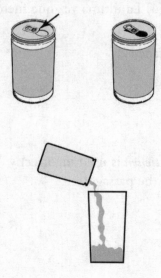

Special Education and Education of Exceptional Students

TEST INFO BOX

Read this section if you are taking one of these tests.

Special Education: Knowledge-Based Core Principles (0351)
60 multiple-choice questions, 1 hour

Special Education: Application of Core Principles Across Categories of Disability (0352)
60 multiple-choice questions, 1 hour

Education of Exceptional Students (0353)
60 multiple-choice questions, 1 hour

PREPARATION TIPS

Chapter 2, "Test-Preparation and Test-Taking Strategies," will help you prepare for the multiple-choice tests and essay items. Chapter 8, "Principles of Learning and Teaching Review," may help you prepare for this test.

Use the following test description as a study guide. It provides important information about test content, format, and scoring.

Complete and score the practice test questions at the end of this section to get a feel for the type of questions you will encounter. The practice questions do not represent the full range of questions on the test. The answers to all practice questions are at the end of the chapter.

TEST DESCRIPTIONS

Special Education: Knowledge-Based Core Principles (0351)

The 60 multiple-choice items on this one-hour test cover the following areas: Understanding Exceptionalities, Legal and Social Issues, and Delivery of Services to Students with Disabilities.

Special Education: Knowledge-Based Core Principles (0352)

The 50 multiple-choice items on this 1-hour test cover the following areas: Curriculum, Instruction, Assessment, Managing the Learning Environment, Professional Rules, Issues, and Literature.

Education of Exceptional Students (0353)

The 60 multiple-choice items on this 1-hour test cover the following areas: Understanding Exceptionalities, Legal and Societal Issues, and Delivery of Services to Students with Disabilities.

PRACTICE QUESTIONS

On the Web

Additional test questions are available free at the ETS Web site. Visit the Tests at a Glance portion of the Praxis Web site at *www.ets.org/praxis/prxtest.html* and click on the title of the test you are preparing for.

Choose the correct answer.

1. Which of the following statements best summarizes the collaborative approach to special education instruction?

   (A) The special education teacher meets with the regular classroom teachers to ensure that the same material is being covered in the resource room.
   (B) Special needs students are mainstreamed for all subjects.
   (C) The regular classroom becomes the home base for the special needs student. Special educators, other professionals, and aides work in support of the regular teachers in this environment.
   (D) The special needs students are mainstreamed for any subject that would not be affected by their disability but stay in the self-contained classroom for subjects related to their disability.

2. "Pull-out" programs for special needs students are beginning to receive much criticism. A valid criticism of this approach is that

   (A) pull-out programs stigmatize students.
   (B) pull-out programs deny students a chance for academic improvement.
   (C) special education teachers give students too much help.
   (D) students need to learn to cope on their own.

3. The Individuals with Disabilities Education Act (IDEA), 1992 was instituted primarily

   (A) because school systems could not carry out all the specifications of PL 94-142 alone.
   (B) to develop clearer specifications for the delivery of educational services to handicapped children.
   (C) to loosen the federal government's control over special education programs and services.
   (D) to exclude limited English proficiency students from the larger "handicapped" label.

4. Which of the following is NOT true about the Individualized Education Program (IEP) for special education students?

    (A) An IEP must be written for every child who receives special education services.
    (B) An IEP does not have to include methods of evaluation.
    (C) An IEP does not have to be of a specific length.
    (D) An IEP must include both long-term goals and short-term objectives.

5. An active, immature third-grade student in your class has an IQ of 125 and achievement test mathematics grade equivalency of 6.0 which puts him at the 80 percentile. You get a call from his parents asking why he is not in the Gifted and Talented program of the school. What would be your best response to their question?

    (A) He did not make the 130 IQ cutoff the school requires.
    (B) He did well, but there were still 20 students who did better and class size is limited.
    (C) His immaturity led the committee to decide he was not a good candidate.
    (D) His disruptive class behavior needs to be improved.

6. Lisa is a special needs student who is referred to your attention because she is not doing well in her English class. After looking at her records, you decide you need more specific information. You receive the teacher's permission to observe Lisa in the classroom. What should be your next step?

    (A) Find a reliable behavioral checklist.
    (B) Talk to Lisa about observing her.
    (C) Get permission from Lisa's parents.
    (D) Choose the behavior(s) to be observed.

7. In order to place a special needs student in a special education program, a proper due process must be followed including all of the following EXCEPT

    (A) parents may be represented at any meeting.
    (B) parents are fully informed of their rights.
    (C) parents have the right to object to any findings.
    (D) parents were called and told about any pending placement.

8. According to federal law, what are the ages during which handicapped persons are entitled to a free public education?

    (A) Ages 5–18
    (B) Ages 3–21
    (C) From age 5 until high school graduation
    (D) From age 3 until high school graduation

9. A student has difficulty processing spoken directions. Which of the following approaches is most likely to help the student?

    (A) Give instructions in written form.
    (B) Speak in a loud, deliberate voice.
    (C) Give directions while writing them on the chalkboard.
    (D) Give instructions in structurally simple, short sentences.

10. Students diagnosed with attention-deficit hyperactivity disorder (ADHD) are often medicated with

    (A) Valium.
    (B) Prozac.
    (C) Ritalin.
    (D) Zoloft.

11. Repeated testing of a fourth-grade student in Ray Maw's class reveals an IQ in the 110–115 range but standardized test scores that are two or more years below grade level. Which of the following is the most appropriate interpretation of these test scores?

    (A) The student is a poor test taker.
    (B) The student's achievement and potential match.
    (C) The student is gifted.
    (D) The student has a learning disability.

12. Which of the following is the appropriate placement for a fifth-grade student who has been classified learning-disabled by the Child Study Team?

    (A) Place the student in a self-contained class with other learning-disabled students and send the student out for music and art specials.
    (B) Place the student in a fifth-grade class with support from a special education teacher.
    (C) Place the student in a self-contained class with other learning-disabled students and send the student to a fifth-grade class for some subjects.
    (D) Place the student in a fifth-grade class and meet with the parents to arrange extra tutoring.

ANSWERS

MATHEMATICS

Mathematics

1. **(D)** 2. **(D)** 3. **(D)** 4. **(C)** 5. **(D)** 6. **(C)** 7. **(D)**
8. **(B)** 9. **(D)** 10. **(D)**

Mathematics: Content Knowledge

11. **(D)** 12. **(A)** 13. **(C)** 14. **(C)** 15. **(C)** 16. **(C)** 17. **(B)**
18. **(A)**

Mathematics: Proofs, Models, and Problems—Part 1
Mathematics: Pedagogy

Show your written work to a qualified professor or teacher and ask that person to rate your responses.

SOCIAL STUDIES

Social Studies

1. **(D)** 2. **(B)** 3. **(A)** 4. **(C)** 5. **(E)** 6. **(D)** 7. **(B)**
8. **(A)** 9. **(C)** 10. **(D)** 11. **(B)** 12. **(C)** 13. **(D)** 14. **(A)**
15. **(C)** 16. **(D)** 17. **(B)** 18. **(C)** 19. **(A)** 20. **(B)** 21. **(A)**
22. **(D)** 23. **(C)** 24. **(A)** 25. **(C)**

Social Studies: Analytical Essays
Social Studies: Interpretation of Materials
Social Studies: Pedagogy

Show your written work to a qualified professor or teacher and ask that person to rate your responses.

SPANISH

Spanish

1. **(B)** 2. **(D)** 3. **(C)** 4. **(A)** 5. **(C)** 6. **(D)** 7. **(A)**
8. **(B)** 9. **(B)** 10. **(B)** 11. **(C)** 12. **(D)** 13. **(B)** 14. **(A)**
15. **(B)** 16. **(C)** 17. **(B)**

Spanish: Productive Language Skills

Ask a professor of Spanish or a teacher of Spanish to listen to your recording and evaluate it.

Spanish: Linguistic, Literary, and Cultural Analysis

ERROR ANALYSIS

Line	Error	Correction
18	No error	
19	por	para
19	estas	estos
20	favoritas	favoritos
21	No error	
22	sus amigos	a sus amigos
23	saliendo	salir

SPECIAL EDUCATION AND EDUCATION OF EXCEPTIONAL STUDENTS

1. **(C)** 2. **(A)** 3. **(B)** 4. **(B)** 5. **(C)** 6. **(D)** 7. **(D)**
8. **(B)** 9. **(D)** 10. **(C)** 11. **(D)** 12. **(B)**

PART VIII

CERTIFICATION, TEST SCORES, AND CAREERS

Praxis Test Scoring and State-by-State Certification Testing Requirements with Passing Scores

---

PRAXIS TEST SCORING

Raw Scores and Scale Scores

Your raw score is the number of items you answer correctly, or the number of points you actually earn. Your scale score converts your raw score to a score that can be compared to everyone else who has taken that test.

It works this way. Test items, test sections, and different forms of the test have different difficulty levels. For example, an item on one form might be harder than a comparable item on another form. To make up for this difference in difficulty, the harder item might earn a 0.9 scale point, while the easier item might earn a 0.8 scale point. A scale score can be compared to the scale score on all forms of a test.

This is the fair way to do it. To maintain this fairness, Praxis passing scores are given as scale scores. All the scores discussed here are scale scores.

Praxis Scale Scoring

The scoring for each Praxis test is summarized on the following pages. The tables show the scale score range and score interval for each test, along with the scale scores at the first quartile, second quartile, and third quartile. An explanation of quartiles is given in the following table.

	Percent of test-takers who scored at or <u>below</u> this scale score.	Percent of test-takers who scored <u>above</u> this scale score.
First quartile	25%	75%
Second quartile	50%	50%
Third quartile	75%	25%

The PLT and most Subject Assessment multiple-choice tests have a scale from 100 to 200 with an interval of 1, for about 100 scale points.

PPST scores range from 150 to 190 for about 40 scale points.

Some tests have a scale from 250 to 990 with an interval of 10, meaning there are about 74 scale points. Constructed response Subject Assessments have a scale from 100 to 200 with an interval of 5, meaning there are about 20 scale points.

You can't compare scale scores on different tests, even if they have the same scale. You can't be sure that a scale score of 400 is twice as "good" as a scale score of 200. And you don't really care. The only thing that matters is if your scale score is at or above the score required by your certification state(s). If it is, you pass.

Passing Scores

No one can be sure what the passing raw score will be. That's because there are many different forms of each test, and the same raw score will earn a different scale score on each form. Besides, the best approach is to just relax and do your best.

You can get an idea of how difficult it is to pass the test in your certification state. Look up the passing score for a test in your certification state. Then compare that score to the quartile scores on the following pages.

Examples

PPST Reading Test for Virginia

Virginia Passing Score	1st quartile	2nd quartile	3rd quartile
178	175	179	182

The Virginia passing score is just below the second quartile. That means that about 50 percent of test takers pass. The test is of average difficulty.

Curriculum, Instruction, and Assessment for Connecticut

Connecticut Passing Score	1st quartile	2nd quartile	3rd quartile
163	170	181	189

The passing score is well below the first quartile score. That means that more than 75 percent of test takers pass. The test is easy to pass.

<u>PLT K–6 for Nevada</u>

Nevada Passing Score	1st quartile	2nd quartile	3rd quartile
169	169	175	183

The Nevada passing score is at the first quartile, meaning that about 75 percent of test takers pass. The test is relatively easy to pass.

Estimating Passing Raw Scores

You may want to use this very general rule of thumb to estimate passing raw scores. However, this method may not apply to your test. A raw score estimated this way may be somewhat higher or lower than the raw score you actually need to pass.

Follow these steps.
Choose the test you have to pass.
Look up first quartile scale score on the following tables of Praxis Scale Scores.
Look up the passing scale score for your certification state.
Assume that a score at the first quartile is about 65 percent to 70 percent of the raw scale points.
Estimate the raw score you will need.
Look at this example.

Example

- **PLT K–6**

- **First quartile scale score for the PLT K–6.**   169

- **Passing score in North Carolina for the PLT K–6.**   160

  The passing score is less than the first quartile score.

  The estimated passing score is 55 percent to 60 percent correct.

- **The PLT has 51 items.**
  $0.55 \times 51 = 28$
  $0.60 \times 51 = 31$

- **The estimated PLT K–6 passing raw score for North Carolina is 28–31 correct. Try to get 32 to 35 correct to be sure.**

PRAXIS SCALE SCORES

TEST NAME (TEST IDENTIFIER)	SCORE RANGE	SCORE INTERVAL	FIRST QUARTILE *	SECOND QUARTILE *	THIRD QUARTILE *
PPST					
Pre-Professional Skills Test: Mathematics (0730)	150–190	1	173	179	184
Pre-Professional Skills Test: Reading (0710)	150–190	1	175	179	182
Pre-Professional Skills Test: Writing (0720)	150–190	1	173	175	178
PLT					
Principles of Learning & Teaching: Grades K–6 (0522)	100–200	1	169	175	183
Principles of Learning & Teaching: Grades 5–9 (0523)	100–200	1	166	175	183
Principles of Learning & Teaching: Grades 7–12 (0524)	100–200	1	171	179	185
SUBJECT ASSESSMENTS					
Art Education (0130)	250–990	10	570	620	680
Art Making (0131)	100–200	1	158	168	177
Art: Content Knowledge (0133)	100–200	1	161	173	183
Art: Content, Traditions, Criticism, & Aesthetics (0132)	100–200	5	135	150	160
Audiology (0340)	250–990	10	610	640	660
Biology (0230)	250–990	10	610	690	760
Biology & General Science (0030)	250–990	10	600	650	700
Biology: Content Essays (0233)	100–200	1	141	151	159
Biology: Content Knowledge, Part 1 (0231)	100–200	1	158	169	179

* EXPLANATION OF QUARTILES:

First quartile   About 25 percent of the scale scores are below this score.

About 75 percent of the scale scores are above this score.

Second quartile   About 50 percent of the scale scores are below this score.

About 50 percent of the scale scores are above this score.

Third quartile   About 75 percent of the scale scores are below this score.

About 25 percent of the scale scores are above this score.

TEST NAME (TEST IDENTIFIER)	SCORE RANGE	SCORE INTERVAL	FIRST QUARTILE*	SECOND QUARTILE*	THIRD QUARTILE*
Biology: Content Knowledge, Part 2 (0232)	100–200	1	135	148	160
Biology: Content Knowledge (0235)	100–200	1	159	167	177
Biology: Pedagogy (0234)	100–200	1	150	156	164
Business Education (0100)	250–990	10	600	640	680
Chemistry (0240)	250–990	10	490	560	630
Chemistry: Content Essays (0242)	100–200	5	145	160	165
Chemistry: Content Knowledge (0241)	100–200	1	136	150	167
Chemistry: Content Knowledge (0245)	100–200	1	156	162	173
Chemistry, Physics, & General Science (0070)	250–990	10	530	580	650
Communication (0800)	250–990	10	650	740	780
Early Childhood Education (0020)	250–990	10	600	650	680
Earth/Space Science (0570)	250–990	10	550	630	700
Economics (0910)	250–990	10	490	570	650
Ed. Leadership: Administration & Supervision (0410)	250–990	10	620	680	730
Education in the Elementary School (0010)	250–990	10	600	640	670
Education of Students with Mental Retardation (0320)	250–990	10	580	630	670
Elem. Ed.: Content Area Exercises (0012)	100–200	1	151	156	164
Elem. Ed.: Curriculum, Instruction, & Assessment (0011)	100–200	1	170	181	189
Elem. Ed.: Curriculum, Instruction, & Assessment (K–5) (0016)	100–200	1	142	151	158
English Lang., Lit., & Comp.: Content Knowledge (0041)	100–200	1	167	178	188
English Lang., Lit., & Comp.: Essays (0042)	100–200	5	155	160	170
English Lang., Lit., & Comp.: Pedagogy (0043)	100–200	5	135	150	160
English Language & Literature (0040)	250–990	10	550	600	650
Foreign Language Pedagogy (0840)	100–200	1	163	173	181
French (0170)	250–990	10	560	630	690
French: Content Knowledge (0173)	100–200	1	169	183	192
French: Productive Language Skills (0171)	100–200	1	170	182	193
Fundamental Subjects: Content Knowledge	100–200	1	162	174	184
General Mathematics (WV) (0067)	100–200	1	163	173	181
General Science (0430)	250–990	10	560	650	730
General Science: Content Essays (0433)	100–200	5	135	145	160
General Science: Content Knowledge, Part 1 (0431)	100–200	1	155	167	177
General Science: Content Knowledge, Part 2 (0432)	100–200	1	146	158	170
General Science: Content Knowledge (0435)	100–200	1	160	170	183
Geography (0920)	250–990	10	600	660	710
German (0180)	250–990	10	530	620	690
German: Content Knowledge (0181)	100–200	1	177	191	197
Government/Political Science (0930)	250–990	10	620	690	750
Health & Physical Education (0850)	250–990	10	560	620	670
Health Education (0550)	250–990	10	650	710	760

TEST NAME (TEST IDENTIFIER)	SCORE RANGE	SCORE INTERVAL	FIRST QUARTILE*	SECOND QUARTILE*	THIRD QUARTILE*
Home Economics Education (0120)	250–990	10	610	660	700
Introduction to the Teaching of Reading (0200)	250–990	10	620	670	700
Library Media Specialist (0310)	250–990	10	630	670	710
Marketing Education (0560)	250–990	10	650	710	760
Mathematics (0060)	250–990	10	560	610	670
Mathematics: Content Knowledge (0061)	100–200	1	121	139	153
Mathematics: Pedagogy (0065)	100–200	5	120	135	155
Mathematics: Proofs, Models, & Problems, Part 1 (0063)	100–200	1	144	163	179
Mathematics: Proofs, Models, & Problems, Part 2 (0064)	100–200	1	131	144	162
Middle School: Content Knowledge (0146)	100–200	1	137	164	174
Music: Analysis (0112)	100–200	1	151	167	178
Music: Concepts & Processes (0111)	100–200	5	140	155	165
Music: Content Knowledge (0113)	100–200	1	155	165	174
Music Education (0110)	250–990	10	570	620	680
Office Technology (PA) (0794)	100–200	1	158	166	171
Physical Education (0090)	250–990	10	590	630	670
Physical Ed.: Content Knowledge (0091)	100–200	1	147	154	161
Physical Ed.: Movement Forms-Analysis/Design (0092)	100–200	1	149	156	164
Physical Ed.: Movement Forms-Video Evaluation (0093)	100–200	5	155	165	175
Physical Science: Content Knowledge (0481)	100–200	1	142	159	169
Physical Science: Pedagogy (0483)	100–200	1	145	159	176
Physics (0260)	250–990	10	480	550	640
Physics: Content Essays (0262)	100–200	5	150	160	170
Physics: Content Knowledge (0261)	100–200	1	114	124	141
Physics: Content Knowledge (0265)	100–200	1	153	156	173
Pre-Kindergarten Education (0530)	250–990	10	690	735	780
Psychology (0390)	250–990	10	580	650	700
Reading Specialist (0300)	250–990	10	570	620	660
School Guidance & Counseling (0420)	250–990	10	620	670	710
School Psychologist (0400)	250–990	10	650	700	750
School Social Worker (0210)	250–990	10	690	760	800
Social Studies (0080)	250–990	10	560	610	660
Social Studies: Analytical Essays (0082)	100–200	5	145	155	165
Social Studies: Content Knowledge (0081)	100–200	1	158	164	180
Social Studies: Interpretation of Materials (0083)	100–200	1	159	167	174
Social Studies: Pedagogy (0084)	100–200	1	167	181	192
Sociology (0950)	250–990	10	600	670	710
Spanish (0190)	250–990	10	520	590	660
Spanish: Content Knowledge (0191)	100–200	1	163	178	189
Spanish: Linguistic, Literary & Cultural Analysis (0193)	100–200	1	160	173	182
Spanish: Pedagogy (0194)	100–200	5	165	175	180

TEST NAME (TEST IDENTIFIER)	SCORE RANGE	SCORE INTERVAL	FIRST QUARTILE*	SECOND QUARTILE*	THIRD QUARTILE*
Spanish: Productive Language Skills (0192)	100–200	1	163	178	193
Special Education (0350)	250–990	10	570	630	680
Special Education: Application of Core Principles Across Categories of Disability (0352)	100–200	1	147	156	161
Special Education: Knowledge-Based Core Principles (0351)	100–200	1	155	162	174
Special Education: Preschool/Early Childhood (0690)	250–990	10	640	680	730
Special Education: Teaching Students with Behavioral Disorders/Emotional Disturbances (0371)	100–200	1	156	164	176
Special Education: Teaching Students with Learning Disabilities (0381)	100–200	1	153	164	176
Special Education: Teaching Students with Mental Retardation (0321)	100–200	1	143	151	165
Speech Communication (0220)	250–990	10	610	670	720
Speech-Language Pathology (0330)	250–990	10	630	670	710
Teaching English as a Second Language (0360)	250–990	10	620	710	780
Teaching Speech to Students with Language Impairments (0880)	250–990	10	610	690	740
Teaching Students with Emotional Disturbances (0370)	250–990	10	620	680	740
Teaching Students with Learning Disabilities (0380)	250–990	10	610	670	730
Teaching Students with Orthopedic Impairments (0290)	250–990	10	650	720	760
Teaching Students with Physical & Mental Disabilities (0870)	250–990	10	650	710	780
Teaching Students with Visual Impairments (0280)	250–990	10	700	760	790
Technology Education (0050)	250–990	10	620	670	700
Vocational General Knowledge (0890)	250–990	10	580	680	750
World & U.S. History (0940)	250–990	10	510	560	630

STATE-BY-STATE CERTIFICATION TESTING REQUIREMENTS

This section shows the Praxis tests and passing scores required in each state. Refer to each state in which you want to be certified and look up the testing requirements.

This listing is current and has been carefully checked. However, certification requirements change constantly. You must contact the appropriate state education departments to receive the most current information. The one exception is if you're attending a college with an approved certification program. Follow the guidelines established by the college, and you'll probably be okay for that state's certification.

Begin your contact by calling the state certification office. These phone numbers may also change. Call information if this happens. Even more frustrating is the busy signal you may hear when you call. Keep trying. If all else fails, write to the certification office.

When you reach or write the certification office, ask for their certification requirements and a certification application. If you're calling, have your questions ready. You may not get another chance to ask them.

Some states have county or regional offices that dispense certification information. If you need to talk to someone and the certification office is always busy, try a general number at the state education department or a local school district to find out about these options.

When a state requires the PLT or Praxis I, you must usually take the test(s) no matter which certificate you want. When a state requires a Subject Assessment, you usually need to take only the test required for the certificate you want.

Example: One person wants elementary education certification and another wants special education certification in Indiana. Indiana requires the PPST, so both will take this test. Indiana requires the Elementary Education Test and a Special Education Test. The person seeking elementary education certification will take the Elementary Education Test. The person seeking special education certification will take the required Special Education Test.

There are three 2-hour testing sessions on each Praxis paper testing day. The first number in each test code shows the session in which that test was given recently.

ALABAMA

Alabama Department of Education	PPST	PLT	Elementary Ed.	
Box 302101	❑ Reading	❑ Early Child.	❑	0011
Montgomery AL 36130-3901	❑ Writing	❑ K–6	❑	0012
(334) 242-9977	❑ Mathematics	❑ 5–9	137	0014
www.alsde.edu		❑ 7–12	❑	0016

ALASKA

Alaska Department of Education	PPST	PLT	Elementary Ed.	
801 West 10th Street	175 Reading	❑ Early Child.	156	0011
Juneau AK 99911-0500	174 Writing	❑ K–6	❑	0012
(907) 465-2831	173 Mathematics	❑ 5–9	143	0014
www.educ.state.ak.us		❑ 7–12	❑	0016

ARIZONA

	PPST	PLT	Elementary Ed.
Arizona Department of Education	❏ Reading	❏ Early Child.	❏ 0011
Teacher Certification Unit	❏ Writing	❏ K–6	❏ 0012
1535 West Jefferson	❏ Mathematics	❏ 5–9	❏ 0014
Phoenix, AZ 85002		❏ 7–12	❏ 0016
(602) 542-4361			
www.ade.state.az.us			

ARKANSAS

	PPST	PLT	Elementary Ed.
Arkansas Department of Education	172 Reading	159 Early Child.	❏ 0011
Teacher Education and Licensure	173 Writing	❏ K–6	❏ 0012
4 Capital Mall	171 Mathematics	164 5–9	❏ 0014
Little Rock, AR 72201-1071		164 7–12	❏ 0016
(501) 682-4342			
www.arkansased.org			

CALIFORNIA

	PPST	PLT	Elementary Ed.
California Commission on Teacher	❏ Reading	❏ Early Child.	❏ 0011
Credentialing	❏ Writing	❏ K–6	❏ 0012
1900 Capitol Avenue	❏ Mathematics	❏ 5–9	147 0014
Sacramento, CA 94244-7000		❏ 7–12	❏ 0016
(916) 445-7254			
www.ctc.ca.gov			

COLORADO

	PPST	PLT	Elementary Ed.
Colorado Department of Education	❏ Reading	❏ Early Child.	❏ 0011
Teacher Education and Certification	❏ Writing	❏ K–6	❏ 0012
201 East Colfax Avenue	❏ Mathematics	❏ 5–9	147 0014
Denver, CO 80203		❏ 7–12	❏ 0016
(303) 866-6628			
www.cde.state.co.us			

CONNECTICUT

	PPST	PLT	Elementary Ed.
Connecticut State Department of Education	172 Reading	❏ Early Child.	163 0011
Bureau of Teacher Certification	171 Writing	❏ K–6	148 0012
Box 150471—Room 243	171 Mathematics	❏ 5–9	❏ 0014
Hartford, CT 06115-0471		❏ 7–12	❏ 0016
(860) 713-6969			
FAX: (860) 566-8929			
www.sde.ct.us/sde			

DELAWARE

Delaware Department of Public
Instruction
Division of Professional
Development
and Certification
Townsend Building, Box 1402
Dover, DE 19903
(302) 739-4686
www.deeds.k12.de.us

PPST	PLT	Elementary Ed.	
175 Reading	❏ Early Child.	158	0011
173 Writing	❏ K–6	❏	0012
174 Mathematics	❏ 5–9	151	0014
	❏ 7–12	❏	0016

DISTRICT OF COLUMBIA

District of Columbia Public
Schools
Educational Credentials
825 Capitol Street NE
Washington, DC 20002
(202) 442-5377
www.k12.dc.us

PPST	PLT	Elementary Ed.	
172 Reading	❏ Early Child.	❏	0011
171 Writing	❏ K–6	148	0012
174 Mathematics	❏ 5–9	145	0014
	❏ 7–12	❏	0016

FLORIDA

Florida Department of Education
Office of Teacher Certification
325 West Gaines, Room 201
Tallahassee, FL 32399
(800) 445-6739
www.fldoe.org/edcert

PPST	PLT	Elementary Ed.
❏ Reading	❏ Early Child.	❏ 0011
❏ Writing	❏ K–6	❏ 0012
❏ Mathematics	❏ 5–9	❏ 0014
	❏ 7–12	❏ 0016

GEORGIA

Georgia Professional Standards
Commission
Two Peachtree Street
Atlanta, GA 30303
(404) 232-2500
(800) 869-7775
www.gapsc.com

PPST	PLT	Elementary Ed.
❏ Reading	❏ Early Child.	❏ 0011
❏ Writing	❏ K–6	❏ 0012
❏ Mathematics	❏ 5–9	❏ 0014
	❏ 7–12	❏ 0016

HAWAII

Hawaii Teachers Standard Board
650 Iwilei Road
Honolulu, HI 96817
(808) 586-2600
www.htsb.org

PPST	PLT	Elementary Ed.	
172 Reading	❏ Early Child.	164	0011
171 Writing	163 K–6	135	0012
173 Mathematics	157 5–9	❏	0014
	157 7–12	❏	0016

IDAHO

Idaho Department of Education
Teacher Certification Division
Box 83720
Boise, ID 83720
(208) 332-6881
www.sde.state.idaho.gov

PPST	PLT	Elementary Ed.
❏ Reading	❏ Early Child.	❏ 0011
❏ Writing	❏ K–6	❏ 0012
❏ Mathematics	❏ 5–9	143 0014
	❏ 7–12	❏ 0016

ILLINOIS

Illinois State Certification and
    Placement Section
100 North First Street
Springfield, IL 62777
(866) 262-6663
www.isbe.net

PPST	PLT	Elementary Ed.
❏ Reading	❏ Early Child.	❏ 0011
❏ Writing	❏ K–6	❏ 0012
❏ Mathematics	❏ 5–9	❏ 0014
	❏ 7–12	❏ 0016

INDIANA

Indiana Department of Education
Professional Standards Board
Room 229, State House
Indianapolis, IN 46204-2798
(317) 232-9010
www.doe.state.in.us

PPST		PLT	Elementary Ed.
176	Reading	❏ Early Child.	165 0011
172	Writing	❏ K–6	❏ 0012
175	Mathematics	❏ 5–9	❏ 0014
		❏ 7–12	❏ 0016

IOWA

Iowa Department of Education
Board of Educational Examiners
Grimes Office Building
Des Moines, IA 50319-0147
(515) 281-3245
www.boee.Iowa.gov

PPST	PLT	Elementary Ed.
❏ Reading	❏ Early Child.	151 0011
❏ Writing	❏ K–6	❏ 0012
❏ Mathematics	❏ 5–9	142 0014
	❏ 7–12	❏ 0016

KANSAS

Kansas Department of Education
Division of Teacher Education
    and Accreditation
120 West Tenth Street
Topeka, KS 66612-1182
(785) 291-3678
www.ksbe.org

PPST		PLT		Elementary Ed.
175	Reading	161	Early Child.	163 0011
174	Writing	161	K–6	❏ 0012
173	Mathematics	161	5–9	❏ 0014
		161	7–12	❏ 0016

KENTUCKY

Kentucky Standards Board
100 Airport Road
Frankfort, KY 40601
(502) 564-4606
www.kyepsb.net

PPST		PLT		Elementary Ed.
*	Reading	❏	Early Child.	❏ 0011
*	Writing	161	K–6	❏ 0012
*	Mathematics	161	5–9	148 0014
		161	7–12	❏ 0016

*Required—score varies by program.

LOUISIANA

Louisiana Department of
  Education
Box 94064
Baton Rouge, LA 70804-9064
(877) 453-2721
www.teachlouisiana.net

PPST		PLT		Elementary Ed.	
174	Reading	❏	Early Child.	❏	0011
173	Writing	161	K–6	❏	0012
172	Mathematics	154	5–9	150	0014
		161	7–12	❏	0016

MAINE

Maine Department of Education
Division of Certification and
  Placement
State House, Station 23
Augusta, ME 04333
(207) 624-6603
www.maine.gov.education.cert

PPST		PLT		Elementary Ed.
176	Reading	❏	Early Child.	❏ 0011
175	Writing	166	K–6	❏ 0012
175	Mathematics	❏	5–9	❏ 0014
		162	7–12	❏ 0016

MARYLAND

Maryland Department of
  Education
Department of Certification
200 West Baltimore Street
Baltimore, MD 21201
(410) 767-0412
www.marylandpublicschools.org

PPST		PLT		Elementary Ed.	
177	Reading	❏	Early Child.	❏	0011
173	Writing	❏	K–6	150	0012
177	Mathematics	❏	5–9	142	0014
		162	7–12	❏	0016

MASSACHUSETTS

Massachusetts Department of
  Education
Office of Teacher Certification
350 Main Street
Malken, MA 02148
(781) 838-3102
www.doe.mass.edu

PPST	PLT	Elementary Ed.
❏ Reading	❏ Early Child.	❏ 0011
❏ Writing	❏ K–6	❏ 0012
❏ Mathematics	❏ 5–9	❏ 0014
	❏ 7–12	❏ 0016

MICHIGAN

Michigan Department of
  Education
Teacher Preparation and
  Certification
Box 30008
Lansing, MI 48909
(517) 373-3324
www.michigan.gov/mde/

PPST	PLT	Elementary Ed.
❏ Reading	❏ Early Child.	❏ 0011
❏ Writing	❏ K–6	❏ 0012
❏ Mathematics	❏ 5–9	❏ 0014
	❏ 7–12	❏ 0016

MINNESOTA

Minnesota Department of	PPST		PLT		Elementary Ed.	
Education	173	Reading	164	Early Child.	❑	0011
Personnel Licensing Team	172	Writing	159	K–6	❑	0012
1500 Highway 36 West	171	Mathematics	155	5–9	145	0014
Roseville, MN 55113			157	7–12	❑	0016

(651) 582-8691
www.education.state.mn.us

MISSISSIPPI

Mississippi Department of	PPST		PLT		Elementary Ed.	
Education	170	Reading	❑	Early Child.	158	0011
Division of Teacher Certification	172	Writing	152	K–6	❑	0012
Box 771	169	Mathematics	152	5–9	153	0014
Jackson, MS 39205-0771			152	7–12	❑	0016

(601) 359-3483
www.mde.k12.ms.us

MISSOURI

Missouri Department of	PPST		PLT		Elementary Ed.	
Education	❑	Reading	❑	Early Child.	164	0011
Department of Elementary and	❑	Writing	❑	K–6	❑	0012
Secondary Education	❑	Mathematics	160	5–9	❑	0014
Box 480			160	7–12	❑	0016

Jefferson City, MO 65102
(573) 751-4212
www.dese.mo.us

MONTANA

Montana Office of Public	PPST		PLT		Elementary Ed.	
Instruction	❑	Reading	❑	Early Child.	❑	0011
Teacher Education and	❑	Writing	❑	K–6	❑	0012
Certification	❑	Mathematics	❑	5–9	❑	0014
Box 202501			❑	7–12	❑	0016

Helena, MT 59620-2501
(406) 444-3150
www.opi.state.mt.us

NEBRASKA

Nebraska Department of	PPST		PLT		Elementary Ed.	
Education	170	Reading	❑	Early Child.	159	0011
Teacher Education and	172	Writing	❑	K–6	❑	0012
Certification	171	Mathematics	❑	5–9	❑	0014
301 Centennial Mall South			❑	7–12	❑	0016

Box 94987
Lincoln, NE 68509
(402) 471-2496
www.nde.state.ne.us/tcert

NEVADA

Nevada Department of
  Education
Teacher Licensure and Education
1822 East Sahara–Suite 205
Las Vegas, NV 89104
(702) 486-6455
www.doe.nv.gov

PPST		PLT		Elementary Ed.	
174	Reading	❏	Early Child.	158	0011
172	Writing	169	K–6	135	0012
172	Mathematics	❏	5–9	148	0014
		161	7–12	❏	0016

NEW HAMPSHIRE

New Hampshire Department of
  Education
Bureau of Teacher Education
State Office Park South
101 Pleasant Street
Concord, NH 03301
(603) 271-2407
www.ed.nh.us/education

PPST		PLT		Elementary Ed.	
174	Reading	❏	Early Child.	❏	0011
172	Writing	❏	K–6	❏	0012
172	Mathematics	❏	5–9	148	0014
		❏	7–12	❏	0016

NEW JERSEY

New Jersey Department of
  Education
Office of Licensing
CN 500
Trenton, NJ 08625-0500
(609) 292-2070
www.state.nj.us/njded

PPST		PLT		Elementary Ed.	
❏	Reading	❏	Early Child.	❏	0011
❏	Writing	❏	K–6	❏	0012
❏	Mathematics	❏	5–9	141	0014
		❏	7–12	❏	0016

NEW MEXICO

New Mexico Department of
  Education
Director, Professional Licensure
  Unit
300 Don Gaspar
Santa Fe, NM 87501-2786
(505) 827-6587
www.sde.state.nm.us

PPST		PLT		Elementary Ed.	
❏	Reading	❏	Early Child.	❏	0011
❏	Writing	❏	K–6	❏	0012
❏	Mathematics	❏	5–9	❏	0014
		❏	7–12	❏	0016

NEW YORK

New York Department of
  Education
Office of Teaching
Cultural Education Center
Empire State Plaza
Albany, NY 12230
(518) 474-6440
www.highered.nysed.gov/tcert

PPST		PLT		Elementary Ed.	
❏	Reading	❏	Early Child.	❏	0011
❏	Writing	❏	K–6	❏	0012
❏	Mathematics	❏	5–9	❏	0014
		❏	7–12	❏	0016

NORTH CAROLINA

North Carolina Department of
  Public Instruction
Licensure Section
301 North Wilmington Street
Raleigh, NC 27601-2825
(919) 807-3310
www.ncpublicschools.org

PPST	PLT	Elementary Ed.
176 Reading	❏ Early Child.	* 0011
173 Writing	❏ K–6	* 0012
173 Mathematics	❏ 5–9	❏ 0014
	❏ 7–12	❏ 0016

* Combined score of 313

NORTH DAKOTA

North Dakota Department of
  Public Instruction
Director of Certification
Bismarck, ND 58503-0585
(701) 328-9641
www.nd.gov.espb

PPST	PLT	Elementary Ed.
173 Reading	❏ Early Child.	158 0011
173 Writing	162 K–6	❏ 0012
170 Mathematics	❏ 5–9	❏ 0014
	❏ 7–12	❏ 0016

OHIO

Ohio Department of Education
Department of Teacher Education
  and Certification
65 South Front Street, Room
  1012
Columbus, OH 43266-0308
(877) 644-6338
www.ode.state.oh.us/tp/ctp/

PPST	PLT	Elementary Ed.
173 Reading	166 Early Child.	❏ 0011
172 Writing	168 K–6	❏ 0012
172 Mathematics	168 5–9	❏ 0014
	165 7–12	❏ 0016

OKLAHOMA

Oklahoma Department of
  Education
Division of Professional Standards
2500 North Lincoln Boulevard,
  Room 211
Oklahoma City, OK 73105-4599
(405) 521-3337
www.sde.state.ok.us

PPST	PLT	Elementary Ed.
173 Reading	❏ Early Child.	❏ 0011
172 Writing	❏ K–6	❏ 0012
171 Mathematics	❏ 5–9	❏ 0014
	❏ 7–12	❏ 0016

OREGON

Oregon Teacher Standards and
  Practices Commission
465 Commercial Street NE
Salem, OR 97310
(503) 378-3586
www.tspc.state.or.us

PPST	PLT	Elementary Ed.
174 Reading	❏ Early Child.	❏ 0011
171 Writing	❏ K–6	❏ 0012
175 Mathematics	❏ 5–9	❏ 0014
	❏ 7–12	❏ 0016

PENNSYLVANIA

Pennsylvania Department of
    Education
Bureau of Teacher Preparation
    and Certification
333 Market Street
Harrisburg, PA 17126-0333
(717) 787-2967
www.teaching.state.pa.us

PPST		PLT		Elementary Ed.	
172	Reading	❑ Early Child.		168	0011
173	Writing	❑ K–6		❑	0012
173	Mathematics	❑ 5–9		❑	0014
		❑ 7–12		❑	0016

RHODE ISLAND

Rhode Island Department of
    Education
Office of Teacher Certification
255 Westminster Street
Providence, RI 02903
(401) 277-2675
www.ride.ri.net

PPST		PLT		Elementary Ed.	
❑	Reading	❑	Early Child.	❑	0011
❑	Writing	167	K–6	148	0012
❑	Mathematics	❑	5–9	145	0014
		167	7–12	❑	0016

SOUTH CAROLINA

South Carolina Department of
    Education
Teacher Certification Section
3700 Forest Drive
Columbia, SC 29204
(803) 734-2873
www.sc.teachers.org

PPST		PLT		Elementary Ed.	
175	Reading	❑	Early Child.	164	0011
173	Writing	165	K–6	145	0012
172	Mathematics	165	5–9	❑	0014
		165	7–12	❑	0016

SOUTH DAKOTA

South Dakota Department of
    Education
Office of Certification
Kneip Office Building
700 Governors Drive
Pierre, SD 57501
(605) 773-3134
www.doe.sd.gov

PPST		PLT		Elementary Ed.	
❑	Reading	160	Early Child.	❑	0011
❑	Writing	153	K–6	❑	0012
❑	Mathematics	153	5–9	140	0014
		153	7–12	❑	0016

TENNESSEE

Tennessee Department of
    Education
Office of Teacher Licensing
710 James Robertson Parkway
Nashville, TN 37243-0377
(615) 532-4885
www.tennessee.gov.education.lic

PPST		PLT		Elementary Ed.	
174	Reading	155	Early Child.	159	0011
173	Writing	155	K–6	❑	0012
173	Mathematics	154	5–9	140	0014
		159	7–12	❑	0016

TEXAS

Texas Education Agency	PPST	PLT	Elementary Ed.
Division of Teacher Certification	❑ Reading	❑ Early Child.	❑ 0011
William B. Travis State Office	❑ Writing	❑ K–6	❑ 0012
Building	❑ Mathematics	❑ 5–9	❑ 0014
1701 North Congress Avenue		❑ 7–12	❑ 0016

Austin, TX 78701-1494
(512) 836-8400
www.sbec.state.tx.us

UTAH

Utah Board of Education	PPST	PLT	Elementary Ed.
Certification and Personnel	❑ Reading 160	Early Child. 177	0011
Development	❑ Writing 160	K–6 150	0012
250 East 500 South Street	❑ Mathematics 160	5–9 150	0014
Salt Lake City, UT 84111		160 7–12	❑ 0016

(801) 538-7500
www.usue.k12.ut.us

VERMONT

Vermont Department of	PPST	PLT	Elementary Ed.
Licensing Office	177 Reading	❑ Early Child.	❑ 0011
120 State Street	174 Writing	❑ K–6	❑ 0012
Montpelier, VT 05602-2703	174 Mathematics	❑ 5–9	148 0014
(802) 828-2445		❑ 7–12	❑ 0016

www.state.vt.us/educ/

VIRGINIA

Virginia Department of	PPST	PLT	Elementary Ed.
Education	178 Reading	❑ Early Child.	❑ 0011
Office of Professional Licensure	176 Writing	❑ K–6	❑ 0012
Box 2120	178 Mathematics	❑ 5–9	143 0014
Richmond, VA 23218-2120		❑ 7–12	❑ 0016

(804) 225-2022
www.per.k12.va.us

WASHINGTON

Washington State Superintendent	PPST	PLT	Elementary Ed.
of Public Instruction	❑ Reading	❑ Early Child.	❑ 0011
Director of Professional	❑ Writing	❑ K–6	❑ 0012
Certification	❑ Mathematics	❑ 5–9	141 0014
Old Capitol Building, Box 47236		❑ 7–12	❑ 0016

Olympia, WA 98504-7236
(360) 725-6400
www.kl2.wa.us

WEST VIRGINIA

Office of Professional Preparation
West Virginia Department of
   Education
Building 6, Room 337
1900 Kanawha Boulevard East
Charleston, WV 25305-0330
(304) 558-7826
www.wvde.state.wv.us

PPST	PLT		Elementary Ed.	
174 Reading	❑ Early Child.	155	0011
172 Writing	165 K–6		❑ 0012
172 Mathematics	159 5–9		❑ 0014
	156 7–12		❑ 0016

WISCONSIN

Department of Public Instruction
Bureau of Teacher Education
Box 7841
125 South Webster Street
Madison, WI 53707-7841
(800) 266-1027
www.dpi.state.wi.us

PPST	PLT	Elementary Ed.	
175 Reading	❑ Early Child.	❑ 0011
174 Writing	❑ K–6	❑ 0012
173 Mathematics	❑ 5–9	147 0014
	❑ 7–12	❑ 0016

WYOMING

Wyoming Department of
   Education
Professional Teaching Standards
   Board
Hathaway Building, 2nd Floor
1920 Thomas Avenue
Cheyenne, WY 82002
(307) 777-6261
www.ptsb.state.wy.us

PPST	PLT		Elementary Ed.	
❑ Reading	❑ Early Child.	160	0011
❑ Writing	❑ K–6		❑ 0012
❑ Mathematics	157 5–9		❑ 0014
	161 7–12		❑ 0016

DEPARTMENT OF DEFENSE DEPENDENT SCHOOLS

4040 North Fairfax Drive
Arlington, VA 22203
(703) 588-3108
www.dodea.edu

PPST	PLT	Elementary Ed.
175 Reading	❑ Early Child.	❑ 0011
174 Writing	❑ K–6	❑ 0012
170 Mathematics	❑ 5–9	❑ 0014
	❑ 7–12	❑ 0016

18 Getting a Teaching Job

I t is never too early to start preparing to get a teaching job. You might as well start now.

There are specific steps you can follow to increase your chances of getting the teaching job you want. There are no guarantees, mind you. But you can definitely improve the odds. Let's begin with a discussion of job opportunities.

WHERE ARE THE TEACHING JOBS?

There are teaching jobs everywhere! This writer served on the board of education in a small suburban town with about 80 teachers in a K–8 school district. It was the kind of place most people would like to teach. There were between two and five teaching openings each year, for six years. But you could hardly find an advertisement or announcement anywhere.

About the only people who knew about the jobs were administrators and teachers in the district and surrounding districts, the few people who read a three-line ad that ran once in a weekly paper, and those who called to inquire about teaching jobs. Keep this information in mind. It is your first clue about how to find a teaching job.

The *Occupational Outlook Handbook*, released by the federal government, predicts that teaching opportunities for elementary and secondary school teachers will increase about as fast as all occupations as a whole during the next 10 years. The book predicts a much faster increase in jobs for special education teachers.

Other sources predict an increased need for mathematics, science, bilingual, IESL teachers during this same period. Experience indicates that the opportunities for teachers certified in more than one area will grow much faster than average as well.

Some publications predict that the population of elementary age school children will increase about 12 percent by 2016. If the number of teachers were to increase at this rate overall, the number of teachers in the United States would grow from about 3,800,000 to about 4,300,000. Teachers are apportioned approximately as follows: elementary school, 1,680,000; middle school, 602,000; secondary school, 1,100,000; special education, 440,000.

Over half of American teachers are older than 40. The number of retirements during the next decade will probably be larger than we have seen in the last 20 years. Knowledgeable sources predict that as many as 2,500,000 people will be teaching in 2016 who are not now teaching.

The growth in the school age population and the retirement rate will produce many teaching jobs during the next decade. You need only one.

HOW CAN I FIND A JOB?

Before discussing this question, let's talk about rejection. Remember, you need only one teaching job. If you are interested in 100 jobs, you should be extremely happy with a success rate of 1 percent. A success rate of 2 percent is more than you need, and a very high success rate of 5 percent will just make it too hard to decide which job to take.

Rejection and failure are part of the job search process. Be ready; everyone goes through it.

Okay, I'm Ready to Begin. How do I Find a Job?

Start now even if you won't be looking for a job for several years.

Begin by deciding on the kind of teaching jobs you want and the geographic areas you are willing to teach in. There is no sense pursuing jobs you don't want in places you don't want to go.

Write your choices here.

These are the kind of teaching positions I'm interested in.

_____   _____

_____   _____

These are the places or locales I'm willing to teach in.

_____   _____

_____   _____

You can change your mind as often as you like. But limit your job search to these choices.

Follow the guidelines presented below. You must actually do the things outlined here. Reading, talking, and thinking about them will not help.

Make and use personal contacts.

Find out about every appropriate teaching position.

Apply for every appropriate teaching position—go to every interview.

Develop a good résumé.

Create a portfolio.

Use the placement office.

Make and Use Personal Contacts

You will not be surprised to learn that many, if not most, jobs are found through personal contacts. You must make personal contacts to maximize your chances of finding the job you want. Take things easy, one step at a time, and try to meet *at least* one new person each month.

Find a way to get introduced to teachers, school administrators, board of education members, and others who will know about teaching jobs and may influence hiring decisions. The more people you meet and talk to, the better chance you will have of getting the job you want.

Get a mentor. Get to know a superintendent or principal near where you want to teach, and ask that person to be your mentor. Tell them immediately that you are not asking for a job in their district. (That will not stop them from offering you one if they want to.) Explain that you are just beginning your teaching career and that you need help learning about teaching jobs in surrounding communities and about teaching in general. Ask your mentors to keep their eyes and ears open for any openings for which you are qualified. You can have as many mentors as you want. Listen to their advice.

You already have a lot of contacts through your friends and relatives. Talk to them all. Tell them you will be looking for a teaching job and ask them to be alert for any possibilities. Ask them to mention your name and your interest in a teaching position to everyone they know.

Find Out About Every Appropriate Teaching Position

The contacts you have and are making each month will help you keep abreast of some teaching opportunities. Follow these additional steps. Look in every paper every day distributed in the places you want to teach. Don't forget about weekly papers.

Call all the school districts where you want to teach. Ask the administrative assistant or secretary in the superintendent's or principal's office if there are current or anticipated job openings in the district. If you are in college or a recent graduate, visit or contact the placement office every week and ask your professors if they know about any teaching opportunities.

Find out about jobs now even if you won't be teaching for several years. This information may help you decide where you want to student teach.

Develop a Résumé

Start working on your résumé right away. Just working on a résumé will help you develop skills and choose experiences that will look good on a résumé.

A good résumé is a one-page advertisement. A good résumé highlights the things you have done that prospective employers will be interested in. A good résumé is not an exhaustive listing of everything you have done. A good résumé is not cluttered.

For example, say you worked as a teacher assistant and spent most of your time on lunch duty and about 10 percent of your time conducting whole language lessons. What goes on the résumé? The whole language experience.

Your résumé should include significant school-related experience. It should also include other employment that lasted longer than a year. Omit noneducation-related short-term employment. Your résumé should list special skills, abilities, and interests that make you unique.

An example of a résumé using a format that has proven successful appears on the next page. This résumé combines the experience of more than one person and is for demonstration purposes only.

An outline of a résumé you can copy, to begin to develop your own résumé, is also included. If you are interested in two different types of teaching positions, you may have two résumés. Go over your final résumé and cover letters with a placement officer or advisor.

Create a Portfolio

A résumé helps get you an interview. A portfolio is what you bring to an interview to show a prospective employer what you have done. Start working on a portfolio right away.

Your portfolio should include the things you do in college classes, in practica, in student teaching, and in any other activity related to teaching. Include lesson plans, unit plans, letters and other communication from teachers, administrators, and parents, examples of students' work, pictures of you working with students, pictures of bulletin boards, documentation of teaching-related activities, and anything else that relates to your work with or about children.

Keep everything in a big folder. Make copies and keep them in a safe place. When you are ready to go on interviews you can decide what to include and put those materials under acetate covers in a professional loose-leaf book.

Some employers will want to see your portfolio, and some will not. But you've got to be ready. Check with your advisor, your professor, your mentor, as well as other teachers and administrators, for more advice about preparing your portfolio.

SAMPLE RÉSUMÉ

Derek Namost
33 Ann Street
Kearning, NJ 99999
(555) 555-5555
derekn@mymail.net

Objective:	Elementary School Teacher	
	Special Education Teacher	
	Secondary School History Teacher	
Education:	BS History—Collegiate College (minor in education)	2003
	MS in Education at Long Key College in progress	
Certification:	Teacher of Special Education	
	Teacher of Elementary Education	

Experience: **Lincoln School District** 2008–present
Elementary School Teacher Fifth Grade
- Teach in a student-centered elementary school
- Prepare and teach individualized lessons geared to student needs
- Use computer software and CD-ROMs to teach mathematics and motivate students
- Prepare and implement whole language instruction
- Integrate instruction in science, language arts, and social studies

Southern Pines School District 2004–2008
Secondary School Special Education Teacher
- Planned and taught modified classes for classified students
- Modified the curriculum to meet the individual needs of students
- Taught modified science and social studies courses to classified students
- Assisted students with class assignments, self-management, and study skills
- Collaborated with class and subject-matter teachers

Watson School Spring 2004
Student Teacher, Preschool Class
- Collaborated in teaching a class of preschool students

Honors:	Kappa Delta Pi, Phi Delta Kappa	
Coaching/	Coach, varsity soccer team	2004–2005
Advising:	Advisor, mathematics team	2003–2004
	Interested in coaching and advising after-school activities	
Special Skills:	Extensive experience using computers, including Macintosh and PCs, multimedia, and CD-ROMs.	
References:	References are available upon request	

Apply for Every Appropriate Teaching Position—Go to Every Interview

When it is time, apply for every teaching position that is of the type and in the location you listed. No exceptions! Direct application for a listed position is probably the second most effective way to get a job. The more appropriate the jobs you apply for, the more likely you are to get one. It is not unusual for someone to apply for more than 100 teaching positions.

Go to every interview you are invited to. Going to interviews increases your chances of getting a job. If you don't get the job, it was worth going just for the practice.

Your application should include a brief cover letter and a one-page résumé. The cover letter might follow this format: The first brief paragraph should identify the job you are applying for. The second brief paragraph should be used to mention a skill or ability you have that matches a district need. The third brief paragraph should indicate an interest in a personal interview. Every cover letter should be addressed to the person responsible for hiring in the school district.

Use the Placement Office

If you are a college student or a college graduate, use your school's placement office. Set up a placement file that includes recommendation letters from professors, teachers, and supervisors. It's handy to have these references on file. If a potential employer wants this information, you can have them sent out from the placement office instead of running around.

College placement offices often give seminars on job hunting and interviews. Take advantage of these.

What Time Line Should I Follow?

Let's say you are looking for a job in September and you will be certified three months earlier, in June. You should begin working on your personal contacts by September of the previous year. You should start looking for advertisements and tracking down job possibilities during the previous January. Have your placement file set up and a preliminary résumé and portfolio done by February. You can amend them later if you need to. Start applying for jobs in February.

Any Last Advice?

Stick with it. Follow the steps outlined here. Start early and take things one step at a time. Remember the importance of personal contacts. Remember that you need only one teaching job. Let people help you.

Index

NOTES

NOTES

NOTES

NOTES

NOTES

NOTES

No One Can Build Your Writing Skills Better Than We Can...

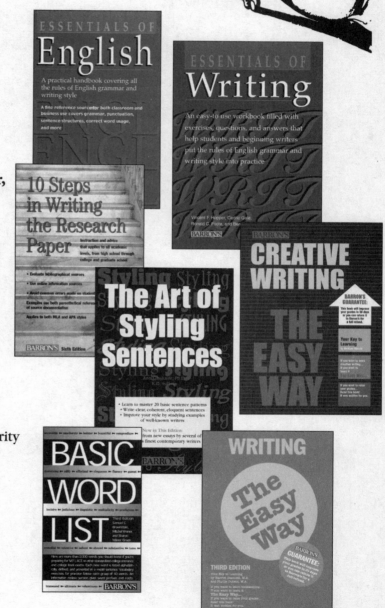

Essentials of English, 5th Edition
(978-0-7641-1367-3)
The comprehensive program for effective writing skills.

Essentials of Writing, 5th Edition
(978-0-7641-1368-0)
A companion workbook for the material in *Essentials of English*.

10 Steps in Writing the Research Paper, 6th Edition
(978-0-7641-1362-8)
The easy step-by-step guide for writing research papers. It includes a section on how to avoid plagiarism.

Creative Writing The Easy Way
(978-0-7641-2579-9)
This title discusses, analyzes, and offers exercises in prose forms.

The Art of Styling Sentences: 20 Patterns for Success, 4th Edition
(978-0-7641-2181-4)
How to write with flair, imagination, and clarity by imitating 20 sentence patterns and variations.

Writing The Easy Way, 3rd Edition
(978-0-7641-1206-5)
The quick and convenient way to enhance writing skills.

Basic Word List, 3rd Edition
(978-0-8120-9649-1)
More than 2,000 words that are found on the most recent major standardized tests are thoroughly reviewed.

BARRON'S EDUCATIONAL SERIES, INC.
250 Wireless Boulevard • Hauppauge, New York 11788
In Canada: Georgetown Book Warehouse
34 Armstrong Avenue • Georgetown, Ontario L7G 4R9

Please visit **www.barronseduc.com** to view current prices and to order books

(#15) R12/07

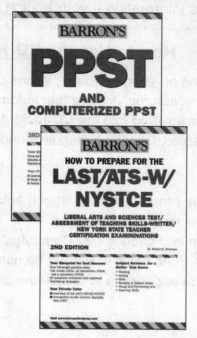

How to Use the CD-ROM

The software is not installed on your computer; it runs directly from the CD-ROM. Barron's CD-ROM includes an "autorun" feature that automatically launches the application when the CD is inserted into the CD-ROM drive. In the unlikely event that the autorun feature is disabled, follow the manual launching instructions below.

Windows®

Insert the CD-ROM and the program should launch automatically. If the software does not launch automatically, follow the steps below.

1. Click on the Start button and choose "My Computer."
2. Double-click on the CD-ROM drive, which will be named **PRAXIS**.
3. Double-click **PRAXIS.exe** application to launch the program.

Macintosh®

1. Insert the CD-ROM.
2. Double-click the CD-ROM icon.
3. Double-click the **PRAXIS** icon to start the program.

SYSTEM REQUIREMENTS

The program will run on a PC with:
Windows® Intel® Pentium II 450 MHz
or faster, 128MB of RAM
1024 X 768 display resolution
Windows 2000, XP, Vista
CD-ROM Player

The program will run on a Macintosh® with:
PowerPC® G3 500 MHz
or faster, 128MB of RAM
1024 X 768 display resolution
Mac OS X v.10.1 through 10.4
CD-ROM Player